# A HISTORY OF THE PEOPLE OF IOWA

BY

CYRENUS COLE

*Write this for a memorial in a book.*—EXODUS XVII, 14.

*I would have every man apply his mind seriously to consider these points, viz., what their life and what their manners were. . .*—Preface to THE HISTORY OF ROME, by Titus Livius.

*To give, in detail, the several motions and resolutions of the time, is not within the plan of this work. . . In this, I apprehend, consists the chief part of the historian's duty: It is his to rejudge the conduct of men. . .*—THE ANNALS OF TACITUS Book III, Section LXV.

CEDAR RAPIDS IOWA
THE TORCH PRESS
NINETEEN HUNDRED
AND TWENTY-ONE

THE TORCH PRESS
CEDAR RAPIDS
IOWA

TO

ANNA LARRABEE

AND TO MY NIECE

MARY COLE

ND TO ALL WHO LOVE IOWA

## BY WAY OF INTRODUCTION

Of course no apology is necessary for writing *A History of the People of Iowa,* and so none will be offered. The author believes his work is not a duplication of any other. Not too much, but too little has been written about Iowa. The people of this state have been neglectful of their own history. Even in their schools they have taught the history of every land except their own.

On one occasion the author interrogated four college girls, senior class students in a university, and was surprised to find that not one of them had a distinct idea of who James W. Grimes was. They had heard of Samuel J. Kirkwood, largely through the fact that Mrs. Jane Kirkwood, the widow of the war governor, was still living in Iowa City. They knew much about the Sabine women, but very little about their own great-grandmothers who had crossed the Mississippi in 1833, and in the years following. They knew what Curtius did in the Roman Forum, but they were wholly ignorant about the Iowa hero who held a fort while General Sherman signalled "I am coming." And yet the lessons derived from human experience might have been garnered from Iowa history as well as from Roman.

The neglect is not unusual. Men are apt to be indifferent to their own historic surroundings. Nor has the material of Iowa history been accessible to the many. Gue's and Brigham's excellent histories are too voluminous. They have become books of reference for students of men and events. The author of the present volume has undertaken to write a history in a form fitted for the general reader who is the average man and woman, and the average school boy and school girl. He has been equally diligent to follow historical accuracy and to avoid historical scholasticism. While his work is complete as to time covered, it is not exhaustive. It would have been easier to have written it in two or three volumes than to condense it into one. For all disputed points he has cited the proper authorities, but he has tried not to make his footnotes burdensome. For a fuller statement of the purpose and the scope of this work, the reader is referred to Chapter XLIII, under the title, "An Interlude the Reader May Skip," beginning on page 257, where these are somewhat fully set forth.

To assist the reader to understand the history of Iowa, which extends over nearly two centuries and a half, or from 1673 to the present time, the author has divided the time into nine periods, each one of which is marked by some distinct achievement. He has also subdivided the periods into many chapters, eighty-five in all, and none of them long. Each chapter is so distinct and specific that the table of contents will serve almost as an index to the work.

All detailed writing has been avoided, for the author has not been able to make himself believe that men and women nowadays have either the time or the inclination for details. Those who want to study any period or any question at greater length — as it is hoped there may be many — will find ample material in other books, and the footnotes in this volume will, in a measure, direct them to those sources. The general reader has not been burdened with facts and discussions that would be suitable to the specific reader. In short, what is printed in this volume is what, in the opinion of the author, every man and woman of Iowa ought to know about his own state.

The author is conscious of many defects, of deficiencies and omissions even. Others may discover errors that escaped him. In making books nothing is ever perfect. The historical judgments expressed are his own, and they are not infallible. He has tried to give to each man his proper place in the history of the state, and to favor none above his deserts. The twenty-eight portraits were selected in the same manner and they are of the men and women who, in the judgment of the author, best represent their times. If there has been any partiality it has been akin to that which Titus Livius ascribed to himself in his Preface to *The History of Rome*, wherein he says, "But either a fond partiality for the task I have undertaken deceives me, or there never was any state either greater or more moral, or richer in good examples, nor one into which luxury and avarice made their entrance so late, and where poverty and frugality were so much and so long honored; so that the less wealth there was, the less desire was there."

The writing of this volume has occupied the spare time, and often more than spare time, of the author for many years. In preparing himself for the work, he believes he read nearly everything that has been written about Iowa. It has been a labor of love, but not without a sense of duty. Iowa has been good to him, and Iowa was good to his parents and grandparents before him. Every Iowan owes his state some service and this work is part of the author's service.

The author is under many obligations to many persons for aid and encouragement. Some of these deserve to be mentioned especially. First of all, he wants to name Luther A. Brewer, with whom he has been long associated in newspaper work. Mr. Brewer has been many things in the preparation of this volume—copy-editor, proof-reader, indexer and publisher. He knows how thankful the author is to him, and others would not understand it if it were expressed in many words. A. N. Harbert, a diligent and intelligent collector of Iowana, has stood by as a *fidus Achates*. Many of the illustrations are reproductions from his private collection. The author is also indebted to Newton R. Parvin of the Masonic Library of Iowa; to Joanna Hagey and Frances E. Wolfe of the Cedar Rapids Public Library; to Dr. Benj. F. Shambaugh of the State Historical Society at Iowa City, and to Edgar R. Harlan and to William H. Fleming, secretary to many governors, of the State Historical Department at Des Moines. And last, to Jacob Van der Zee, associate professor in political science at the State University, for a final reading of the proof sheets. Mr. Van der Zee, burdened as he has been with his own work, has not been able to do enough to be held responsible for the results, but he has done enough to entitle him to more than a mere acknowledgement — he is a man from whom Iowa still has much to expect as a writer and historian.

But beyond and above all, both as a source of information and as an inspiration, the author is indebted to his own mother, who was one of the pioneer women of Iowa—and to her he has paid a filial tribute in the last chapter of this volume, under the title of "A Postscript Personal."

# CONTENTS

## PORTRAITS



## MAPS AND ILLUSTRATIONS

# PART I

## Discovery and Possession

(1673-1804)

# CHAPTER I

## "In the Beginning"

To find a beginning for a history of Iowa one must go to old Quebec, the capital of New France. It was there the plans were made, in the seventeenth century, for the discovery and the exploration of the Mississippi Valley. The first white men came to what is now Iowa in boats, using the St. Lawrence, the Great Lakes, and the Fox, the Wisconsin, and the Mississippi rivers as their highways. They came as explorers and as adventurers, as men seeking fame and fortune, as missionaries of the church, and as trappers and traders. They were all Frenchmen, or French-Canadians. Their speech was easily blended with the dialects of the Indians, but it did not remain to become the language of those who came later to till the lands and build cities. The men who came by way of Quebec were merely the pathfinders.

But for the student of history who seeks causes and motives, even Quebec is not an acceptable starting point. It was only a stopping place on a great historical highway, a new and a temporary center where certain human energies were re-formed and reorganized for new achievements. He who studies history must go still farther back. He must sojourn in London, in Paris, in Madrid, and in The Hague, capitals in which the old world's unrest and the new world's aspirations found expression in the centuries out of which America was born.

There are no events that are detached from other events. Everything that happens in this world is part of a stupendous whole. It is at once bound to something that preceded it and related to something that is to follow it. This constitutes the chain of inevitable world destiny. If human history were made up of accidental and inconsequential happenings it would hardly be worthy of study and its recording would be a futile and fruitless task.

We may find, nay, we shall find, that our fragment of American history is part and parcel of a great moral and intellectual upheaval in Europe. In the sixteenth and seventeenth centuries there was a renaissance, a re-birth in the old world. Out of it the boundary lines of nations were recast, and for the minds of men there were new flights of freedom. Efforts to make certain beliefs final and certain intellectual conceptions static had failed. The unceasing purposes of progress and development could not be thwarted. And so there came into being a new Europe to undertake the subjection and civilization of the new world which had been discovered. In the meantime, for more than a century the new land which Columbus had revealed remained unexplored and unused. It is true that the Spaniards, in the wake of the discovery credited to them, put forth some efforts in America, but they were without adequate or permanent results. They laid the foundations of St. Augustine in Florida, a city that was born only to languish; they despoiled the native civilizations of Mexico and of Peru; Ponce de Leon in his old age sought for the fabled fountains of youth; and De Soto along a trail of desolation sought for a golden empire to find only a grave in the Mississippi River which he re-discovered and to which, as if in mockery, the Spaniards had given the name of the River of the Holy Ghost.[1]

Spain had played a glorious part indeed. By her strength she had stopped the Moslem tide westward bound, thereby saving Europe for Christianity. And as her supreme gift to mankind she had added a new world to the old. But when all this had been accomplished, a blight fell upon her. It may have been in the blood of the Hapsburgs which was mingled with the blood of Isabella, the sainted. Her explorers despoiled the new world which had been discovered, and in the old world her rulers sought to fasten on subject races the new forged

[1] Rio del Espiritu Santo. Alvarez de Piñeda reached it in 1519; De Soto, marching overland from Florida, in 1541. It is said the river was known to the Spaniards as early as 1513.

shackles of the most cruel Inquisition ever devised from the malice of men. To America the Spaniards brought the torch and the sword. They killed and they plundered. Unfitted for the sublime work of leadership in the land which Columbus had discovered, Spain herself had to be broken as a world power before other nations could perform that service for mankind.

It is the imperishable glory of a small country, of Holland, built half in the sea and half on the land, that she challenged the supremacy of the Spain which sought to fasten the Inquisition on a people who boasted that they had never worn a yoke. By the middle of the sixteenth century the two nations, so unequal in all respects, and so unlike also, were engaged in the great war in which it was to be determined whether Europe should become modern or remain medieval. Two generations, and almost a third, fought in that war. But the outcome was as definite as it was inevitable. Human progress may be delayed but it cannot be stopped; right may tremble before might, but might must in the end bow before right. By the outcome of that war the nations of north-western Europe were set free, and then those freed nations prepared themselves to enter America.

Under these new moral stimulations and with these new intellectual conceptions, England, Holland, and France almost simultaneously sent their exploring and colonizing ships across the Atlantic. In the first decade of the seventeenth century they founded settlements along the coast from the James River to the St. Lawrence. In the great world race, Holland soon fell by the wayside by reason of her own physical restrictions, and France was eventually hampered under the sway of an absolutely monarchy by which the aspirations of her colonists were suppressed and crushed. Her subjects in the new world had no freedom left for their own development. And so it became England's destiny to shape the course of empire in North America, until she too through a bigoted ruler more than a century later sought to restrict and to restrain the liberties that belonged to the old races in a new world.

America became the first heir of this renaissance in Europe. The time was propitious for the birth of new nations. The seventeenth century began well and became another golden age in the world. In Holland, Grotius formulated international law from which ultimately will come international peace; the poet Vondel preceded Milton; and Rembrandt created a new art in which he depicted the common people who were to be glorified in the new world. In France, Descartes founded almost a new science of the mind, and Molière, Corneille, and Racine followed with a literature for whose like we must go back to classic Greece. But most of all, the new thought blossomed in England where Bacon entered new avenues of thought and where Shakespeare summed up all human knowledge and adorned it with beauty everlasting in works that are still almost beyond man's comprehension.

Shakespeare closed his career with *The Tempest*, in which one may find a forecast of the new world. In this play "the poet's eye in fine frenzy rolling" caught a glimpse of all the marvelous things to be. Caliban, a creature of the primeval darkness, learned a new language and a new service, and Ariel, a creature of spiritual skies, was set free to fill the world with music and with beauty. The drunken shipwrecked sailors talked of laying ten doits "to see a dead Indian," while the nobles in the scene dreamed of a land where the grass grew "lush and lusty;" in which they saw "every thing advantageous to life," and where, they were told, the clouds "would open and show riches ready to drop" upon them. And the "admired Miranda! Indeed, the top of admiration!" on her father Prospero's "still-vex'd Bermoothes,"[2] exclaimed, "O brave new world, that has such people in't!"

Does it not read like a dream of the new world, and is it not the prelude to America?

[2] The Bermudas.

# CHAPTER II

## The French Look Westward

While Shakespeare was still writing, the English founded Jamestown in 1607; the French, Quebec in 1608; and the Dutch made a beginning on the island of Manhattan in 1609. If there is added to these the founding of Plymouth in 1620, we have the genesis of the American nation, including Canada. The settlements were made by small groups of men, but the stamp of each remains on them even to this day. Within a period of two years the foundations of America were laid and the strife begun for the mastery of the opportunities which the sailor of Genoa had revealed to the world more than a century before.

It was then far away to what is now Iowa, which is the theme of this history, but the discovery of this distant land was very directly connected with those primary settlements on the Atlantic seaboard. The French had been on the Hudson long before the Dutch settled on Manhattan Island. They had abandoned it, and in the final lottery they drew the St. Lawrence instead of the Hudson. They were not satisfied with their allotment. Quebec commanded one of the great rivers of the continent, but its climate was one of long winters and of an ice-bound river. And so the founder of the colony, Samuel de Champlain, cast longing eyes southward and dreamed of sunny skies and warm waters like those of his homeland. In the pursuit of his quest he reached the beautiful lake which still bears his name, but which was then known as the Lake of the Iroquois. He was within reach of the Hudson in the very year that the Dutch anchored the Half Moon in its waters. But his quest was ill-omened. Chance, fate, destiny, Providence, what was it? On the lake, in the vicinity of the modern Ticonderoga, he came in contact with some Mohawk Indians. He did not know how to make peace with them and so he made war on them. The little skirmish that followed has been called one of the decisive battles of America.[1] It was fought by a few men, white and red, on the thirteenth of July, 1609. The French combatants in their boats, lying far enough off shore to protect themselves against the primitive weapons of the savages, used muskets to win a victory that was their greatest defeat in America. They vanquished their adversaries of the forests on that summer day, but for a century the vanquished pursued the victors, confining them to the country of the St. Lawrence. It was the day of doom for the southward extension of their empire. But for the battle on the lake, they might have reigned on the Hudson and changed the course of American history!

Stopped on the south by hostile Indians, the French moved in the only direction that was left them, that is, up the St. Lawrence and around the Great Lakes. Quebec became a missionary colony and the Jesuit priests marched westward with the trappers and the traders; with the adventurers of the woods and of the waters. None dared more and none suffered or achieved more than those who, bent on long and hazardous journeys, bore no weapons except a staff and wore no insignia except that of the cross. Around their names are woven many of the romances of the interior of the continent. They left their impress on vast regions; not only on those of the St. Lawrence, but on those of the Mississippi and all its tributaries, and northward on lands whose rivers flow to Arctic seas.[2] The transcripts of the transactions of these missionaries were published annually in Paris under the title of the *Jesuit Relations*. These printed reports, together with the original materials on which they were based, are great storehouses of history, of romance, and of adventure. It is to those sources that every historian must go for his informa-

[1] "It made the Iroquois the allies first of the Dutch and afterward of the English; and this is one of the great central and cardinal facts in the history of the New World." — John Fiske in *The Dutch and Quaker Colonies of America*, Vol. I, Chapter IV.

[2] "Not a cape was doubled nor a stream discovered that a Jesuit did not show the way." — Bancroft.

tion and inspiration when he would write the history of the Mississippi Valley.

Champlain died in 1635. He had been no farther west than Lake Huron. But he knew there was a farther west and he must have longed to explore it. What he could not perform himself, he sent others to accomplish. In 1634 Jean Nicollet passed through Lake Michigan, traversed Green Bay and entered the Fox River, coming within a few days' journey of a great river to the west of which the Indians had told the French. Nicollet, and others also, thought that the water to the west was the Chinese Sea. When he went on his journey he not only believed in that myth, but he literally clothed himself in his belief. He went expecting and prepared to meet the Chinese. He is described by one of his contemporaries, who says that "he wore a grand robe of Chinese damask, all strewn with flowers and birds of many colors." [3] And so arrayed, he wandered through the wilderness of lakes and rivers and forests. According to the same account, Nicollet was well received among the Indians. Their chiefs entertained him lavishly, serving at one feast one hundred and twenty beavers. But he did not go far enough to find the Chinese Sea.

The great quest did not die with Champlain, nor did explorations end with Nicollet. In due time there came to New France a dreamer who was also an organizer. This was Jean Talon, who became intendant of the province. He realized perhaps more fully than others that the nations of Europe were contesting for the mastery of the American continent. He knew what the English and Dutch were doing on the Atlantic seaboard and what the Spanish were doing in the south. For France he coveted the interior of the continent and he thought out ways to achieve it. He went to Paris and laid his plans before the rulers, where they were well received, and he was assured that the government deemed "nothing more important for the colony than a passage to the South Sea." To find that way became the great desire of his life.[4]

New light had been thrown on the unexplored country.

[3] Thwaites's *The Jesuit Relations*, Vol. XXIII, p. 279.

[4] *Ibid.*, Vol. LI, p. 53.

The Jesuits had a mission at La Pointe, at the tip of Lake Superior. To it Indians came from afar to trade. In the *Jesuit Relation* of 1666-1667 there appeared the statement that Father Claude Allouez had talked with red men who lived "toward the great river named Messepi," which is said to be the earliest printed form of the modern Mississippi. Some historians believe that Allouez himself may have looked upon the river in some of his journeyings.[5]

When Talon returned from France he at once proceeded with his plans to discover the mythical river and to find the South Sea passage which was so important. In 1670 he sent Daumont de Saint-Lusson to take possession of the undiscovered country. With Lusson went Nicholas Perrot, a noted *coureur de bois* and Indian interpreter, and also Louis Joliet,[6] an explorer and hydrographic engineer. On the fourteenth of June, 1671, at the Sault Ste. Marie, holding a piece of sod in one hand and his drawn sword in the other, he took possession of the country "in the name of the most high, mighty and redoubted Monarch, Louis XIV." It was a French proclamation that included "all countries, rivers, lakes, and streams contiguous and adjacent . . . both those which have been discovered and those which may be discovered hereafter, in all their length and breadth, bounded on the one side by the Sea of the North and of the West, and on the other by the South Sea;" and "all other potentates, princes, sovereigns and republics" were warned against trespassing on the lands on the peril of his majesty's "resentment and efforts of his arms."

By that proclamation what is now Iowa became French territory, June fourteenth, 1671. To this process, Talon desired to add the rights of discovery and occupation. For this he found two men. One was René Robert Cavelier, Sieur de la Salle, known in American history as La Salle, and the other was Louis Joliet. Both had studied for the Jesuit priesthood but had been lured from those studies by the lust of trade and

[5] Shea's *Discovery and Explorations of the Mississippi Valley*, pp. xviii, xxv.

[6] The French spelling of this name was Jolliet; Father Marquette in his *Journal* rendered it Jollyet.

exploration. La Salle was of a distinguished family, born in Rouen, France, 1643, while Joliet was the son of a humble wagon-maker in Quebec. He was born in 1645. La Salle was ambitious and became a man of many enterprises, while Joliet, more deficient in imagination, lacked the dramatic touch that brings with it the repute of glory. La Salle drew the lesser assignment, to begin with. He was sent southward and explored the Ohio and the Illinois, events which do not concern this history. To Joliet fell the discovery and exploration of the river of which Father Allouez and others had heard.

In New France, the church marched with the state, if it did not lead it. And so Father Dablon, who was the head of the Jesuit Missions, designated Père Jacques Marquette, one of the younger but most enterprising missionaries, to accompany Joliet, and to look after the spiritual welfare of the new tribes that might be encountered. Marquette was a man well fitted for the work. He was born in Laon, France, in 1637. As a young man he had read the *Jesuit Relations*, and they had fired his heart with the zeal of the missionary. In 1666 he was sent to America, where he speedily inured himself to the hardships of pioneer life and acquainted himself with many of the Indian dialects. One of the first things he must have heard was the mention of the "Great River" of the west, for it was in the *Relation* of 1666-1667 that the name "Messepi" appeared for the first time. The name was made up of two Indian words, mesi or missi, signifying great, and sepe or sepo, meaning river. But the great river of the west remained still only a name, for in the *Relation* of 1669-1670, Father Dablon wrote that "To the south flows the great river, which they call the Missisipi, which can have its mouth only in the Florida Sea, more than 400 leagues from here." The mystery of the river was still unsolved.

It is possible, however, that two French wood rangers had already reached the river as early as 1659, and some think, 1655. There is a brief reference to them in the *Relation* of 1660. It is now accepted that this reference was to Pierre d'Esprit Radisson and his less enterprising brother-in-law, Medard Chouart des Groseilliers. These men seem to have been regarded as outlaws, because they conformed neither to the civil nor to the ecclesiastical authorities at Quebec. The treatment they received may have driven them to Boston, where they revealed secrets of their explorations that led the British to Hudson Bay, making that region British instead of French. While under this influence, Radisson seems to have written an account of some of their travels, in very poor English, in fact in a mixture of many languages, including Indian dialects. This now constitutes his *Journal*. The manuscript found its way to England where it was buried in the archives of the Hudson Bay Company where it was found almost two centuries later in some waste papers.

The publication of this belated *Journal*[7] led to bitter discussions which divided the mid-western historical world into two factions, the one rejecting and the other accepting the discoveries of Radisson. The most essential part of the Radisson account is to this effect: "We were four months on our voyage without doing anything but goe from river to river . . . We met several sorts of people . . . By persuasion of some of them we went into ye great river that divides itself into 2 . . . the forked river . . . so called because it has 2 branches, the one towards the west, the other towards the south, which we believe runs toward Mexico, by the tokens they gave us."[8] This forked river with two branches has been accepted as the Mississippi and the Missouri. Radisson also speaks of the Illinois Indians and of the Sioux and of the "Maingonas,"[9] probably the same Indians which Father Marquette was soon to designate as the "Moingouena." But whatever conclusions we may come to now about the discoveries of these rangers, neither Joliet nor Marquette in 1673 had any knowledge of them.

Before 1673 Marquette himself had heard much of the unexplored river. In 1669 he was at La Pointe, where he had succeeded Father Allouez. While there he met many Indians of the Illinois tribe, who came there to trade. They told him that they lived on a great river which was thirty days' jour-

[7] The *Journal* was first printed in 1885 by the Prince Society of Boston.

[8] Prince Society's reprint of Radisson's *Journal*, pp. 151, 152.

[9] Lacnas Gifford Weld in his *On the Way to Iowa* accepts this as the first record of the word from which the name Des Moines was derived.

ney to the southwest. Filled with the desire to go and preach to them, he acquainted himself with their dialect. In writing about this information, Marquette said "it is hard to believe that the great river discharges its waters in Virginia, and we think rather that it has its mouth in California." He hoped some day to have "full knowledge either of the South Sea or of the Western Sea." Geographic conceptions were hazy in those days.

When Marquette had been apprised by Joliet of their assigned journey, the two men spent the winter at St. Ignace, making preparations for their undertaking. From such knowledge as they had they made crude maps of the region to be traversed. They built two boats of birch bark, with splints of cedar and ribs of spruce, strong enough to resist the currents and yet light enough to be carried over the portages. For food they provided themselves with smoked meats and corn. Five hardy and trustworthy *voyageurs* were selected to assist them.

For them the winter was an anxious season of waiting; one of solemn anticipations. The spirit of a great adventure was upon them. Father Marquette wrote of the "happy necessity" of exposing his life for the discovery of new lands and the salvation of strange peoples still living in darkness. In his daily prayers he placed their expedition under the protection of the Virgin Mary, and to her he dedicated whatever they might achieve.

# CHAPTER III

## The Discovery of Iowa

On the seventeenth of May, 1673, Joliet and Marquette left the Mission of St. Ignace and set out on their immortal journey of discovery, "firmly resolved," says the record, "to do all for so glorious an enterprise." They followed the northern shore of Lake Michigan, and passing through Green Bay soon entered the Fox River which they ascended until they came to a narrow neck of land that separates it from the headwaters of the Wisconsin. They had passed the limits of known explorations by white men. The Indians whom they met tried to dissuade them from going farther. They told them of ferocious tribes who murdered all strangers who came among them, and that without either cause or provocation; of frightful monsters in the river which devoured both men and their canoes; of demons whose roaring could be heard afar; and of heat on treeless plains so intense that all perished in it. But undismayed, having carried their boats and stores across the portage, on the tenth of June they started down the Wisconsin River, leaving "the waters which flow to Quebec . . ." to follow those which would lead them "into strange lands."

On the seventeenth of June they reached the mouth of the Wisconsin River, and then, looking across what was the "Great Water," they discovered Iowa. It was with a joy, says Father Marquette, which he could not express. He bestowed on the river the name "de la Conception," in honor of the Virgin Mary, and in conformity with his oft-repeated vows. As they floated out upon the river they looked and listened, but there was no human sight or sound; no evidence that any man had ever frequented the place. It was a great and primeval solitude of silence. The place of discovery has been called "one of the noblest scenes in America."[1] Rugged cliffs, deep fissured, with trailing vines and towering trees rose like mountains above them as they neared the western shore. The deep waters were beneath them, the blue sky was over them, and the loveliness of June was all around them! The wonder and the awe that must have been depicted on their faces are themes for painters and poets!

They soon turned their boats down stream, for it was their assigned task to determine the course and the outlet of the river which they had rediscovered. The first written description of any part of what is now Iowa was recorded by Marquette in his *Journal*.[2] It was to the effect that "on the right is a considerable chain of very high mountains." They were not mountains, nor the foot-hills of mountains, but merely the bluffs where the prairies descend abruptly to meet the channel of the river. Fortunately the name which was bestowed on the river hardly survived Marquette's own journey on its waters, and the one which the Indians had given to it, the Messipi — the Mississippi — the Great Water, clung to it, a name as fluent and as majestic as its own course and current through the heart of a continent.

They had not gone far when the scenery changed. "There is now almost no wood or mountain," Marquette wrote, "and the islands are more beautiful and covered with finer trees." But still they saw no human beings on either shore. They saw "nothing but deer and moose, bustards and wingless swans." The latter, says the account, "shed their plumes in this country." In the water they encountered cat-fish of

[1] By Thwaites in his *Father Marquette*.

[2] Both Joliet and Marquette made records of their journey. Joliet lost his papers on the return trip in a wreck in the La Chine rapids. This accident lost him much of the credit that was his due. The details of the expedition history owes to Marquette's *Journal*, or report which he made to Dablon, the supervisor of the Jesuit missionaries at Quebec. Dablon forwarded a copy of it to Paris where it was printed in Thévenot's *Receuil des Voyages Curieux* in 1681. The original MS. remained in Quebec until in 1842, when it was removed to St. Mary's College, Montreal. In 1853, Dr. John Gilmary Shea published it in his *Discovery and Exploration of the Mississippi Valley*, from which the quotations in this chapter are taken.

such size that one, mistaken for "a large tree," threatened to "knock" them "to pieces." They saw also "a monster with the head of a tiger, a pointed snout like a wild cat's, a beard and ears erect, a grayish head and neck all black," which has been interpreted to mean a tiger-cat crouching on the water's edge. The explorers were looking for unusual things and often they gave unusual descriptions of what they beheld. Farther down the river they saw flocks of wild turkeys and herds of bison, or buffalo, which Marquette called *pisikious,* and which he described somewhat grotesquely.

Day followed day as they floated down the river, but still they saw no human beings. None the less they were constantly on their guard against surprises. When they made landings to cook their food they built but little fire, lest the smoke should attract the savages, and at night they slept in their boats far enough from shore for safety. And yet they must have longed for the sight of men, to learn from them something about the strange country through which they were passing.

Father Marquette's account then continues: "At last, on the twenty-fifth of June, we perceived footprints of men by the water side, and a beaten path entering a beautiful prairie. We stopped to examine it, and concluding that it was a path leading to some Indian village, we resolved to go and reconnoiter; . . ." Leaving the men to guard the boats . . . "then M. Jollyet and I undertook this rather hazardous discovery for two single men who thus put themselves at the discretion of an unknown and barbarous people. We followed the little path in silence, and having advanced about two leagues, we discovered a village on the banks of the river, and two others on a hill, half a league from the former."

The place of this landing is still in dispute. Clearly, it was above the mouth of a river flowing into the Mississippi not far below. Marquette's meager description of the country might fit any one of several streams. But he says it was in latitude "40 degrees and some minutes, partly by southeast and partly by southwest, after having advanced more than sixty leagues since entering the river, without discovering anything." We have here the latitude and the distance below the mouth of the Wisconsin, as reckoned by the explorers. Their observations of distances and directions were very accurate, as may be noted from the fact that the course of the river as laid down on Marquette's map corresponds closely with the actual course of the Mississippi as now known. From the map we know also that it was on the west or Iowa side of the river they made their landing. The name given to the group of three villages which they discovered is Peourea, and the name Moingouena appears on the map near the same river. The first of these names was transferred to Illinois as Peoria and the second became identified with the Des Moines River. From this association it was generally assumed by the early writers that the villages of the Peourea were on the bank of the Des Moines. But when Francis Parkman and John Gilmary Shea, in the middle of the last century, began to write history more critically both were impelled to the belief that the river was one farther north.

More recent and also more critical examinations of the maps and the descriptions have given added credence to the conjectures of Parkman and Shea.[3] The sixty leagues of Marquette correspond to about two hundred and seven miles, which is not the distance from the mouth of the Wisconsin to the mouth of the Des Moines, but which is almost the exact distance from the first river to the mouth of the Iowa, which by modern steamboat charts is two hundred and twelve miles from Prairie du Chien. By the reckoning in leagues the place was therefore at the mouth of the Iowa River. But the "40 degrees and some minutes" of Marquette correspond with the mouth of the Des Moines. His leagues and his latitudes are clearly at variance with each other. In which was he in error? Did he miscount the leagues, or misread the latitudes? It must have been the latter, for it is found that all except one of Marquette's latitudes are in error and the error is always the same, one degree. The exception is the Akensea, or Arkan-

[3] The most lucid statement of this controversy may be found in *The Iowa Journal of History and Politics*, Vol. I, No. 1, p. 3, by Laenas Gifford Weld.

sas River, which is correctly given as thirty-three degrees and forty minutes. The Wisconsin, the Illinois, the Missouri, and the Ohio on his map all enter the Mississippi one degree too far to the south. The error may have been due to a defect in the instrument which was used. Adding this one degree to Marquette's "forty degrees and some minutes," we have the latitude of the mouth of the Iowa River, by degrees of latitude. But if the historic meeting with the Illinois Indians took place on the Iowa instead of the Des Moines, it was at least on what is now Iowa soil.

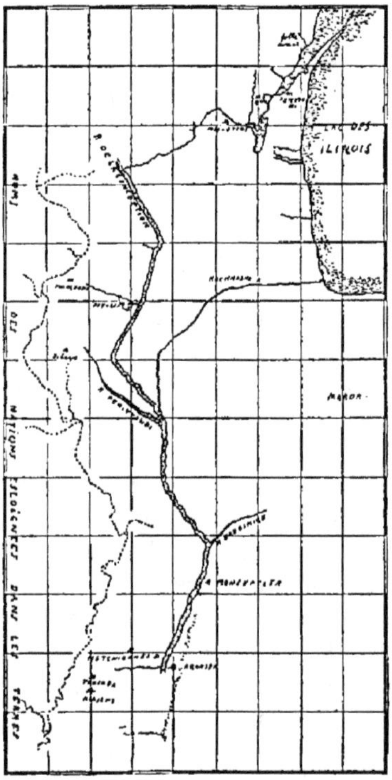

Marquette's Map.—Dotted line shows correct course of Mississippi.

Without being seen, the two explorers entered the first of the villages until they were so near one of the cabins that they "even heard the Indians talking." They then announced their presence by calling to them in a loud voice. "At this cry the Indians rushed out of their cabins." Their attitude was that of friendliness. After conferring, they deputed four of their oldest men to meet the white visitors. Of these four, "two carried tobacco-pipes well adorned and trimmed with various kinds of feathers." They approached slowly, frequently "lifting their pipes toward the sun, as if offering them to him to smoke, but without uttering a single word."

When they reached their unbidden guests, the Indians stopped to consider them attentively. Marquette spoke to them first, asking them who they were. "They answered that they were Ilinois and, in token of peace, they presented their pipes to smoke." Happily Marquette at La Pointe had acquainted himself with the dialect of these Indians.

The two explorers were then conducted to the village where all awaited them impatiently. They were taken to the cabin of an old man who received them standing "perfectly naked, with his hands stretched out and raised toward the sun." This patriarch said to them: "How beautiful is the sun, O Frenchman, when thou comest to visit us! All our village awaits thee, and thou shalt enter all our cabins in peace!"

They were then conducted to the cabin of the great sachem, who lived in one of the other villages. He summoned a council before which Father Marquette presented their joint mission, as emissaries from the government of New France and from God. In reply the chief said: "I thank thee, Blackgown, and thee, Frenchman . . . for taking so much pains to come and visit us; never has the earth been so beautiful, nor the sun so bright, as today; never has our river been so calm, nor so free from rocks, which your canoes have removed as they passed; never has our tobacco had so fine a flavor, nor our corn appeared so beautiful as we behold it today. Here is my son, that I give thee, that thou mayest know my heart. I pray thee to take pity on me and all my nation. Thou knowest the Great Spirit who has made us all; thou speakest to him and hearest his word: ask him to give me life and health, and come and dwell with us, that we may know him." [4]

These are indeed words of surpassing beauty — but we dare not doubt that Father Marquette was a faithful reporter of them. No fairer or nobler words have ever been spoken since in Iowa, and civilization and Christianity have been able to add nothing to that Indian's conception of God and man's relation to Him.

A feast was soon spread for the visitors, which was served in four courses, the first of which was of corn boiled in water and flavored with grease, the second of fish, the third of dog's meat, which was removed when the guests indicated they could

[4] Longfellow's paraphrase of this speech is one of the most beautiful passages in his *Hiawatha*. See Canto XXII of poem.

not partake of it, and the last, of the fattest portions of buffalo meat. They exchanged presents, one of the gifts from the Indians being a calumet, or peace pipe, with which the travelers later won the favor of hostile tribes. They made a round of visits in the villages and when the white men departed they were accompanied to their canoes by nearly six hundred natives who showed "every possible manifestation of joy."

Neither Joliet nor Marquette ever again returned to the Iowa country. They went down the river as far as the outlet of the Arkansas where they were able to satisfy themselves that it emptied into the Gulf of Mexico. On their return they passed up the Illinois River and down the Chicago to Lake Michigan. Father Marquette, true to his vows, returned to the Illinois Indians to preach to them and, exhausted by his labors and the many hardships he had borne in wild lands, he died on the site of the present city of Ludington, Michigan, May eighteenth, 1675. Later the Indians took his remains, followed by a retinue of canoes, back to the Mission at St. Ignace. Joliet lived many more years and made many more explorations, some of them in the Hudson Bay country. He was rewarded with offices and with the island of Anticosti. He died, according to the meager accounts, "some years prior to 1737,"[5] being old in years.

[5] Shea's *Discovery and Exploration of the Mississippi Valley, 1852*, p. lxxx. According to other authorities, Joliet died much earlier.

## CHAPTER IV

### IOWA UNDER FRANCE

La Salle, who had been on the Ohio and on the Illinois, was one of the first to grasp the meaning of the identification of the Mississippi River with the Gulf of Mexico. He saw on it the empire in America of which other Frenchmen had dreamed. He was in many ways, if not in all ways, the greatest man in French-American explorations. He had a vast and a speculative mind. He was bold in his conceptions and daring in his executions. He was ambitious and he was greedy. He thought of France, but also of himself; of riches and an illustrious name. But as an administrator he was a man of many defects. He was proud and taciturn. He was unable to trust others, and he was not trusted by them. He aroused hatreds that he could not subdue and he created antagonisms that he could not surmount. He became a magnificent failure in the midst of magnificent victories.[1]

Jean Talon, who had grasped from afar the whole scheme of the Mississippi Valley, was not permitted to remain in New France long enough to see the realization of his plans. He left his work to Frontenac, who became the greatest of the French governors in America. Frontenac was dazzled by the discoveries of Joliet and Marquette and of La Salle. For a time Frontenac and La Salle coöperated in great undertakings. Both were opposed by the Jesuits, who saw their power declining in the presence of two such dominating minds. The traders of Canada constituted the third side of the complicated triangle of ambitions and authority. They feared that the opening of the Mississippi would divert the trade of which they had enjoyed a monopoly. In one thing the three conflicting forces were united, namely, resistance to the English

[1] For the life and achievements of La Salle see Francis Parkman's *La Salle and the Discovery of the Great West.*

and the Dutch on the Atlantic seaboard. They must be kept out of the west. To further this end, Frontenac, aided by La Salle, concluded a spectacular peace with the Iroquois Indians who had so long been the enemies of the French. They were to constitute a red barrier to those who might come through the mountains into the Mississippi Valley.

La Salle then went to Paris with fulsome letters from Frontenac. There he was well received. His achievements were acclaimed and his plans were approved. Louis XIV bestowed upon him almost unlimited powers. He could build forts and he could make wars. But colonists for the new empire had to be approved by imperial authority. When La Salle returned to America, he sent Father Hennepin up the Mississippi while he himself proceeded toward the gulf, which he reached on April ninth, 1682. They sang Te Deums and cried "long live the king," as he called the region Louisiana, and in the name of Louis the Grand took possession of "the seas, harbors, ports, bays, adjacent straits, and all nations, peoples, provinces, cities, towns, villages, mines, minerals, fisheries, streams and rivers within the extent of the said Louisiana," and it extended in the parlance of that day to "the farthest springs of the Missouri." Eleven years before, Lusson had made the Iowa country part of New France, and now La Salle re-made it part of Louisiana. But it remained French.

Once more La Salle returned to France to procure men and materials for his empire. To the financiers he talked of buffalo hides and beaver skins; of wool and gold and precious stones. All the wealth of a continent would be poured into the lap of France! Dazed and dazzled by anticipated riches they placed men, money, and materials at the disposal of the prospective empire builder. With four laden ships La Salle returned to America. Women were included in the cargoes. They were to become the pioneer mothers of the French in Louisiana. The ships sailed for the mouth of the Mississippi. They were well armed to resist the Spaniards who might be found in those waters. But they were not worsted by Spaniards, but by stormy seas and by crews that mutinied and by captains who deserted. They failed to find the mouth of the Mississippi. They sailed far past it and made a landing "somewhere between Matagorda Island and the Bay of Corpus Christi," on the coast of Texas. They sought in vain for the mouth of the river they had passed; they were four hundred miles away from it. One of the four ships was wrecked in the surf and one of the captains, Beaujeau, sailed his ship back to France, taking the cannon and munitions with him. The others landed and built what they called a fort, to protect especially the women while La Salle and a company of men started overland to find the Mississippi. They sought in vain. Those in the fort perished and La Salle himself was murdered by one of his own men, probably on the nineteenth of March, 1687, and somewhere on the southern branch of the Trinity River. Even burial was denied him. His body was left to be devoured by wolves and vultures. Such is the glory of man. He who would have founded an empire was not able to find a grave in the land of his dreams.

Of La Salle's overland companions many perished in the wilderness, but a few found their way back to the Mississippi and ultimately to the St. Lawrence, after toilsome journeys by water and by land, often bereft of food and always beset by Indians. No one has written their Odyssey or their Anabasis for there was no Homer or Xenophon among them, nor could the Greek poets and historians have written them adequately.

It was not until 1718 that La Salle's city at the mouth of the Mississippi was founded, when Sieur de Bienville made a beginning at New Orleans. But then, at last, France stood guard at the mouths of the two great rivers of the continent, the Mississippi and the St. Lawrence, and bending around the Great Lakes stretched the empire of her dreams — but it was vacant and void. Near the center of this region was what is now Iowa — for we must not lose sight of the theme of this history.

Then for a while nothing prospered or even went well in Louisiana, in New France, or in Old France. The last years of the grand monarch, Louis XIV, were as disastrous as his earlier years had been glorious. In 1697 he was compelled to sign an ignominious peace at Ryswick, dictated by the allied nations under the leadership of little Holland. He died and Louis XV came to the throne. He aped the grandeur of his predecessor, but he wielded none of his power. It was said of him that he spent thirty-six millions of francs on a strumpet, but he could not find a franc for those who would have built a French empire in America. When he had impoverished the treasury of his country, he empowered John Law, an escaped murderer from Scotland, to issue unlimited quantities of paper money against the unknown and unrealized resources of Louisiana. When the "Mississippi Bubble" burst, the wreckage filled France and Europe. If Louis XIV had said, "L'état, c'est moi," Louis XV was at least able to say, "Après moi, le déluge."[2] France was headed for the Revolution.

In America, Frontenac, with a short interim, was able to hold out until 1698, when he died. He had become an irascible man who quarreled with everyone, fate not excepted. Quebec remained a village while New Orleans almost perished, and no lands were tilled or cities built between the two outlets. Only trappers, traders, and missionaries traversed the vast realms of New France and of Louisiana. The colonists were treated like the slaves of their government, the government that should have nursed and nurtured them. It was the law that none might enter or leave New France without the permission of the government in Paris, a government so incompetent that it could not meet the needs of those who lived under its own shadows. Those whose religious views were not approved might not trap nor trade in the realm. "No farmer could visit Montreal or Quebec without permission." When the dispersed Huguenots wanted to settle on the Mississippi, they were forbidden to enter. The king declared that he had not driven heretics out of old France to let them build a republic in New France. But they were made welcome on the Atlantic seaboard, from South Carolina to Massachusetts, where they added their splendid alloy to the American race

[2] "I am the State," "After me, the deluge."

that was then forming. Instead of Huguenots who were masters of all arts and trades, New Orleans received a cargo of distressed women from the streets of Paris who became the wives of distressed men. To each woman the king presented a chest of clothes and trinkets. Gayeties followed in New Orleans, but there was no industry up and down the Mississippi.

Those whom we now call Americans soon began to find their way westward through the Allegheny Mountains. They were hardy and daring men; men of courage and of convictions; free men and splendid men; men fit to subdue the wilderness and to found new states. The farther west they came the more they ceased to be Europeans and the more they became Americans. By 1754 there were more than a million of such men in the Atlantic colonies, while the French from Quebec to New Orleans and back again did not number more than a hundred thousand.

When they clashed, as soon they did, there was no question of the outcome. The French claimed all the valley country to the Alleghenies, but the English-Americans insisted that their provinces extended westward to the Mississippi. Soon we catch a glimpse of George Washington as the bearer of a dispatch from the governor of Virginia to the French on the Ohio. The French answer was Fort Duquesne and the English reply was Fort Necessity. Israel Putnam moves upon the scene as a private soldier and John Stark as a lieutenant.

The decisive action between the contending races took place in Canada, when the English general, Wolfe, defeated the French general, Montcalm, on the Heights of Quebec in 1759. It was only a skirmish, but like the skirmish on Lake Champlain a century and a half before, it decided much. Canada and the St. Lawrence ceased to be French and became English. Louisiana was not affected, but fearing that the English might seize it also, Louis XV secretly transferred it to Spain, in 1762, three years after the surrender at Quebec. It was the deluge of loss and decay. France woke up with nothing left in America except a few fishing islands. And with Louisiana, the Iowa country passed under Spanish dominion.

# CHAPTER V

## AS PART OF A SPANISH PROVINCE

So unpopular was the transfer of Louisiana to Spain that the French governor was permitted to remain until 1768, when he was succeeded by the Spaniard, Antonio d'Ulloa, who, being a man of letters and of science, ruled temperately. It was while the French were still in control of the province that St. Louis was founded, in 1764. During the American Revolution the Spanish governors were friendly to the Americans, primarily because they wanted to be rid of their British neighbors, and they helped themselves to Florida, including a strip along the coast connecting the peninsula with Louisiana. The Spanish possessions then extended from the Atlantic to the Pacific and as far north as the headwaters of the Mississippi.

But the region lying between the Allegheny Mountains and the Mississippi River was in dispute. In the treaty of peace at the close of the Revolutionary War, Great Britain ceded it to the United States. The British had always claimed that their seaboard colonies extended westward to the Mississippi, and whatever claims the French had to any of the lands were ceded to them with Canada. On this theory the American general, George Rogers Clark, during the Revolution, acting on a commission of the governor of Virginia, organized Kentucky as a county of that state, and defended it with arms. He took Kaskaskia in Illinois in 1777 and Vincennes in Indiana in 1779, and he built at the mouth of the Ohio a fort which he called Jefferson.

In many ways the Spanish sought to gain control of that region. They offered help to the struggling colonists if they would stop at the Allegheny Mountains. But that price was too dear to pay. "Poor as we are," Benjamin Franklin wrote to John Jay who was in Europe, "yet as I know we shall be rich, I would rather agree to buy at a great price the whole of their right to the Mississippi than sell a drop of its water." He said that "A neighbor might as well ask me to sell my street door." The simile was an apt one. Franklin saw even then that the Mississippi would be a street door for the republic. Spain, reluctant to give up the region, finally proposed to run a boundary line one mile east of the Mississippi River to keep that stream as a Spanish highway. Later she used all manner of intrigue to win over the western settlers and to alienate them from loyalty to the United States. But it was all in vain.

In the meantime settlers were pouring through the Alleghenies. In 1780 there were few white men in Kentucky, but by 1784 there were twenty thousand of them and in that year thirty thousand more are said to have entered the land. A few years later there was a similar stream of immigrants into Ohio, many of them coming from the New England states. If they were often dissatisfied with the government of the United States, still they were and they remained Americans. The Spaniards were aliens to them.

But the trans-Mississippi country, especially north of St. Louis, remained a sealed and unsettled area. "Now and then some weather-beaten trapper," says McMaster, "came from it to the frontiers of the states with stories of great plains as level as the floor, where the grass grew higher than the waist, where the flowers were more beautiful than in the best kept gardens, where trees were never seen, and where the Indians still looked upon the white man as a God." [1]

Out of the multiplication of population and discontent, what was believed to be a full settlement was finally evolved, in 1795, when Spain conceded to the Americans the right not only to navigate the Mississippi, but to deposit and reship their goods at New Orleans. Spain was at the time willing to enter into such an agreement for troubles were brewing for her in Europe. Out of the turmoil of the French Revolution

[1] McMaster's *History of the People of the United States*, Vol. I, p. 4.

Napoleon Bonaparte had risen to become not only the master of France but the potential master of Europe. To save herself Spain made a treaty with France that angered England to the point of declaring war on her. Spain now became as anxious about Louisiana as France had been a generation before. She even feared an Anglo-American alliance that might oust her from all her possessions on the Gulf of Mexico and on the Mississippi River. It was America's opportunity. Thomas Pinckney was the American minister at Madrid. He was ready to open negotiations, but he insisted that rights on the Mississippi must be the basic considerations. When Spain hesitated to concede what he wanted from her, he adroitly asked for his passports. Did that mean he would go to London and make an American pact with the British? If he did, it might transfer the war between England and Spain to America with Louisiana in the balance. In that fear Spain entered into a treaty with the United States, making the Mississippi River the boundary between them on the west, and on the south the thirty-first parallel of latitude. And the port of New Orleans was made free to American commerce.

But what Spain had saved from possible British seizure, she was not able to defend against Napoleon in whom the old French ambitions of an empire in the Mississippi Valley had reappeared. Would it not make him stronger in France to restore to her what Louis XV had lost in America? He had the power to dictate and Spain did not have the power to resist, and so on the first of October, 1800, by the secret treaty of San Ildefonso, Spain ceded back to France all of Louisiana. The consideration named was trivial enough, the recognition of the Duke of Parma, a son-in-law of the king of Spain, as king of Tuscany. It was an American empire exchanged for a European title!

When the contents of the treaty became known in the United States there was great alarm over it. America did not covet the powerful and ambitious Napoleon as a neighbor on the west and south. The impotent kings of Spain were more to be desired as such neighbors than the ambitious French usurper. The American state of mind was aggravated by the arbitrary, unwarranted, and unauthorized action of the Spanish intendant at New Orleans in refusing to permit the Americans to use the Mississippi River and the port of New Orleans for their commerce. The western settlers clamored for redress, and when the government at Washington seemed impotent or neglectful, they threatened to take matters in their own hands by organizing an army of frontiersmen to go down the river. And some talked of seceding from the United States and setting up a western government of their own.

Congress was greatly perturbed. Some members denounced the western settlers as turbulent and disloyal, but others as strenuously defended them. The Federalists, who were always unreconciled to President Jefferson, made an issue of the matter. They were for war on Spain, that much they loved the western Americans! The president procrastinated for he did not believe the matter was as serious as it was reported. In the senate James Ross of Pennsylvania made a two days' speech on the question and moved that the western militia be called out and five millions of dollars be appropriated to meet the situation.[2] No price was too high to pay for American rights and honor! The resolution was defeated and the house passed one of confidence in the executive. The president was authorized to use a provisional army in the west, but he had other plans. As a remedy he named a minister extraordinary, James Monroe, to go immediately to Madrid to settle the matter. These negotiations led up to the purchase of Louisiana by America, but before we proceed with those transactions, we must recount what had been happening specifically in the Iowa country under one hundred and thirty years of French and Spanish dominion, for these things are important in this history.

[2] Hosmer's *The Louisiana Purchase.*

# CHAPTER VI

## In the Iowa Country from 1673 to 1804

Following Joliet and Marquette, Nicolas Perrot, who had been a wood ranger, was sent to the Mississippi Valley as the commandant of the west. The Quebec government instructed him to promote peace and trade with the Indians. Somewhere below the Wisconsin, in 1685 or 1686, he built a trading post which also served as a fort. According to evidence, it was on the eastern side of the Mississippi, but he carried on much trade with the Indians on the Iowa side. A Miami chief presented him with some specimens of lead ore, conveying probably the first knowledge among white men of the mineral deposits in that region. The name of Perrot's Mines long remained attached to the country on both sides of the river.

In 1699 Pierre Charles Le Sueur came to the Mississippi River, but he did not spend much time in the Iowa country. In his notes, however, he referred to the "Ayavois" Indians. A young man named Jean Pénicaut accompanied him on some of his tours.[1] He referred to the "Rivière Moingona, the name of a nation of savages who dwelt on its banks." He found the grass of the prairies abundant and likened it to sanfoin. Wild animals without number thrived on it. The mines of Perrot and the "mountain" of Marquette, opposite the mouth of the Wisconsin, were noted in their reports.

The map makers kept pace with the explorers. On one of Franquelin's maps, made in 1688, appears the "Rivière des Moingona." On a more ambitious map, made in 1703, by William de L'Isle, a noted French cartographer, we find the river designated as "des moingona," which suggests the origin of the modern name Des Moines, while the Little Sioux is called

[1] *Wisconsin Historical Collections*, Vol. XVI, pp. 175-177.

the river "des Aiaouez." On the same map there was laid down a route across what is now northern Iowa, starting at the Mississippi, below the mouth of the Wisconsin, and ending on the Missouri River. This first river-to-river road was called the "Chemin des Voyageurs," meaning the road of the traders. It ran to the south of the group of lakes in what is now Dickinson County. In the vicinity of the lakes the map maker located villages of "Aiaouez" and "Paoutez," indicating that the Iowa Indians were then known by those two distinct names. From these maps and descriptions a modern man begins to feel at home in the Iowa of two centuries and more ago.

But all that was written about the country in those days was not correct. Many wrote themselves up and wrote others down. Father Louis Hennepin did this. He accompanied La Salle, and was sent up the Mississippi River, which he explored as far as the Falls of St. Anthony. He was at one time taken prisoner by a band of Sioux Indians, from whom he was rescued by Daniel Greysolon Du Lhut, or Du Luth, a noted explorer. He wrote a book which he called a *Description of Louisiane,* which is still valuable. But carried away with success in writing, he wrote two others, which he called *Nouvelle Decouverté* and *Nouveau Voyage,* in which he exploited many things which he had not done nor seen.[2] In the latter he sets himself out as the discoverer of the mouth of the Mississippi, a fact which, he says, he had concealed until then, 1698, out of regard for La Salle, who had coveted all the glory for himself. He even attempted to rob Joliet of his credit on the Mississippi. Father Hennepin, however, had very little to do with the Iowa country.

But the writings of another romancer have a great deal to do with the Iowa country, for he made the Des Moines the central river of the heart of the American continent. This writer was Baron de Lahontan. He wrote a book that became the popular one of its day.[3] It was printed in many languages and in many editions. Many contend that he himself was

[2] See Thwaites's *Hennepin's, A New Discovery.*

[3] *New Voyages to North America* by the Baron de Lahontan.

never farther west than Mackinac, where he may have spent one winter, and that his information was gleaned from others, or conjured up out of his own imagination. In the new land he pretended to have discovered a new river to which he gave the name Rivière Longue, or Long River. It is this that has been identified with the Des Moines. On its banks lived nations in Arcadian simplicity, without courts or laws or policemen. All men were free, and even their marriage relations were hampered with no "fettering covenants" that lasted through life. Of one of the chiefs he wrote, "When he walks, his way is strow'd with leaves of Trees," but usually he was carried about by six slaves! Another chief presented the baron and his retinue with "a great many Girls." Of course, all this is fiction, although it was taken for truth in Europe, which was then ready to believe anything about the new world. He anticipated Swift's *Gulliver's Travels.* By some his chapter on the Long River has been interpreted as "a satire upon European life and civilization." [4]

But that Lahontan's tales were accepted as facts is shown by a map drawn on a terrestrial globe in 1720 by a Capuchin monk, Philip Legrand of Chalon, France.[5] On this map the Des Moines is made the central river to the continent, with the Missouri and the Mississippi as two distorted forks. The Des Moines was not only the central river, but it was represented as Amazonian, extending far into the northwest where it drained lakes as vast as inland seas.

Among the writers of romance may be placed also the explorer Radisson, reference to whose diary in English has already been made. He wrote things that almost discredit his veracity and his standing as an explorer. "The country is so pleasant," he recorded in his broken English, "so beautiful & fruitfull," that it grieved him that the poverty stricken hordes of Europe "could not discover such inticing country to live in." He spoke of new kingdoms that "are so delicious & under such temperat a climat, plentifull of all things, the earth bringing foorth its fruit twice a yeare, the people live

[4] Thwaites's *Lahontan's New Voyages*, p. xxxvi.

[5] *Annals of Iowa*, Third Series, Vol. III, p. 175.

long & lusty & wise in their way." By coming to these new lands "what laborinth of pleasure should millions of people have," he exclaimed, "instead that millions complaine of misery & poverty!" This reads like an account of a visit to some fairy land.

When Father Charlevoix came to travel in the country, he left us more definite information about it. He says that the clay from which calumets were made "is found in the country of the Ajouez," which is another name for the Iowa Indians. Going up the Mississippi, he writes, "On the Left . . . we see the Moingona come out of the Midst of an immense and magnificent Meadow, which is quite covered with Buffaloes and other wild Creatures. At its entrance into the Mississippi it has little water, and is also but narrow: It has nevertheless a course, as they say, of two hundred and fifty leagues, winding from the North to the West . . . . In going up the Moingona, they find a great deal of coal."[5] He mentions the rapids above the mouth of the Des Moines and those in the vicinity of Rock Island. Of the lead mines he says they were "discovered formerly by a famous Traveller of Canada, named Nicolas Perrot," and that they still bore his name.[6]

So many came to the Iowa country in those days and so many left bits of writing about what they did and what they saw that we shall not attempt to follow them all. This is not a catalogue of details. Only those men and things are cited that have a curious interest or that serve to make an impressionistic picture of the country. Some came to trap and some to trade and others to preach. Every river bore its *voyageurs*, and the language spoken was French, when it was not some Indian dialect. But none came to till the soil or to build cities. There was not a plow in the Iowa country in those days, neither were there horses nor oxen. Strong arms and oars were the motive power on the streams, and along the "Chemin des Voyageurs" men went afoot. The time for settlements had

[5] *Letters to the Dutchess of Lesdiguieres; Giving an Account of a Voyage to Canada, and Travels Through that Vast Country and Louisiana, to the Gulf of Mexico*, by Father Charlevoix, London, 1763, p. 295.

[6] *Ibid.*, p. 296.

not yet arrived. The French did not settle; they roamed. And John Law's Mississippi Company which became the "Mississippi Bubble" had brought the whole region into great disrepute, and associated it with bankruptcy and distress. It was " only after the lapse of a century," said Barbé Marbois, who was Napoleon's minister of finance, and became an historian, "that the real prosperity of the country has effaced the infamy connected with its name." [7]

And if the French had been disposed to become settlers they had too many growing troubles both in America and in France to undertake the work at that time. They were about to lose New France to England and at home they were drifting toward the Revolution. In the Mississippi country their troubles in the first half of the eighteenth century came from the Fox Indians, then a turbulent and warlike tribe. In Wisconsin they lived on the river which still bears their name and which was part of the great highway to the west. For decades they kept that region embroiled in tribal wars. The French finally drove them out, pursuing them to the Rock River, and some think to the Illinois, where they were almost annihilated. So pitiable was their condition for a time that the Sacs, another warlike tribe, began to sympathize with them and, finally, when in fear of punishment for the killing of a prominent French official, one de Villiers, by a Sac warrior, they made common cause with the Foxes, which was the commencement of the coöperation between the two tribes which became associated under the name of Sacs and Foxes.

To maintain their prestige in the country and to protect their Indian allies, the French determined to make war on the allied Sacs and Foxes who thereupon took refuge in the Iowa country, on the Wapsipinicon River, which the French called "la Pomme de Cigne," meaning the river of the swan-apples, a species of roots that grew on its banks. The punitive expedition was placed under the command of Captain Nicholas Joseph de Noyelles, who left Montreal in 1734 and eventually marched with eighty Frenchmen and more red allies, many of whom proved unfaithful. He was instructed to spare the Sacs

[7] Marbois's *History of Louisiana*, Vol. I, p. 111.

if they would leave the Foxes, but if not to destroy both tribes and "to let our savages eat them up." Before they reached the Wapsipinicon, they learned that the Sacs and Foxes had left the country and had gone to the "Rivière sans fourche," meaning the river without a fork, a name often applied to the Des Moines. But their flight did not protect them. The French commander led his little force over the prairies, crossing the Cedar, the Iowa, and the Skunk rivers. It was in midwinter and the men suffered terribly. They were poorly clad and so lacking in food that at one time they subsisted for four days on the meat of twelve dogs and one dead horse. They overtook the enemy on the Des Moines, sixty leagues above its mouth, probably in the vicinity of the present city of Des Moines, where an indecisive battle was fought in which two Frenchmen were killed and many more Indians. The battle took place on April nineteenth, 1735.[8]

But the battle, while it proved the endurance and prowess of the French, did not decide anything. Two years later, in 1737, Pierre Paul, Sieur Marin, was sent to the west to separate the two tribes and to keep them from molesting the Illinois Indians who were allies of the French. Marin built a fort on Magill's Slough, which is on the Iowa side of the river below the mouth of the Wisconsin. He is credited with having established peace among the tribes, but it must have been a very temporary one, for the Sacs and Foxes continued to molest the Illinois and finally drove them out of the region, perhaps almost annihilating them. And the same fate befell the Mascoutins, from whom the name Muscatine was derived. The Sacs and Foxes eventually made themselves masters of the whole Mississippi from the Wisconsin down to the Illinois.

After Canada became British in 1759, and Louisiana Spanish in 1762, the Americans, who were still British subjects, soon found their way to the Mississippi, where they coveted part of the Indian trade. Jonathan Carver of Connecticut,

[8] De Noyelles's report of this expedition, found in the *Wisconsin Historical Collections*, Vol. XVII, pp. 224-229, is reprinted in *The Iowa Journal of History and Politics*, Vol. XII, pp. 245-261, edited by Jacob Van der Zee.

was one of these pioneers. He describes himself as a captain in the French wars, but he may have been a shoemaker who had an interest in the fur trade. He spent three years, 1676 to 1678, in the new country. He came down the Wisconsin River, near the mouth of which he saw "a mountain of considerable height," the McGregor bluffs which had similarly deceived others. He crossed the Mississippi, and proceeded to "a small river . . . which the French call Le Jaun Rivière, the Yellow River." He left there the traders who had accompanied him, while he himself ascended the Mississippi River. He speaks of Prairie du Chien as "the great mart, where all the adjacent tribes, and even those who inhabit the most remote branches of the Mississippi, annually assemble about the latter part of May, bringing with them their furs to dispose of to the traders."[9]

A few years later there came into the country another man from Connecticut, Peter Pond. In 1773 he established himself in the Iowa country opposite the mouth of the Wisconsin. He is the author of one of the earliest fish stories told in Iowa. He wrote it in the spelling of an illiterate man. "We put our Hoock and Lines into the Water and Leat them Ly all nite. In the Morning we Perseaved thare was fish at the Hoocks. . . Thay Came Heavey. At Length we hald one ashore that wade a Hundred and four Pounds—a Second that was One Hundred Wate—a third of Seventy-five Pounds." He says that the men who were in camp with him and near him were glad to see this for they had been a long time without either meat or fish. We will let him finish the story for it shows how men lived in Iowa in those days: "We asked our men How meney Men the Largest would Give a Meale. Sum of the Largest Eaters Sade twelve men Would Eat it at a Meal. We agread to Give ye fish if thay would find twelve men that could undertake it. Thay Began to Dres it. The fish was what was Cald the Cat fish. It Had a large flat Head Sixteen Inches Betwene the Eise. They Skind it—Cut it up in large Coppers Such as we have for Youse of our men. After it was Well Boild thay Sawd it up and all Got Round it. Thay Began and Eat the

[9] Jonathan Carver's *Travels Through the Interior Parts of North America, in the years 1676, 1677, 1678.* Third edition, pp. 50, 51.

hole without the least thing with it But Salt and Sum of them Drank of the Licker it was Boild in. . . Thay all Declard thay felt the Beater of thare Meale Nor Did I Perseave that Eny of them ware Sick or Complaind.''[10]

Peter Pond was equally apt in describing the life at Prairie du Chien in those days: ''The french Practis Billiards—ye latter Ball. Hear the botes from New Orleans Cum. Thay are navagated By thirtey Six men who row as maney oarse. Thay Bring in a Boate Sixtey Hogseats of Wine on one. . . Besides Ham, Ches &c—all to trad with the french & Indians.'' The ham and the cheese were the incidentals.[11] In this case other times did not have other customs. The Prairie du Chien which he described was in those days one of the gateways to the Iowa land.

During the American Revolution there were many American traders in the Mississippi Valley and through their activities the war for freedom had its reflection on the shores of Iowa. The British, the Spaniards, and the Americans contended for the control of the country. The Indians were divided in as many ways. The fame of Boston had been carried far for the Americans were sometimes called ''Bostoniens.''[12] It was largely a traders' war on the Mississippi. In April, 1780, a barge loaded with goods belonging to American traders was seized and plundered at the mouth of the Turkey River.[13] A little later a number of Spaniards and Americans were made prisoners at the lead mines. In a letter George Rogers Clark was advised that ''people from Michilimackinac are at the River des Moins,'' stirring up the savages against him.[14] It was Iowa's share in the American Revolutionary War.

When peace came, the Americans and Spaniards stood confronting each other along the Mississippi. The Spaniards then began to see the advantages of developing their lands. To that end they proceeded to encourage settlements on them. But their ideas were not fitted to American conditions. Their

10 *Wisconsin Historical Collections*, Vol. XVIII, p. 338.
11 *Ibid.*, Vol. XVIII, p. 339.
12 *Ibid.*, Vol. XVIII, pp. 404-406.
13 *Ibid.*, Vol. XI, p. 151.
14 *Ibid.*, Vol. XVIII, p. 405.

conceptions and systems were still feudal. They thought in estates instead of in homesteads. They made princely grants of land, the grantees to hold the Indians in fealty to their king and to promote trade for the benefit of the government. In the Iowa country three grants made at that time are of historic interest. The first of these was made to Julien Dubuque, the second to Louis Honoré, or Tesson, and the third to Basil Giard.

Julien Dubuque was in many ways one of the remarkable men of his times in the west. He is the most picturesque figure in the early history of Iowa. He was a French-Canadian, born in the province of Quebec in 1762, as a British subject. He received a good education in the parish and other schools. He was suave of manner and fair of speech. At the age of twenty-three, or in 1785, he came to Prairie du Chien, seeking fortune and adventure. He soon crossed the river and ingratiated himself into the friendship and favor of a band of Fox Indians who had their village on Catfish Creek, just below the city that now bears his name. He had the adaptability of his race for friendships and associations with the red men. He was both wise and crafty. He was also a snake-charmer and a magician. He made the Indians believe that he had almost supernatural powers. He alternately cajoled and threatened them. But always he held them under his will. In his presence they were child-like, superstitious and simple. At one time he is said to have threatened to set Catfish Creek on fire, and he made his threat good by having his men pour oil on the water above the village to which he set fire as it floated down on the current.[15] In due time he got from them what he wanted, the control of the lead mines. He himself drew up the document which the Kettle Chief and his associates signed by making their marks on a piece of paper the contents of which they did not understand, except as he explained it to them. It was stipulated, among other things that they sold and abandoned to him "all the coast and contents of the mine discovered by the wife of Peosta [16] so that no

[15] M. M. Ham's "Julien Dubuque," in *Annals of Iowa*, Third Series, Vol. III, p. 329.

[16] Peosta was a Fox chief who owes his fame to his wife.

white man or Indian shall make any pretensions to it without the consent of M. Dubuque."

Thus secured in his occupancy, Dubuque proceeded to develop the mines. He built cabins for his men and a smelter for his ore which he carried down the river to St. Louis in his own boats. For overseers he employed French-Canadians, but the bulk of the work in mining and transporting the lead was performed by squaws, who were often paid in mere trinkets. The work was all done in primitive ways, but they succeeded in taking out large quantities of ore. As he prospered, Dubuque thought to make himself more secure in the possession of the mines, and so having re-named them "The Mines of Spain," he appeared before the governor-general at St. Louis as his "Excellency's very humble, and very obedient, and very submissive servant," asking for a grant of the lands he had obtained from the Indians. Carondelet, the governor-general, made the grant with the restriction that he should not trade with the Indians except with the permission of one Don Andreas Todd to whom a monopoly of the trade in Upper Louisiana had been given. Dubuque's lands were princely in their extent, twenty-one miles up and down the river and nine miles in depth.

The grant to Basil Giard, who was one of Dubuque's associates, was made by the lieutenant-governor of the province, Delassus, in 1796. It was for 5,680 acres of land including part of the present city of McGregor. His tract extended east and west six miles and was one mile and a half in width. Giard lived upon his land and brought some of it under cultivation, but he devoted more time to trade than to farming. In 1799 Louis Honoré, or Tesson, received permission to occupy 7,056 arpents of land, about six thousand acres, lying about six leagues above the mouth of the Des Moines River, including the present town of Montrose in Lee County. One of the conditions was that he should make himself "useful in the trade in peltries in that country, to watch the savages and to keep them in the fealty which they owe his majesty," the king of Spain. Tesson planted on his land an orchard of apple trees which was frequently mentioned in the writings of the early travelers.

# CHAPTER VII

## The Louisiana Purchase

Having noted the chief happenings in the Iowa country under France and Spain, we must now proceed to consider a national transaction that ranks in American history next to the Declaration of Independence—the purchase of Louisiana. To settle disputes with Spain over the navigation of the Mississippi, President Jefferson, as already stated, was not minded to use the military authority which had been voted him by congress. He held the closing of the river to be the ill-advised act of the intendant at New Orleans, instead of a hostile policy of the government at Madrid. The president obtained from congress two million dollars to buy a shipping site at New Orleans, and he sent James Monroe as envoy extraordinary and minister plenipotentiary to deal with both France and Spain, since the transfer of Louisiana from Spain to France had not yet been completed. There was at that time no thought in the president's mind of the purchase of Louisiana. On the contrary, Monroe was authorized to guarantee to France the undisputed possession of the west bank of the Mississippi in consideration of granting the Americans the right to navigate the river and to re-ship their goods at New Orleans.

But in Paris Robert R. Livingston, one of the great American diplomats, had outlined a more ambitious policy. Talleyrand, Napoleon's crafty and unscrupulous minister of state, was opposed to Livingston's policies. But the American succeeded in laying his plans before Napoleon through the intercession of Joseph Bonaparte, with whom he was on terms of personal friendship. He proposed that France should sell to the United States all of Louisiana lying north of the Arkansas River. Such a cession, he argued, would leave France enough lands to support fifteen million people, while it would set up an American barrier between France in Louisiana and England in Canada. In numerous notes this proposition was set forth, but without any replies from Napoleon.[1]

Soon, and suddenly, Livingston was aided by an event in Europe—a war between France and England over Malta. England had a fleet in readiness and Napoleon was thrown into a panic of fear over the probable seizure of Louisiana. What the American diplomat had so often pressed may have recurred to him. Would it not be better to sell the province to America than to have it seized by England? He would sell not a part but all of Louisiana. When he proposed this to his ministers they opposed it. They said that even then preparations were under way to send colonists to New Orleans to lay the foundations of the long desired and coveted French empire in America. But Napoleon persisted. He said Louisiana was already lost to France and it was only a question whether it should be to England or to America. "They ask of me one town in Louisiana," he said, "but I already consider the colony as entirely lost, and it appears to me that in the hands of this growing power, it will be more useful to the policy and even to the commerce of France, than if I should attempt to keep it."[2]

His mind made up, he acted in haste, all the time in the fear of England seizing New Orleans. On the tenth of April, 1803, he said to his ministers: "I renounce Louisiana. It is not only New Orleans I will cede, it is the whole colony, without any reservation. I know the price of what I abandon . . . I renounce it with the greatest regret. To attempt obstinately to retain it would be folly. I direct you to negotiate this affair with the envoys of the United States. Do not even await the arrival of Mr. Monroe."[3] But he cautioned Marbois to get enough for the colony so he would not have to levy new taxes to carry on the war with England.

1 Hosmer's *The Louisiana Purchase.*

2 Barbé Marbois's *The History of Louisiana, Particularly of the Cession of the Colony to the United States of America,* Philadelphia, Lea & Carey, 1830, p. 264.

3 *Ibid.*, p. 274.

When Napoleon's decision was communicated to Livingston he could not believe in its sincerity. When Monroe arrived on the scene, on the twelfth of April, he also was perplexed. He had come to buy a city and he was offered a province. Neither he nor Livingston had authority to act on such a proposition. But Napoleon insisted on action. The American diplomats did not want England to seize Louisiana, for then, with Canada, their empire would encircle the United States, and control the mouth of the Mississippi. They decided to give their country and the future the benefit of the doubt and do a thing still unthought of in America, one without warrant in the constitution. The Americans offered twenty million francs for the province, and the French negotiators asked a hundred and twenty-five million. The price finally agreed upon was eighty million, including certain war debts which France owed to Americans.

The final papers for the transfer were signed on thirtieth of April, 1803, by Barbé Marbois for France, and by Monroe and Livingston for America. Napoleon himself added the stipulation that the people in the transferred province should be entitled "to the enjoyment of all the rights, advantages, and immunities of citizens of the United States;" and that they should in the meantime, "be maintained and protected in the free enjoyment of their liberty, property, and the religion which they profess." When it was all done, Napoleon said, prophetically, "This accession of territory strengthens for ever the power of the United States; and I have just given to England a maritime rival, that will sooner or later humble her pride."[4]

When the news of the purchase of Louisiana reached the United States, consternation filled many minds. President Jefferson was most of all perplexed. He could find in the constitution no authority for such an act. He thought of amending the instrument, but his wisest advisers persuaded him that what was so manifestly for the welfare of the nation could not be unconstitutional. So the president accepted the purchase as an accomplished and inevitable fact and asked congressional ratification of it.

[4] Marbois's *History of Louisiana*, p. 312.

But the Federalists who had been willing to vote one-third of the purchase price to go to war with Spain or France over American rights on the Mississippi refused to be reconciled to paying three times as much for the possession of the whole province. They said that the debt incurred, fifteen million dollars, could never be paid. The interest on it would be $2,465 a day! How could a nation meet such a daily bill? Also, they said that it would be folly to extend the boundaries of the United States west of the Mississippi River. The people living on two sides of the river would never be able to agree with each other, their interests would be so diverse. And would not the older states be depopulated to supply the new areas with settlers? Nor were all the fears in the minds of the Federalists and New Englanders. James Madison, Jefferson's secretary of state, shared in some of them and he feared that a separate government west of the river might be inevitable.

Upon the summons of the president, congress met in October and on the nineteenth of that month the purchase was ratified. Provisions were at once made for the government of the new lands. The province was divided into two parts along the thirty-third degree of latitude. All south of that line was called the Territory of Orleans, and all north of it, the District of Louisiana. The latter, of which Iowa was part, was attached to the Territory of Indiana for purposes of government.

All this was done before the transfer of the province from Spain to France had been accomplished. That transfer was made on November thirtieth, and from France to the United States on December twentieth, at New Orleans; and at St. Louis the respective transfers were made on the ninth and tenth of March, 1804, when Iowa became American territory.

# CHAPTER VIII

## Louisiana as an Ugly Duckling

In the east there was universal as well as profound ignorance of the trans-Mississippi country which had been acquired. By many also the region was held in contempt. President Jefferson himself while seeking to enlighten the people but added to the prevailing ignorance. He transmitted to congress for publication what purported to be "An Account of Louisiana." In his message transmitting these letters and reports, he said: "You will be sensible from the face of these papers . . . that they are not and could not be official." He said they were the result of the best inquiries that different individuals had been able to make.[1] Among other things there were accounts of Indians of giant stature, of a mountain of salt one hundred and eighty miles long, forty-five miles wide and of towering height. Such a phenomenon, it was admitted, might be doubted "were it not for the testimony of several respectable and enterprising traders who have visited it." And as for the salt, were not samples of it to be seen in St. Louis? But the critics of the purchase refused to be sensible about the matter and so they heaped new ridicule on the president and on Louisiana.

The president acted more wisely when he appointed Meriwether Lewis and William Clark to explore the Missouri River and the country through which it flowed, for which congress had made a modest appropriation. These enterprising explorers ascended the Missouri and descended the Columbia to the Pacific Ocean, adding to American explorations and discoveries one of their most brilliant chapters. What they contributed to Iowa history is slight, but still not inconsequential. As they passed up the river in the summer of 1804, they made

[1] *Annals of Congress*, 2nd Session, 8th Congress, pp. 1498-1578.

entries in their journals of the "Ayauway Nation" and their village near the headwaters of "Charaton" River. The Oto and Missouri tribes having asked for mediation with the Mahas, or Omahas, a conference was held and the place was called Council Bluffs, in what is now Nebraska, which they thought a favorable place for a fort, with timber and clay for brick available to it "and the air being pure and healthy." At the mouth of the "petite Rivière des Sioux," being the Little Sioux, they heard of the "Lac d'Esprit" on the Dog-plains, meaning Spirit Lake on the prairies, which was drained through that river. Below the mouth of the river to which they gave his name, Sergeant Charles Floyd, a member of the expedition, died of a fever, and they buried him on a high bluff on which a monument was afterwards erected by a grateful state and nation.[2] Of such modest things were the beginnings of Iowa history along the Missouri.

While Lewis and Clark were on their journey, a somewhat similar expedition was sent up the Mississippi River, in the autumn of 1805, under the command of Zebulon M. Pike. This undertaking was under the direction of General James Wilkinson, who was then in command of the army of the west. It may have been part of the Burr conspiracy in which Wilkinson was implicated, but Pike himself was loyal as well as a brave officer. In his journal he gave currency to the belief that the river called "de Moyen" was the "river of the monks," unmindful of the fact that the name may have been derived from the Moingouena Indians which Father Marquette had located on its banks almost a century and a half before.[3] Pike tarried on the site of the future Fort Madison, but he did not recommend it for a fort. He bestowed that honor on a high eminence that is now part of Crapo Park in the city of Burlington. He called that "a very handsome situation for a garrison." He met the Sac and Fox Indians above the Rock

[2] The monument was dedicated in 1901.

[3] In *Annals of Iowa*, Third Series, Vol. III, p. 554, Charles R. Keyes says the name *de Moyen* was often used by French traders returning to St. Louis, and when so used meant "of the middle," meaning the country between the Mississippi and Missouri rivers, drained by the Des Moines.

River, but he made no reference to Black Hawk who said afterwards that the gallant American lieutenant asked them to haul down their British flag and to give up their British medals, which they refused to do, preferring to have "two fathers." At The Mines of Spain he met "Monsieur Dubuque" who received him with salutes from a field piece and with many obsequious attentions. But when the lieutenant sought information about the mines, the pioneer settler of Iowa became "the evasive Mr. Dubuque," for he was not certain as to his status under the new American government and he did not want to give up his secrets. Another advantageous site for a fort was reported north of the present city of McGregor, which is still known as Pike's Hill.

The people of the District of Louisiana, which included what is now Iowa, were not satisfied with the government which congress had given them. They wanted a larger measure of participation, but their ideas of self-government included primarily the right to own slaves. Congress heeded part of their petition and on the fourth of July, 1805, the District of Louisiana became the Territory of Louisiana, but with no provision for slavery, but as that institution was not expressly forbidden the settlers took their slaves with them into the territory. When Louisiana was admitted as a state, the Territory of Missouri was organized, June fourth, 1812, of which Iowa was a part. In due time the territorial legislature asked for admission as a state. This was in 1818. An acrimonious debate ensued, principally over slavery. When Maine asked to be set up as a state, the two propositions were linked together. To admit Maine it would be necessary to admit Missouri with slavery. With the amendment that thereafter slavery would be prohibited in all territory north of thirty-six degrees and thirty minutes of latitude, the free soil advocates yielded to the contention of the South. Missouri was admitted as a slave state and territory north of it was cast off in 1821, without any form of organized government, and so remained for thirteen years. The future Iowa was not only a wilderness, but a waif. No one cared for her still unborn soul. Why should any one care? The belief was still prevalent that somewhere in what is now Iowa the Great American Desert began. And the whole trans-Mississippi region was still held in contempt by many.

The contempt was most violently expressed by Josiah Quincy of Massachusetts in congress on the fourteenth of January, 1811, when the admission of Louisiana as a state was under consideration. "If this bill passes," he said, "the bonds of this union are virtually dissolved; that the states which compose it are free from their moral obligations, and that, as it will be the right of all, so it will be the duty of some, to prepare definitely for a separation—amicably if they can, violently if they must."[4] This declaration caused confusion in the house. Well it might. But when Mr. Quincy was able to proceed, he said: "This constitution never was, and never can be strained to lap over all the wilderness of the west, without essentially affecting both the rights and convenience of its real proprietors. It was never constructed to form a covering for the inhabitants of the Missouri and the Red River country. And whenever it is attempted to be stretched over them, it will rend asunder." He declared that the rights, the liberties, and the property of the people could not be thrown "into a hotch-pot with the wild men on the Missouri . . ." The framers of the constitution never contemplated such a thing for "they were not mad men" and "they had not taken degrees in the hospital of idiocy." He said he had already heard of six states which were to be set up across the Mississippi, and he declared the question was "whether the proprietors of the good old United States shall manage their own affairs in their own way, or whether they and their constitution and their political rights shall be trampled underfoot by foreigners introduced through a breach of the constitution." Of the six ugly ducklings about to be hatched out of the Louisiana Purchase, Iowa was one.

The belief that the center of what is Iowa was a desert region lingered at least until 1819, when the admission of Missouri was under debate. So eminent a statesman as Thomas H. Benton at that time wrote: "After you get forty

[4] *Annals of Congress*, 3rd Session, 11th Congress, p. 525.

or fifty miles west of the Mississippi, the arid plains set in. The country is uninhabitable except upon the borders of the rivers and the creeks. The Grand Prairie, a plain without wood or water, which extends to the northwest farther than hunters or travelers have ever yet gone, comes down to within a few miles of St. Charles[5] and so completely occupies the fork of the Mississippi and Missouri rivers that the woodlands for three hundred miles of each forms a skirt from five to twenty miles wide, and above that distance the prairie actually reaches the rivers in many places."[6] According to this description there was a tapering strip of fertile land along the Mississippi, and another similar strip along the Missouri, and all the rest of Iowa was "a plain without wood or water."

And the much traveled Lieutenant Pike admitted the existence of these deserts, but out of them he comforted the people of the east by saying: "From these immense prairies there arises one advantage to the United States, viz., the restriction of our population to some certain limits, and thereby a continuance of the Union." He was enabled to reach this conclusion by the following reasoning: "Our citizens, being so prone to rambling and extending themselves on the frontiers will, through necessity, be constrained to limit their extent on the west to the boundaries of the Missouri and the Mississippi, while they leave the prairies, incapable of cultivation, to the wandering and uncivilized aborigines of the country."[7]

Such was the knowledge, and such was the vision of the west in that time. How unwise they were and how unprophetic! It was the Grand Prairie indeed, but not the Great Desert. The untrodden and untraversed land, lying enfolded in the mighty arms of the two great rivers of the continent, was not a Sahara, but a Mesopotamia; God's meadow and man's garden to be.

[5] St. Charles is on the Mississippi, twenty miles north of St. Louis.

[6] Printed in the *Missouri Republican*.

[7] Elliott Coues's *The Explorations of Zebulon Montgomery Pike*, Vol. II, p. 525.

# PART II

## THE INDIANS

(1804-1833)

# CHAPTER IX

## The Indians in Iowa

When the Indians came to Iowa is unknown. Nor does any one now know whence they came. Ethnologically they bore many resemblances to Asiatic races, and theologically many of their traditions and practices resembled those of the ancient Hebrews. That they were of a common origin with the races of the old world can hardly be questioned.

The earliest evidences of human beings in what is Iowa are found in mounds of earth which lie scattered over wide areas. In these mounds weapons of war and utensils of domestic life have been abundantly uncovered. Many of the materials found in them are not native here, such as copper and mica and obsidian. The people who left them must have understood trade and transportation as well as the fabrication of metals and cloth. The men who devised the mounds may have had a knowledge of geometry, and they must have had conceptions of both government and religion. "They were acquainted," says one investigator, "with the seven planets and the twelve signs of the Zodiac."[1] They practiced picture-writing, but they also wrote in syllabic characters. If the mounds were built by the ancestors of the Indians, then there must have been racial retrocession instead of progression. The Indians who were living here when the white men came on the scene could tell nothing about the mounds or about those who have been called the Mound Builders. They could not give an intelligent explanation of their own origin. Even their own great grandparents had become mythical beings to them.

The past of the human race in America is a mystery that may never be solved. Those who like to speculate on such

[1] See article by Professor G. Seyffarth, Ph. S., Th. D., in the third volume of the *Proceedings of the Davenport Academy of Sciences.*

things are left free to do so. They may think of the past of what is now Iowa in waves of human migrations that swept over these lands through thousands of years. They may think of races living here before Babylon fell or Adam sinned—back to the time when there were men and women who lived in the Land of Nod. They may draw word-pictures or thought-pictures of cultivated fields and templed towns in this land of ours; of caravans of commerce and armies marching in the panoply of proud war; of bridal processions and funeral marches winding through ancient temples; or of tasseled corn in the valleys, and on green slopes flocks and herds that made husbandmen rich and glad ages ago. But it will be only speculation. No one knows—and it may not matter much.

All that we know is that the Indians were here when the white men came as discoverers and explorers. At first all these red men looked alike, but those who remained to study their dialects, characteristics, and institutions soon separated the native populations not merely into tribes, but the tribes into racial groups. In what is now Iowa there were two distinct races. One of these is now called Algonquian, and the other Siouan, race names derived from the predominating tribe in each group. Probably the former came from the east and the latter from the west. Both came in quest of food, of which there was an abundance, provided by the grass-eating and the meat-bearing animals that had preceded them. Coming from the east and from the west, presumably, they clashed here in the Mississippi Valley, and neither being strong enough to conquer the other, both were deflected southward, the one down the Mississippi and the other down the Missouri. Between them and before them they may have crushed the superior races which built the mounds, races that may have come up long before from the south where civilizations were found far advanced. But all this is speculation. We are still living in ignorance of the past.

When Joliet and Marquette came here in the seventeenth century, the Indians they found along the Mississippi were Algonquian, and those of which they heard along the Missouri were Siouan. When the Americans came in 1804, Algonquian tribes were still along the Mississippi and Siouan along the Missouri, and they were still hostile to each other.

The Indians living in the Iowa country in 1804 may be divided into four groups: the Sacs and Foxes along the Mississippi; the Iowas along the Des Moines, east and south of the center of the state; the Otoes, Missouris, and Omahas along the Missouri; and the Sioux in the north and west, from the Big Sioux River to the upper Des Moines and thence to the Mississippi in an attenuated line.[1] The white settlers came in contact with the Sacs and Foxes, chiefly; much less with the Iowas; hardly at all with the three tribes on the Missouri; and not with the Sioux until fifty years later.

In the four groups there were probably not more than fifteen thousand Indians, and some writers place their combined numbers as low as twelve or even ten thousand. If they had cultivated the soil they could have lived comfortably in any one of the ninety-nine counties of the present state, and they might have subsisted on the products of one or two civil townships. "Their cultivated fields," said John Quincy Adams in a speech delivered in 1820, "their constructed habitations, a space of ample sufficiency for their subsistence, and whatever they had annexed to themselves by personal labor, was undoubtedly by the law of nature theirs. But what is the right of a huntsman to the forest of a thousand miles over which he has accidentally ranged in quest of prey?"

If possession means the use of the lands, then the Indians were not dispossessed of any except small areas. Viewed from this standpoint, the processes by which the European races acquired the lands of America do not seem very unjust or cruel, if so at all. They merely took what the native races were not using, and what they appropriated they converted to human needs and human development. But the red man did not view the matter from the same angle, and we must give his viewpoint also some consideration.

[1] The Winnebago and Pottawattomie tribes who sojourned in Iowa later lived on reservations provided by the government.

# CHAPTER X

## The Iowa Indians

In any history of Iowa the Indians from whom the state derived her name are entitled to primary consideration. On Father Marquette's map these Indians are set down as the Pah8tet, which rendered into modern spelling is Pahoutet. He knew them only by hearsay. The first white man who seems to have come in contact with them was Father Louis André, who met them at Green Bay in 1676, where they came to trade.[1] "This year," so reads the account, "we have among the puants 7 or 8 families from a nation who are neutral Between our Savages and the nadoessi, who are at war. They are aiaoüa, or nadoessi mascouteins," meaning Sioux of the prairies, indicating both their race and their location. André placed them two hundred leagues to the west, and he said their greatest wealth consisted of "ox hides and Red Calumets." In 1682, La Salle referred to them as the Aiounonea. About 1700, Le Sueur used the name Ayavois. He is said to have supplied them with their first fire-arms. A little later D'Iberville called them the Ayooues, and on de L'Isle's map we find the names Aiaoues, Paoute, Paouttaoua and Aioureoua, probably all referring to the same Indians. Father Gabriel Marest, about 1700, may have been of the opinion that the Ayavois and the Paoutees were two distinct tribes. In American times, Lewis and Clark used the spellings Ayauway, Iawai and Iaway, and Lieutenant Pike, Ioway and finally, Iowa.[2]

From these citations, and scores of others that might be made, it appears that these Indians were known under two

[1] Thwaites's *Jesuit Relations*, Vol. LX, pp. 203-205.

[2] For these and other spellings see the article on the "Iowa Indians" in the *Handbook of American Indians*, in two volumes, of the Bureau of American Ethnology, published by the government in 1910.

names, and it is from one of these names the modern word Iowa was evolved. The first name, Pahoutet, is rendered in various forms and spellings—and these variations are not to be wondered at, for the early writers were not always etymologists nor did they render the same Indian sounds into the same French syllables. This name was written Pahucha by Schoolcraft in his *Indian Tribes*, published in 1853.[3] But later etymologists have extended it to Pähutch'ac.[4] This is given as their own name for themselves. The other name by which they were known was given to them by Frenchmen who are said to have first heard of these Indians through the Sioux, who called them Ayúhäpä or Ayúhbä. The guttural ending of this word, it is believed, was for the French so difficult to render that they took the first two syllables, "Ayu," and added to them one of their own terminals, "vois" or "ouez," making Ayuvois or Ayuouez, as they changed Iliniwuk to Illinois.[5] The American Board of Indian Ethnology accepts this as the origin of the word Iowa.[6]

The Sioux name, Ayúhbä, is said to be equivalent in meaning to the Iowa name Pähutch'ac. To find the meanings of these words we must go to the origin of the tribe itself. The tradition is that the Iowa Indians sprang from the Winnebagoes. The linguistic relationship is offered as proof of this. On one of their many extensive migrations the parent tribe remained on Lake Michigan, while a band of them pushed on

[3] Henry Schoolcraft was employed as an Indian agent, became a pioneer law maker and a noted writer on Indian subjects.

[4] See the reprint of Thomas Foster's *Indian Record and Historical Data*, 1876, edited by William Harvey Miner, published by the Torch Press, Cedar Rapids, 1911, under the title *The Ioway*, p. 6.

[5] Miner's *The Ioway*, pp. 2 and 3.

[6] In a letter to the author dated August 11, 1919, H. W. Dorsey, chief clerk of the Smithsonian Institution, Washington, says, "J. N. B. Hewitt, ethnologist of the Bureau [American Ethnology] informs me that the name Iowa is from the Sioux term A-yu-hba, meaning Sleepy Ones." Cato Sells, commissioner of Indian Affairs, also in a personal letter to the author, dated August 6, 1920, after thorough study of the records, says his department concurs in the conclusions of the bureau of ethnology, and the commissioner says personally, "I am inclined to think that the weight of authority supports this view."

southwestward until they came to the Mississippi River. There another separation took place, some continuing on their journey until they came to the Missouri where they became known as the Missouri and Oto tribes. Those who remained on the Mississippi were the ancestors of the Indians we know as the Iowas. The tradition is that "The Iowas encamped on a sand-bar, and that the dust blew into their faces, and they received the name of Pahucha, or 'Dusty Men.'"[7] We are also told, "They are called Iowas only by other tribes and the whites." Another tradition is that they received this name after bathing in the waters of a muddy river, which may have been the Missouri, and permitting the sediment to dry in their hair and on their faces.[8]

The Sioux, their kinsmen, translated the name Pahucha into their own equivalent in meaning, Ayúhäpä, or Ayúhbä. The theory is that the French took this name, dropping the guttural ending and changing it to Ayuvois — with many variations — and from that the name Iowa was then evolved. How the meaning "Drowsy ones," or "Sleepy ones,"[9] was derived from this word is not clear, unless dusty suggested grayness, and this in turn, age and drowsiness.

But it soon came about that the white men, being proud of their state, were not satisfied with such meanings and they proceeded to think out more poetic ones. The explorer, Major

[7] See Schoolcraft's *Collections*, Vol. III, I, p. 262, where this explanation or theory is set forth in a paper prepared by Rev. William Hamilton and Rev. Samuel McCleary Irvin, two Presbyterian missionaries to the Iowa and Sac and Fox Indians. These missionaries were diligent in tribal research. They established what was known as an Iowa and Sac Mission Press, from which were issued among other volumes *An Ioway Grammar* (1848) and *The Ioway Primer*. In a letter written from the Omaha Mission, March 4, 1868, Mr. Hamilton repeated this statement, for which see volume one of *The Transactions and Reports of the Nebraska State Historical Society*, edited by Robert W. Furnas, p. 47.

[8] This explanation was given to Dr. Thomas Foster in 1873, by a Winnebago ex-chief, a half-breed whose name was Baptiste, and who had spent much time among the Iowas. See Miner's *The Ioway*, p. 7.

[9] Dr. Stephen R. Riggs, an authoritative man, made a Dakota-English dictionary, which was published in 1853, by the Smithsonian Institution, Washington, in which he gives the following: "Ayuhba, Sleepy Ones, the Iowa Indians."

Stephen H. Long, interpreted it to mean "Gray Snow." But he is said to have confused the two Indian words "pa" and "pah," the former meaning snow, and the later nose or face, and in the case of animals, the whole head.[10]

But while gray snow was more poetic, the Americans who loved their state sought still more romantic meanings for the name. "It is conceded," wrote one of the pioneers, in 1868, "that the name of Iowa arose in this way: Many years ago . . . some Indians in search of a new home, encamped on a high bluff of the Iowa River near its mouth . . . and being much pleased with the location and country around it — in their native dialect exclaimed — Iowa, Iowa, Iowa (beautiful, beautiful, beautiful), hence the name Iowa to the river, and to those Indians. . ."[11] Unfortunately, this writer does not state by whom this was conceded. Other writers, with no more authority, had assumed similar meanings. One legend is that the Sacs and Foxes invented the name when they came to Iowa, meaning "this is the place."[12] But we have already seen that when these Indians came to Iowa they were in flight before the French, and if they used any exclamations they may have been those of fear

[10] This explanation of Long's error is given by William Hamilton in his letter of March 4, 1868, already cited. W. W. Hildreth, one of the early American writers on the subject, in the *Annals of Iowa*, April, 1864, accepts this meaning, treating the name Iowa as evolved directly from Pyhoja.

[11] William L. Toole in the *Annals of Iowa*, 1868, p. 48.

[12] Found in Niles's *The Weekly Register*, Vol. LVI, p. 48, reprinted from a letter in the Buffalo, New York, *Journal*, in part: "Taking into consideration the soil, the timber, the water, the climate, Iowa Territory may be considered the best part of the Mississippi Valley. The Indians so considered it, as appears from the name they gave it. For it is said that the Sioux [Sac] and Fox Indians, on beholding the exceeding beauties of this region held up their hands and exclaimed in an ecstacy of delight and amazement, I-O-W-A, which in the Fox language means, 'this is the land'." Gue in his *History of Iowa*, Vol. I, p. 67, credits to Theodore S. Parvin, a high authority, this legend: "This tribe [the Iowas] separated from the Sacs and Foxes and wandered off westward in search of a new home. Crossing the Mississippi River they turned southward, reaching a high bluff near the Iowa River. Looking off over the beautiful valley spread out before them they halted, exclaiming, 'Iowa!' or 'this is the place'."

instead of admiration. And why should another tribe, an unrelated one, have been given the name of a Sac and Fox exclamation? A still more modern writer derived the name from the Sac and Fox word kiowa, meaning again "this is the place," as applied to a desirable place for camping or fording a river.[13] But if these Indians had such a word and so used it, there is no connection showing its application to the Iowa Indians. As late as 1890, additional vogue was given to these theories in a government publication [14] wherein the statement was made that "Some of the neighboring Algonkins called them Iowas, a name originally applied to a river and said to mean 'beautiful land.'" This writer, evidently, confused the words Iowa and Ohio, the meaning of the later being "beautiful river."

There seems to be no evidence, etymological or other, to support the theory that Iowa means either "this is the place" or "the beautiful land." Dusty men, or men with dusty faces, would seem to be the etymological meaning of the name.[15] But as it is a name evolved from an Indo-French term, with hardly a semblance to the original, except in sound, it is doubtful if any derived meaning is applicable to the word. But if etymologically and historically there is no basis for the adjective beautiful, there is scenically and geographically. If the Indians did not call Iowa the beautiful land, there is no reason why the white men may not do so, if it pleases them.

Historically the Iowa Indians do not fill a large place in the story of the state that was named after them. Our interest in them is largely through their name. They do not seem to have been at any time a numerous or powerful tribe, although they had the usual traditions that at one time they had been

[13] L. F. Andrews, *Annals of Iowa*, Third Series, Vol. II, p. 465. As his authorities he cites Antoine Le Claire, the Sac and Fox half-breed and interpreter, and Taylor Pierce, long connected with the trading post at Fort Des Moines.

[14] In the Eleventh Census of the United States, Indian volume, p. 322.

[15] The *Encyclopedia Britannica* and the *National Geographic Magazine*, August, 1920, accept this meaning, but the *Century Dictionary* gives "gray or dusty noses."

of great importance.[16] They may be spoken of correctly as a minor tribe of many migrations. In 1848 sixteen of these migrations were traced on a charcoal map by an aged Iowa brave, Wawnonqueskoona.[17] According to this map they sojourned more often in northern Missouri than in Iowa. But they were sufficiently identified with the state that was named after them. Father Marquette located them within its present boundaries in 1673, and the Americans found them on the Des Moines when they entered the land. In nearly all the treaties made with the Indians affecting the southern half or two-thirds of the state, from the Mississippi to the Missouri, the government recognized they had an undefined and undivided interest in the lands.

Their most notable chief in historic times was Mahaska. His father was Manhawgaw, who was killed by the Sioux, and his son was the younger Mahaska, who did not reach his father's greatness, though his mother was Rantchewaime, one of the most notable among Indian women in Iowa. She is spoken of as having been a woman of physical comeliness and moral excellence.

[16] In the *Indian Tribes of North America*, Vol. II, p. 267, Schoolcraft says the Sacs believed the Iowas existed through their kindness to them, while the Iowas believed they found the Sacs almost exterminated by the Sioux, and that they gave them women for wives and rescued them from extinction.

[17] The map was included in Schoolcraft's *Collections*, Vol. III, p. 256.

# CHAPTER XI

## The Sacs and Foxes, and a Treaty

How the Sac and Fox Indians came to the Mississippi River country has already been told, in connection with the military expedition of de Noyelles in 1734. The proper name of the Sacs is Sauks, and of the Foxes, Musquakie, or Meskwaki.[1] Closely as the two tribes were associated, they did not constitute a confederacy. Each retained its own tribal organization. Racially both were Algonquian. Jointly they claimed the country on both sides of the Mississippi, from the Wisconsin and the Upper Iowa to the Illinois and the Missouri. The Foxes had their principal village on the Iowa side of the Mississippi, near the site of the present city of Davenport, and the Sacs on the Illinois side, above the mouth of the Rock River. The former city was called Musquakinuk, and the latter Saukenuk.

Among Indian villages, Saukenuk was a city, and a wonderful one too. It is described by the early writers as well laid out and well built up. It had streets, even if they were not always straight, and open spaces for assemblies and games. They had houses, called hodensotes, as well as wikiups. Their houses were pretentious ones for red men. Some of them were a hundred feet long by forty feet wide. The frames were made of poles tied with thongs and the coverings were of elm bark. To obtain this, they girdled big trees and stripped off the bark in sheets. The hodensotes were divided into apartments which were occupied by related families. Some of the apartments were used in common for storerooms and fire places. They had also houses for public discussions and tribal councils, in which all questions affecting the good

[1] See *Handbook of the American Indians,* articles on Sauks and Musquakies.

of the tribe were debated by the chief men. "Indeed, I have seen many Indian villages," wrote Major Forsyth, an agent among the Sacs, to Governor Clark in St. Louis, in 1817, "but I never saw such a large one or such a populous one" as Saukenuk.[2]

In this wonder city of the Sacs, two remarkable Indians were born, men destined to become rivals for power and to play important rôles in the history of the future Iowa. The elder of the two was born in 1767 and he was called Makataimeshekiakiak, meaning the Black Sparrow Hawk, and known in history as Black Hawk, a name once dreaded, but now respected. The name of the younger, who was born in 1780, was Keokuk, who was called the Watchful Fox, because he was alert and a member of the Fox clan. He became the orator of his tribe, and the friend of the white man. In 1804 both men had already won many distinctions.

The Americans had hardly taken over the government of the Louisiana Purchase when they came in contact with the Sacs and Foxes through a tragedy the evils of which kept repeating themselves through a generation. On the Mississippi, in what is now the state of Missouri, there was a rough frontier settlement called Cuvier. There one night in the spring of 1804, a dance was given in a white man's cabin to which an Indian brought his daughter, who is described as a comely maiden.[3] In those days white men danced with Indian women. While the daughter danced, the father drank whiskey. He became what they called *esquaby*, meaning drunk. But he was not too drunk to resent an insult of some kind given to his daughter by a white man, who also may have been *esquaby*. Red men in those days had morals of sex, even if white men sometimes had not. A quarrel and a fight ensued. The Indian father was kicked out of doors. Outside he laid in wait for vengeance. When his white assailant stepped out of the cabin he felled him with a tomahawk. The red murderer

[2] See Irving B. Richman's sketch of Saukenuk in his *John Brown Among the Quakers and Other Sketches*, 1894.

[3] Perry A. Armstrong's *The Sauks and the Black Hawk War*, p. 58.

fled to Saukenuk. It was a crime that the white man's government could not overlook. The Sacs, acting according to their conceptions of tribal justice, surrendered the murderer to the soldiers who pursued him. He was imprisoned at St. Louis. His tribesmen then sent a delegation of five principal men to intercede for him. Among the five were Pashipaho and another chief, Quashquamme, a relative of the imprisoned murderer.

As soon as the Sac delegation reached St. Louis they learned that nothing could be done to save their kinsman; there was only one tenable punishment for the murder of a white man by an Indian and that was death. But they remained in the city, hoping still for some more favorable decision. They were befriended by Auguste Chouteau, the French trader, or at least he extended credit to them. On this credit they lived well and drank a great deal of fire-water, and they adorned themselves with clothes and trinkets, until their debts amounted to $2,234.50. Chouteau was willing to have them indebted to him for he knew that they owned many lands and he hoped by this lavishness to bind them to him and to draw them from the British traders at Mackinac.

While the five Indians still tarried there, William Henry Harrison arrived in St. Louis. He was governor of Indiana Territory and by virtue of that office had been made governor of the District of Louisiana and commissioner of its Indian affairs. He had received instructions from Washington to write treaties of trade and amity with the tribes. Chouteau presented him with the opportunity for negotiating such a treaty with the Sacs and Foxes through the presence of the five delegates. He may have pressed it on him for he saw thereby an opportunity to collect his debts. The Indians were promised, among other things, the release of their prisoner if they would enter into a treaty. So, on the third of November they made their marks on a piece of paper the contents of which it was afterwards said they did not understand.

This is the famous treaty of the third of November, 1804. By its terms the Sacs and Foxes were represented as selling all their lands lying on the east side of the Mississippi, from the Wisconsin to the Illinois, and a tract on the west side lying between the Missouri River on the south and the Jeffreon River on the north, but as there was no known river of that name at that time the boundary was indefinite.[4] The two tracts contained fifty-one million acres of the best lands on the continent. And for this they received the cancellation of their debts, $2,234.50, annuities of $1,000 for an unnamed number of years — and the release of a prisoner. The murderer was released, according to promise, but he was immediately shot down, presumably by a relative of the white man whom he had killed. The only merciful provision in the treaty was that the Indians might occupy their lands until such time as they would be required for actual settlers. The Indians also were promised a trading post at which goods would be sold at reasonable prices, while the government coupled with that the right to erect a fort at or near the mouth of the Wisconsin.

All these transactions over, the five Indians returned to Saukenuk. But they remained for some time outside the village. It may have been to sober off, or out of the realization that they had made a bad bargain on which they dreaded to make a report to the tribe. When they did enter and when they had told what they had done in St. Louis, there was both wailing and indignation in Saukenuk. The Indians realized they had lost their lands and had not saved their kinsman. Black Hawk afterwards said the returned men "appeared to be dressed in fine coats, and had medals."[5] He said also that it was soon learned that they had been drunk most of the time in St. Louis. Neither Pashipaho nor Quashquamme, nor any of the others, could give a clear statement of what they had done. They admitted they had sold some lands, but they always insisted that no lands north of the Rock River had been so sold. But they had no authority to sell any lands. They had been delegated to secure the release of a prisoner, not to dispose of lands. Such dispositions could be made only by tribal action.

[4] On some early maps this name was given to a small stream in northern Missouri.

[5] Black Hawk's *Autobiography.*

# CHAPTER XII

## The Building of Fort Madison

It was not until 1808 that the government undertook to build the trading post promised the Indians in the treaty of 1804, and then it was made a mere annex to a military fort. Late in the summer of that year Lieutenant Alpha Kingsley, of the First United States Infantry, was sent up the Mississippi with about fifty men. In selecting a site he paid no heed to the recommendations that had been made by Lieutenant Pike three years before—and time was to prove that his choice of a place was unfortunate.

The Indians from the first resented the presence of soldiers on their lands. Even if they had accepted the validity of the treaty, it contained no stipulation for a military establishment on the site of what became Fort Madison. The lieutenant sought, but in vain, to pacify them by statements to the effect that it was the purpose of the government to maintain only a few soldiers there, to keep the traders company. His first report to the government was made from the "Garrison at Belle Vue, near river Le Moine, 22 November, 1808," in which he stated that on account of the lateness of the season he had been compelled to erect temporary buildings for his men, and that he had surrounded them with a low stockade as a protection against possible attacks by the Indians, who had appeared very unfriendly.[1]

During the winter months that followed he set his men at work cutting logs for the permanent blockhouses and pickets for a higher stockade. Being without horses or oxen, the men were compelled to drag the timbers over the snow by their own strength. On the nineteenth of April, 1809, another report

[1] *Annals of Iowa*, Third Series, Vol. III, pp. 97-110, for the official records in the war department concerning Fort Madison.

was made, which was dated "Fort Madison, near Le Moin," James Madison in the meantime having been elected and inaugurated as president of the United States. This time he reported that he had erected the permanent buildings and stockade in great haste, with the men sleeping on their arms, for he had received warnings of possible Indian attacks. These warnings have been attributed to "a beautiful Sac maiden" who had fallen in love with one of the soldiers which her tribe hated.[2] But *A Personal Narrative*, written by a sutler, has recently thrown new light on this incident, as well as on other matters connected with those stirring scenes.[3] By what inspiration did a somewhat illiterate man make a record of his experiences, and by what providence were his mutilated sheets preserved through subsequent flight and fire?

According to this narrative the British traders of Canada were the instigators of much of the Indian unrest in the Mississippi Valley in those years. They wanted to keep for themselves the trade which they had long enjoyed. The Indians had more faith in the British than in the Americans, for they sold them better goods. The British sold goods made to meet the wants of the red men, while the Americans sold them what was left over in trade. The American blankets were small and thin, their cotton goods flimsy and decayed, their traps had weak springs and their powder would not always explode. "The British made a handle of it," says the account. They not only decried their goods, but they derided the Americans. They added to them the evil insinuations that while they, the British, wanted only to trade with the red men, the Americans were plotting to get their lands—and the building of Fort Madison was held up as a first step in this

[2] A Sac woman carried a warning to the fort preceding the attacks in 1811, for which John Beach, a Sac and Fox agent, is cited as authority in Stevens's *The Black Hawk War*, Vol. I, p. 40.

[3] Jacob Van der Zee of the State Historical Society found this narrative among the *Michigan Pioneer Collections*, Vol. VIII, pp. 662-669, and Vol. XII, pp. 438-450, and with permission printed it in *The Iowa Journal of History and Politics*, October, 1913, under the title: "Old Fort Madison; Some Source Materials," with explanations and comments on the text. His paper is one of the notable contributions to early Iowa history.

process of dispossession. The Indians eagerly absorbed all this mental poison and were turned "against the new traders and Big Knives," as the Americans were called. Among those most hostile was "a young chief of great influence with the braves of the Sauks and Foxes . . . a daring and reckless spirit," whose name was Black Hawk.

In the autumn of 1808, when the Indians went down the river to their winter hunting grounds below the Des Moines, they stopped at the new fort to take credit, that is to buy goods to be paid for the following spring out of the proceeds of their hunting. Their spies at the same time gathered what information they could about the fort and its surroundings. They made a poor hunt during the winter. They were restless and they held many councils as to the best method of attacking Fort Madison before the permanent structures could be completed. The plan that was finally decided upon was Black Hawk's, and he was placed in command of the undertaking, with Pashipaho as second in authority.

While the Indians were still plotting, a young man of the Iowa tribe came to the fort and told their secrets to the sutler, who many years before had befriended this Indian in some way at Detroit. If an Indian did not forgive an injury, neither did he forget a benefit. The object of the young warrior was not to betray the Indians so much as it was to save the life of his friend, whom he warned to leave the place. It was, no doubt, on this information that Lieutenant Kingsley had hastened his building operations. In May the young Iowa Indian made another visit to the sutler to tell him that on the following day the Sacs and Foxes would come up the river and stop at the post to pay their debts. After that they would ask permission to give a dance, ostensibly for the entertainment of the soldiers, within the stockade and during the dance, upon a given signal, they would murder all the men, using weapons which they would have concealed in their clothing. All the information given proved correct. The Indians came up the river early and hastily discharged all their debts and that without any haggling. Then Pashipaho went within to ask permission to give a dance, while Black

Hawk and his warriors remained outside pressing around the entrance. But instead of the coveted permission, which was asked on the allegation that the ground outside was too full of stumps for the warriors to give the dance, they were confronted with a garrison ready for defense. "Bayonets bristled through the doors and windows," and a "six pounder stood . . . directly in front of the gate, loaded with balls," and "near the cannon stood a man with port fire in hand waiting for orders." If the order to fire had been given, half of Black Hawk's warriors would have been blown to atoms, so closely were they packed around the entrance. Realizing that their plans had been betrayed, "Pashipaho waved his hand as a signal for retreat." The weapons for the intended massacre were soon disclosed. Even the squaws, who had accompanied the warriors to ward off suspicions, had concealed in their clothes pack ropes with which they had intended to tie up the goods in the post after the garrison had been murdered. After Lieutenant Kingsley had rebuked the chiefs and warned the warriors to keep the peace, he permitted them to proceed to Saukenuk, but Black Hawk was in such a rage over his defeated plans that he organized a war party of about fifty braves "against the Osages, 300 miles away," to be revenged on them. In response to persistent appeals for reinforcements, Captain Horatio Stark was sent up the river in August with additional men, until the whole number was increased to more than eighty, Stark assuming command of the fort.

The Indians remained in a hostile attitude, but for more than two years they kept peace. For Black Hawk these intervening years must have been momentous ones. He still insisted that the sale of their lands in 1804 was not valid, and he continued to look upon Fort Madison as a menace to his people. One may think of him as sitting often on the high bluff above Saukenuk, which is still known as Black Hawk's Watch Tower, smoking and thinking, for so he speaks of himself in his *Autobiography*. He was that kind of an Indian, a dreaming, brooding Indian. And as he sat there, he overlooked the village of his people and their cultivated fields and saw beyond them the great river flowing on its way to the gulf.

They were all intertwined in his affections, for he was a lover of nature and of his race. These noble qualities were not denied him even by his severest detractors.

In those days runners often came to him from the Wabash and whispered of a great Indian uprising under Tecumseh, the Shawnee chief, and his brother, Elskwatawa, the Prophet. They too were dreaming Indians and their dream was of driving the white men out and restoring the land to the red men to whom the Great Spirit had given it. "If you do not join your friends on the Wabash," the Prophet himself said to Black Hawk, "the Americans will take this very village from you."[4] Tecumseh's dream became his dream, and Tecumseh's ambition his ambition. Whatever else one may think of the ill-fated Sac brave, there is something noble if not majestic in this magnificent Indian sitting on his Watch Tower smoking and thinking; grieving over the wrongs of his race and dreaming of righting and redressing them. This glimpse of him in these years will enable one to understand better the things which he is still to do.

And the time has come to take another and a last look at Julien Dubuque at The Mines of Spain. The careers of Giard and Tesson as claim holders along the Mississippi have already been closed. In 1803 Tesson's lands were sold for one hundred and fifty dollars to Joseph Robidoux, a creditor.[5] The sale was made under the old Roman law at the door of the parish church in St. Louis. Giard ceased to cultivate his lands probably in 1808.[6] Dubuque had prospered more. Some years he had taken as much as forty thousand pounds of lead out of his mines. Twice a year he had gone to St. Louis to sell his ores and his pelts acquired in Indian trading. He brought rich wares to the city and bought cheap merchandise and trinkets for the Indians. He danced with the rich and he fiddled for them. They flattered him by night and probably

[4] Black Hawk's *Autobiography.*

[5] When Robidoux died, Thomas F. Reddick acquired the claim, and his heirs in 1839, after much litigation, secured a favorable decision in the Supreme Court of the United States.

[6] His heirs sold their rights to James H. Lockwood and Thomas P. Burnett of McGregor, for $300.

fleeced him by day. He transacted a large business, but gradually he ceased to prosper. Finally his debts to Chouteau were so great that he was unable to pay them, and he had to assign to his creditor seven-sixteenths of his domain, and later he assigned to him the remaining nine-sixteenths to be delivered in event of his death. All his planning and all his working had been for his creditors.[7]

His end of all things earthly was at hand—he died on the second day of March, 1810, some said "a victim of his vices," but others more merciful, said of pneumonia. He left no heirs; only assignees. His marriage with a woman of the Fox tribe is denied by later historians, though often reiterated by the earlier ones. But for two and twenty years he had held the confidence of the Indians whom he had beguiled with fair words and crude magic. So high had he stood in their esteem that they buried him with all the honors they bestowed on their chiefs. Their orators praised him and their musicians chanted weird dirges over his body and over his grave. To them he seemed so supernatural that for a long time they believed that he would return from the dead and live among them again. His burial place was on a high bluff overlooking the river, just below the city that was afterwards named for him. If he had failed, it was a fine failure to make. He was the first white man in those regions who did certain things and they were things which will always be retold in Iowa history. He was a pioneer settler and business man. His boats loaded with ores and merchandise were the richest argosies on the upper Mississippi during those years. He did not belong to Iowa, nor to America. He was a remnant of the old French days, a relic of the empire of which Jean Talon and La Salle and Frontenac had dreamed.

But men die and the world moves on to new events. On the seventh day of November, 1811, General William Henry

[7] The heirs of Chouteau made many attempts to make their claims valid; in 1836, after the town of Dubuque was platted they had recourse to the courts, but the Supreme Court of the United States, in a decision in 1853, held that Dubuque's rights were those granted him by the Indians, that is peaceable possession to work the mines; see *American State Papers*, Public Lands, Vol. III, p. 678.

Harrison defeated Tecumseh's Indians, under the command of the Prophet in the battle on the Tippecanoe. Two hundred Winnebago Indians from the Rock River participated in the disastrous battle and twenty-five of them were killed. Black Hawk himself may have been present—and if he was not in body, he was so in spirit.[8] When the survivors returned home, war parties were organized to wreak vengeance on the Americans along the Mississippi. One party went to Prairie du Chien, one to the mining regions, and another operated against Fort Madison. Black Hawk accompanied the latter. A reign of terror was inaugurated, with murder and fire and pillage, from Prairie du Chien to Fort Madison. Only a few Americans outside of the fort escaped. Among those who reached safety was one George Hunt who has been identified as the sutler who wrote the *Personal Narrative* of these stirring times, and who in the meantime had become engaged in trade in the mining regions.[9] The Winnebagoes mistook him for a Saginash, that is an Englishman, and it was only Americans who had forfeited their lives for the events on the Wabash. His escape is a thrilling tale of Indian fidelity and of a white man's courage and hardihood in a flight in mid-winter of over two hundred and fifty miles.

The attacks on Fort Madison at that time were personally directed by Black Hawk, whose hatred for the place had not been abated by time. He anticipated modern warfare by concealing himself in a hole in the ground, camouflaged with brush, from which vantage point he directed the attacks. The fort was well defended by Lieutenant Thomas Hamilton, who had succeeded Captain Stark in command, and by Lieutenant Baron Vasquez, a competent gunner. The Indians fought until their ammunition was exhausted.

[8] Black Hawk in his *Autobiography* makes no mention of having been with Tecumseh, but many early writers believed he participated in the battle of Tippecanoe.

[9] *The Iowa Journal of History and Politics*, October, 1913, p. 542.

# CHAPTER XIII

## FORT MADISON AND THE WAR OF 1812

In the War of 1812, between the United States and Great Britain, Fort Madison was destined to play an important part. In April, 1812, the state of Louisiana was admitted into the Union, and what had been the Territory of Louisiana, including what is now Iowa, was reorganized as the Territory of Missouri, of which William Clark, of Lewis and Clark fame, was made governor. On the eighteenth of June, of the same year, congress declared war on Great Britain. What was a war for American freedom on the seas, in the west became a contest for trade. The British traders had almost monopolized the traffic with the Indians. They hoped now to expel the Americans entirely. They had the confidence of the Indians, and as soon as war was declared, they summoned them to their aid. Tecumseh was made over into a brigadier-general and Black Hawk donned a red uniform and was dubbed a colonel of the British army. Tecumseh remained long enough in the service to lose his life, but Black Hawk soon tired of the white man's warfare. He spoke contemptuously of men standing up in rows to be shot down; he preferred the red man's stealth and strategy.

But Black Hawk was absent long enough to give his rival, Keokuk, a longed-for opportunity for tribal advancement. The Sacs, in fear of an American attack upon their village, were in readiness to abandon Saukenuk and to seek refuge in the Iowa country. Keokuk entered the council chamber and dissuaded them from such a course. He talked himself into such favor that he was placed in command of the situation. He prepared Saukenuk for a defense against an attack that was never made. When Black Hawk returned he was chagrined to find a strong faction of his tribe under Keokuk in favor of keeping peace with the Americans. The rivalry between the two men became more intense. The Fox Indians also were almost wholly devoted to peace. Wapello, whose village was on the east side of the river, was of one mind with Keokuk, and the chief Black Thunder took his band up to Prairie du Chien to keep them out of the war.

But the British Indians, as they were called, once more centered their hatred on Fort Madison, the sole remnant of the American power in that region. The British themselves of course were ready to encourage and help them. On the fifth of September the Indians made an attack on the place. Most of them were Winnebagoes, but many Sacs were among them. In their first assault they killed John Cox, a soldier who was caught outside the stockade. Lieutenant Hamilton was still in command, aided by Lieutenant Vasquez, the gunner. They found that Fort Madison was disadvantageously located for either defensive or offensive warfare. High bluffs stood immediately back of it and deep ravines approached it. The Indians skulked in the ravines and from the bluffs they hurled burning timbers on the buildings below, without exposing themselves to fire. For four days the two hundred or more red men kept up their attacks. One account states that "they threw upwards of 500 pieces of burning timber on the roofs of the houses; and when the attack commenced there was no spot about the fort that did not emit a continued sheet of fire from guns, fiery arrows and brands." The soldiers made syringes of their gun barrels and were hard put to it to keep the fires down. Lieutenant Hamilton, at a time when the wind was favorable, ordered the factory building, which was nearest the bluffs, to be burned. The garrison was not able to attack the Indians beyond "knocking over such red skins as had the impudence to peek over the bank." On the fourth day the firing was slight, and on the fifth, which was on the ninth of September, 1812, the Indians disappeared, recrossing the river.[1]

During the winter of 1812-13, Lieutenant Hamilton appealed for reinforcements for Fort Madison, but he did so in vain.

[1] Niles's *The Weekly Register*, October 31, 1812, Vol. III, p. 1.

The government was in the midst of a war that was taxing its resources. Instead of strengthening the fort, the war department seems to have considered abandoning it altogether. General Benjamin Howard, then in command at St. Louis, opposed that course on the ground that it would serve to embolden both the British and their Indian allies in the entire upper Mississippi Valley and enable them to carry their warfare against settlements farther east. Instead of withdrawing the garrison at Fort Madison, he was in favor of establishing an additional one at Prairie du Chien. In April the general himself was at Fort Madison. But nothing came of the Prairie du Chien project that year, and in July, 1813, the Indians reappeared at Fort Madison and in the first surprise of their attack killed a corporal and three privates.

Still unable to take the place by assault, they then laid siege to it and did that so effectively that the garrison was penned up in the stockade. Both supplies and munitions in the fort were low and the situation became so critical that Lieutenant Hamilton decided to save at least his men. On the third of September he set them to work to dig a trench from the southeast block house to the river, the men working on their hands and knees to conceal their movements from the besiegers. In the night time, having first transferred what provisions they needed to their boats, they quietly slipped out into the river, the last men to leave the fort setting fire to all the buildings. Before the Indians, who were within gunshot of the scene, realized what had been done the fort was wrapped in flames and the garrison was safe on the waters of the wide Mississippi. When the sun rose, there was nothing left of Fort Madison except two charred chimneys, and after that the Indians called it Potowonock, meaning the place of the fire.

But the Americans were not yet persuaded to give up the whole upper Mississippi Valley to the British and the Indians. In May, 1814, Governor Clark outfitted an expedition consisting of a gunboat and barges and one hundred and fifty volunteers and sixty regulars, and proceeded to Prairie du Chien where he established a garrison in what was called Fort

Shelby. Soon after his return to St. Louis, he sent Captain John Campbell up the river with reinforcements and supplies. Before they could arrive on the scene, on the seventeenth of July, the British and their allies attacked Fort Shelby and captured the place. On the next day when the forces under Campbell reached the vicinity of Rock Island they were furiously attacked by the Indians under the command of Black Hawk. Sacs and Foxes and Winnebagoes participated in these operations. A storm drove one of the boats on an island which still bears the name of Campbell. Many of the men, including the commander, were wounded and nine were killed. Black Hawk boasted that he himself prepared the fiery arrows with which they set fire to the stranded boat. The other boats managed with difficulty to pick up the men who had borne the brunt of the attack and, having done that, they beat a hasty retreat down the river. When the British commander at Prairie du Chien heard of this victory he called it "perhaps the most brilliant action fought by Indians only, since the commencement of the war." This was a tribute to Black Hawk.

Still determined to win back what they had lost, the Americans in September, 1814, sent a much stronger expedition to operate on the Mississippi. It was placed under the command of Major Zachary Taylor. Three hundred and thirty-four officers and men accompanied him. The Indians when apprised of their coming, appealed to Prairie du Chien for aid. The British sent down a small force of men with three guns, a brass three-pounder and two swivels. According to the British accounts the Americans came up the river in eight boats, with a white flag hoisted over one of them, for which they later substituted a war flag. The British resisted them on the fifth of September, when the severest fighting was done on Credit Island, which is now part of the suburbs of the city of Davenport. On the morning of the sixth, the British and their red allies landed the three guns on the Iowa shore and under the protection of the ground opened fire on the boats. The Indians are said to have manned the guns with glee. It was a rare as well as a new sport for them. The

American boats were soon made helpless in the water. Major Taylor in his report says that they held a council in which they decided that they could not risk an engagement with the enemy, whose numbers they estimated at more than a thousand. So they withdrew down the river. On the Iowa shore the British and the Indians followed them, dragging their guns through the grass, until the ground became too broken for them to keep up with the boats. The Americans had eleven men wounded, three of them mortally. It was a part of the War of 1812 which was fought on Iowa land.

The withdrawal of Taylor's expedition left the British and the Indians in control of the entire upper Mississippi Valley. At New Orleans they were making preparations to conquer the rest of it. Early in December, 1814, Sir Edward Pakenham entered Lake Bargne and landed ten thousand British veterans of European wars within ten miles of New Orleans. So confident were they of being able to take the city that they brought with them civil administrators to set up a new government for the entire Mississippi country. But they omitted some things in their calculations.

The Americans were not only preparing to defend New Orleans, but to reconquer the valley. Their commander was Andrew Jackson of Tennessee, a frontiersman, an Indian fighter, and to his detractors only a "blackleg" lawyer. He succeeded in getting together a force of about seven thousand men. Below New Orleans, from the river to an impassable swamp, he threw up barricades of bales of cotton. On the right he had Louisiana Creoles and river pirates; in the center, a force of regulars; and on the left, frontiersmen mostly from Tennessee. They were fighting men who could shoot straight. Unseen and in silence they waited behind their barricades on the eighth of January, 1815 — a memorable date in American history. Sir Edward led his own troops. When they thought the Americans had fled without firing a shot, the attack on them suddenly began. So deadly was the American fire that hundreds of the British fell. Three times they rallied their forces, but it was of no avail. Sir Edward Pakenham was among the dead. The battle of New Orleans had been won by the Americans, but before it was fought peace between the United States and Great Britain had already been agreed upon. If there had been telegraph wires in those days to carry the news the battle would not have been fought and Andrew Jackson might have missed the presidency of the United States.

When the British commander at Prairie du Chien told the Indians of the peace that had been made, with American victory, Black Hawk "cried like a child."[2] He had staked his fortunes on the British, and had lost. But it was different for Keokuk. He was elated. He had cast his fortunes with the Americans.

[2] Salter's *Iowa the First Free State in the Louisiana Purchase*, p. 100.

# CHAPTER XIV

## The Readjustment of Indian Affairs

In making the treaty of peace after the War of 1812, the British protected their late Indian allies to the extent of insisting that the American government should restore them to "all the possessions, rights, and privileges which they may have enjoyed . . . previous to such hostilities." Having used them, the British did not desert them. The Americans at first objected to such a provision in the treaty, but later they accepted it. The president appointed William Clark and Ninian Edwards, the governors of Missouri and Illinois, and Auguste Chouteau, the St. Louis merchant, to negotiate new treaties with all the tribes whose relations had been disturbed by the war. To facilitate these negotiations a great conference was held at the Portage des Sioux, above the mouth of the Missouri River, in June, 1815. Only the Sacs of the Rock River failed to respond to the summons. The commissioners treated all the tribes as if they had been engaged in hostilities against the United States. This was resented by those who had not taken part in the war, and especially by the aged chief of the Foxes, Black Thunder, who had taken his band to Prairie du Chien to keep the peace.

To the extent that they were concerned, the tribes were required to affirm the provisions of the treaty of 1804. But it was not until the following year that the Sacs of the Rock River went to St. Louis to make a new treaty, and they were then represented as "imploring mercy, having repented of their conduct, and anxious to return to peace with the United States." In the treaty which they signed the sale of their lands in 1804 was specifically reaffirmed. The names of both Black Hawk and Keokuk were affixed to this document, but afterwards Black Hawk still insisted that when he had "touched the goose quill" on that occasion he did not know that he had assented to the sale of their lands.

When the Sacs returned from St. Louis they found workmen engaged in building a fort on Rock Island, a fort to which they gave the name of Armstrong, in honor of the secretary of war. Black Hawk and his band deeply regretted this. It was to them another invasion of their lands and one that boded no good. To Black Hawk the island was sacred ground for it was the abode of a good spirit which "was white with large wings like a swan's, but ten times larger."[1] The noise of saws and hammers drove out that spirit and an evil one came in place of it. He speaks of the island as their garden where they gathered berries and fruits and nuts.

The building of Fort Armstrong brought to the future Iowa one of her noted pioneers, George Davenport, after whom the city was named. Davenport was an Englishman of education and many talents. He was born in 1783. A brave deed brought him to a brave new land. He was injured in trying to rescue a passenger who had fallen overboard and was landed in New York for recovery. He became an American in fact. He fought against his own native land in the War of 1812. He helped to carry General Scott from the field at Lundy's Lane, where he was wounded. He fought with General Jackson at New Orleans. His increasing weight compelled him to leave the active service, and he was sent to Fort Armstrong as an army commissary. He soon set up as an independent trader and prospered greatly in business, standing out as an influential man of his times.

In 1820 there came across the Mississippi a man who has been called the first American settler in Iowa — Dr. Samuel C. Muir. He was a Scotchman by birth and a squaw-man by marriage. He was an army surgeon and when the government for the good of the service forbade and annulled Indian marriages among officers, he refused to comply. "God forbid," this noble man said, "that a son of Caledonia should desert his child or disown his clan." Dr. Muir built a cabin for his dusky brood on the site of the present city of Keokuk. If the

[1] Black Hawk's *Autobiography*.

squaw-men were barred as army officers, the half-breed children were so many that they became a problem for both races. Most of them grew up as savages for they naturally associated most with their mothers. Their social status was uncertain; often it was miserable. But the Indians were loyal to all who were of their blood. It was at their own suggestion and insistence that the tract of land lying between the Des Moines and the Mississippi rivers, above their confluence, was set aside for these half-breeds and it was known as the Half-Breed Tract. But those for whose good it was intended reaped few benefits. As soon as they acquired titles they disposed of their lands and long litigation followed.

At peace with the American government, the Indians continued to carry on tribal wars. Even the Sacs and Foxes attacked the Iowas with whom they had so long lived in peace. The amity between these tribes, perhaps, accounted for by their common hatred of the Sioux, may have been strengthened by an act of generosity related by Black Hawk. A Sac had killed an Iowa. Under tribal laws the murderer had to pay the penalty with his own life. Being too ill to go to meet his fate, his brother went in his stead. Black Hawk was one of the party that escorted him to the Iowa village. The escorting party halted at some distance, while the victim alone proceeded to the village, singing his death song as he went. When the Iowas had dug his grave and were about to fell him with their tomahawks, they learned that he was not the murderer, but his brother, offering himself as a sacrifice. For this they admired him so much that instead of killing him they sent him back with two ponies, one for himself and the other for his brother. The Sacs admired the act. But in 1823 the friendship came to a sudden ending. The Iowas at that time had their principal village near the present town of Eldon, on the site of the old Iowaville. They were fond of horse races and they maintained near their village a race track that was somewhat famous. One day while the warriors unarmed were engaged in this sport, a band of Sacs under Pashipaho rushed from the woods where they had been concealed, while at the same time another band under Black Hawk attacked their village. The massacres that followed left the Iowas irretrievably broken in both strength and spirit. It is alleged that the Sacs had heard that the Iowas intended to attack them, and so they attacked first.[2]

In an attempt to put an end to such suicidal wars, the American government in 1825 summoned the tribes to another great council of peace, to be held at Prairie du Chien. Lewis Cass of Michigan Territory, and William Clark, governor of Missouri, appeared as the leading negotiators. At the appointed time the tribes came from all directions. They came from the forests of the north and from the prairies of the south. There were Chippewas and Winnebagoes and Pottawattomies, Sacs and Foxes, and Iowas and Sioux. All came to make a great league of perpetual peace among them. "But no tribes," said Schoolcraft, who was present,[3] "attracted as intense a degree of interest as the Iowas, and the Sacs and Foxes. . . They came to the treaty ground armed and dressed as a war party. . . They bore flags of feathers. They beat drums. They uttered yells, at definite points. They landed in compact ranks. They looked the very spirit of defiance. Their leader stood as a prince, majestic and frowning. The wild native pride of man . . . was never so fully depicted to my eyes." Compared with these prairie tribes those from the forests seemed at a disadvantage. "Their martial bearing, their high tone, and whole behavior during their stay, in and out of the council, was impressive and demonstrated, in an eminent degree, to what high pitch of physical and moral courage, bravery and success in war may lead a savage people. Keokuk who led them, stood with his war lance, high crest of feathers, and daring eye, like another Coriolanus, and when he spoke, in the council, and at the same time shook his lance at his enemies, the Sioux, it was evident that he wanted but an opportunity to make their blood flow like water." And the chief Wapello of the Foxes stood back of him in like defiance.

But in spite of these hostile manifestations, a peace spirit

[2] Barrows's *History of Scott County*, Chapter IV.

[3] Schoolcraft's *Personal Memoirs; Thirty Years with the Indian Tribes*, Philadelphia, 1853, pp. 215-216.

prevailed at last. As the negotiations that followed affected the Iowa country, the chief result was the drawing of a division line between the Sioux on the north and the Sacs and Foxes and Iowas and other tribes on the south. This line began at the mouth of the Upper Iowa River, ascended that stream to the source of its left fork, from which point it ran in a direct line to the upper fork of the Des Moines, and thence in another direct line to the lower fork of the Big Sioux and down that stream to the Missouri. As between the Iowas and the Sacs and Foxes, there was a stipulation that they should occupy their lands in common "until a satisfactory arrangement can be made between them for a division of their respective claims." A similar stipulation ran to the benefit of the Otoes and Missouris.

One hundred and thirty-four chiefs signed the peace stipulations, and others signed it in the following year. When they parted, it is recorded, Sac and Sioux actually shook hands! But an imaginary line was soon far too thin for red men to recognize. The old tribal feuds were still too strong. In the spring of 1828, Sioux, Winnebagoes, and Menomonees made an Indian agent at Prairie du Chien the unwitting means of another massacre. Through him the Fox Indians living in the lead regions of Julien Dubuque were invited to a council where the tomahawk was to be reburied. Unsuspectingly, the Fox chiefs and braves proceeded to the proposed tribal trysting place. On the second night out, when at some distance below the Wisconsin River, they were surprised by a war party composed largely of Sioux and all but two were massacred. The survivors carried the news to the village, which thereupon was abandoned in fear of an attack to follow. They fled down to Rock Island. There a war party was formed and placed under the leadership of a half-breed named Morgan. Their lamentations were soon changed to war cries. "With blackened faces, chanting the death song," they started up the Mississippi to be revenged for their kinsmen.[4] Sioux and Winnebagoes and Menomonees lay encamped almost under the guns of Fort Crawford. In the night time the

[4] Barrows's *History of Scott County*, Chapter IV.

Foxes, stripped for war, and with their canoes in waiting, crept upon their enemies, killed all in the camp and escaped down the river. They returned to Rock Island with their canoes lashed together and with the scalps and heads of their enemies borne aloft on poles. The village in the mining regions was permanently deserted and what is now Davenport was called Morgan in honor of the chief who had led them.

To prevent such occurrences the government in 1830 made still another treaty with the tribes, by which the boundary line between them was expanded into a strip forty miles wide to which the name of the Neutral Ground was given. It extended from the mouth of the Upper Iowa to the Des Moines. The Sioux on the north and the Sacs and Foxes and other tribes on the south each donated twenty miles to this strip, which thereby became the property of the United States. On this ground all might hunt, but none might molest the other. At the same time and place, the government acquired by treaty from the Otoes, Missouris, and Omahas, and from other tribes as they had interest in them, all the lands lying on the Missouri slope of what is now Iowa, as far north as the Sioux boundary. The purpose of the government was not to open these lands for white settlements, but to use them for reservations for tribes to be removed from the east side of the Mississippi. President Jackson had followed John Quincy Adams in recommending that the Iowa country should be used for Indian reservations, a fate that later befell what is now Oklahoma. But the turbulent Black Hawk was about to start a war that was to obliterate the plans of presidents.

# CHAPTER XV

## THE SACS ARE REMOVED TO IOWA

The Rock River and Rock Island region soon began to attract the attention of white men. They coveted the fertile fields which the Indians had brought under cultivation, and the presence of Fort Armstrong made it a safe place. As early as 1827 a number of squatters appeared on the scene. They were adventurers, and some of them may have been fugitives from justice. The Indians still denied the validity of the treaty of 1804, but even under that treaty they were entitled to the use of their lands until they should be surveyed and sold to actual settlers. Clearly the white men were trespassers, not only in the eyes of the Indians, but under the law of congress, passed in 1807, forbidding settlers on public lands until the same were offered for sale. But the provisions of that law had been notoriously disregarded, and at that time red men had few rights that white men felt bound to respect.

It is hard now to realize the attitude of the settlers toward the Indians. Many of them thought it both right and proper to kill savages as they killed wolves and rattlesnakes. Following the disturbances and massacres during the War of 1812, the territorial legislature of Illinois, sitting at Kaskaskia, passed "An act to promote retaliation upon hostile Indians, and to encourage the bravery and enterprise of our fellow citizens," which was approved by Governor Ninian Edwards on the twenty-fourth of December, 1814. "Bravery" and "enterprise" as defined in that act were nothing less than murder. It was provided that any one who had obtained a proper license from some commanding officer, "who shall kill a warrior, or take prisoner a squaw or child," was entitled to a reward of $100 in each instance. If these deeds and achievements were on the part of rangers, hunting in parties of less than fifteen, the reward was only $50 per head![1] The law recognized a difference between wholesale and retail killing!

Such an act would now be inconceivable. But those were different times. Men and women did not think then of Indians as they do now. They had many reasons to think otherwise. Had not the red men plundered and murdered white men up and down the whole Mississippi? Were not the massacre at Fort Dearborn and the burning of Fort Madison fresh in their minds? Who among them had not seen the charred cabins of white pioneers, or possibly the bodies of scalped men, or even of women and children? To them the only good Indian was a dead one. One's sympathies now are with the Indians, but the settlers must not be left without justification. Their viewpoint must not be lost sight of entirely, if at all. They were doing part of the world's greater work. They were subduing the wilderness. They were living under the laws of the jungle. It was kill or be killed. It was still merely the survival of the fittest.

In 1828 more white men came to Saukenuk and new Indian fears and even hatreds were aroused. In 1829 before the tribes had returned from the winter's hunting some of the white men took possession of part of the village and its cultivated fields. A man named Joseph Vandruff established a saloon on an island in the Rock River. Black Hawk said that they made his warriors drunk to rob them of their traps and guns. To comply with the provisions of the treaty, the lands were thereupon ordered surveyed and sold to settlers. George Davenport in many ways interceded for the Indians. He was on terms of friendship with the president, but no concessions could be obtained, except that they might remain on their lands until the first of April, 1830. Those who remained after that date would be driven out.

Keokuk accepted this ultimatum. Before the stipulated day he went to the west side of the river and established a new village on the south bank of the Iowa River, a few miles above its mouth. Black Hawk refused to leave, although he

[1] *The Life and Times of Ninian Edwards*, by his son, Ninian W. Edwards, p. 163.

was urged to do so by Davenport and also by others who were his friends. When he returned with his band in the spring of 1831, he went again to Saukenuk. They used some force, but committed no murders. Black Hawk and a few of his men went to Vandruff's island and emptied the whiskey barrels with the contents of which they were debauching his men.[2] The squatters then appealed to Governor Reynolds, who seems to have been a vain and officious man who coveted military glory — and, it is said, the presidency. He listened eagerly to the appeals and issued a call for seven hundred volunteers to drive out the invaders of the state. Major-General Edmund P. Gaines, then in command of the troops of the west, also had been informed and came up the Mississippi River from St. Louis with a force of men. Aid was summoned from Fort Crawford. In all, General Gaines had about a thousand regulars under his command and he had no need of the volunteers. The general held a series of councils. When Black Hawk had entered one of these councils with his men in full war regalia, General Gaines either through ignorance or in contempt asked, "Who is this Black Hawk? Is he a chief? By what right does he appear in council?" The brave thereupon withdrew, fearing to speak in the anger which had been aroused in him. The next morning he returned and said, "My father, you inquired yesterday, 'Who is Black Hawk? — why does he sit among the chief men?' I will tell you who I am. I am a Sauk, my father was a Sauk — I am a warrior, so was my father. Ask these young men who have followed me to battle, and they will tell you who Black Hawk is! Provoke our people to war, and you will learn who Black Hawk is!"

General Gaines informed him that he had not come to parley. He was there to carry out the orders of the government. He gave him two days in which to remove his band to the west side of the river — after that, force would be used. When the two days were up, Black Hawk and his band were still in their village. General Gaines then moved up the

[2] In one of the petitions sent to the governor it was alleged that the Indians went to "a house, rolled out a barrel of whiskey and destroyed it."

Rock River with a boat loaded with soldiers and displaying a big gun. The Indians offered no resistance and manifested no fear whatever. They said in effect, these are our lands; we are living here peaceably; shoot us if you will. General Gaines was touched by their devotion to their village and their fields. He hesitated to use force. He believed they would leave eventually, as inevitably they must. But for Black Hawk the situation was suddenly changed when his spies brought news of the approach of a multitude of pale-faces on horses — these were Reynolds's volunteers. He knew the attitude of the settlers toward the Indians and he realized that they would be under no restraints from their commanders. In fear of them he decamped with all his band, crossing the Mississippi on the night of the twenty-fifth of June in the face of a terrific storm. In the morning there was not an Indian left in the village. General Gaines marvelled at the celerity of their removal, and their crossing of the river in a storm. He knew then Black Hawk was a great commander. The volunteers were so chagrined over the escape of their victims that to be revenged they burned the village of Saukenuk and tramped down with their horses the growing crops.[3]

The flight and the revenge constituted what has been called the Black Hawk War of 1831. The fleeing Indians were brought back and made to sign somewhat drastic "articles of capitulation," which were called a treaty.[4] Among other things, Black Hawk agreed to remain on his own side of the river. He was no stranger in the Iowa country. He had lived and hunted there. It was part of his ancestral domain, as much so as was Illinois.

Black Hawk was sixty-five years of age. He was discouraged as well as old. Tribal power had slipped away from him. Left to his own meditations he might have given up the struggle for supremacy. But his young warriors were still warlike and the squaws wailed for the return to their corn fields in Illinois. He soon fell under the evil counsels of two

[3] Ford's, *History of Illinois*, 1854, p. 109.

[4] This treaty was never officially published; if it was submitted to the president it was not ratified.

men, Nahpope, or Neapope, meaning Soup, and Waupesek, or Winneshiek, who passed among his people as a prophet. He was half Sac and half Winnebago and illegitimately born. He practiced incantations, claimed supernatural powers and spoke oracularly. Every Indian crisis seems to have had such a man connected with it. The chiefs used them to influence their warriors. Nahpope is described as a liar and a mischief-maker. He had both malice and imagination. He was a red-skinned Iago to a red-skinned Othello.

Nahpope went on a long journey in the course of which he is said to have visited the British in Canada and the tribes in Illinois. He came back with glowing reports of a possible Indian restoration under Black Hawk. He told him all he had to do was to raise the war-whoop of the Sacs and the tribes would march to battle under his banner, while the British would come down from the north to help them. Black Hawk hesitated but was at last seduced. He was no longer able to think clearly. He himself went north. He talked with his friend Davenport and with the British commanders, all of whom gave him good advice, that is, not to go to war again. He was persuaded to leave it all to the great father in Washington. Through Keokuk he sought permission to go east to talk over his grievances. But nothing came of it. It is a long story of dreams and intrigue, of wounded pride and the eternal desires of the Indian for revenge. In the spring of 1832, Black Hawk was determined to reënter Illinois. His warriors were scattered. He made "an encampment on the Mississippi, where Fort Madison had stood," he says in his *Autobiography*. He admits he "again tried to recruit some braves from Keokuk's band . . . but could not."

The Black Hawk War was fought in Illinois and in Wisconsin, but it was planned in what is now Iowa and it was to this state that the stragglers returned. The outcome of the war was of much more meaning to the Iowa of the future than to either Illinois or Wisconsin. It was the very beginning of Iowa. If the other states have erected monuments to the Indian who waged that war, Iowa herself is the monument of his last great adventure.

## CHAPTER XVI

### The War Dance on the Iowa

When Black Hawk said that he "again tried to recruit some braves from Keokuk's band . . . but could not," he did not tell all the story. He was habitually reticent about his own defeats, and that effort was one of his greatest defeats. He went to Keokuk's village with a band of his warriors,[1] and erected his war post, around which his braves danced themselves into a state of delirious exhaustion, reënacting all the mimicries of savage warfare, and after that the chief made one of his most notable speeches, a speech in which he recounted all their wrongs, and invoked all the savage vengeance of his race. Keokuk's men were at first swept off their feet and they demanded of him that he lead them into Black Hawk's proposed war. For Keokuk it was one of the most critical hours in his career, but by his wisdom and adroitness as a speaker he succeeded in turning it into a triumph for himself. As an oratorical achievement it was superb.

What knowledge history has of this weird war dance on the Iowa River, and of the speeches of the rival leaders, was derived from a spy, Josiah Smart, who was in the confidence of Keokuk. He had come to the village to confirm the reports made to the whites about the movements of Black Hawk. He came dressed as an Indian, but Keokuk fearing that his disguise would not protect him during the war dance, had him concealed in some camp equipage, which happened to be near

[1] Isaac R. Campbell, an authoritative early settler, claimed the chief assembled his band near or on the site of Fort Madison. Perry A. Armstrong in his exhaustive book, *The Sauks and the Black Hawk War*, says Black Hawk's village was on the Iowa River a few miles above Keokuk's village and that he started on his invasion of Illinois from that point. Armstrong as a boy saw something of the war. He spent years in col-

the place where Black Hawk erected his war post, enabling him both to see and to hear what was going on. Smart was a squaw-man, married to a woman of the Sac tribe and was fully conversant with their dialect.[2] According to his accounts the dance was a savage orgy supreme, every effort being put forth to arouse the war instincts of Keokuk's pacific band. Finally, Black Hawk commanded silence, and began his speech, appealing for recruits.

"Head-men, Chiefs, Braves, and Warriors of the Sauks," he said,[3] "for more than a hundred winters our nation was a

lecting the materials for his book. Arthur Springer in his *History of Louisa County* says the war party moved down the Iowa River. William L. Toole, after whom an old town at the mouth of the river was named, in the *Annals of Iowa*, January, 1868, speaking of the trail along the Iowa River, says: "And on this trail the warriors of those villages passed to the Masso-Sepo with their ponies, and across it to the upper sand banks (New Boston), some going in canoes down the Iowa, taking their arms, ammunition, etc., preparatory to the war of 1832." John B. Newhall in *A Glimpse of Iowa in 1846*, says Black Hawk resided on the Iowa "until the Indian hostilities in 1832" and "It was here that he sounded the war-whoop, . . to that last deadly conflict." Jesse Williams in his *Iowa*, in 1840, speaking of Florence and the Iowa River country, says: "Here the Indian chief Black Hawk resided until the Indian hostilities of 1832 . . . and it is here he gave the war whoop and rallied forth his countrymen to the last deadly struggle in defense of . . . the home of their ancestors." These men were almost contemporaneous with the events of which they wrote and their testimony is therefore good. Undoubtedly, some of his band may have been on the Mississippi at that time and so Mr. Campbell also may have been justified in his conclusions.

On the first of August, 1920, eighty-eight years after the events enacted there, the author in the company of Hon. H. O. Weaver, Mrs. Weaver and William Weaver, their son, visited the sites of the villages, Keokuk's at what is called Florence, six miles below Wapello, and Black Hawk's, five miles above that city, labeled "The Site of an Indian village," on the early maps.

[2] For an account of the services of Josiah Smart, written also Swart, see Armstrong's *The Sauks and Black Hawk War*, p. 283. Smart continued as interpreter, succeeding Le Claire, for many years. In Galland's *Iowa Emigrant*, 1840, he is listed as Joseph Smart.

[3] The quotations from the speeches of Black Hawk and Keokuk are taken from Mr. Armstrong's *The Sauks and The Black Hawk War*, but, unfortunately, he does not always acquaint his readers with his sources or authorities, and he was also addicted to verbal embellishments.

powerful, happy, and united people . . . Our children were never known to cry of hunger, and no stranger, red or white, was permitted to enter our lodges without finding food and rest. Our nation was respected by all who came in contact with it, for we had the ability as well as the courage to defend and maintain our rights of territory, person and property against the world. Then, indeed, was it an honor to be called a Sauk, for that name was a passport to our people traveling in other territories and among other nations. But an evil day befell us when we became a divided nation, and with that division our glory deserted us, leaving us with the hearts and heels of the rabbit in place of the courage and strength of the bear."

Then he retold the story of the coming of the white men, whom he termed the "Long Guns." "Why did he [the Great Spirit] send the pale-faces across the great ocean to take it [their country] from us? When they landed on our territory they were received as long-absent brothers whom the Great Spirit had returned to us. Food and rest were freely given them by our fathers, who treated them all the more kindly on account of their weak and helpless condition. Had our fathers [had] the desire, they could have crushed the intruders out of existence with the same ease that we kill the blood-sucking mosquitoes. Little did our fathers then think that they were taking to their bosoms, and warming them into life and vigor, a lot of torpid, half-frozen and starving vipers, which in a few winters would fix their deadly fangs upon the very bosoms that had nursed and cared for them when they needed help.

"From the day when the pale-faces landed upon our shores, they have been robbing us of our inheritance, and slowly, but surely, driving us back, back, back toward the setting sun,

He spent years in collecting his materials, sparing no pains or money to gather his data, visiting the scenes described, as well as the living witnesses of the events. He says "Jo Smart was the only white man" present and "from his description of the topics handled, and the order in which they were considered," the substance of his account was made up. Armstrong also acknowledges his indebtedness to Bailey Davenport, son of George Davenport, who was old enough to remember the events of the war. See *The Sauks and the Black Hawk War*, p. 641. Armstrong's sources are credible.

burning our villages, destroying our growing crops, ravishing our wives and daughters, beating our papooses with cruel sticks, and brutally murdering our people upon the most flimsy pretenses and trivial causes.''

The orator then recited what had happened recently at Saukenuk, beginning with the treaty made by the ''cowardly and treacherous Quashquamme,'' until ''they burned down our ancient village and turned their horses into our growing corn.'' And, ''They are now running their plows through our graveyards, turning up the bones and ashes of our sacred dead, whose spirits are calling to us from the land of dreams for vengeance on the despoilers. Will the descendants of Nanamakee [4] and our other illustrious dead stand idly by and suffer this sacrilege to be continued? Have they lost their strength and courage, and become squaws and papooses? The Great Spirit whispers in my ear, no! Then let us again be united as a nation and at once recross the Mississippi, rekindle our watch-fires upon our ancient watch tower, and send forth the war-whoop of the again united Sauks, and our cousins, the Masquawkees, Pottawattamies, Ottawas, Chippewas, Winnebagoes, and Kickapoos, will unite with us in avenging our wrongs upon the white pioneers of Illinois. When we recross the Mississippi with a strong army, the British father will send us not only guns, tomahawks, spears, knives, and ammunition in abundance, but he will also send us British soldiers to fight our battles for us.

''Then will the deadly arrow and the fatal tomahawk hurtle through the air at the hearts and heads of the pale-faced invaders, sending their guilty spirits to the white man's place of endless punishment, and should we, while on the war-path, meet the Pauguk, our departing spirits will be led along that path which is strewn with beautiful flowers, laden with the fragrance of patriotism and heroism, which leads to the land of dreams, whence the spirits of our fathers are beckoning us on, to avenge their wrongs.''

In the midst of the indescribable tumult that followed Black Hawk's speech, Nahpope spoke and repeated the delusions and lies about the help that would come to them from

4 Black Hawk's mythical ancestor.

their cousins and from the British, naming even the vessel upon which the latter would be transported to Milwaukee. Accepting these assurances and grasping at the visions which Black Hawk had conjured up, the Indians abandoned themselves wholly to the war spirit. Keokuk's band joined the others, out-vying and out-doing them. Almost with one voice his head-men and his braves demanded of him that he should lead them on the war-path with Black Hawk's men. For Keokuk it was a critical and even a dangerous moment. To have resisted his men,. even to have refused to do what they demanded of him, might have meant death for him at their hands, so infuriated were they. He was too wise, too cautious to do that. Instead he seemed to acquiesce in the spirit that had overwhelmed them. When they demanded that he speak, he advanced to the war post and laid his hand upon it without striking it. They listened. He watched every expression on their faces. He knew every secret of the human heart, for as a diplomat and orator he had made such things his study.

"Head-men, Chiefs, Braves, and Warriors of the Sauks," he began, speaking with studied deliberation, "I have heard and considered your demand to be led forth upon the war-path against the pale-faces, to avenge the many wrongs, persecutions, outrages, and murders committed by them upon our people. I deeply sympathize with you in your sense and construction of these terrible wrongs. Few, indeed, are our people who do not mourn the death of some near and loved one at the hands of the Long Guns, who are becoming very numerous." And then he adroitly pictured their numbers and their strength. "Their cabins are as plenty as the trees in the forest," he told them, "and their soldiers are springing up like grass on the prairies. They have the talking thunder, which carries death a long way off, with long guns and short ones, long knives and short ones, ammunition and provisions in abundance, with powerful war horses for their soldiers to ride." And then still more adroitly he told them: "In a contest where our numbers are so unequal to theirs we must ultimately fail. All we can reasonably hope or expect is to wreak the utmost of our vengeance upon their hated heads, and fall, when fall we must, with our faces to the enemy. Great is the undertaking and desperate must be our exertions. Every brave and warrior able to throw a tomahawk or wield a war-club must go with us. Once across the Mississippi, let no one think of returning while there is a foe to strike or a scalp to take, and when we fall—if our strength permits—let us drag our feeble, bleeding bodies to the graves of our ancestors, and there die, that our ashes may commingle with theirs, while our departing spirits shall follow the long trail made by them in their passage to the land of spirits.

"It is my duty as your chief to be your father while in the paths of peace, and your leader and champion while on the war-path. You have decided to follow the path of war, and I will lead you forth to victory if the Good Spirit prevails. If not, and the Bad Spirit rules, then will I perish at my post of duty. But what shall we do with our old and infirm, our women and children? We cannot take them with us upon the war-path, for they would hamper us in our movements and defeat us of our vengeance. We dare not leave them behind us, doomed to perish of hunger or fall captive to the pale-faces, who would murder the old and the young, but reserve our wives and daughters for a fate worse than death itself."

And then Keokuk dramatically stated the supreme requirement on which he would lead them in war: "I will lead you forth upon the war-path, but upon this condition: That we first put our wives and children, our aged and infirm, gently to sleep in that slumber which knows no waking this side the spirit land, and then carefully and tenderly lay their bodies away by the side of our sacred dead, from whence their freed spirits shall depart on the long journey to the happy home in the land of dreams beneath, beyond the Evening Star.[5] For we go upon a long trail which has no turn,—from which in a few short moons, we shall follow them, but they must not follow us. This sacrifice is demanded of us by the very love we bear those dear ones. Our every feeling of humanity tells us we cannot take them with us, and dare not leave them behind us."

[5] According to Sac belief, the hereafter was located in the west.

The half-drunken and delirious men are pictured as standing cowed in the presence of the sacrifice which Keokuk had required of them. As he looked into their faces, he knew his advantage and he realized his power over them. Then turning suddenly toward Black Hawk, he said: "To you, venerable Chief, do I appeal for an answer to what I have said. Your long experience upon the war-path tells you I have spoken the truth, yet with all your wonderful eloquence, you have urged us to this terrible sacrifice. Brooding over the oft repeated wrongs committed by the pale-faces upon you and your people, your mind has grown weak, until you have lent a willing ear to the whisperings of evil counsellors, who cannot speak the truth, because their tongues are forked, like the viper's. They came to you under the guise and pretense of friendship and by the use of base flattery and hypocrisy gained your confidence, only to lead you in the crooked path of ruin and destruction. They are enemies of yours and your band, instead of friends. They first told you the British father has promised you aid and assistance, in warriors as well as in guns, tomahawks, spears, knives, ammunition, and provisions, as soon as you should recross the Mississippi at the head of a hostile army. Why has he not furnished you these things, to enable you to raise, arm, and equip your army, ready for war? This fact proves the whole story a lie, prepared no doubt by Nahpope or his cunning brother, Winnesheik [Waupesek], for the sole purpose of deceiving and misleading you and your band. The British Father is at peace with our Great Father in Washington, and neither knows of nor cares for you or your grievances. The same evil counsellors have told you that the moment you shall sound the war-whoop east of the Mississippi all the Indian tribes between that and the Illinois River will rise up as a single warrior and unite with you, and under your banner, to avenge their wrongs upon the white pioneers. What wrongs have they to avenge? They are on terms of peace and good will with these white settlers, and have no cause of complaint or grievance whatever. Yet they have told you that these Indians across the river were not only ready but eager to join you in a general massacre of the frontier inhabitants of northern Illinois, and are now only waiting for your signal fires to be rekindled upon the watch tower at Saukenuk to begin their slaughter. If this be true, why are not their great war-chiefs here tonight? Where are Wauponsee, the Red Devil, Big Thunder Shaata, and Meachelle? Why are they not here in person, or by their representatives, if it be true they are anxious to go upon the war-path with you? Their absence is proof conclusive that they have no intention or desire to join you in this suicidal undertaking. You have been deceived,—aye, cruelly deceived—by those counsellors with a forked tongue, who are leading you into the crooked path of the Bad Spirit, and have no love for you, or respect for your gray hairs or good name."

Still more sure of himself and of his power over those who were listening breathlessly to him, Keokuk addressed himself even more personally to Black Hawk, saying: "I beseech you, by the noble character you have always borne, by the honors and trophies you have won upon the war-path, by the love you bear your gallant little band, by everything you hold sacred and dear, abandon this wild, visionary and desperate undertaking, and return to your village. Seed time is here, but your grounds have not been prepared for the planting. Go back and plant the summer's crop. Arise to the dignity and grandeur of your honored position as the father of your gallant little band; shake off the base fetters of the Bad Spirit which bind you hand and foot, and turn your feet from the crooked war-path into the path that leads to peace. In this way only can you save your true and trusty band from certain defeat, if not utter annihilation. If you still persist in going on the war-path against the white people, then indeed may we bid farewell to Black Hawk, whose protecting spirit has forsaken him in his old age, and suffered his star of success—which has led him in triumph to a hundred victories on the war-path—to go down behind a cloud, never to rise again; and when the Pauguk comes, his lofty spirit will depart, groping its way doubtingly along the dark and crooked path to the land of dreams, unhonored, unlamented, and unwept."

Keokuk's speech might have been delivered by Mark Antony

in the Roman Forum, instead of in an Indian village along the banks of the Iowa. The Roman orator did not more adroitly win over his enraged auditors than did the Indian the infuriated warriors. Our version of his great speech is manifestly imperfect, but there is enough of it to stamp it with grandeur. Not in the capitol on the Iowa, nor in the capitol on the Des Moines has a greater or more purposeful speech been delivered since. It was Keokuk's supreme effort and his greatest oratorical achievement. And the place in which it was delivered may not have been far from the scene in which Joliet and Marquette had their famous interview with the Illinois Indians one hundred and sixty-nine years before. In Iowa history those six or ten miles along the Iowa River are sacred ground.

The effect of the speech, as described by Josiah Smart, the spy and squaw-man, was profound. Drunken men were made sober and infuriated men were pacified. In a few moments with adroit and eloquent words, Keokuk had shattered the whole fabric of his rival's dreams. The vision of his Indian Confederation had vanished—nothing but a wild and desperate undertaking remained. Black Hawk himself could make no reply — he made none. He was a defeated leader on the eve of his greatest war.

With those of the tribe who remained faithful to him, Black Hawk proceeded on his way to Illinois. If he had misgivings and fears, he was too proud an Indian to turn back. Better to go to defeat and to death with all his followers than to live humiliated and ridiculed. Fate beckoned him on and the doom of defeat hovered over him. The melancholy Indian riding at the head of his long file of warriors on ponies, up the Mississippi toward Fort Armstrong and the site of the ancient Saukenuk, is one of the saddest pictures in the history of his race.

# CHAPTER XVII

## The Black Hawk War

The Black Hawk War was fought by Indians then living in what is now Iowa, It was an effort to recover lands in Illinois which they had lost. On the part of the red men it soon became a retreat in flight with a few brilliant rear guard actions, and on the part of the white men it was a series of massacres, committed by volunteer soldiers poorly organized, or by regular soldiers poorly commander. The so-called battles of the war were fought in Illinois and Wisconsin, and the details of them do not concern this history, but in its consequences the war, as already noted, was more vital to Iowa than to Illinois. For Illinois it was riddance of a few Indians, but for Iowa it was the prelude to settlements by white men. The war therefore has an important place in Iowa history. It also has a peculiar general interest, derived from the later prominence of many men who participated in it.

First of all comes Abraham Lincoln, then unknown to fame. He entered as a volunteer, a tall and lank young man on a horse. The records do not show that he took much part in the actual fighting, if any at all. The future president was mustered into the service by Major Robert Anderson who is known in history as the defender of Fort Sumter at the beginning of the Civil War.[1] Jefferson Davis, who became president of the Confederate States, was at that time a lieutenant in the regular army, stationed at Fort Crawford, near Prairie du Chien. When the war began he was absent on leave, but he returned in time to participate in it and he had charge of Black Hawk after his surrender.[2] Zachary Taylor, another future presi-

[1] See letter by Robert Anderson to Perry A. Armstrong, May 10, 1870, printed in Armstrong's *The Sauks and the Black Hawk War*, p. 370.

[2] *The Life of General Albert Sidney Johnston*, by William Preston

dent, was the commander at Fort Crawford. General Winfield Scott, of Mexican War fame, who was sent from the east to take command of the troops, arrived on the scene in time to help write the treaty of peace. Albert Sidney Johnston, the Confederate general of Shiloh fame, and Philip Kearny and William S. Harney, who became famous Indian fighters, were also among the participants in the war.

Black Hawk's movements were well known to the American authorities. Keokuk had kept them fully informed of all his plans. General Henry Atkinson at Jefferson Barracks had early news of the impending outbreak, and at once started up the river with a force of men, while troops were also summoned from Fort Crawford. Governor John Reynolds of Illinois, issued another call for volunteers to which the settlers responded with alacrity.

Nevertheless, when Black Hawk on the sixth day of April, crossed the Mississippi the settlements were filled with the wildest alarms. Runners were sent in all directions. Those who could do so, fled to Fort Armstrong where a strong stockade was built for their protection, and others rushed eastward, leaving their cabins and all their effects. The rumors that ran through the settlements pictured a general uprising of the Indians and a British army moving down from the north to aid them. The newspapers printed the most sensational matter, tales of burning settlements and massacred settlers. Many things were told that never happened. While the settlers were in flight and the nation in an uproar, General Atkinson was coming up the river with boats not far behind the canoes in which were carried Black Hawk's non-combatants. Keokuk also, with a band of his trusted warriors, was hurrying up the river, about one day behind Black Hawk, on the opposite shore. He wanted to save both his white friends at the fort and the Indians who were going to attack it, the one from massacre and the other from committing an act of folly under Black Hawk's leadership.[3] Josiah Smart was with him. They were

Johnston, Appleton, 1878, p. 36; also, *Jefferson Davis; a Memoir by His Wife.*

[3] Armstrong's *The Sauks and the Black Hawk War*, p. 285.

much impeded by swollen streams. But somewhere they were picked up by General Atkinson who overtook them with his boats. For Keokuk these were troubled times for he was in effect openly arrayed against his rival.

Waupeseck, the Prophet, who had been at the fort in the guise of a friend, but in the disguise of a spy, met Black Hawk down the river. He had promised the trader, Davenport, and the interpreter, Antoine Le Claire, that he would try to dissuade him from his foolish purpose, but he did no such thing. On the contrary, he filled his mind with new hopes by telling him of the weakness of Fort Armstrong and the paucity of its defenders. So Black Hawk hastened on. His plans and purposes are not clearly stated anywhere. His apologists say he was of peaceful mind, that he only wanted to return to his old lands to plant crops. He himself told President Jackson afterwards that he had taken up the war hatchet to redress the grievances of his people.[4] The fact that he had encumbered himself with his non-combatants has been used as proof of his peaceful intentions. But he probably intended leaving them at Saukenuk, while with his men he should destroy the fort, which was to be the signal of the great uprising of red men of which he was still dreaming. His whole undertaking was sheer madness. It is unaccountable. But before he could make his attack, General Atkinson arrived at the fort and with him were Keokuk and his men. Black Hawk had been beaten and defeated.

Thus frustrated, two ways remained open to Black Hawk. He could return to Iowa, or he could go up the Rock River to the country of the Winnebagoes. Nahpope, still bent on evil, advised the latter course, while Philip Kearny, acting as a messenger for General Atkinson, warned him to return to the trans-Mississippi country. Black Hawk followed the bad advice. In haste he proceeded up the Rock River. He found scant welcome among the Winnebagoes who had no desire to engage in his wild adventure, which to them appeared already as a failure. Black Hawk then realized that he had been deceived. "The supplies that Nahpope and the Prophet had

4 *Fulton's Red Men of Iowa*, p. 213.

told us about," he said later in his *Autobiography*, "and the reinforcements we were to have, were never more heard of." He was soon pursued by soldiers sent by General Atkinson, but these were so delayed by floods that he was able to keep far ahead of them. In the vicinity of Dixon he was overtaken by a force of volunteers under the command of two political colonels, named Stillman and Bailey, who had been sent forward by Governor Reynolds to do so extraordinary a thing as capture Black Hawk and his band, an achievement that would have filled the country with the glory of his name. And they might have done it without striking a blow! Black Hawk was ready to quit and anxious to return to the Iowa country. So he sent messengers with a white flag to intercept Colonel Stillman's "column." Those who saw the white flag thought it was a piece of Indian trickery. They made prisoners of the messengers, subsequently killing one of them. The truth is that some of Stillman's soldiers may have been intoxicated. Black Hawk through his spies was soon informed of the treatment given his peace envoys. He says he had only forty men with him, but he laid in ambush for his white pursuers. When the warriors leaped from their hiding places, with war-whoops and deadly shots, the "column" not only staggered, but fled in a rout which became a riotous retreat. It was thirty miles to Dixon, but the reeling volunteers did not stop until they got to that place, where they told the most astounding stories of their encounter with thousands of red-skins. This event is known as the Battle of Stillman's Run.

At Dixon the volunteers entrenched themselves in the fear that thousands of warriors would soon be upon them. Governor Reynolds sent urgent appeals to General Atkinson to hurry up with his regulars before there was an annihilation of them all. When the general came up, being an engineer instead of an Indian fighter, he added to the entrenchments. And the volunteers and the regulars sat behind their embankments and waited patiently for the Indians to attack them. But Black Hawk in the meantime was hastening away, hoping to regain the west bank of the Mississippi by a circuitous route northwestward. His only hope was to keep ahead of the soldiers. His way lay across the Wisconsin. But when the incompetent commanders had recovered from their fright at Dixon, they started in pursuit. For the Indians the flight became one of the most tragic episodes in American history. Black Hawk had the women and children to look after. He did not dare to leave them behind. Soldiers who paid no heed to white flags would hardly spare the helpless! They were without food much of the time. They subsisted on roots and on the bark of young trees. Many starved by the wayside. Their trail could be followed by the buzzards that hovered over it. Their crossing of the Wisconsin under fire was called by Jefferson Davis a brilliant military achievement.

Finally they reached the Mississippi, "nearly opposite the mouth of the [Upper] Ioway," according to Atkinson's report. It was where the Bad Axe River enters the Mississippi. The pursuing soldiers were upon them, and on the river a boat from Fort Crawford challenged their crossing. They were not to be permitted to return to their Iowa country. Black Hawk once more raised the white flag of surrender. The Winnebago interpreter on the boat misinterpreted or misrepresented Black Hawk's request, and so the flag was not respected. He was given fifteen minutes to get their women and children out of the way and then they "let slip at them a six-pounder," says the report of Captain Throckmorton. From the shore and the boat they shot those who were struggling in the water. General Atkinson estimated the killed at one hundred and fifty. "The precise number," he reported, "could not be determined as the greater portion of them were slain after being forced into the river." One devoted and noble mother swam the river bearing her papoose in her teeth as cats carry their kittens. The babe grew up under the name of Two Scars, and became a chief. Her name was Nawasa — a name that deserves to be remembered. Nor did all those who reached the western bank escape. There Sioux and Menomonee Indians, who had been summoned for that work by the Americans, tomahawked and scalped many of the helpless ones. The Battle of Bad Axe lasted two days. It was a massacre, though called a battle.

Black Hawk and those who fought around him made no attempt to cross the Mississippi. They had tarried too long. When it was all over, they fled down the Mississippi. They took refuge "on some islands above Prairie du Chien," [5] where they were overtaken by a squad under Jefferson Davis. They had hoisted another white flag which was this time respected. Two disreputable Winnebago Indians, Decorie, or Decorah, the One-eyed, and Cheators, claimed the reward that had been offered for the capture of the leader. Lieutenant Davis says that he "reported to Colonel Taylor" his "disbelief in the Winnebago story." To this Taylor replied: "They want the credit of being friendly and to get the reward, let them have it." [6] Black Hawk, his two sons, Nahpope, the Prophet, and nine others were held as prisoners. The fallen leader was placed in irons, which were ordered removed by General Street, the agent of the Winnebagoes.[7] He told General Street that he had done nothing "for which an Indian should be ashamed;" he had fought for his country, his squaws and papooses against the white men who came year after year to cheat them and to take their lands. Under the escort of Lieutenant Jefferson Davis, the prisoners were taken down the Mississippi to Jefferson Barracks. Of the band with which Black Hawk had invaded Illinois on the sixth of April, probably many more than half were dead, and the living were leaderless and hopeless derelicts on the prairies of Iowa.

[5] *Life of General Albert Sidney Johnston.*

[6] *Jefferson Davis; Memoir by His Wife,* Vol. I, p. 141.

[7] Life of Street, *Annals of Iowa,* Third Series, Vol. II, p. 92.

# CHAPTER XVIII

## The Black Hawk Purchase

It cost two million dollars to wage the Black Hawk War, and the lives of a thousand men, women, and children, of whom four-fifths were Indians.[1] It changed the status of both races along the Mississippi River. General Scott, who had been delayed by outbreaks of cholera among the troops, arrived at Rock Island in time to take charge of the peace negotiations. Associated with him in that work was Governor Reynolds of Illinois. On account of the prevalence of cholera on the island, their conferences with the Indians were held on the Iowa side of the river, on the site of the present city of Davenport. There they met the Sacs and the Foxes, and the Winnebago Indians who lived south of the Wisconsin River, who had become more or less involved in the war.

On the fifteenth of September these Winnebagoes signed a treaty by which they ceded to the government all their lands and accepted in lieu of them annuities and lands in the Iowa country, in the east end of the Neutral Ground, which now constitutes northeastern Iowa. On the twenty-first of the same month a treaty was concluded with the Sacs and Foxes, the latter being made to share part of the blame for the war in which some of their men and chiefs, notably Poweshiek, had participated. In this treaty they reaffirmed the treaty of 1804, and ceded a strip of land lying on the west side of the river, extending north and south from the Neutral Ground to the boundary of Missouri, and of an average width of about fifty miles. To form the western boundary of this strip, the treaty-makers, and after them the map-makers, measured fifty miles from the Mississippi along the southern boundary of the Neutral Ground, and a like number of miles from the same river

1 *Wisconsin Historical Collections*, Vol. XII, p. 261.

along the northern boundary of Missouri, and from these two points they drew two direct lines to a point on the Cedar River where it is "forty miles from the Mississippi." This strip, containing about six millions of acres, was at first called Scott's Purchase, but later it was called the Black Hawk Purchase, and still later the name of the Iowa District was given to it. It was the nucleus of the present state of Iowa. The cession was demanded from the Indians "partly for indemnity for the expenses incurred [in the war] and partly to secure the future safety and tranquillity of the invaded frontiers." Out of it, however, there were reserved for the Indians four hundred square miles lying on either side of the Iowa River, which became known as Keokuk's Reserve.

Because of the extent of the cession, the Sacs and Foxes received compensation, $20,000 to be paid them annually for thirty years, the payment of their debts to Davenport and Farnham, the traders, amounting to $40,000, the maintenance at government expense of an additional blacksmith and gun shop, and "forty kegs of tobacco and forty barrels of salt" annually, the same to be delivered at the mouth of the Iowa River. Out of the negotiations, largely at the suggestion of Keokuk, the interpreter, Antoine Le Claire, received two sections or square miles of land on the Iowa side, one of which is now part of the site of the city of Davenport and the other at the head of the rapids, which is now part of the town of Le Claire.

The treaty was signed by "Keo-o-kuck, or He Who Has Been Everywhere," and eight other Sacs, and by "Wau-pe-lo, or He Who is Painted White," and by twenty-three other Fox Indians. Black Hawk was not made a party to the treaty. He was at that time at Jefferson Barracks, "wearing the ball and chain," an indignity for which he reproached General Atkinson, and that justly, for he was a prisoner of war — not a convict. Keokuk, it is said, out of the kindness of his heart for his fallen rival, but probably more to increase his tribal prestige, immediately intervened for the release of Black Hawk. Personally he accompanied the wife and daughter of the fallen brave to Jefferson Barracks, and pledged himself for the good behavior of the prisoners, if they should be released.

But heedless of these appeals and pledges, the government ordered Black Hawk, his sons and sub-alterns to be taken to Fortress Monroe for safe keeping. When Black Hawk was presented to Andrew Jackson, then president, after gazing curiously at each other, the Indian said to him, "I am a man, and you are another," expressive of his sense of racial equality. The president's fellow feelings may have been aroused, for on the fourth of June, upon renewed assurances of Keokuk, who pleaded for their families, the prisoners were ordered to be taken back to their own country where they were to be released. They were first escorted through the principal cities of the east, in charge of Major John Garland, so that they might realize the numbers and might of the Americans. The president and the Indian met again at Baltimore, where Black Hawk admitted that he had invaded Illinois, that is taken up the hatchet, to redress the grievances of his people. They passed through Philadelphia and New York, where many attentions were paid them, for Black Hawk had become a national character. They returned to the west by way of Albany, Buffalo, Detroit, and Prairie du Chien, and thence down the Mississippi to Rock Island.

The chief men of the Sacs and Foxes were summoned to meet Black Hawk, to bind them mutually to keep the peace. Keokuk came up the river with a retinue in barbaric splendor, for he was fond of magnifying his office. He himself was seated on a platform built over two boats lashed together. He had three of his wives with him and over him floated the stars and stripes, for he boasted of his Americanism. His followers are said to have filled twenty canoes. They stopped on the Iowa shore, "for arranging their dress, painting their faces and equipping themselves with the implements of war."[2] Thus arrayed they went to the island to greet the fallen man. When the rival leaders met they shook hands, smoked and talked, after which Keokuk with his retinue returned to the Iowa shore until the following day when the formal release was to take place. For these ceremonies, Keokuk sat with the aged Pashipaho on one side of him and Wapello on the other. Black Hawk entered in deep dejection. Major Garland then

[2] Salter's *Iowa the First Free State in the Louisiana Purchase.*

read to them the conditions surrounding the release of the prisoners. Black Hawk was told that thereafter he must listen to Keokuk. These words aroused the old fire in Black Hawk. "I am a man—an old man," he said in indignation, "I will not conform to the counsels of any one. I will act for myself—no one shall govern me. I am old—my hair is gray—I once gave counsel to young men. Am I now to conform to others? I shall soon go to the Great Spirit, when I shall be at rest. What I said to our great father in Washington I say again—I will always listen to him. I am done."

The scene created was momentarily intense and full of pathos. Major Garland was so touched by it that he modified his statement, and Keokuk spoke in a spirit of conciliation, after which Black Hawk asked that the words he had spoken in anger should be blotted out, if they had been written down. In the evening, Major Garland received the Indians at his quarters. They smoked together and drank some wine. Many speeches were made. Black Hawk when he rose to speak remembered that his wife and children had been well cared for by his rival, Keokuk, during his absence. "I thank them for it," he said. "The Great Spirit knows I thank them. Before the sun sets behind the hills tomorrow, I shall see them; I want to see them. . . I shall soon be far away. I shall have no village, no band; I shall live alone." To Major Garland, who had treated him with consideration on the long journey, he said: "When you come upon the Mississippi again, you must come to my wigwam. I have none now. On your road home, you will pass where my village once was. No one lives there now; all are gone. I give you my hand; we may never meet again; I shall long remember you. The Great Spirit will be with you, and with your wives and children. Before the sun rises I shall go to my family."

Black Hawk was sixty-six years old when he wended his way back to the Iowa River. He had only a few more years to live. He had already prophesied his own going. "Tell him," he said, "that Black Hawk's eyes have looked upon many suns, but they shall not see many more, and that his back is no longer straight as in his youth, but is beginning to bend with age. The Great Spirit has whispered among the tree tops in the morning and in the evening, saying, Black Hawk's days are few, he is wanted in the spirit land." Keokuk himself could not make use of more beautiful words. They are words that leave in our minds the stamp of his native and innate nobility of soul.

Realizing that he did not have long to live, and mindful of the many misunderstandings among white men concerning him, he asked that the story of his life should be written down and printed, so that he might be judged fairly by posterity. His wishes were gratified. Antoine Le Claire acted as an interpreter and J. B. Patterson, a newspaper man of Oquawka, Illinois, as amanuensis. These three men produced what is known as Black Hawk's *Autobiography*, dated the tenth moon, that is the month of October, 1833. Le Claire and Patterson were known among all men as both competent and honest, and they certified under legal forms that what they printed was the veritable and authentic account of the great Indian's life, as told by himself.

The end of Black Hawk is so near that it may be well to complete here the story of his life. In 1836 he was present at the sale of Keokuk's Reserve, in which he took no part. In 1837 he went once more to Washington. Keokuk and other chiefs had been summoned there by the government, and they did not dare to leave him behind in Iowa, lest his relentless followers should make tribal troubles under his leadership. Upon his return, he lived for a while on Devil's Creek in Lee County, and in the spring of 1838, he went farther west, to Davis County on the Des Moines River — where he built a cabin in which he lived a half savage and half civilized life. On the Fourth of July of that year he was invited to be the guest of the city of Fort Madison. After they had eaten, he was introduced as "the illustrious guest," in response to which he made his last speech as follows:

"It has pleased the Great Spirit that I am here today. I have eaten with my white friends. The earth is our mother — we *live* on it, with the Great Spirit above us. It is good. I hope we are all friends here. A few summers ago I was fighting against you. I did wrong, perhaps. But that is past and buried. Let it be forgotten. Rock river was a beautiful country. I liked my villages, corn fields, and the home of my people. I fought for it. It is now yours. Keep it as we did — it will produce you good crops. I thank the Great Spirit that I am now friendly with my white brethren. We are here together; we have eaten together; we are friends. It is His wish and mine, and I thank you for your friendship. I was once a great warrior. I am now poor. Keokuk has been the cause of my present situation — but I do not attach blame to him. I am now old. I have looked upon the Mississippi since I was a child. I love the great river. I have dwelt upon its banks from my infancy. I look upon it now. I *will* shake hands with you, and as it is my wish, I hope you are my friends."

The speech, or portions of it, was first printed in the Fort Madison *Patriot*. There are minor variations in the copies that have come down to us, in punctuation and also in the meanings given to certain words. But the sentiments expressed are the same in all the versions extant. They are definite and they partake of the beauty of Indian oratory. Tried in many wars and subdued in peace, in his last speech Black Hawk combined the Christian philosophy of the white man with the resignation and stoicism of the Indian.

In the following September, he was taken ill while on a journey to Rock Island. He returned to his cabin where he died on the third of October, 1838. He was buried partly in the uniform of an American soldier. Many of the presents he had received from American statesmen and soldiers, and of which he had been proud, were deposited in the grave with him. But even in death he found no rest for his worn out body. His bones were stolen, probably for purposes of exhibition. They were carried to Illinois, whence they were returned upon the demand of the territorial governor of Iowa, Robert Lucas. His relatives feared to have the stolen bones returned to their grave, and so they were kept in Burlington, where they were eventually consumed in a fire. It was the completion of the tragedy of his life.

# CHAPTER XIX

## Black Hawk and Keokuk

The names of Black Hawk and Keokuk must be included in any list of great American Indians. And measured by what they were and by what they did, their names must stand near the top of such a list. They suffer in comparison with none. That out of a tribe numbering only a few thousand persons two such men should have been developed at one time is in itself remarkable. Perhaps their environment had much to do with that development; they lived in stirring times for their race; they became the expressions of the attitudes of the inferior race that had to give way to a superior one.

The rôles played by these two Indians are diametrically opposed to each other. Black Hawk's part was that of unavailing protest, and Keokuk's that of equally unavailing acquiescence. Black Hawk resisted, while Keokuk compromised. Keokuk's course was based on an intelligent calculation of consequences, while Black Hawk followed the instincts and aspirations of his race regardless of consequences. It came about that Keokuk was pleased with the praise of white men, while Black Hawk found no pleasure in anything except a satisfied racial conscience. Black Hawk died nobly in the virtues of his own race, while Keokuk passed out in many of the vices of the white man. History may praise Keokuk, but it must admire Black Hawk.

First of all and most of all, the historian wonders how these two men out of their meager opportunities gathered so much human wisdom, and how out of their miserable surroundings they garnered so much human nobility. If it is true that many of their acts were brutal, it is also true that many of their thoughts were lofty. The beautiful imagery of many of their spoken words betokens both wealth of mind and health of heart. Only fine instruments produce fine music. In their speeches one comes often upon the evidences of a rare appreciation of nature, and of a philosophy of life that is almost profound. One discovers also the evidences of manners and morals, of things ethical and religious, and of that fairest of all human qualities, charity. Embittered rivals, they forgave each other. Keokuk intervened for Black Hawk when he was down and out, and Black Hawk in his swan song, said, "Do not blame him," after he had depicted Keokuk as the cause of his great undoing.

Black Hawk and Keokuk read no books and yet they knew and uttered the things that are written in books. But if neither one could read or write in any human language, is it not true that all the books are not printed ones? Is not wisdom expressed also in fields and in forests, in meadows and in streams, in clouds and in stars as well as in books and pictures? What writers and artists garner for others, these Indians may have garnered for themselves out of the bounteous nature around them. It is worth while to study the man in the forest as well as the man in the library, the savage as well as the civilized man, the primal as well as the final man.

Black Hawk was all Indian, but Keokuk had in him an admixture of Caucasian blood. Black Hawk speaks of his father, Pyesa, but his mother remained nameless; Keokuk's father has no name that survives, but his mother was La Lott, a half-breed.[1] Among Indians he bore the distinction of blue

[1] Keokuk's white blood is no longer a matter of conjecture; it is fully attested in a letter written by the agent, Thomas Forsyth, to William Clark, governor of Missouri, under date of June 9, 1830. Forsyth represents that on that day, Keokuk and others appeared before him asking him to protest to the governor against abuses that were practiced in the Half-Breed Tract, through the encroachments of white men and whiskey. Among other things asked is that an allotment of lands should be made to La Lott, "the mother of Keokuk." The fact that she was entitled to such lands as well as her French name are conclusive as to her origin. The letter, signed by Keokuk, was printed in *The Iowa Advocate and Half-Breed Journal*, then edited by Dr. Isaac Galland, of August 16, 1847, being No. 2 of that publication, of which few copies have survived, one of them being in the Historical Department at Des Moines, reprinted in *Annals of Iowa*, Third Series, Vol. X, p. 455.

eyes. But Keokuk regarded himself as an Indian. He was a Sac, and that meant a proud Indian. Physically as well as mentally and in their careers, the two men were opposites. Black Hawk was probably five feet and eight inches in height, thin and wiry; Keokuk stood nearly six feet in height, and robust and massive. Black Hawk had an aquiline nose and his eyes are spoken of as the most piercing ever seen in a human head. Keokuk was described as a "magnificent specimen" of manhood, and when he was wrought upon, as in speaking, he is said to have "looked like thunder."

Neither Black Hawk nor Keokuk was born a chief. Both rose to the distinctions and powers of leadership through their own exertions. By some writers they have been called usurpers of tribal powers. But such conclusions are based on misapprehensions and misinterpretations. Among the Sacs — and it is also true of other tribes — government was democratic, not monarchial. There were ruling clans, or families, and to be born of them was an advantage, but even the disadvantage of birth could be overcome and Keokuk at least did so. The son of a chief could not assume his father's office unless he could do his father's tasks. The sagacious and the daring became leaders among them. The primal test was, of course, physical courage, the courage that is esteemed among all achieving peoples. The Indians exalted physical courage. To kill and to scalp an enemy was the highest expression of this quality. It was the ambition of every young Indian. Their mothers taught it to them. At fifteen Black Hawk distinguished himself in war, and at seventeen he led a war party. Keokuk was only fifteen when he unhorsed a Sioux. But physical courage was not all. Sagacity, cunning, and eloquence were also esteemed qualities. At Saukenuk there was a council lodge in which all tribal questions were discussed and voted upon. The man who could sway a council was an acclaimed leader. Oratory was the Indian's inheritance, and the first American orators were the red men.

Black Hawk inherited from his father the mysterious medicine bag which was among them the symbol of some occult power. But Keokuk, of humbler birth, had to beat down the tribal organization to win advancement. When he had worsted his Sioux enemy — they rode at each other like knights of old, with leveled spears — a great feast was prepared for him, he was admitted to the society of the braves, and it was especially decreed that on all public occasions thereafter he might appear on horseback, an honor of which he was never unmindful. When the artist, Catlin, had depicted his rugged face, his vanity was not satisfied until he had been painted on horseback also. But it was on diplomacy that he relied most for his advancement. He was made tribal guest-keeper which enabled him to dispense tribal hospitality, which he did with a lavish hand.[2] He was not always scrupulous in the use of power. His mind was always alert. It was filled with schemes and strategems. He made use of intrigue. In his own tribe he played one faction against another. Black Hawk was almost wholly lacking in these arts. He was crafty in war, but not sagacious in diplomacy. Keokuk avoided obstacles in his way, Black Hawk combatted them. Black Hawk defied fate and Keokuk defied chance. Black Hawk was mentally and morally too honest to strive with Keokuk. Black Hawk was defeated by his own convictions, and Keokuk's victory was the compensation of his compromises. Keokuk may be praised for his abilities, but Black Hawk for his stabilities. Both were great orators. The supreme contest between them was around the war post on the Iowa River, where Keokuk won the victory by his adroitness. To Black Hawk oratory was a means to an end, while Keokuk must often have indulged in it for its own sake. Black Hawk's speeches were direct and incisive; Keokuk's elaborate and ornate. Black Hawk's words were few and terse; Keokuk's many and beautiful. Keokuk's gestures were like the waving of the tree tops; Black Hawk's were like the snapping of branches.

As an orator, Keokuk was indeed supreme. Black Hawk spoke of him contemptuously as a great talker. But it was not his contempt; it was his glory, and his power, and it became his immortality. His flights of oratory must have been

[2] See article on "Keokuk" in the *Handbook of American Indians*, Bulletin 30, American Bureau of Ethnology.

magnificent. All the early writers speak of them. One who heard him, wrote of him: "A glance at his bearing, his self possession, his intellectual and expressive countenance, at once revealed his great superiority over his fellows. . . His individuality was marked, his oratory was proverbial — so intense and energetic were his words and gestures when aroused, that he could carry his audience with him, whether they understood a word or not."[3] Another, writing of him on one occasion, said: "Keokuk . . . slowly rose to his feet, letting drop his blanket from his shoulders. . . His manner was dignified. All eyes were turned upon him, and a smile of satisfaction, if such a thing could be seen upon the face of an Indian, could be traced, as this great orator began his speech. . . As he warmed up with the subject he became animated and even eloquent. His speech was clear and distinct. He spoke fast, so much so, that Mr. Le Claire, the interpreter, had frequently to stop him. His lofty bearing, his earnest, intelligent look and his well-timed gestures, all told that he was one of nature's orators."[4]

On his eastern tours, made generally on business connected with the government, multitudes flocked to hear him. When he appeared before committees of congress, or before the commissioners of Indian affairs, judges of the supreme court and other high officials adjourned their business to hear him speak. He was conscious of his powers. He was even vain of them. We have only fragments of his great speeches. But as every fragment of Sappho has been called a poem, so every fragment of Keokuk may be called an oration. Every piece glows with the colors of the prairies and we can almost hear in it as we read it the rustling of the leaves of the forest. Or, it is the rippling of a brook, followed by the crashing thunder from the clouds over it! There were then no men in Iowa who could report him adequately. Those who performed these services for history were all lingually and mentally his inferiors.[5] Keokuk himself realized their deficiencies, and in his

[3] Recollections of Hon. Alfred Hebard, in *Annals of Iowa*, Third Series, Vol. I, p. 401.

[4] Willard Barrows's *History of Scott County*, Chapter IV.

[5] That Keokuk understood English is the testimony of Caleb Atwater, who was employed by the government to negotiate with the Indians in

vanity he grieved over the fact — he had the desires of immortality.

Of Black Hawk, whole speeches have been preserved. His swan song at Fort Madison is one of these. It is as perfect as anything that could have come from Keokuk. But Black Hawk left more — his *Autobiography*, translated by Le Claire and transcribed by Patterson. Those who had not dealt justly with him sought to discount this book; they even called it a spurious concoction of white men for commercial purposes.[6] But the best answer is not the affidavits of the translator and transcriber, but the contents of the book. No one but an Indian could have supplied those. They are the memories and the images; the impressions and the philosophy of a red man. The tints and taints of the minds of the white men through which they passed are visible, but the essential things in the book are those of the Indian, of Black Hawk. There is probably no other such record of the mind of an Indian. It is a truly remarkable book — an Indian classic. It is also an Iowa book, for Black Hawk was at that time a resident of Iowa, and Iowa had always been part of his homeland.

As history, Black Hawk's *Autobiography* bears the stamp of truthfulness. There are things that he avoids, for an Indian like Black Hawk could never consent to humiliate himself. But if he does not always tell the whole truth, he at least never tells anything that he did not believe to be true.

1829. On one occasion, he says, "Taking Keokuk aside, and alone, I told him in plain English, all I wanted of him, what I would do for him, and what I expected from him and his good offices. He replied in good English, 'I understand you sir, perfectly, and it shall all be done.' It was all done faithfully, and he turned the tide in our favor." See Atwater's *Remarks Made on a Tour to Prairie du Chien*, 1831 edition, p. 70.

[6] Reynolds in his *History of My Own Times*, called the book "a catchpenny publication," with which Black Hawk himself had little to do. Reynolds speaks of Black Hawk as "a treacherous and evil disposed Indian." Governor Ford, who took part in the war, passed a better judgment of him. He says, "Black Hawk was distinguished for courage and for clemency to the vanquished. He was an Indian patriot, a kind husband and father, and was noted for his integrity in all his dealings with his tribe and with the Indian traders." See Ford's *History of Illinois*, p. 109.

Black Hawk

Keokuk

Mahaska

Rantchewaime

But it is not all composed of history. He moralizes much. "The path of glory is rough," he says, "and many gloomy hours obscure it." He mingles tradition with history, mythology with theology, and superstition with science. He tells us what Indians believe and what he thinks white men believe. He portrays Indian manners, customs, morals, etiquette, and law. He relates folklore and fairy stories that seemed to him as real as nursery tales to children.

If Keokuk had dictated his autobiography, it would have resulted in a different book. There would have been in it more of pomp and ceremony. He might have been loquacious where Black Hawk was reticent. Keokuk's book might have been seasoned with humor, for he had a fine sense of it. When a Sioux chief in a Washington conference said that one could not put wisdom in the head of a Sac or Fox unless he bored his ears with a wooden stick, Keokuk replied quickly that to perform the same operation on the head of a Sioux, one would need hot irons. When Joseph Smith, the Mormon, invited him as a leader of one of the lost tribes of Israel to go in quest of a land flowing with milk and honey in the west, Keokuk replied that Indians preferred annuities to honey and whiskey to milk.

Black Hawk and Keokuk were Indians, and they were called savages. They walked by other lights and they wrought according to other standards. But they stand out as men of heroic proportions, morally as well as physically. Nor do they suffer greatly when measured by the standards of the race that called itself the superior one. There is an historic fascination about them, and they have left the glamor of some romance on the land in which once they lived.

# CHAPTER XX

## THE INDIANS IN PASSING

The Indians are about to pass out of Iowa. Remnants of the tribes will linger on the scene a few years longer, and a few will remain indefinitely. But the defeat of Black Hawk was their day of doom. They have already lost the Missouri River slope as far north as the lands of the Sioux, the Mississippi bank has passed out of their control, while across northern Iowa the government owns the Neutral Ground, stretching from the great river westward to the Des Moines. White settlers are on their way to the Iowa country. They will replace the trappers and the traders. Before taking up their story, it may be well to make some note of the red men, how they lived here, what they believed and what they did besides making tribal wars and signing treaties drawn up for them by the government, for this is a history of the people of Iowa, and the Indians were the first people who lived here.

In those times the two races did not understand each other. The differences between them were irreconcilable. To the Indian the white man was a despoiler, and to the white man the Indian was an incumbrance on the land. Those who sought to do something for the Indian tried to teach him to read religious tracts, and those who robbed him, first offered him whiskey. The red man laughed at the tracts and drank the whiskey. Those who merely wrote about them depicted them as morose, cruel, and relentless savages. There were exceptions. George Catlin, the artist, who came to live among them, insisted even in that day that the Indians were human beings. The other writers saw them only on the frontiers where all the vices of the two races were intermingled. But Catlin lived with them back of the frontiers. There he found them a happy, sociable, and even jovial people. There they were neither taciturn nor morose. They laughed and talked a great deal. The women gossiped and the men boasted of their exploits. They told stories and sang songs. To Catlin they were kind, generous, and even courteous. And so they were among themselves. They had things in which they believed and institutions that they prized. But the white men sneered at their beliefs and trampled on their systems of government. They met the white man's ridicule with the red man's resentment. They saw the faults in the beliefs and practices of the white man. "The whites may do wrong all their lives," said Black Hawk in his *Autobiography*, "and then if they are sorry for it when they are about to die, all is well, but with us it is different. We must continue to do good all our lives." And what was his conception of doing good? "If we have corn and meat," he says, "and others have not enough, we divide with them. If we have more blankets than we absolutely need, and others have not enough, we must give to those who want."

Such was their religion in practice. Their theoretical religion, according to Catlin, was an indefinite form of Theism. He saw the Indian as "a moral and religious being, endowed by his maker with an intuitive knowledge of some great author of his being and of the universe." They prayed much and they fasted often. Black Hawk said of himself that he never took a drink of water from a spring without being mindful of the Great Spirit. They had thoughts of a hereafter, but the so-called Happy Hunting Ground was largely a white man's creation for them. The future world was to them hardly more distinct than a land of dreams. Keokuk spoke of it as lying around the evening star, and so dying was "going west." Their priests were their medicine men. They believed in spirits, the good and the evil. Curing the sick was a process of casting out the evil spirits. To appease these spirits they made supplications and sacrifices. If they placed food in graves or made fires near them, it was to sustain and light the spirits of the dead on their long journeys. Even their most abhorrent practice, that of scalping the dead, had a religious significance. The soul of the scalped enemy could not leave the dead body and so could not confront them in the hereafter to plague them. They believed in good and bad luck, venerated many animate and inanimate beings, and practiced magic. Ignorance and superstitions abounded among them.

According to Mr. Catlin their alleged debasement of women was greatly exaggerated. If their women appeared as drudges, it was still not an entirely unfair division of labor. If the women had to prepare the food, the men had to provide it. It was the duty of the men to hunt and fish, to defend their lodges and their lands. These duties meant that they had constantly to be in readiness. The women among them had many rights and they used them. They ruled in the cabins. They drove the drones out of them, the men who did not do their share of the work of providing food and defense. It was the constant aim and desire of every ambitious chief to win and hold the sympathy and support of the women. It was also part of the duties of the women to educate the children. Black Hawk says that they taught the boys to be brave and the girls to be virtuous. Their domestic relations were well regulated and they observed a great deal of tribal etiquette.

They did not live like beasts, nor did they mate like birds. On the contrary, marriages were subjects of many laws and regulations. The mothers were almost the contracting parties. Among the Sacs and Foxes, what is known as the Crane Dance was a matrimonial ceremony. In this dance, in the spring of the year, the marriageable ones appeared in their gaudiest costumes. When a young man's fancy was fixed on a maiden, he told it first of all to his own mother, and then she went to the mother of the girl and made the necessary arrangements, provided there were no impediments, such as consanguinity of blood. When approved by both mothers, the young man went the next evening to the girl's cabin. With flints he would strike a light, which he held first before his own face, so that she might see him, and then before hers. If she blew out the light, he was accepted; if not, he was refused. The rejected lover could return on the following day to play love tunes on a pipe or flute. If, in response, she showed herself, the suitor was invited to return in the evening with the flints, "when his suit was usually successful," says Black Hawk. The Indians had ceased to be cave men.

They practiced trial marriages. Those who found they were unhappily married could separate at the end of the first year. Black Hawk thought this system wiser than that of the white men with its many infidelities and much unhappiness. For marital infidelity the man might kill the woman. "But no indiscretion," says Black Hawk, "can banish a woman from her parental lodge; no difference how many children she may bring home she is always welcome — the kettle is over the fire to feed them." The mothers prepared the "beautifully ornamented cradles which they carried on their backs," says Catlin. Indian children never cried. They seldom died of diseases, but many were killed in accidents.

Of the Indian women who lived in Iowa, few are remembered by their names. Rantchewaime, or the Female Flying Pigeon, the wife of the elder Mahaska, and the mother of the younger Iowa chief of that name, is perhaps the best known of all their women. She is described by the early writers as a woman of unusual comeliness and many virtues. In 1837, she accompanied her husband to Washington. She followed him and insisted on her right to go with him — it is said with a club held over him. In Washington she attracted much attention and many artists painted her picture, portraying her as an aboriginal madonna. Upon her return from that eventful trip, she assembled the women of her tribe and lectured them on the evils of the fads and foibles of the white women. She was killed by falling from her horse. After her death her husband often spoke in praise of her. He boasted that she was so good that when the needy came to her she let everything slip through her hands as through a sieve.

Many red men had many wives, but Black Hawk, with the moral austerity of his race, had only one. He was ever true to her and she was always devoted to his welfare. One of the missionaries, the Rev. Cutting Marsh, in a memoir of those times, speaks of a visit he made to this chief's cabin. He says he "was well received by the children," the parents being away. The cabin itself was surrounded with a neat fence. Within, he says, he "never before witnessed such a specimen of neatness and good order in any Indian lodge." One of Black Hawk's daughters was Nauasia — by some called Nemaqua. She is spoken of as a girl of remarkable beauty. William Carroll, an early settler and an elder in a church, has left some glowing accounts of her. His testimony is that Nauasia was one of the prettiest girls he had ever seen. Her beauty, he said, was such that it would attract attention in any circle.[1] When the family lived on Devil's Creek, in Lee County, she often came to Fort Madison with her father. The father and daughter were greatly devoted to each other. When a new hotel was erected in the place, she participated in many of the dances that were given there. She was always the belle of the ball, according to the elder. "And what a dancer!" he exclaimed many years afterwards. He says that "she was as spry and agile as a fawn," and so light on her feet that "she would leap high in the air and whirl around and cut fancy capers until she had beaten every other dancer in the settlement." The young men, he adds, "would stand around, and look eagerly until they had mustered up courage to ask her for a dance, and then everybody envied them." A young white man from the east fell in love with Nauasia, some accounts say he was from Baltimore, but Elder Carroll says he came from New York, but his friends and relatives shamed him out of the proposed marriage by calling him a "squaw man." He fled the country and the girl eventually was married to a man of her father's band.

The Indians indulged in a great deal of music. They used primitive wind-instruments and drums. The Iowas for a drum used a hollowed log with a rawhide stretched over it. To give a liquid note to the tones they kept a quantity of water in the log. They had many songs, repetitive in words

[1] William Carroll came to Iowa in 1835 and was well acquainted with Black Hawk and his family. He wrote his reminiscences in his old age, but his memory was still good at the time. They were printed in the Burlington *Hawk-Eye*, March 24, 1897. Fulton, in *The Red Men of Iowa*, gives the daughter's name as Nemaqua, and her suitor as a young man from Baltimore.

and monotonous in music. They had men who composed words and music for special events. The Iowas had a song and dance of welcome, during the rendering of which all stood up. For the home-coming of their warriors they sang:

"How-a! How-a!
O-ta-pa!
I am proud of being at home.
I am proud, O-ta-pa.
I am home, my enemy ran.
I am proud, I am proud, O-ta-pa." [2]

For warriors going to battle they had many songs. One was called a Wolf song and another the Eagle song with the following words:

"I am a war eagle.
The wind is strong, but I am an eagle.

* * * *

I see my enemy below me.
I am an eagle, a war eagle."

They had sports and games of many kinds and they devoted much time to these. Many of their games were played with balls, some of which were similar to football. The Iowas were especially fond of horse races. Gambling devices and games were many. One was called a Moccasin Game, similar to the white man's shell games. For this they sang:

"Take care of yourself. Shoot well or you lose.
You warned me, but see, I have defeated you.
I am one of the Great Spirit's children.
Wa-kon-da I am. I am Wa-kon-da."

Some investigators say that in music the Sacs and Foxes were as far advanced as were the Romans in the days of Julius Caesar. They had a crude drama, both comic and tragic. They had a voluminous oral literature, in which were imbedded many fairy stories of surpassing beauty. Even the great war chiefs indulged in these tales. "I will relate," says Black Hawk gravely, "the manner in which corn first came." Corn was something almost sacred among them. It was their sustenance, the highest material expression of the Great Spirit himself, the Wa-kon-da of the Iowas. "Once

[2] These translations are taken from Catlin.

upon a time," according to a story related by the chief, "a beautiful woman was seen to descend from the clouds and to alight on the earth, by two of our ancestors who had killed a deer, and who were sitting by a fire roasting part of it to eat." They went to her and offered her the choicest morsels of the venison. She thanked them and told them that if they would come to the same place at the same time next year, "they would find the reward for their generosity and kindness." When they told their story they were laughed at, but when they returned at the appointed time they found "where her right hand had rested on the ground corn was growing, where her left hand had rested, beans, and where she had been seated, tobacco." Corn and beans for succotash, and tobacco for peace and solace!

The Pottawattomies, who lived a while in Iowa, believed that the first human beings were destroyed because of ingratitude. When the Great Spirit had created a second man, they said he was so lonesome that the Great Spirit sent him a sister who was so ravishingly beautiful that many suitors came to woo her. The first of the suitors was Usama, or Tobacco; the second Wapko, or Pumpkin; the third, Eshmossimin, or Melon; the fourth, Kokees, or Beans, but she refused each one and each one dropped dead when he was refused. Then came a fifth suitor, Mondamin, or Corn, whom she accepted. Mondamin then buried all the dead suitors and from them sprang tobacco, the pumpkin, the melon, and the beans, while Mondamin himself became the father of all the Indians.

All the products of the earth, and all the manifestations of nature were thus symbolized and turned into fairy stories. Such tales invariably have marked the first dawn of human development. Some believe that such tribes as the Sacs and Foxes were on the threshold of a great mental development when the white men came to interrupt their racial course. That is speculation. They had a well ordered system of government, an extensive literature and an expressive drama, but they had not yet discovered the secret of the circle — they did not know that a wheel was more serviceable for transportation than the end of a pole!

# PART III

## Settlements and Territorial Governments
## (1833-1846)

## CHAPTER XXI

### The Prairies Primeval

The white men who crossed the Mississippi on the first day of June, 1833, came to a beautiful country. It was a grass-land, but it was not treeless. The meadows were vast, but the wood-lands also were extensive. The settlers called the wood-lands timber and the grass-lands prairie, a name that was derived from the French word *pré*, meaning a meadow. This word of foreign origin became particularly and peculiarly mid-western American. The Iowa prairies they entered were not level and flat, but for the most part successions of hills and valleys. The new country afforded everything that pioneering races needed or desired — wood, water, and fertile soil. For immediate sustenance there was an abundance of fish and of game that cost no more effort than the throwing of a hook or the aiming of a gun. In summer time there was a succession of wild berries, fruits, and nuts. The land was a wild paradise made beautiful by a profusion of flowers of every form and hue.

The historian must take all these things into consideration, for the nature of a country and its natural products have much to do with the development of the race that is to occupy it. Do not the seas and the mountains and the prairies and the plains in some manner and to some extent transform men into their own likenesses? The mountaineer is one man and the plainsman is another. Did not the people of Holland become patient and sturdy by their contact with the ocean, and the Scotch peoples frugal and thrifty on the stingy hills from which they had to wring their sustenance? How shall we measure the influence of the bleak shores and hills of New England and of the semi-tropical luxuriance of the south-lands on the development of an American national character?

And what is to be the final influence of the fertile and liberal prairies of the Middle West in the last national equation? Here men became free and unconventional; hospitable and generous; eager to receive new ideas and ready to try new experiments in thought as well as in government. But, fortunately, no part of our common country has been able to live its own life. Railroads and printing presses, telegraphs and telephones have mingled the peoples and intermingled their thoughts.

And, perhaps, it would not be right to proceed to people this beautiful state of which the Black Hawk Purchase in 1833 was the nucleus without taking some thought of how it came to be and how it was so well fitted for human uses and development. This is the story of the geologists.

In the beginning—if there ever was a beginning—their story is that here there was an open sea, and that the waters came and receded many times, leaving their deposits. The evidences of marine life are abundant, although one may have to delve deep into the earth to find them. When was it the waters flowed over this land? Who can compute time? Then, so the geologists say, there was an upheaval. The land beneath the waters was lifted up. That may have been part of the great catastrophe that in the farther west mingled the rocks of the earth with the clouds of the sky, forming the Rocky Mountains. In those days a celestial on-looker might have believed that God was destroying the earth—but He was making it. In due time vegetation must have spread over the new-made lands. And then animal life followed. The climate must have been sub-tropical for the remains are of plants and animals that belong to such climatic conditions. The fig tree and the magnolia and the cinnamon grew here; the tapir and the tiger and the panther roamed through the land. Huge reptiles and unnamed mammoths floundered in the jungles. Birds of brilliant plumage and monkeys may have flitted and chattered in the trees. The earth was prodigal and all things that flourished in it were luxuriant. It was a riot of living things. And thousands of years passed away. It may have been a thousand centuries of time, or many thousands of them, in each process. It is all inculculable and inconceivable.

Gradually or swiftly, the climate of the land changed from sub-tropical to sub-Arctic. It became as cold as it had been hot. All the life that had existed perished or departed from the land. Deep snows fell and vast fields of ice pressed down from the north to the south. Under their grinding weight rocks were pulverized and hills were tumbled into the valleys. One glaciation followed another. One is supposed to have extended as far south as the mouth of the Missouri and the last one may have extended only half way across the present state of Iowa, from north to south. What caused these great changes in climate is not known. There may have been changes in the angle of the axis of the earth.

Through countless years the accumulated ice and snow melted when the climate changed again from sub-Arctic to that which has prevailed since. The freed waters cut the channels of new rivers, leaving the surface as it still remains, except as it has been modified by subsequent erosions. The pulverized soils of the prairies remained and here and there deposits of granite boulders which had been carried down with the ice from quarries of the north. The last glaciation may have been a hundred or two hundred thousand years ago, and it may have been as recent as fifty thousand years. But it was in modern times, geologically speaking.

New forms of vegetation came. Nature may have evolved them out of her infinite processes, or the seeds of them may have been carried by wind and by water. The grasses and the trees, the flowers and the herbs, the mosses and the fungi—all spread over the land. Animal life must have followed quickly and most of it was made up of grass-eating ruminants. Through countless centuries more the processes of growth and decay of both vegetable and animal life enriched the earth for the coming of man. No one knows now when he came. But when he did come it was as the inheritor of a part of that region of the earth of which De Tocqueville said that it was, on the whole, best adapted for human habitation.

# CHAPTER XXII

## The First American Settlements

Before the first of June, 1833, there were a few Americans living in what is now Iowa — probably only forty or fifty. Nearly all of them lived in the Half-Breed Tract, between the Des Moines and the Mississippi rivers, above their confluence. This tract was not included in the Black Hawk Purchase. It had been reserved for those who were of mixed blood. But they were a shiftless race, inheriting the vices rather than the virtues of the two parent races. They cared more for whiskey than for lands. They permitted white men to live among them, whether for favors bestowed or benefits expected. The Indians who had donated these lands to the half-breeds viewed the presence of these settlers with misgivings. In 1830 they entered a protest against the white men and their whiskey on the reservation. This protest, which was in the form of a letter written by their agent, Thomas Forsyth, to Governor Clark of Missouri, was signed by Keokuk and other chief men of the Sacs.[1] But no heed seems to have been paid to it.

The Indian traders living in Iowa at that time continued to be mostly French. They understood the red men better than the Americans. They were more facile in the use of their dialects and in adapting themselves to the customs of the natives. One of these traders is reputed to have been a scion of the French nobility, a man who fled from his native land during the French Revolution to become a wanderer in the wilds of the west. He was called Chevalier Marais. He is said to have taken for his wife the daughter of an Iowa chief and to have made his home on Buck Creek in what is now

[1] See footnote, p. 108.

Clayton County. His career is mythical. On the Missouri River slope, Peter A. Sarpy had a much more real existence. He established himself there in 1824 and became one of the noted characters in those parts.

The first real settlers made their homes in the Half-Breed Tract, in what is now Lee County. Isaac R. Campbell, a somewhat noted man in those early times, writing of his first visit to the Iowa country, which was in 1821, said that "The only indication of a white settlement . . . was the cabin built by Dr. Samuel C. Muir on the site of the present city of Keokuk." He built his cabin in 1820, when he left the army and crossed the river because he would not desert his native wife and their children. Isaac Galland, another credible writer, says that "Morrice Bloudeau, a half-breed of the Sauk Indians, opened the first farm, enclosing his field with a log wall, on the bank of the Mississippi, and the balance with a worm fence, and caused it to be ploughed and cultivated in corn, in the usual way."[2] That was prior to 1829, when Mr. Galland himself with his family settled in the same vicinity. The place was then called Ahwipetuk, meaning at the head of the rapids — the Des Moines rapids in the Mississippi River. At about the same time, according to his account, Moses Stillwell and Otis Reynolds made settlements at the foot of the same rapids, which was called Puckeshetuk. Ahwipetuk became Nashville, and Puckeshetuk, Keokuk. At different times attempts were made to make settlements at Fort Madison, Burlington, and Dubuque, but these efforts were frustrated by the military forces, which patrolled the Mississippi until 1833, when the Indian title to the Black Hawk Purchase expired. Mr. Galland estimates that fifty white persons were living in Iowa in 1832.

At Ahwipetuk and Puckeshetuk, others soon joined the first settlers, and so two primitive villages came into being and the villagers learned to think of their settlements as future cities, with a developed spirit of rivalry between them. Puckeshetuk was the more favored by location, for there the boats had to lighten their burdens before they could ascend

[2] Galland's *Iowa Emigrant*, 1840, p. 7.

the rapids, but Ahwipetuk had in Dr. Galland a man of many activities and enterprises. He was in some ways one of the most notable men of that period. He was a writing-man, and he became a publisher to whom history is indebted for many things. But his chief claim to immortality in local history lies in his connection with the founding of the first school in Iowa. As he was blessed with children of his own, and was mindful of the children of other parents living on the frontier, he realized the need of education. A young Kentuckian, Berryman Jennings, was converted into a teacher, while the kitchen of the Galland cabin was made over into a temporary school room.[3] The benches and the desks as well as the school room itself were made out of hewn logs. Eight pupils were enrolled, ranging in ages from six to sixteen. Reading, beginning with the A-B-C's, writing, and arithmetic were taught in crude ways—it was all humble and meager, but it was a beginning, and around that schoolhouse at Ahwipetuk hangs the romance of first things in a new land. All this happened in the month of September of 1830. When the settlers at Puckeshetuk heard of the school, they immediately established one of their own, of which I. W. Robinson was the teacher. And so community rivalry promoted progress even in those early times.

At about the same time Americans tried to gain a foothold in the mining regions. After the death of Julien Dubuque, in 1810, the Fox Indians had permitted no white men to enter their country. The squaws and old men of the tribe worked the mines in crude ways and took out considerable ore which they sold to the traders on the Mississippi. But in 1828, after the Sioux and Menomonee massacre, and the counter massacre under the half-breed chief Morgan, they abandoned their village and remained with their kinsmen on the site of Davenport which was then called Morgan. Knowing that the Indians had left the region, in 1829 James L. Langworthy, a Galena miner and a man whose name is noted

[3] See Parvin's *History of the Early Schools and Education in Iowa, 1830-1859;* also, *Annals of Iowa,* Third Series, Vol. III, p. 445. The first schoolhouse *proper,* was built in Burlington, 1833.

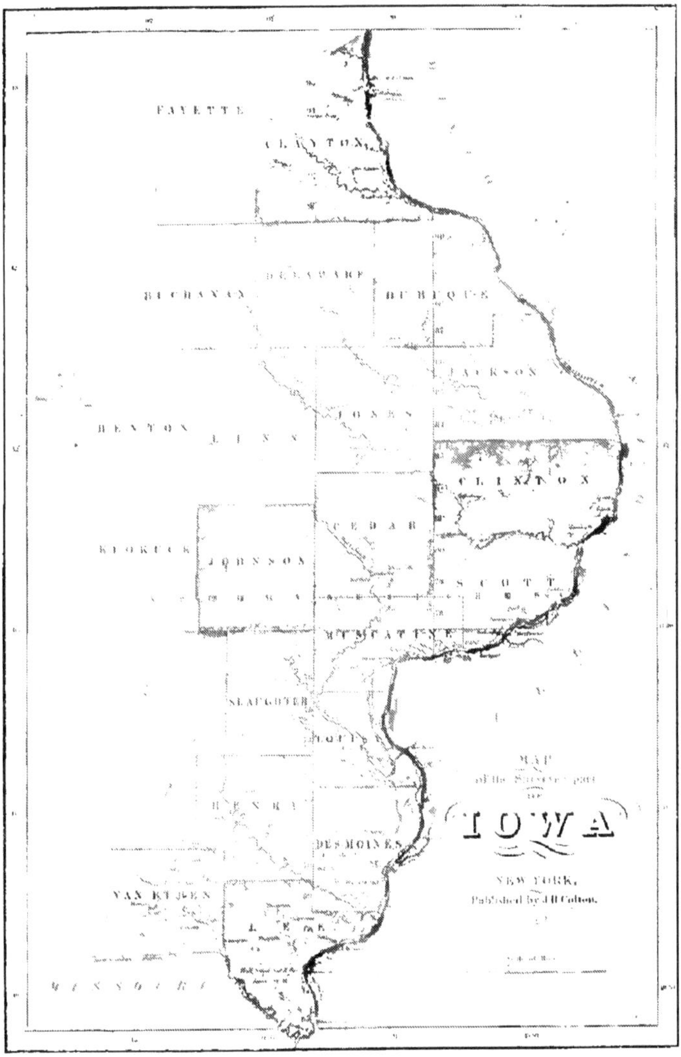


MAP SHOWING FIRST COUNTIES ALONG MISSISSIPPI

in early history, crossed the river to explore the abandoned mines.[4] He was so well pleased with the prospects that in the following year he returned, accompanied by his brother, Lucius H. Langworthy, and by many others.

They entered the country in an orderly way. One of the first things they did was to draw up "articles of agreement," prescribing for themselves a form of government. Sitting on a cottonwood log in the environs of the present city of Dubuque, they constituted what has been called the first legislative assembly held on the soil of Iowa. The scene is at least not without some historic picturesqueness. In their articles they placed limitations on their own greed. It was provided that no man should hold more than two hundred feet square of the mineral lands, equivalent to about one acre, and that to hold even that much he must work on it at least one day out of six. All differences and disputes were to be settled by arbitration, and those who asked for "letters of arbitration" were bound to abide by the decision of the arbitrator. The first executive officer of this miniature and voluntary government was Dr. Francis Jarret, or Jarote, according to some records. But they were not long permitted to remain on their seized possessions. When Colonel Zachary Taylor at Fort Crawford heard that they had crossed the river he sent a squad of soldiers under Lieutenant Jefferson Davis to drive them out.[5] The lieutenant seems to have acted with tact, assuring them that when the lands were opened for settlement their claims would receive due consideration. After the treaty for the Black Hawk Purchase had been signed in 1832 another attempt was made to occupy the mines, but it was again frustrated. The government wanted to keep faith with the Indians so that the Indians could have faith in it.

But at last, on the first of June, 1833, all restraints were removed. The Indians had withdrawn to the reservation on the Iowa River and the soldiers who had patrolled the west

[4] See "The Langworthys of Early Dubuque and Their Contributions to Local History," in *The Iowa Journal of History and Politics*, Vol. VIII, No. 3.

[5] See *Jefferson Davis; a Memoir, by His Wife.* Mrs. Davis was the daughter of Zachary Taylor.

bank of the Mississippi had departed. In the earliest dawn of that historic day the invasion of the Black Hawk Purchase by white men began. It was literally an invasion, for under a law of congress passed in 1807, settlers were forbidden on the public domain until the lands had been surveyed and were offered for sale. But the provisions of that law had at no time or anywhere been enforced, and the migrating settlers of those days regarded the public lands as the property of those who could use them, or seize and hold them. Being trespassers, they formed for their protection a system of land government that reached institutional significance. Each man "blazed" or "staked out" his own piece of land; if trees were convenient he marked his boundaries on them, and if not he used stakes driven into the ground. Those who came after him respected the enclosed ground as his "claim." At first this was done by mutual consent and consideration, but eventually organizations known as Claim Associations were perfected until they had the form and authority of a constituted government. Township and even county maps were made on which all recognized claims were marked. Records of transfers were kept, for claims were bought and sold and money was borrowed on them. These associations had administrative officers who could summon any force necessary to defend the rights of the members. As civic organizations they had a marked influence in the development of the settlers in local self-government and they also affected their attitude toward the national government. The preëmption and homestead laws were in many respects outgrowths of them.

The number of settlers who came to the Black Hawk Purchase in 1833 cannot have been very large, for three years later when the first census was taken, the total population had barely passed ten thousand. Nearly all of them were native-born Americans and most of them were western Americans, men from Illinois, Indiana, and Ohio, and from the more southern states, Missouri, Kentucky, and Tennessee. There were among them also many who came from the New England states, New York and Pennsylvania, and from Virginia and the Carolinas. Their three principal crossings of the Mississippi were at Burlington and Dubuque and in the vicinity of Rock Island, where the ferries were located. Settlements were made at many points, but the two principal centers were Burlington and Dubuque. Burlington was then known as the Flint Hills, but the name of Dubuque was from the first associated with the lead mines, where a small city came into being almost as if by magic. It was the only recognized industrial center in the new country and it received a motley population.

The early settlers shunned the open prairies; they clung to the rivers and streams. They built their cabins in the timber and cultivated the clearings. One reason for this was that most of them were timber people. They had lived in the wooded lands, not on the prairies. In their new country they followed the instincts and traditions of their ancestors. Another reason was that the timber afforded fuel and building materials; in summer time, shelter against the hot suns and in winter against the cold blasts and blizzards. So strong was the idea among them that the open prairies were impossible as human habitations that for many decades they remained almost untenanted.

There was little planting in 1833. The season was too far advanced when the first settlers arrived on the scene. Many had brought provisions with them and what they lacked they could procure from boats on the river. Nor did they need much. They lived in a country where fish abounded in the rivers and where the land was filled with game, from quail to deer and bear. The procuring of necessary food involved but little work.

But as the days began to grow shorter and the cold winds to sweep across the prairies, many returned to the Illinois side of the river to await the coming of the spring. This was especially true of the women and children. In the settlement at Dubuque not a woman was left when winter came. Those who went away fared better than those who remained. The first winter was one of great severity and the snow fell so deep that even the wild game disappeared. The winter was long, and before new supplies of food could be obtained almost famine conditions prevailed. The situation was probably the worst in Dubuque, where sufferings were great and the deaths many. In that community five hundred men were inadequately housed, cooped up in crowded cabins. Partial starvation confronted them before new supplies could be brought up. The one thing they had enough of was whiskey, and of that they had too much. "The demon of intemperance," wrote one who survived the hardships of that season, "stalked everywhere during those long winter evenings and short bleak days." Poor food and too little of it, and bad whiskey and too much of it, left them a prey to many diseases, the last and worst of which was an outbreak of what was called in those days in the west Asiatic cholera. "The sick lay down to die," says our chronicler, "with no gentle hand to nurse them, no medical aid to relieve them, and no kindred or friends to mourn their untimely fate." Dubuque became a village of stranded and hopeless men. They died miserably where they had hoped to begin life over, if not to acquire riches out of the fabulous mines which had lured men since the days of Nicolas Perrot.

But spring came again—and was it ever more welcomed in Iowa? And with the grass men's hopes revived. Men who had vowed that they would return to "civilization" so soon as the routes back were open and they were able to travel in them, remained to try their luck anew. The grass as it crept in green over the hills and the birds as they came back from the south-land made all men glad again. But better than birds or flowers was the return of the women. And with them came a horde of new settlers. Soon the sound of the woodman's axe was heard in the forests up and down the rivers, and the crack of the whip in the hands of the pioneer ploughmen who broke up the age-old prairie sod to make way for the crops of man. Log cabins were "raised" and wheat and corn were planted. The men and women had come to remain in the land, and to help lay the foundations of a new commonwealth.

# CHAPTER XXIII

## A Government Without Laws

The first settlers were squatters. Regarding them as trespassers, congress made no provision for their government. In 1821, when Missouri was admitted as a state, the residue of the territory of that name was literally cast off. No government was deemed necessary for a region in which no white men lived and much of which was then regarded as a desert.

But if the people were without law, they were not lawless. What congress denied them they provided for themselves. Under the Claim Associations they developed a good system of land tenure. Each man protected his own rights by helping to protect the rights of all others. They enforced law and order in the same way. The wrong-doers of that time were apt to be either horse thieves or the passers of counterfeit money. As they had no jails those who were not wanted in the settlements were escorted to the Mississippi River and sent "back to where they came from." Men who harbored, aided, or abetted in any way such suspicious "characters" were in danger of the same treatment.

When more serious crimes were committed, the people provided their own courts. On the nineteenth of May, 1834, Patrick O'Connor murdered his mining partner, George O'Keaf, near the village of Dubuque. O'Connor was a man of bad character and he committed his crime without provocation. When he was questioned about it, he said it was his own business. But the people made it their business also, and on the following day he was tried before a jury selected by common consent, with Woodbury Massey as foreman. Two men of repute acted as counsel. Few witnesses were heard. The accused admitted his guilt, but insisted he could not be tried for there was no law in the land, and no government. He forgot that the people can make laws for their own protection. He was found guilty and by the jury sentenced to be hanged.

The carrying out of the sentence was delayed to give O'Connor time to appeal, first to the governor of Missouri and then to the president of the United States. Both disclaimed jurisdiction in the Black Hawk Purchase, President Jackson on the ground that the laws of congress had not been extended over the territory. He suggested that the proper pardoning power was the one that had sentenced him. But that power was relentless. A rumor was circulated that men were coming from Galena, where O'Connor had lived, but in bad repute, to rescue him. The people of Dubuque prepared to meet them with a company of one hundred and sixty-three men, armed. It was under the escort of this company that the sentence was carried out on the twentieth of June, in the presence of probably a thousand persons, boats bringing crowds of spectators from Galena and Prairie du Chien. The condemned man rode in a cart, sitting on his own coffin, Father Fitzmaurice by his side. They halted in sight of a gallows and of a grave. He was blindfolded, the noose was placed around his neck, and upon the signal the cart was moved and the man dropped to his death. The effect of this drastic punishment was said to have been wholesome throughout that region.[1]

A few other crimes were committed in the mining regions where a turbulent population had been brought together under chaotic conditions. In a quarrel over the possession of a claim, two men named Smith, father and son, known as "bad characters," shot Woodbury Massey, who was a good man defending a just cause. The perpetrators of this crime were brought before Judge Irvin at Mineral Point, but were discharged for want of jurisdiction. They had the good grace to leave that part of the country, but later when Massey's younger brother met the elder Smith in Galena he took revenge and killed him. The justness of his act was so apparent to the men of that day that they did not even arrest Massey. In due time the younger Smith returned to Dubuque, determined to have revenge for his father's death.

[1] See article on "The Execution of O'Connor," in the *Annals of Iowa*, October, 1865, by Eliphalet Price, an eye-witness of the event.

The news of his coming and his intentions reached Louisa Massey, who is described as "the fair-haired, blue-eyed sister . . . just verging into womanhood." Perplexed over the sorrows of her ill-fated family, she determined to give her own life, if necessary to save her brother. Smith was pointed out to her. He was well armed and surrounded by a concourse of men. Undaunted, the girl stepped up to him and in a tremulous voice exclaimed, "If you are Smith, defend yourself." In the same instant she shot him down. She made her escape and he recovered from his wound. The woman was secreted from arrest and sent into Illinois among relatives where later she was married and lived happily. When the gallant law-makers of Iowa Territory were creating their county system they bestowed on one of them the name of Louisa, in honor of this girl, and by reason of that fact a sentimental interest will always be attached at least to one of the older counties. No county was more nobly named.[2]

But not many crimes were committed. Outside the mining regions there were but few bad men among the squatters, and public sentiment was wholesome. Life was reduced to its simplest if not its sweetest forms. The conditions must have been somewhat Arcadian. A witness of good repute testified afterwards: "Nowhere has ever such a state of society existed for honesty, integrity, and high-tone generosity . . . No need here for locks to keep out burglars. We had none. No fear of being injured by others. It was never done."[3] In those days the doors of all cabins stood open to wayfarers and there was food on all the tables for those who were hungry. But such conditions were not universal. A traveler in 1835 spoke of Keokuk as "the lowest and most blackguard place," infested with coarse and ferocious watermen. In "Dubuques" he found "a parcel of blackguard noisy miners," who slept three in a bed, when drunk.[4]

[2] George W. Jones in his *Autobiography* mentions this incident as "a powerful argument in favor of the bill to create the Territory of Iowa."

[3] See footnote 4, p. 129.

[4] Murray's *Travels in North America*, Vol. II, pp. 98, 151.

# CHAPTER XXIV

## UNDER MANY GOVERNMENTS

Congress was at last moved to provide a government for the people who had dared to cross the Mississippi. In June, 1834, the whole region lying between the Mississippi and the Missouri rivers and extending from the state of Missouri on the south to the British possessions on the north was annexed to Michigan Territory. Stevens T. Mason, who was governor, was well disposed towards the settlers of the west. In calling an extraordinary session of the territorial council to provide for their wants he referred to them as "an intelligent, industrious, and enterprising people," which was the first official praise bestowed on them. When the council met in September, the Black Hawk Purchase was divided into two counties, the division line running due west from the lower end of Rock Island. The northern county was called Dubuque and the southern Demoine. Each county was made a township, the former called Julien and the latter Flint Hills. For judicial purposes the two counties were attached to what was Iowa County, Michigan Territory. In court parlance the three counties thus united were called the Iowa District, of which David Irvin was made judge. It was in this manner that the name Iowa was first applied to any part of the present state of that name. The Michigan county was so named in 1829 at the suggestion of Henry R. Schoolcraft, the noted explorer and Indian writer, who was then a member of the legislature of that territory. He must have chosen the name for its own sake, for it had no special significance as applied to that region.

The first civil officers in the Black Hawk Purchase were appointed by Governor Mason. They were John King chief justice of Dubuque County, and Lucius H. Langworthy sheriff. After the people of Demoine County had designated them in an election, the governor appointed William Morgan chief justice, Solomon Perkins sheriff, and William R. Ross clerk of that county. As an assurance of peace on the frontier, the war department stationed three companies of the First United States Dragoons on the Iowa bank of the Mississippi River, a short distance above the mouth of the Des Moines. This was called Camp Des Moines. For the discipline of the troops and the moral effect upon the Indians, the Dragoons in the spring of 1835 were sent on a long expedition through the Indian country west and north of the Black Hawk Purchase. Under the command of Lieut.-Colonel Stephen W. Kearny they left Camp Des Moines on the seventh of June. The three companies were under Captain Nathan Boone, a son of Daniel Boone, and Lieutenants Albert M. Lea and H. S. Tanner. Officers and men they numbered about one hundred and seventy. Provisions were conveyed in five commissary wagons each drawn by two spans of mules. Beef was provided for the journey on the hoof in the form of a herd of cattle. But there was such an abundance of wild game in the country that they had little need of the domestic animals.

The Dragoons followed the divide between the Des Moines and Skunk rivers. They proceeded northwestward until they reached the mouth of a river to which they gave the name of Boone. Then they turned and went east by north until they reached the Mississippi River, north of the present boundary of Iowa. After they had received fresh provisions, which had been sent up in a boat, they turned westward again and proceeded through what is now southern Minnesota. A hat-shaped lake to which they gave the name of Chapeau was afterwards called Lake Albert Lea. When they reached the headwaters of the Des Moines they had an encounter with the Sioux. They then followed the course of that river, crossing and recrossing it many times, until they came to the fork of the Raccoon. From that point Lieutenant Lea was ordered to go down the Des Moines to its mouth, to ascertain its flowage and resources. Accompanied by one private and an Indian guide, he descended the river in a hollowed cottonwood log. The Dragoons completed their march of eleven hundred miles without the loss of life and with their animals in better condition than when they started, which they attributed to the nutritiousness of the native grasses. Shortly after his return to Camp Des Moines, Lieutenant Lea resigned from the army and in the following year he published in Philadelphia a notable little book on the Iowa District.

The first general elections were held in October, 1835, when George W. Jones as delegate in congress and four members of the Michigan territorial council, Allen Hill and John Parker from Dubuque County and John B. Teas and Jeremiah Smith from Demoine, were elected. The council of which they were members met at Green Bay in January, 1836, but before any important business could be transacted the territory was dismembered by the admission of Michigan as a state. For the second time the settlers were left without a government. When congress was memorialized to set up another territorial organization for them there was objection to it on the part of many southern members who looked with alarm on the growth of free states in the northwest. In this juncture John M. Clayton, a senator from Delaware, earned the right to have a county in the future state of Iowa named after him by championing the settlers.[3] He protested against "citizens of the United States living in its territory . . . unprotected by its courts of civil and criminal jurisprudence." On April thirteenth, 1836, congress yielded to the protests and appeals and created Wisconsin Territory, which included Iowa.

Henry Dodge, who was appointed governor of the new territory, was a man of many titles and many deeds. He was, in fact, one of the most remarkable men of that period. He was a product of the frontier, having been born in Post

[3] George W. Jones in his *Autobiography* says he used his best efforts with Iowa legislators to have a county named after him and also one after his state, Delaware. "For similar reasons," he says, "I had counties named for my devoted friends, Dr. Linn (senator from Missouri), General Jackson, James Buchanan, Thomas H. Benton, General Lewis Cass, Martin Van Buren, Robert E. Lee, and others." Others believe Lee County was named after Albert M. Lea, through misspelling of his name.

Vincennes, Indiana Territory, in 1782. His war record was distinguished. He served in the War of 1812, was brigadier-general of the militia of Missouri, and the commander of a volunteer force in the Black Hawk War. When the government organized a mobile force known as the mounted rangers, he was placed in command of them and in that capacity he helped to keep the peace in the Indian country as far west as the Rocky Mountains. The red men both feared and respected him, and among white men he was proclaimed the "captain of an aggressive civilization." He was the Colonel Roosevelt of that era and his rangers were its Rough Riders. He had also abilities as a diplomat and a statesman. He helped to write good Indian treaties and to make the constitution of Missouri.[4]

One of his first official acts was to cause a census to be taken of the territory. This was done in 1836, when the four counties east of the Mississippi River returned a population of 11,687, and the two counties west, 10,531, of which 6,257 were in the county of Demoine and 4,274 in Dubuque. The apportionment for the election, which was held in September of that year, was based on this population, for Demoine County ten members in the two houses of the territorial legislature and for Dubuque County eight, making eighteen members in all against nineteen elected from the east side of the river. In that election George W. Jones was returned to congress. The council elected met at Belmont in what is now Wisconsin, October fifth, 1836, when Peter Engle of Dubuque County was elected president of the lower house.

At this session Demoine County was sub-divided into counties as they now exist, except that the southern part of what is Scott County was then called Cook. A separate judicial district was created for the west side of the river, of which David Irvin was made judge. But the principal business of

[4] George W. Jones in his *Autobiography* says that Governor Dodge could have been elected president of the United States in 1844 instead of J. K. Polk, if he had consented to allow his name to be used. He was deaf to all importunities. Speaking of others in that campaign, he said, "They want the office and are qualified to fill it. I do not want the place and am not qualified for it."

the session was the location of a capital. It was assumed that at least two states would be created out of the territory. and that the Mississippi River would be the dividing line between them. It was therefore determined to find a location which would remain suitable for the future state of Wisconsin. Belmont and Madison contested for the honor. Belmont had hardly buildings enough to house the council of thirty-nine members and Madison was still a wild paradise embowered in its four lakes. The Dubuque members supported Belmont and the Demoine members voted for Madison, which won the victory, while Burlington was made the temporary capital. The defeated ones charged political trading and even corrupt practices on the part of the victors, but they were comforted with a few crumbs. Dubuque was given one of the three banks chartered, which became the Miners Bank, and the Dubuque & Belmont Railroad was created on paper. It was provided that this first railroad might be double tracked, if the traffic should warrant it, and that on it could be used either horse or steam power. Passenger rates were limited to six cents per mile and freight rates to fifteen cents per ton per mile.

In the meantime the Sacs and Foxes on Keokuk's Reserve, the ten mile strip for forty miles up and down the Iowa River, had been made so uncomfortable by being completely surrounded by white men that they were willing to sell their lands and take up others farther west. So Governor Dodge concluded a treaty with them on the twenty-seventh of September, 1836. The Indians, who had previously sold their tepees to squatters as "improvements," received from the government what was equivalent to about seventy-five cents an acre, $50,000 for payment of their debts to the traders, $30,000 in cash, and $100,000 in ten annuities. In the making of this treaty, Keokuk was the chief spokesman for the tribes. He came to the conference with all the prestige of his office as chief. When his time came to speak—for where Keokuk was there was always oratory—he advanced, shook hands with Governor Dodge, fell back a few paces and then his voice "rang clear as a trumpet." Black Hawk also was there, but only as a looker-on. "The poor dethroned monarch," Catlin wrote of him on that occasion, "looked like an object of pity." He wore "an old frock coat and a brown hat," and he carried "a cane in his hand." With him were his two sons and also Nahpope and the Prophet of the evil days. They all stood "in dismal silence." They were not consulted, and they were not allowed to sign the treaty.

But there was another man in that historic group who needs to be pointed out, for he is destined to play an important part in the history of Iowa. His name is James W. Grimes.[5] He is young, hardly of legal age. He is there to act as secretary to the governor. He is an ardent Whig, a Yankee from New Hampshire, and just why the Democratic governor had selected him for that office is not explained. It was probably in recognition of his well marked abilities. He had come to Burlington in the spring of the same year, bringing with him nothing except the traditions of a New England home, a college education, and almost enough knowledge of the law to be admitted to its practice.

In the following year, 1837, the chiefs of the various Indian tribes interested were summoned to Washington where they negotiated another treaty with the government by the terms of which they ceded a million and a quarter more acres, lying in a triangular strip west of the original purchase. This was called the Second Black Hawk Purchase. The bulk of the lands was in what are now Linn and Johnson counties. Settlers immediately entered the new country and squatters appeared on the sites of Iowa City and Cedar Rapids in 1838. The Sacs and Foxes went to the Des Moines River country and a few bands ascended the Iowa and the Cedar.

On the sixth of November, 1837, the first legislative body met in what is now Iowa, being the second session of the first territorial council of Wisconsin. A temporary building had been erected for the purposes of this meeting, but after it was destroyed by fire the council met in a Methodist church to which the name of Old Zion was given. At this session Dubuque County was sub-divided into the smaller counties as

[5] Salter's *Life of James W. Grimes*, p. 11.

they now exist. But not a great deal of business was transacted. Everyone recognized that the government as it existed was a temporary one. Many members of the council participated in a delegate convention which was held in October. This convention, with the concurrence of the members from the east side of the river, prepared three memorials to congress, for preëmption rights for the settlers, for the settlement of the Missouri boundary dispute, and for a separate territory west of the river.[6]

In the memorial on preëmptions, congress was reminded that "Twenty-five thousand people have settled on lands in Wisconsin Territory west of the Mississippi River, in what is called the 'Iowa District,' improved farms, erected buildings, built towns, laid out cities and made valuable improvements, but have not yet been able to secure any kind of title to their homes and farms." In the memorial for a separate territorial government, congress was told that "Perhaps no territory of the United States has been so much neglected by the parent government, so illy protected in the political and individual rights of her citizens."

The creation of a new territory was opposed under the leadership of John C. Calhoun of South Carolina, who considered every public question from the standpoint of the slaveholders. Speaking against preëmption rights, he said that if he had been rightly informed "the Iowa country had already been seized upon by a lawless body of armed men, who had parcelled out the whole region, and had entered into written stipulations to stand by and protect each other" in their seized possessions. That was an interpretation of the Claim Associations. Henry Clay of Kentucky confirmed those views and Thomas Ewing of Ohio offered the consolation that the eastern states were well rid of the men who had crossed the Mississippi — in his opinion it was worth a thousand dollars each to be rid of them in that way. So poorly did grave and reverend senators understand the men of the west!

[6] The matter of a name was also discussed, some favoring Washington, and others Jefferson. "And after considerable debating, skill, log-rolling, &c., Iowa was decided upon." See Wm. L. Toole's article in *Annals of Iowa*, 1868, p. 45.

It was in vain that Delegate Jones assured Senator Calhoun that slavery as an institution had nothing to fear from the men of the Iowa District, for the majority of them had come from southern states or were southern-minded men. To this Mr. Calhoun replied: "Wait until western Ohio, New York and New England shall pour their populations into that section, and you will see Iowa grow some day to be the strongest abolition state in the Union."[7]

So inplacable was Senator Calhoun in his opposition to the Iowa proposals that Mr. Jones did not dare to bring them up while he was in the senate. He therefore had recourse to strategy. He was on intimate terms with the Calhoun family and a great admirer of the senator's daughter, Anna Calhoun, who was more kindly disposed toward the west than her father. Mr. Jones tells the story in his own memoir: At his request, Miss Calhoun one day asked her father to meet her in the Congressional Library. As soon as Mr. Jones saw the senator had left the chamber, he had Senator Clayton call up the Iowa bill, which had already been passed by the lower house, and it was passed without debate. When the South Carolina senator returned from his visit, the deed had been done, and whatever chagrin he may have felt over it was lost in admiration for the clever trick that had been played to overcome his prejudices, or the prejudices of his slavery constituents. "Oh, Anna, you bad girl," the father is represented as having said, "you have prevented my making a speech to oppose that bill, as I would have done and done successfully, as the time for the consideration of territorial bills has passed."[8] A few years later an Iowa county was named Calhoun — let it be believed that it was named in honor of Anna Calhoun, who did something for Iowa worth remembering, and not for her father, with whose views this state had so little in common.

On the twelfth of June, 1838, President Martin Van Buren signed the bill by which Iowa Territory came into existence on the fourth of July of that year.

[7] Jones's "Autobiography," reprinted in Parish's *George Wallace Jones*, pp. 128-130.

[8] *Ibid.*, pp. 127-128.

# CHAPTER XXV

## The First Territorial Government

Iowa Territory extended from the Mississippi to the Missouri, and from the state of Missouri on the south to the British possessions on the north. But the settled portion was still confined to a narrow strip along the Mississippi. Of this vast domain President Van Buren made Robert Lucas of Ohio governor and William B. Conway of Pennsylvania secretary. As judges of the supreme court the president appointed Charles Mason chief justice and Joseph Williams and Thomas S. Wilson associate justices.

Robert Lucas came into his office well qualified for its duties. He had been for many years in the public service. He had helped to make many laws in Ohio and for four years he had been governor of that state. He was also a soldier, having served in the War of 1812. Born in Virginia in 1781, he emigrated to Ohio early enough to participate in its pioneer life. He was a frontiersman, and the trans-Mississippi country to which he was sent presented to him no new or untried problems. But unfortunately he was so old and so experienced that he assumed toward the people of Iowa, most of whom were young men, a paternal and dictatorial attitude which they soon resented. He pitted his experiences against their aspirations. Politically he was a Democrat of the Andrew Jackson type. Religiously he was a Methodist. He was a sturdy man, but also an opinionated one. He was stern, sedate, and serious. His friends said he was also modest and unassuming. He was a strict moralist. He abhorred the two prevalent vices of the west, drinking and gambling, and announced that he would appoint to office no man addicted to these habits.

Of Secretary Conway not so much can be said in praise.

Robert Lucas

Theodore S. Parvin

Albert M. Lea

George Davenport

The new secretary was a politician who believed with Andrew Jackson in the spoils of office. He was not always scrupulous. He was vain, pompous, and verbose. He employed intrigue and he made mischief. There was no bond of sympathy possible between the governor and the secretary and their differences marred the politics of the first years of the territory.

Governor Lucas did not reach Burlington until the middle of August. He was accompanied by two young men, Jesse Williams, who served as clerk of Indian affairs, and Theodore S. Parvin, who had an undefined status as private secretary to the governor, an office for which no provision had been made in the territorial act. Mr. Parvin was destined to render so many services in so many ways to the territory and the future state that note must be taken of him. He was born in New Jersey in 1817. He studied law in Cincinnati, where he met Governor Lucas on his way to Iowa. The two men were drawn together in mutual admiration. They were unlike and yet they had much in common. For Iowa the coming of this enthusiastic young man was a good fortune, for he did here many things that no other man could have done. He became a man of many callings — lawyer, judge, teacher, professor, collector, historian, librarian, and the founder of libraries.

But while the coming of the governor was delayed, that of the secretary was not. As soon as Mr. Conway arrived on the scene he proceeded to act. He assumed virtually the office of governor, for which he found some warrant in the territorial act, which provided that the secretary should act as governor during the absence of that official. As governor *pro tempore* he divided the territory into judicial districts and he assigned the judges to their places; he went to Davenport and entered into negotiations to make that town the capital, and he was on the point of issuing a proclamation for legislative elections when the actual governor arrived on the scene. By so much as he had exalted himself, Governor Lucas proceeded to debase Secretary Conway. After that there was no peace nor harmony between them.

Governor Lucas, accompanied by Mr. Parvin, at once made a journey up the Mississippi to acquaint himself with the territory and its people, and to locate the temporary capital, as was required of him. Dubuque was then the largest city on the river. It was a place of much commercial importance. While they tarried there they met a young man who unfolded to them his plans for a trans-continental railroad, from the Great Lakes to the Pacific Ocean. This young man was John Plumbe, Jr. His townsmen said he was crazy, at least on that subject.[1] He was simply thinking twenty years ahead of his time. Bellevue in Jackson County was already well established. There was a settlement at Lyons, but Clinton was still unknown. Davenport was a new town, the creation of Antoine Le Claire and the trader after whom it was named. Rockingham opposite the mouth of Rock River and Buffalo a few miles lower, still regarded themselves as rivals of Davenport. Muscatine was then called Bloomington. Below Burlington, Fort Madison and Keokuk were prosperous places. In 1834, at a meeting held in the saloon of one John Gaines, Puckeshetuk had cast off one Indian name to assume another, the name of the orator of the Sacs. Having in a casual way considered the claims of all the towns, Governor Lucas made Burlington the temporary capital of the territory.

The first election in Iowa Territory was held on the tenth of September, 1838, when W. W. Chapman as delegate in congress and thirty-nine members of the First Territorial Assembly were elected, of whom thirteen were members of the upper house and twenty-six of the lower. Of the thirty-nine men, twenty-one were natives of southern states, showing a preponderance of influential men from the South. Only four of them were lawyers, but one of them was the young Mr. Grimes whose coming had already attracted more than local attention.

When the legislature met, serious differences with the governor soon arose. The executive assumed *quasi* legislative powers. He had the power of absolute veto and he used it unsparingly, often accompanying his veto messages with remarks that gave great offense to the law-makers. Secretary

[1] Morcombe's *Life and Labors of Theodore Sutton Parvin*, p. 65.

Conway also treated the legislature with some contempt. Under the act of congress he was the disbursing officer for the national government, and when they asked for penknives and tin cups, he sent them slighting if not sneering messages instead. The men of Iowa resented it, finally passing a resolution to the effect that they would "not tamely submit to the insults and derisions of any officers of the territory." The secretary took the hint and made his peace with the law-makers and then in many ways he added to the differences between them and the governor. It is a long story, but the secretary finally informed the president that Governor Lucas was "vexatious, ill-mannered and dogmatical," while the legislature resolved that Robert Lucas was "unfit to be the ruler of a free people," and on the last day of the session the president was memorialized to remove him from office. Governor Lucas was not removed. He made explanations that were satisfactory to the president, but the organic act was so changed that the legislature could pass acts over the governor's veto, and certain offices that had been appointive were changed to elective ones. Before these troubles were over, Secretary Conway died, leaving the affairs of his office in bad shape. He was succeeded by James Clarke, editor of the Burlington *Gazette*, who made a more capable and less fractious officer.

In spite of all these quarrels the First Territorial Assembly enacted a body of laws that stood the test of time. His admirers subsequently gave much of the credit for this to James W. Grimes, and less to S. C. Hastings, who were the chairmen of the judiciary committees of the two houses. The southern bias of that initial law-making body was shown in several enactments. Black men were denied the right to vote, and after the first of April, 1839, negroes and mulattoes were denied the right to live in the territory without "a fair certificate" of "actual freedom." Those who held such certificates were placed under bonds of $500, and in default of bonds they were to be "hired out" by the county commissioners "for the best price in cash," constituting a form of slavery.[2]

But the first supreme court redeemed the honor of the terri-

[2] *Laws of Iowa*, 1838-1839, p. 65.

tory by a decision in the case of "Ralph." This Ralph — he had no other name — was a Missouri slave who in 1835 had contracted with his master for his freedom at the price of $500. His master permitted him to go to the Dubuque lead mines to earn the money with which to discharge his debt. In 1839, when the debt was still unpaid, the master sent slave catchers to carry him back into slavery. They captured him at the mines and while conveying him to a boat below the town of Dubuque, to avoid publicity, the sympathies of a farmer named Alexander Butterworth were so aroused in behalf of the black man that he applied for a writ of habeas corpus. The case was deemed one of such importance that it was immediately heard before the supreme court. The opinion was delivered by the chief justice, his associates concurring. It was to the effect that human beings could not be treated as property in Iowa, where free soil made free men. With his former master's consent, Ralph had entered Iowa, or what was then Michigan Territory. He owed that former master a legal debt but for the non-payment of that debt he could not be seized and carried out of the territory, and back into slavery.

# CHAPTER XXVI

## Iowa City and Land Titles

Burlington was only a temporary capital. The governor himself brought up the matter of a more central location for a permanent seat of government. But the towns of prestige were still all on the river. Mount Pleasant was the only interior town worthy to be called such, but it was too far south. A legislative contest resulted in which scores of ballots were taken. Burlington, compelled to give up hope for itself, favored Mt. Pleasant, but Bloomington, now Muscatine, with hopes of its own, made overtures to the northern voters of the territory. The idea of creating a new city was finally borrowed from Illinois history.[1] The credit for this belongs to Thomas Cox of Jackson County. It was enacted that commissioners to be elected should "meet at the town of Napoleon," on the first of May, 1839, "and proceed to locate a seat of government at the most eligible point within the present limits of Johnson County." In a supplementary act, Mr. Cox moved to insert the words "to be called Iowa City."

On the first of May only one of the commissioners, Chauncey Swan, made his appearance at Napoleon, which was a place of only two or three log cabins, one mile and a half south of the present Iowa City. A messenger who rode thirty-five miles and back in twelve hours, saved the situation by bringing John Ronalds of Louisa County, who seems to have forgotten about the matter, to the meeting before the fateful hour of midnight on that day — it may have been later. The third member, John Ralston of Des Moines County, may have been willing to see the plan fail by default. Within the allotted time the two commissioners selected the sightly location on

[1] The town of Vandalia was an open prairie when it was designated as the capital of Illinois in 1818.

the Iowa River — and in that hour Iowa City was born. Six hundred and forty acres of mingled woodland and prairie were at once laid off in town lots, the first of which were offered for sale in August. From the proceeds of these sales, together with a federal appropriation of $20,000, the construction of the old capitol building, which still stands as the central building of the State University group, was undertaken. The corner stone was laid on the fourth of July, 1840, with Governor Lucas as the orator of the day. The stars and stripes were hoisted from a tall oak which had been stripped of its branches. Tradition has attributed the design of the building to a Catholic missionary, an Italian scholar who understood architecture, Samuel Charles Mazzuchelli. There is no record of his services in the matter, and he does not mention them in his own memoirs, but the building itself is perhaps the best evidence of his mental presence; the building is classical, not western.[2]

The city had a rapid growth. A visitor in May, 1840, counted one hundred buildings either completed or in course of construction.[3] One man boasted that the house in which he was then living "five days ago was in the woods growing." But the capitol building was not so easily erected as a log cabin. The stone for it had to be quarried from the hills along the river, and some of it was brought from quarries far away from the site. The timbers were cut from the white oak groves of the surrounding hills. The money soon gave out, and more was hard to get. There were the inevitable delays, defaults, and even defalcations, and the usual investigations followed. With the aid of a loan from the Miners Bank at Dubuque the building was finally completed far enough for occupancy in 1842. In 1841 the meetings of the Fourth Territorial Assembly were held in a temporary building known as Butler's Capitol.

An event of more importance to the squatters was the be-

[2] In his *History of Iowa*, Vol. I, p. 214, Gue says that Father Mazzuchelli furnished the design for the building, while John F. Rague was the first architect. Gue came to Iowa in 1853 and his information may have been based on direct testimony.

[3] John B. Newhall.

ginning of the land sales in 1838, five years after the first settlements had been made. In the intervening years the lands had been held under the Claim Associations. The first surveys, however, had been made as early as 1836. But in 1838 the lands were actually offered for sale. For this purpose two land offices had been established, one at Burlington with Augustus C. Dodge, a son of Henry Dodge, as registrar, and Ver Planck Van Antwerp, a relative of President Van Buren, as receiver, and the other office at Dubuque with B. R. Peterkin and Thomas McKnight in charge. Many days before the sales began the two cities presented the appearance of armed camps. The settlers came in numbers and also in might. The lands would be offered at public sale and it was rumored that many "outsiders" and "speculators" would be present to bid them in, thus stealing the improvements that the squatters had made on them.

In many places the disputes over claims had brought on serious troubles. William L. Toole, who was one of the first settlers near the mouth of the Iowa River, wrote that "great strife was kept up here in those early days, through conflicting interest in claims or the encroachments of unprincipled adventurers. Cabins were burned, torn down, or unroofed, and the lives of persons frequently in jeopardy in consequence of these contentions for claims." He relates that at one time, in 1836, contending parties numbering twenty or thirty on each side, met near his settlement, which became known as Toolesboro, "on a disputed piece of land, armed with guns, pistols, knives, &c., intending to decide the right of possession by a battle, the victors to be the possessors." A good old man, named E. Hooke, composed their differences more peacefully.[4] But when the lands were offered for sale, the Claim Associations through their constituted officers were strong enough to be in control of the situation.

When town lots were disposed of some serious troubles ensued. In 1836, the territorial delegate in congress, Mr. Jones, secured grants to a number of cities, including Peru, Dubuque, Bellevue, Burlington, and Fort Madison in Iowa, of

[4] *Annals of Iowa*, 1868, p. 48.

six hundred and forty acres of land. These lands were thereby made the property of those communities and the proceeds of the sales of lots were to be used for the development of the towns. It was provided that no claimant should be allowed to preëmpt more than "one-half acre in in-lots and not more than two acres of out-lots," and that *bona fide* settlers should have the preference. It was further provided that the preëmptions should be approved by commissioners who were to be appointed by the president of the United States. But in spite of all precautions many conflicts arose. In Dubuque at one time a mob was formed that threatened to tear down the land office of the federal government. The sales had to be suspended and appeals had to be made to Washington. Adjustments were in due time made, but the final settlements left many bad feelings in the communities. Speculators and even "usurpers" were in many instances benefitted, if not favored.[5]

The methods of the Claim Associations were much better. Through their officers they took virtual control of the sales of land, and in this they had the coöperation of the land officials, many of whom were anxious not only to serve the people, but to merit their aid in future aspirations. With an ample force of men back of them, both armed and unarmed, "official bidders," appointed by the Claim Associations, appeared for the settlers. So soon as a piece of land was offered, one of these bid for it the minimum price of the government, $1.25 an acre, in the name of the claimant recorded on his plat, and the bid was accepted immediately. Only a few outside bidders appeared, and some of those were so roughly treated that they were glad to make their escape. The government price had to be paid in cash. After three, four, or even five years of work on the land many settlers still did not have enough in actual money to pay the $200 or the $400 for a quarter or half a section. Those who were compelled to borrow had to pay exorbitant rates of interest.

The validity of the transactions under the Claim Associations was soon tested in the supreme court of the state, result-

[5] Parish's *George Wallace Jones*, p. 154.

ing in a notable opinion which was written by Chief Justice Mason and concurred in by his two associates. The title of the case is Hill *vs.* Smith. In this transaction, Hill had sold a piece of land to Smith for $1,000 and had taken his note in payment. After Smith had secured his title from the government he refused to pay the note which he had given. It was argued that Hill had been a trespasser on the public domain, that he had seized and sold what did not belong to him, and that the whole transaction was contrary to law and the note not collectible.

Justice Mason in his opinion said that the act of congress passed in 1807, forbidding settlers on the public lands until the same had been surveyed and were offered for sale, was against "intruders in those cases where public policy would require; but never to disturb the peaceful and the industrious, whose labor was adding so much to the public wealth, changing the barren wilderness into fertile fields." Referring to the act itself and its attempted enforcement at that time, the court said, it would be "contrary to that spirit of Anglo-Saxon liberty, which we inherit, to revive without notice, an obsolete statute, one in relation to which long usage and a contrary policy had induced a reasonable belief that it was no longer in force." It was held that "if custom can make laws, it can, when long acquiesced in, recognized and countenanced by the sovereign power, also repeal them." The government had at no time and in no place enforced this act and it was therefore "wholly inoperative and void."[6] This decision was vital. It carried with it the validity of all the transactions that had been made under the voluntary associations by which the squatters had protected their property.

[6] Morris's *Iowa Reports*, p. 70.

# CHAPTER XXVII

## The Boundary and Banditti Wars

The dispute between the state of Missouri and the territory of Iowa over their boundary line came to a culmination in 1839. Governor Lucas had participated in a somewhat similar controversy between Ohio and Michigan and his experience as well as his disputatious disposition gave him courage to defend what he believed to be the rights of the territory. It is a somewhat comical episode in Iowa history, and it has been so treated by many of the writers, but none the less it achieved something for Iowa that might have been lost by a less determined executive.

The boundary trouble dated back to events that happened in 1808 when the Osage Indians ceded certain lands to the United States. In 1816 John C. Sullivan made a survey of the lands. His starting point was at the mouth of the Kansas River. He ran a line due north for one hundred miles, and from that point he ran another line eastward to the Des Moines River, a few miles above its mouth. This line was laid down slightly north of due east. It was called the Sullivan or the Indian boundary line. When Missouri was admitted as a state the designated northern boundary was "the parallel of latitude which passes through the rapids of the river Des Moines, making the said line to correspond with the Indian boundary line." The intention of congress clearly was to follow the Sullivan line.

In 1836 Missouri asked for the coöperation of the United States and Wisconsin Territory to redetermine her northern boundary, but as neither complied with the request, she proceeded with that work unassisted. The surveyor who directed the work, J. C. Brown, then began by looking for "the rapids of the River Des Moines" in the Des Moines River, evidently ignorant of the fact that the rapids so-called were in the Mississippi River above the mouth of the Des Moines. There are no rapids in the lower Des Moines River, but about sixty miles above its mouth, near the great bend, Brown found some ripples that he mistook for the rapids designated in the congressional act and ran a line westward to the Missouri River. This line was from ten to thirteen miles north of the Sullivan line. On February 11, 1839, the Missouri legislature accepted it as the northern boundary of the state. In the meantime settlements had been made in the Black Hawk Purchase down to the Sullivan line. When the tax collectors of Clark County in Missouri came into Van Buren County, Iowa Territory, the settlers protested and appealed to Governor Lucas for protection. Among other things they said that they did not want to be made part of a slave state. When the dispute reached Washington, the president appointed Albert M. Lea, an eminent authority, to determine the proper boundary line. Lea reported that in his opinion the Sullivan line was the proper one, and no doubt the one intended, but the language of the congressional act was so vague that it would require another act to interpret its meaning. But congress took no action in the matter.

A series of proclamations by the two contending governors followed. Finally the sheriff of Van Buren County arrested the sheriff of Clark County and brought him to Burlington. He was afterwards taken to Bloomington for safe keeping, but he was not imprisoned, nor did he resist the restraint that was placed upon him. In the meantime also the governor of Missouri called out some militiamen to uphold "unsullied the honor and dignity" of his state. Governor Lucas replied by sending the United States marshal to the scene of combat, assuring him that in the way of "armed men" he could summon to his aid the whole military strength of the territory, to act however only as a *posse comitatus*. Much blustering on both sides of the line ensued. In Iowa the excitement ran high and war preparations were made.

In Iowa at that time there existed a military force composed of three generals of some kind, without colonels, captains, lieutenants, or the necessary privates. On December seventh Governor Lucas called upon his three generals to create an army. The generals, figuratively at least, put on their gaudy uniforms and buckled on their swords and proceeded to act. It was in the midst of a hard winter and at first there were few responses, but the war fever worked itself into a frenzy and enlistments were made throughout the territory as far

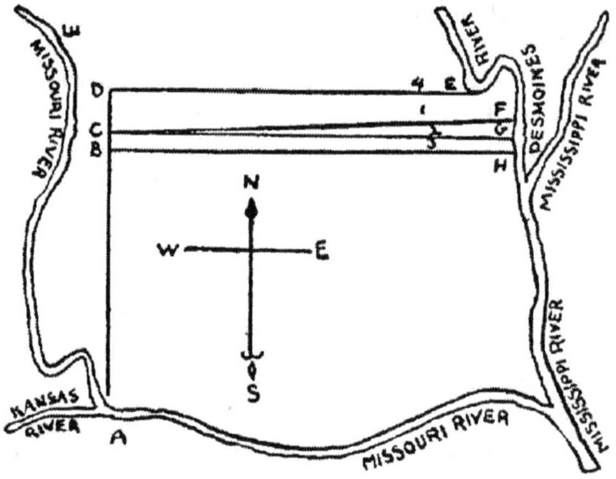


D-E represents line finally claimed by Missouri; B-H line claimed by Iowa; C-F the Indian line survey by Sullivan, and C-G the correct due east and west line, which Sullivan should have followed, and which would have been the correct southern boundary of Iowa.

north as the Turkey River, where a company of hunters, recruited over a barrel of whiskey, got lost on the way to Dubuque. The number of volunteers is variously given from five hundred to a thousand men. That the whole matter was a serious one may be inferred from the fact that men made such sacrifices in the middle of winter and from the further fact that men like Augustus C. Dodge, James W. Grimes, and S. C. Hastings appeared as officers of the expedition. The uniforms and the equipment, furnished by the volunteers, were varied and grotesque. Falstaff himself might have gloried in them. There were muskets left over from the Revolution. The newspaper wags made all manner of paragraphs about them. One man is said to have marched with "a ploughshare carried in a link of a log chain" at his side, and another with a "sheet iron sword about six feet in length, fastened to a rope shoulder strap."[1] In the way of provisions plenty of whiskey is invariably enumerated.

While this military furor was at its height the Second Territorial Assembly was in session at Burlington. Having inherited from the preceding assembly some of the dislike of the governor, a resolution to stop hostilities was passed. Governor Lucas indignantly vetoed this resolution, informing the assembly that the dispute with Missouri was one between that state and the United States government and that the governor and not the Iowa assembly represented the government in Washington. The assembly smiled and passed the resolution over the governor's veto.

About that time a bright, or at least a sane, idea got into the head of the United States marshal, and as a result he sent a delegation to the enemy's camp. In due time Augustus C. Dodge, the head of the delegation, returned with the startling news that they had not been able to find the enemy's camp. The truth was that the governor of Missouri had thought better of making war and had permitted his militiamen to return to their homes. There being no enemy to fight, there was nothing for the Iowa army to do but to return to their homes as best they could. There was no final demobilization, the men just returned. The whole episode was then turned into a jest and a joke. Mock heroic rhymes appeared in many newspapers and mock banquets were given in many places to welcome the warriors home again. Governor Lucas was blamed by many, but if he had not acted determinedly a strip of southern Iowa might have been lost to the state. And it still adds a bit of variety to the peaceful course of Iowa history.

[1] See Willard Barrows's *History of Scott County*, Chapter IV.

After Iowa was admitted as a state, by an act of congress, the dispute was taken to the supreme court of the United States on an agreed case, August fourth, 1846.[2] The decision of the court was that the Sullivan line was the proper boundary, having been recognized in fifteen Indian treaties. Commissioners were appointed to mark that line, and upon their report, in 1850, a final decree was entered.

But if the boundary war was a bloodless one, the "Battle of Bellevue" which followed close on its heels was bloody enough. If the events of the boundary war would have delighted Washington Irving, those of the Bellevue episode would have pleased Fenimore Cooper, although no Indians took part in it.

The whole new west was at that time infested with bad men. They were so many and so well organized that they became known as "The Banditti of the Prairies."[3] Most of them were counterfeiters and horse thieves. In the vicinity of Burlington, as early as 1833, the first year in the Black Hawk Purchase, the settlers had organized themselves for mutual protection against such bands. They had no jails and no government and so they had to fall back on the primitive processes of justice. Bad men, it was agreed among them, should "be delivered with such refugees on the other side of the river." They might have hanged them, but they preferred to send them back "to where they came from" where laws existed for their proper punishment.

To operate in a sparsely settled region the bandits formed organizations of their own, extending through southern Michigan, northwestern Ohio, Indiana, and Illinois, finally reaching out into the Iowa District, as soon as there were people enough to make plundering worth while. They seem to have been most numerous in Jackson County where the broken and wooded country afforded them opportunities of concealment. The first settlers came to Jackson County in 1833. In 1834 the town of Bellview, later spelled Bellevue, was laid out, and

[2] *United States Statutes at Large*, Vol. IX, p. 52.

[3] *The Banditti of the Prairies* is the title of a book written by Edward Bonney of Lee county, who as a detective ferreted out many of their crimes.

Sabula, first called Carrollport and then Charleston, was founded in 1836, while in the same year settlements were made at the forks of the Maquoketa. In 1837 there arrived at Bellevue from Michigan a party of more than twenty men whose leader was one W. W. Brown, who purchased a building in which he began to operate a hotel. Brown is described as the ideal villain of fiction, "a tall dark complexioned man." The men cut wood for Mississippi River steamers and prospered. As a landlord, Brown was one of the most polite men in the west. He also kept a store and a meat market. He was polite in business, generous in credit, and the friend of the poor. But as time passed many "strange characters" passed through his hostelry and additional suspicions were aroused when counterfeit money and stolen horses were traced to them. Even men disappeared mysteriously. There were arrests and even trials, but it was never possible to convict any of the men who had the advice and the protection of Brown, who himself appeared as a lawyer. When a man named Groff was tried for shooting and killing a reputable citizen named James Davis on the streets of Bellevue, he was acquitted on the grounds of insanity. To protect themselves, in 1839, the settlers of Jones, Cedar, and Linn counties organized a Citizens' Association at Linn Grove in Linn County. They did not propose to deal gently with the marauders. But Brown himself had many adherents. He sought to have himself made sheriff and on forged petitions he won a nomination for the legislature and secured a commission as justice of the peace. To steal horses, to pass counterfeit money and dispense justice did not seem incongruous to this many-minded man of evil deeds.

Eventually the suspicions were so many and so direct that social ostracism was visited on Brown and his men. When Jackson's Day, the eighth of January, 1840, was celebrated, as was the custom in many of the settlements, with a ball, no member of the "gang" was invited. Resentful and drunk, while the ball was in progress, James Thompson and a few associates went to the home of James C. Mitchell, a prominent man and leader of the opposition, who had previously branded

Thompson as a thief and counterfeiter, and robbed the house and insulted or assaulted a woman, a Miss Hadley, a relative of Mitchell, who remained at home on account of an illness. In scant attire she made her way to the ballroom and gave the alarm. Mitchell and Thompson soon met on the street and Thompson was killed by Mitchell, for which he was arrested and placed in irons by the sheriff, William A. Warren. A feud was the result, and further clashes were feared. There being no jail, Mitchell was kept under guard in his own home. Crimes multiplied, and to avert a feudal war the sheriff and others went to Dubuque where they obtained warrants for the arrest of Brown and twenty-two others, all of them being charged with thieving, counterfeiting, and committing other depredations to the detriment of the public. The warrants were defied by Brown so far that he placed a red flag in front of his hotel with the inscription of "Victory or Death" on it. The sheriff thereupon authorized Thomas Cox, then a member of the territorial legislative council, and a man of sterling courage and leadership, to collect a posse of at least forty armed men. The men were readily obtained and it was hoped that the community would rid itself of all the bad men. Some parleying ensued, but eventually, on the first of April, 1840, the "Battle of Bellevue" began. A frontal attack on Brown's hotel, where the men were concealed, was determined on. The sheriff and Cox called for forty volunteers and as many promptly stepped forward, although they were warned that some of them would probably be killed. Brown and one of his men met them at the front door with lifted guns. It was believed that he intended to surrender, but the accidental discharge of a gun, the ball passing through Cox's coat, started the war. Brown was one of the first men killed. The "gang" retreated to an upper room and the posse withdrew. Several had already been killed on both sides. Then fire was set to the building and the bandits were forced out upon the roof of a rear building where the shooting was resumed on more equal terms. Some made their escape, but thirteen were captured, after four members of the posse had been killed and three of the bandits, and several more on each side had been wounded, for whom doctors had to be summoned from Dubuque.[4]

Many were for lynching all thirteen of the captured bandits, but the sheriff and Cox pleaded for the processes of law. So on the next day the prisoners were assembled in the presence of the people by whom their fate was to be decided. There was sorrow over the dead and indignation ran high. But it was decided to take a vote of the citizens. For this white and red beans were used, red beans for whipping the scoundrels and white beans for hanging them. Many of the culprits begged for mercy, confessing their crimes freely. "White beans for hanging, red beans for whipping," was the injunction as the men stepped up to cast their votes. When the beans were counted there were found forty-two red ones and thirty-eight white ones, indicating a verdict for whipping, which upon much urging was made unanimous. The thirteen men were then tied to trees and lashed and that without stint, after which they were placed in skiffs without oars, and with frugal provisions sent down the river under their promises never to return to the county. Brown and his men left some adherents in the community, men who had been benefitted by their presence, and apologists in Dubuque wrote indignant letters to Governor Lucas over the breakdown of law and order and the establishment of mob law in Jackson County, but eventually the citizens who had taken the law into their own hands were profusely upheld. The effect and influence of the Bellevue War were salutary throughout that region. Thomas Cox was returned to the legislature and became speaker of the house, and eventually a commemorative monument was erected over his grave near Maquoketa.

[4] The best account of the Bellevue War may be found in Reid's *Life of Thomas Cox.*

# CHAPTER XXVIII

## Territorial Politics

Politically, Iowa Territory was strongly Democratic. The democracy was southern in its antecedents and Jacksonian in its declarations. There existed a weak, but often wavering, Whig minority. When delegates to the first constitutional convention were selected, twenty-one out of seventy-two were Whigs, but the ratio of strength between the two parties was probably not so pronounced as those statistics would indicate. There were southern Whigs as well as northern, and northern Democrats as well as southern, but most of the Iowa Whigs came from northern states and most of the Democrats from southern states. Pro-slavery sentiments were prevalent, if not controlling.

But in the earlier years of the territory political lines were not tautly drawn. In fact such lines were often disregarded entirely. The voters were largely controlled by local interests. There was considerable rivalry between the north end and the south end of the Iowa District. This rivalry appeared in the first legislative session held at Belmont when Burlington and Madison combined to defeat Dubuque and Belmont.

The reign of geographical politics was for a few years almost supreme. The Mississippi was lined with mushroom towns striving for favors. The bitterest of the contests probably were waged in Scott County. When Davenport was surveyed, in 1836, and named in honor of the Indian trader, at the suggestion of his friend, Antoine Le Claire, the interpreter, the town of Rockingham, a few miles below, had already attained considerable growth. Scott County was created in 1837, and in 1838 an election was held to locate the county seat. Rockingham, confident of victory, cast an honest vote, but Davenport contracted with a man named Bellows of Dubuque for the delivery of a certain number of votes, or perhaps an indefinite number, at so much per head, board and whiskey and other entertainment to be furnished. Bellows brought eleven sleigh loads of the most wretched looking rowdies and vagabonds that had ever appeared on the streets of Davenport.[1] They were the dregs of the mining district, "filled with impudence and profanity, soaked in whiskey and done up in rags." They cost Davenport $3,000, but they did not win the victory, for Governor Dodge, when informed of the facts, refused to issue the certificate of election. Another election was held in the following August. It was provided that the sheriff of Dubuque County should count the votes in the presence of commissioners. The election tide ran high. Building lots were offered for votes. The ballot boxes were stuffed and Rockingham that time outdid Davenport. It was afterwards explained that the judges at Rockingham had taken an oath that they should "to the best of their ability see votes enough were polled to elect Rockingham the county seat." Votes enough were cast, but when the polls had been "purged" Davenport was declared the victor by a majority of two. The courts reversed that verdict in favor of Rockingham. The legislature being at the time in session, passed an act for another election, but before it was held Rockingham succumbed, the condition being that Davenport should erect the county buildings at its own expense.

Such bitter geographical contests left little room for the play of party politics. But in 1840, when county questions had been disposed of, a wave of partisan politics swept over the country and Iowa Territory, which had no voice in national affairs, fell under the spell. Politics that year amounted to hysteria. Eight years of Andrew Jackson and four years of Martin Van Buren with the panic of 1837 thrown in, created a widespread feeling for a change. Arguments were not necessary — a coon skin and a miniature log cabin at the head of a procession and cries of "Tippecanoe and Tyler too!" were sufficient to arouse the people.

The Democrats in Iowa seem to have seen the storm coming

[1] Barrows's *History of Scott County*, Chapter III.

for early in January of that year they issued a party call in which it was "deemed highly necessary that immediate steps be taken to effect a permanent organization of the party." In response, perhaps early in April, the Whigs held a meeting at Burlington in which they denounced these partisans steps as attempts "to draw the lines of party distinction . . . mischievous in . . . tendency, and wholly uncalled for." But they seem to have been willing to participate, for in June they held a convention in Wapello in which they deplored that "the administration friends have raised the standard of party, lit its smouldering fires and have thrown down the gauntlet of defiance at our feet by calling conventions to nominate candidates to be supported on partisan grounds." The "smouldering fires" and "the gauntlet of defiance" were somewhat incongruous as figures of speech, but the responses were such that a "congress of the people," composed of Whigs, was held at Bloomington where a party organization was perfected and Alfred Rich was nominated as the party candidate for delegate in congress. The Democrats nominated Augustus C. Dodge for the same office, and an active partisan campaign was carried on, as a result of which Dodge was elected by a majority of six hundred and fifteen votes. But out of the thirteen members of the upper house of the assembly, the Whigs elected seven, the only Whig majority in either house of the territorial assemblies. For the lower house that year the Whigs elected eleven members and the Democrats fifteen.

"Politics began to be a grand staple commodity of the times," says James H. Langworthy, writing of that period. "To be a good unterrified Jackson Democrat, unchangeable as the leopard's skin, was the best trade, and rather the surest road to political preferment."

President William Henry Harrison knew Governor Lucas and did not like him. He lived only one month in office, but that month was long enough for Lucas to be deposed and John Chambers of Kentucky to be appointed governor in his place. The new governor was a personal friend of the president. John Chambers was not a seeker of the office and he was reluctant to accept it when it was tendered him. He was past sixty years of age and he did not covet a governorship in the turbulent trans-Mississippi region. He was an experienced and qualified man for public service, but with a somewhat marked contempt for politicians. He was a lawyer by profession. He was fearless and outspoken, sarcastic and often cynical.

He took the oath of office at Burlington on May thirteenth, 1841. His reception in the territory was less cordial than that which had been extended to Governor Lucas and he was entirely indifferent to that fact. There were political reasons for this attitude, but a stronger reason was that the young men of the territory had grown restless under governorships by old men sent to them from other states. Governor Lucas had worn out their welcome. In a letter written at that time we find these words: "Col. Neally has just given the Gov. the keys of the hog trough—the d--n Yankees are coming daily." There is a great deal of history in that sentence. It is descriptive of the state of mind of many. The Yankees were the northern men whom Calhoun had feared would take possession of the country. The new governor, however, sought to identify himself with the people over whom he was governor. He was a just man and he thought more of the people than he did of the politicians. But this did not help the governor, for the people were an abstract entity while the politicians were a concrete force. Among his detractors were some of the politicians of his own party, while the Democrats in their next convention denounced him as an enemy of the west and of its settlers and their interests. Governor Chambers did not like the new Iowa City and so he provided himself with a country place near Burlington which he called Grouseland, where he spent much of his time in bucolic pursuits and in growing fruits and flowers.

Governor Chambers's administration is chiefly associated with three things: the removal of the territorial capital to Iowa City in 1841-1842, in connection with the meeting of the fourth assembly, the enlargement of the Indian boundaries to the west, and the discussions that preceded statehood. Many had advocated statehood as early as 1838, but the majority of the people were content with a territorial government. Why go to the expense of maintaining a state government out of taxes levied on the people, who were poor in money, when the national government in Washington was ready to pay the expenses of such government as was needed? What more could an elected governor do for the people than one appointed by the president? Would it help any one except the politicians? The pioneers were a parsimonious people and the question of taxes was a nightmare with many of them. The Whigs had political reasons also for being opposed to statehood. They did not care to vote to create offices for Democrats to fill.

Governor Lucas himself was one of the earliest advocates of a state government. In his message to the Second Legislative Assembly he recommended a memorial to congress on that subject and the calling of a constitutional convention. On these recommendations the assembly submitted the matter to the voters in the regular election of 1840 when it was defeated by a decisive vote of 2,907 to 937. In the face of such an adverse vote the question was dropped. But the Whigs changed their attitude materially under Governor Chambers. The politicians among them were tired of alien governors. In 1842 the question was again submitted to the people in the August elections of that year. But it was again voted down. The people still refused to see the necessity of burdening themselves with what to them looked like a costly state establishment. But the question would not rest. An immense impetus was given to it by the Indian treaty of 1842, by which the area of the territory was more than doubled in size while the population grew by leaps and bounds. As a result of this new interest the question was again submitted in April 1844, when it was carried by a majority of 2,745, a somewhat sudden and overwhelming change in the attitude of the voters. In the August elections following, seventy-three delegates to a constitutional convention were elected. Before we proceed with the consideration of a state constitution, we must review the status of the Indians who remained in Iowa, how the Mexican War affected Iowa, and the conditions under which the people lived in territorial days.

# CHAPTER XXIX

## About Many and Various Things

On the Fourth of July, 1834, the first American flag was hoisted over the Black Hawk Purchase. It was in recognition of the action of congress in establishing a territorial government for the people. The flag was raised by Nicholas Carroll in Dubuque, who is said to have paid ten dollars for it. It is also said that the flag was the work of a black woman who had been a slave.[1]

Almost two years later, or in May, 1836, the first newspaper was printed in the Iowa country. It was called the *Dubuque Visitor* and was published by John King, who was a Virginian by birth. In one of the early issues of this paper there was a reference to "the future state of Iowa," and when the paper was sold to William W. Corriell, he changed the name of it to *The Iowa News,* and some of the credit for the naming of the state is claimed for this incident. In 1837, *The Western Adventurer and Herald* was printed on the site of old Camp Des Moines, where, it was announced, "a town will soon be laid out, to be called Montrose." It was a real estate promoter's paper. But as the town did not grow up, the publisher removed his paper to Fort Madison, where it was called *The Patriot.* James G. Edwards soon acquired control of the paper. He was a man of ability and became the most vital editor of early Iowa. Anticipating a division of Wisconsin Territory, he proposed, March twenty-fourth, 1838, that "Iowans take the cognomen of Hawkeyes . . . and we shall rescue from oblivion a memento, at least, of an old Chief." On July fourth Black Hawk made his last speech, in Fort Madison. In the autumn of the year Edwards removed his paper to Burlington, and in the issue of September

[1] Eliphalet Price in *Annals of Iowa,* 1865, p. 538.

fifth added the name *Hawk-Eye* to it. There is a tradition that the idea was suggested by David Rorer, a lawyer of Burlington, but this is not supported. It is possible that it arose from the fact that Rorer may have suggested to Edwards to use the cognomen for his paper.[2] In the same city James Clarke, who became governor, had already started *The Gazette*. Edwards and Clarke were the two outstanding editors of their time. They were Whig and Democrat. Many newspaper altercations arose between them. *The Gazette* thrived on official patronage and *The Hawk-Eye* played the rôle of a free lance, which resulted in at least one personal encounter between Edwards and Augustus Caesar Dodge.

The first paper printed in Davenport was *The Sun*, in 1838, but it soon ceased to shine. As soon as Iowa City came into being two papers appeared there, the *Iowa Capitol Reporter* and the *Iowa Standard*, the former a Democratic organ and the latter, Whig. For a time the ubiquitous Ver Planck Van Antwerp, graduate of West Point and relative of President Van Buren, appeared as editor of the *Reporter*. His pomposity and self-sufficiency made him the target of the wit, and the malice even, of a young man named William Crum, who expounded the Whig doctrine in the *Standard*. The verbal flings and attacks that these two editors indulged in at each other's expense and dignity are now almost beyond comprehension. But that was journalism in those days — nor has it become wholly extinct. To Mr. Crum the stately "general," as Van Antwerp was called by courtesy, was "the thing which says it edits that filthy and demagogical sluice of Loco-focoism, the *Reporter*," while to the man in "red hair and spectacles," silk gloves and silk hat, the other editor was "Silly Billy . . . the last crum of creation."

But these old papers are to the present the mirrors that reflect the true life of the past. In those faded sheets of long ago lies the information that even historians now covet. After 1840 papers sprang up in all parts of the territory. In an enumeration made a few years later, of twenty papers in existence, nine were Democratic, eight espoused the doctrines of

[2] Fort Madison *Patriot*, March 24, 1838.

the Whigs, one was content with liberty as a political creed, while religion and agriculture had the benefit of one paper each.

On the twentieth of June, 1840, the first steamboat ascended the Iowa River to Iowa City, ushering in what was believed to be a new era. "This arrival," said the *Standard* newspaper, "has effectually changed the relation in which we formerly stood to the other towns of the territory." The event was celebrated in a mass meeting of the citizens, where one of the speakers declared that "Ere another month shall elapse the performance of the gallant *Ripple* shall be emblazoned to the world in letters of living light."[3] A committee was appointed to investigate and promote steamboat traffic. At about the same time, keel boats were ascending the Cedar River with some regularity as far as Ivanhoe, only a few miles removed from Iowa City. Robert Ellis, who found his way on foot to Cedar Rapids in the spring of 1838, thought he saw great possibilities in river traffic. He constructed a number of flatboats in the vicinity of Palo. These boats were sixty feet long, sixteen feet wide and drew three feet of water. On one of them he succeeded in taking four thousand bushels of wheat to Burlington. A Mississippi River stern-wheel boat, bearing the name of the *Maid of Iowa*, finally ascended the Cedar as far as Cedar Rapids, "probably in June, 1844."[4] "The people flocked to the river for miles around to see it." During the same years a large and almost regular traffic was carried on the Des Moines as far as the Raccoon Forks, where keel boats and flatboats were superseded in 1843.

The whistles of those boats "were the grandest music" they "had ever heard." And it is not strange, for the rivers were their great avenues of traffic in those days. Boats meant a good deal to men who habitually transported their products and their merchandise to the Mississippi in wagons drawn by oxen. The *Ripple* made Iowa City believe it was destined to be the commercial as well as the political center

[3] Iowa City *Standard*, June 24, 1840.

[4] Carroll's *Pioneer Life in and Around Cedar Rapids*, p. 215, also "Early Steamboating on the Cedar," by Barthinius L. Wick, in *Proceedings Historical Society of Linn County*, Vol. I, p. 87.

of the future state. Land trade routes were projected from that ambitious city in all directions. Travelers to and from Dubuque often lost their way between the two settlements and so one Lyman Dillon of Cascade was employed to turn a furrow between the two places, following a line surveyed by a government engineer for a military road.[5]

Those territorial roads, and early state roads, are still the best favored. They were laid out from one center to another by the shortest and most available ways. They kept to the high lands, the ridges that still overlook the beautiful valleys, for in those early days there were no section lines to be followed. Under road laws enacted in 1838, a highway could be established upon the petition of fifteen householders.[6] In 1840 the county commissioners were empowered to create road districts and to provide for the maintenance of roads. A fine was provided for those who were selected but refused to act as road supervisors. Three days of labor, later reduced to two, were exacted from each male resident between the ages of twenty-one and fifty. In 1842 the first road taxes were imposed on both personal and real property, with the provision that such taxes could be paid in labor on the roads at one dollar a day.[7] The taxes paid in money were used for culverts and bridges and for tools for road working. But not many bridges were built in those years. Small streams were forded and larger ones were supplied with ferries. The ferries were constructed under exclusive rights conferred by the territorial legislatures and later by the county commissioners. The hours of operation and the fees charged were all regulated by laws.

Perhaps not far from the ferries the first mills were built along the streams. Even the larger creeks were utilized for such purposes, for the primitive mills did not require a great deal of power to turn them. Even horse power was used for many of them. Dams were made of brush, wooden cribs, or stone, but as every river was then regarded as potentially

[5] See letter of Edward Langworthy, published in the *History of Johnson County*, p. 235.

[6] *Laws of Iowa Territory*, 1838-39, p. 427.

[7] *Ibid*, 1842, p. 69.

navigable, locks had to be provided for boats to pass. Mills were declared "public" by the first territorial legislature. Their operations were minutely regulated by law. All millers had to grind grain in the order that it was brought to them and they must grind it "as well as the nature and condition of his mill will permit." The tolls were fixed. A water or steam mill was allowed to charge one-eighth of bolted wheat and one-seventh of corn, oats, barley, or buckwheat not bolted. Mills operated by horse or ox power were allowed to charge up to one-fourth of the total grists.

But boats and roads and ferries and mills did not constitute all of pioneer life. The education of their children was a problem that troubled many. School houses and teachers were not always available in scattered settlements. Many mothers taught their own children, and grandmothers, who lingered in the early cabins like blessings from God, often devoted themselves to such work. The first laws as to schools were permissive, not mandatory. They might, but they did not have to build them. In 1844 the first school house was built and paid for out of public taxes, and that honor, as so many other first things, belongs to Dubuque. There were at that time over forty thousand school children in the territory —and there was only one school house paid for out of taxes! But many private, or rate schools, were found in the towns. The records of one of these schools, taught by Jesse Berry at Iowa City in 1840, have been preserved.[8] They are now curious documents. Among the entries are the charges against one pupil "up to the time he ran away." In payment of tuition, for money was scarce, are the following entries: "By 100 bricks, 60 cents;" "By washing one pair of pantaloons, \$1,"—a menial service performed by a devoted mother in that long ago for the education of her child; "By 1 chicken, 12½ cents;" "By 1 pound of candles, 25 cents." From other entries it appears that tuitions were paid for by four bushels of potatoes and thirty-four bushels of rutabagas. The rates may be inferred from the statement of \$3.25 paid for forty-

[8] Shambaugh's *Iowa City, a Contribution to the Early History of Iowa*, p. 75.

eight and one-half days of schooling, and $8 for one hundred and twenty days, which was at the rate of six and one-fourth cents a day, which was then called half-a-bit, a bit being twelve and a half cents.

But in those days, if there was not a schoolhouse on every hilltop, there was at least a saloon in every valley. They were called "groceries," and a "grocery" was legally defined as "any house or place where spirituous or vinous liquors are retailed by quantities less than a gallon."[9] At first the traffic in such liquors was wholly unregulated, and as a result drunkenness was general. The evil became so flagrant that temperance societies to combat them soon came into existence, the first of these to be organized being at Fort Madison, in April, 1838.[10] On November twenty-eighth, 1839, there was a convention of such societies, held at Burlington, over which Chief Justice Charles Mason presided and where Governor Lucas was one of the speakers. In 1841 the *Miners' Express,* a newspaper printed at Dubuque, said that strong drink was "periling every interest of society." Soon after that the Sons of Temperance, a nation-wide organization, gained a strong hold in Iowa. The pledges signed by members recited that "no brother shall make, buy, sell, or use as a beverage any spiritous or malt liquors, wine or cider." But while these voluntary societies accomplished a great deal of good in checking the drinking evils, they accomplished more in preparing public sentiment to combat them through laws which were soon to be enacted.

[9] *Laws of Iowa Territory,* 1838-39, p. 27.
[10] The Fort Madison *Patriot,* Vol. I, No. 6.

# CHAPTER XXX

## The Indians in Territorial Days

The Indian population of Iowa was materially increased when the Winnebagoes and Pottawattomies were removed from Illinois and Wisconsin, the former being located on the eastern end of the Neutral Ground, what is now northeastern Iowa, and the latter in southwestern Iowa, centering in what is now Pottawattamie County. These transfers were not completed until prior to 1840. The Sioux were hostile to both tribes, and to protect them against attacks, the government established two forts, Fort Atkinson on the Turkey River, in what is now Winneshiek County, and Fort Croghan near the site of the present city of Council Bluffs.

In 1842 Captain James Allen with Company I of the United States Dragoons, was ordered to march from Fort Leavenworth to Fort Atkinson. It was a military diversion intended to impress the Indians with the power of the United States. Captain Allen is an interesting figure in Iowa history. He was a graduate of West Point. He participated with Henry R. Schoolcraft in the discovery of the sources of the Mississippi. From Fort Atkinson he took his men to the Sac and Fox Agency, on the Des Moines River, twenty miles west of Fairfield, where he established Fort Sandford, named after an Indian trader whose cabins were used for soldiers' quarters. In the following year, following the departure of the Sacs and Foxes from that region, he moved up the Des Moines to the Raccoon Forks, where he established what became Fort Des Moines. In the following year he made a military tour to the headwaters of the Des Moines, returning by way of the Little Sioux.

But forts were not enough to protect the red men. They were at that time being destroyed by "the water that burns," the whiskey of the white traders. The humane designs of the government were "counteracted and thwarted by a horde of unprincipled and mercenary whiskey sellers."[1] What was called the Winnebago School at one time numbered one hundred and twenty pupils, and one little Winnebago girl made enough progress to write an essay, beginning, "I like to see another Spring come; I love to see all the beautiful flowers growing. I like to take a walk in the woods, and hear the birds singing upon the trees. . . I like to go and live in a new bark wigwam."[2] But in his message of 1845, Governor Chambers complained that among the Winnebagoes, "the chase is almost abandoned and the council fires, if kindled at all, seem only intended to light up the wretched scene of their drunkenness and debauchery."

The one man of that time who had a proper conception of the Indian and his needs was Joseph M. Street, who was agent to the Winnebagoes and later to the Sacs and Foxes. He stands out as a just man in protest against a multitude of scoundrels who traded among the red men. Street was a Virginian of Revolutionary stock. He came west, read law with Henry Clay in Kentucky, and became editor of *The Western World,* a paper that did much to expose the Aaron Burr conspiracy. But Burr's friends were so numerous and so powerful that he found it convenient, if not necessary, to leave Kentucky, going to Illinois. In 1827 he was appointed agent to the Winnebagoes and that brought him in contact with the events of the Black Hawk War. It was to him that the fallen chief made his speech of surrender. He stood for honest practices and the traders were soon arrayed against him. He was sustained by three presidents, John Quincy Adams, Andrew Jackson, and Martin Van Buren, but his enemies were powerful enough to have him transferred from the Winnebagoes to the Sacs and Foxes, which happened in 1835. He sought to change the whole attitude of the government toward the Indians. He wanted the traders abolished and the sales of whiskey and luxuries and trinkets abated. "Teach

[1] Newhall's *A Glimpse of Iowa in 1846,* p. 38.

[2] *Ibid.,* p. 39.

him, agriculture and his family domestic economy," was Street's advice to the government. His efforts were without avail. The government was not yet ready for an enlightened Indian policy and the traders continued to debauch those whose annuities they coveted. General Street, utterly worn out, died in 1840, but his failure continues to wear the glory of a success. It was noble and heroic to die trying to do a fine thing! Among the Sacs and Foxes he was loved with the strange devotion of savages. At their request he was buried on Indian ground, at Agency City, a few miles east of the present city of Ottumwa. The Indians presented his widow with a tract of land, so that their friend might lie buried in Indian soil. Two years later when the chief Wapello was about to die he requested to be buried by the side of the man who had been their "father and friend." The request was complied with and there the two still sleep side by side, in memorial of a pathetic friendship.[3]

The Sacs and Foxes did not prosper. They spent more than their annuities. They became heavily indebted to the traders and the white frontier was pressing harder and harder against them. Keokuk was still their chief, but not wholly respected by his own people. He lived in barbaric luxury and he was charged, perhaps unjustly, with misappropriations of tribal moneys. The Black Hawk faction, under the leadership of Hard Fish, was still bitter toward him. Appanoose, the son of Taimah or Tama, and Kishkekosh were prominent minor chiefs. Poweshiek was still living. He had his village on the Iowa River, above Iowa City.

In 1841 Governor Chambers held a conference with them about their debts and lands. It was explained to them that the traders wanted their debts paid and the settlers wanted their lands. But the Indians refused to sell. They were of one mind on that. When the governor investigated their debts to the traders he found they amounted to $312,366.24. Among the items charged against the Indians were looking glasses at $30 each — what did red men in tepees want of them? There

[3] A monument over their remains is still maintained by the Chicago, Burlington & Quincy Railroad Company about six miles east of Ottumwa.

were also charges for "Italian cravats" and "satin vests" at $8 each, "dress coats" at $45, "super fine cloth coats" at $60! The governor protested against such sales and charges and he succeeded in having the debts sealed down to $258,564.34, much of which still represented waste and extravagance and robbery.

But the debts had to be paid and the red men had nothing to pay them with except their lands, and the land-hungry horde was pressing on the lines. So in October, 1842, the Sacs and Foxes were summoned to another conference. The chief men came decked out in all the cheap fineries the traders had sold them. They spread their tents over half a mile of land, "making as pretty and romantic a scene as eyes could rest upon," according to one who beheld the scene and described it in one of the territorial newspapers.[4] The same writer described the Indians as still "a brave, high-minded, honorable set of fellows," and as being the "finest looking Indians on the globe." Keokuk came in pomp and Kishkekosh as a savage Beau Brummel, carrying a cane instead of a tomahawk. They seemed in high spirits, too, all of them except a son of Black Hawk, who stood aloof, grieving as his father might have done over the impending fate of his race. This melancholy Indian is described as so fine a specimen of his race that he attracted the attention of all.

The conference was held in a tent. Governor Chambers, arrayed in the uniform of a brigadier-general, sat on a raised platform in front of which was an open space for the Indian orators, many of whom appeared to make speeches, chief among them still "the princely Keokuk," of whom the chronicler already cited, wrote, "There are few men in this world equal to the celebrated Keokuk." The negotiations lasted many days, for many of the minor chiefs were loathe to part with more lands. There was even some haggling about prices. But on the eleventh of October a treaty was signed by the terms of which the government bound itself to pay all the accumulated debts of the tribes and $40,000 a year in annuities, being five per cent on the esti-

[4] Burlington *Territorial Gazette and Advertiser*, October 15, 1842.

mated value of the lands, $800,000. For that consideration the Indians on that day sold nearly a third of the present state of Iowa, the very heart of it. The tract extended from the boundary line of the Second Black Hawk Purchase westward to where the waters begin to fall into the Missouri River and north and south from the boundary of the state of Missouri to the Neutral Ground. Under the terms of the treaty the Indians were to vacate the lands as far west as a line running due north and south through the Red Rocks in Marion County by the first of May, 1843, and the remainder of their lands in 1845. After that treaty was signed no Indian lands were left in Iowa except those of the Sioux.

In the spring of 1843 thousands of settlers westward bent began to assemble on the border and Captain Allen's soldiers were hard put to it to restrain them from entering the lands of "The New Purchase" as it was called, before the designated first of May. The west had seen nothing like it before. At midnight on the thirtieth of April the opening of the lands was announced by the booming of cannon and by signal fires on the hills. A contemporaneous account says that "For weeks and months previous to the 1st of May the whole frontier border was lined with settlers, who, with their families, had made encampments in sight of the 'promised land.' So great was their anxiety to secure an eligible spot for their future homes, that from 12 o'clock, midnight, until sunrise of May the 1st, the whole country was literally settled up with claims. The tide of emigration poured in like the 'rush of mighty waters,' and well might the wayfarer exclaim, in the language of holy writ — 'Who hath heard such a thing? . . . Shall a nation be born in a day?' "[5]

What is now Wapello County is said to have received a thousand settlers in a single day, and the city of Ottumwa, said to mean at the rapids — came into being as if by magic.

[5] Newhall's *A Glimpse of Iowa in 1846*, p. 40.

# CHAPTER XXXI

## During the Mexican War

In the presidential election of 1844 James K. Polk defeated Henry Clay. A free soil ticket headed by Martin Van Buren helped to keep the greatest of the Whig leaders out of the presidency. Governor Chambers at once asked to be relieved from office. He was in low health and office holding had no attractions for him. But it was not until the third of December, 1845, that he was so relieved, when James Clarke, who was editor of the Burlington *Gazette* and had been secretary of the territory under Governor Lucas, succeeded him. The new governor was well equipped for the office, but he was not destined to hold it long, for statehood was impending.

In the meantime a war with Mexico was brought on over the annexation of Texas which had won its own freedom and desired to become part of the United States. The war was one of invasion and it became one of conquest. It was popular in the south and also in the west for the coveted territory belonged to both the west and the south. For the advocates of slavery it meant an extension of territory to offset the growth of new states in the northwest. The same reasons that made the war popular in the south made it unpopular in the north. To prosecute the war the president called for fifty thousand volunteers of which Governor Clarke was asked to raise one regiment in Iowa Territory. On the first of June, 1846, the governor issued a call for this regiment and the twelve companies to make it up were speedily offered him. But it was in vain that the governor tendered them to the national government. The records are vague, almost wholly lacking, but a letter written by the secretary of war, W. L. Marcy, to Governor Clarke has been preserved. In this letter it was stated that the national government could not accept the Iowa troops "consistently with the claims of other states." That is, so many men from the other states had volunteered that there was not room in the army for all. The war was looked upon as a popular adventure and men were clamoring to get in.

But a place was found in the army for an independent company organized by Edwin Guthrie of Fort Madison and Frederick D. Mills of Burlington, which became Company K of the Fifteenth United States Infantry. This company reported for service at Vera Cruz, July tenth, 1847, and took part in several important engagements. Mills, who became major of a regiment, was killed at San Antonio Jacinto, August twentieth, 1847. His military career was brief, but it was distinguished. Guthrie, who was captain of the company, died of wounds received in the service. A few years later two of the new counties of the state of Iowa were named after these men.[1]

Another soldier who distinguished himself in this war in the name of Iowa, was Captain Benjamin S. Roberts, who became General Roberts during the Civil War. He was born in Vermont and educated at West Point.[2] He was assigned to the First Dragoons at Camp Des Moines in 1835. He had ups and downs in army and civil life. In 1843 he was practicing law in Fort Madison. He entered the Mexican War in which he became captain of a mounted rifle regiment which did brave service at the siege of Vera Cruz and the storming of Cerro Gordo. He led the party which captured Chapultepec, and he led the advance of the army that entered the City of Mexico, and to him was allotted the honor of raising the American flag over the palace of the Montezumas. He presented to the state the sword of General Torrejon. He was brevetted major, and a few months later, lieutenant colonel, and the state of Iowa by resolution of January fifteenth, 1849, presented him with a sword. In the Civil War he became a brigadier general.

A Mormon battalion of five hundred men may also be cred-

[1] *Annals of Iowa*, Third Series, Vol. II, pp. 200-201.

[2] *Annals of Iowa*, Third Series, Vol. III, pp. 358-363.

ited to Iowa in the Mexican War.[8] The Mormons, driven out of Illinois, were at that time crossing the territory on the migration to Utah. While many men were eager to go to Mexico City, there were not so many who were willing to march across the plains to California where troops were needed. The Mormons were called upon to furnish men for such purpose. Captain Allen, then at Fort Des Moines, was ordered to secure among them the desired enlistments. Many of the Mormon leaders at first demurred. They were asked to serve a government which had not protected them, either in Missouri or Illinois. Captain Allen proceeded to Mount Pisgah and then to Kanesville, or Council Bluffs. Brigham Young saw monetary and political advantages in complying with the requests of the government. Upon his approval the five hundred men were soon found. Captain Allen felt it was a hardship for their families to be thus deprived while on the arduous journey to the west. His attitude was so sympathetic and his treatment of the men so just that he made himself greatly beloved among the Mormons. He himself accompanied the battalion to Leavenworth where, unfortunately, he died of a fever. The Mormon Battalion participated in no battles, but it was marched across the plains, suffering many hardships, but with a death list of only nine men. They helped to win California for the United States. Part of the force was mustered out at Los Angeles, July, 1847, and the remainder at San Diego, March, 1848, and from those places most of the men subsequently found their way to Salt Lake City, Utah. No men in the Mexican War rendered more arduous services to their country than the Mormon Battalion.

While the Mexican War was in progress Iowa was born as a state, but before we proceed to tell the story of that birth we must pause a bit to see how the people lived in the territorial days that were passing away, and inquire into the influences by which their future was being shaped.

[8] See article by D. C. Bloomer, *Annals of Iowa*, Third Series, Vol. II, p. 554.

# CHAPTER XXXII

## Moral and Spiritual Influences

The first meeting house in Iowa was built in 1834, in Dubuque, under Methodist auspices.[1] The building was one story high, twenty by twenty-six feet. It was made of logs and had a batten door and five windows. The Rev. Barton Randal boasted that this edifice was "raised without spirits of any kind," meaning that those who assisted in the work were not regaled with whiskey as was the custom of the country in those times. But he acknowledged that he received assistance from "friendly sinners" in his undertaking, and that of his paltry salary of $100, which enabled him to live on his own "boughten feed," ten dollars were contributed by a gambler. The cost of the first church was $225.

In the same year the noted Peter Cartwright crossed the river and held services at Flint Hills, now Burlington, in response to the pleadings of those who were in moral and spiritual distress over the irreligious conditions of the settlers. He used a bent sapling as a pulpit. He was soon followed by Barton H. Cartwright who remained on the Iowa side. He was a unique and eccentric preacher. He spoke of himself as one who "went about breaking prairie and talking to the people—they called it preaching." He made his living with his plow. He is described "in plain linen pants, home-made cotton vest, common shoes without socks, with no coat and a common chip hat." He was so well qualified that he could "make bass enough for a whole congregation and sustain a prayer meeting to the end without fear, favor or affectation." The settlers heard such men gladly. They expressed in their sermons their own ruggedness.

[1] Newhall's *A Glimpse of Iowa in 1846*, p. 77; also "The Makers of Iowa Methodism," by Aaron W. Haines, p. 24.

In 1835 the Rev. Elnathan Gavit of the Ohio Conference came to Rock Island, where George Davenport provided him with a log cabin. In that or the following year he preached the first sermon, formed the first class, and established the first Sunday School in what is now Davenport.[2] He was made the circuit rider of the whole region from the Missouri state line to the Falls of St. Anthony. He traveled in his extensive circuit, "carrying food in his saddlebags and bivouacking at night on the prairie, seeking people to whom he could preach the scriptures," Indians not excluded. He was on friendly terms with Black Hawk and Keokuk and he was listened to by Zachary Taylor.

In 1837 a leader of the Episcopal church, Bishop Chase, came to the same city, perhaps the first of his faith in the territory. In his notes, which have been preserved,[3] he speaks of preaching in Davenport on the fifteenth of July, 1837. Later he preached in Rockingham. He was impressed with the importance of the future of these places. He wondered what would be the character and destiny of those then growing up "if nothing more be done than now appears to form their manners and their hearts anew."

For many years the meeting houses were few and the only preachers were circuit riders, men who went from settlement to settlement, generally on horseback. Most of them were men of native abilities but not of much learning. They lived simply and endured many hardships. They used no soft words, nor did they make fine phrases. They talked to sinners of sin, and of hell to the unrepentant. Of the early preachers and their doctrines a vivid account has been left by one who attended the first religious service held west of the Des Moines river, in 1837.[4] The meeting was held under an old elm tree, above the mouth of Chequest Creek in Van Buren County. The announcement of the coming of a preacher stirred the whole surrounding country. On the Saturday

[2] Downer's *History of Scott County*, p. 99.

[3] *Ibid.*, p. 98.

[4] See "Frontier Church Going," by George C. Duffield, in *Annals of Iowa*, Third Series, Vol. VI, p. 266.

before the important Sunday many preparations were made. Sunday clothes that had long reposed in chests were taken out and the children had their hair cut. There must have been some salvation even in these formalities. It was a beautiful Sunday morning in August when the people began to assemble under the elm tree, the women wearing sun-bonnets and the men in coats. Although the day was hot, one man came wearing "a tall bell-crowned black fur hat; a stock that kept his chin in the air; a dicky hiding his flannel shirt front, and boots of great size and strength." Nor should a "wescot" of "spotted fawn skin" be omitted from the picture of this worshiper, and the fact that he came in an ox-wagon adds something to the setting and the incongruity of it all. The preacher belonged to the "Baptist persuasion." A hundred or more were in attendance. The women with the children around them sat down on the grass, but many of the men stood somewhat aloof, as if not certain that they wanted to be preached to. The preacher read the first hymn in a "slow quaint inflection," including:

"Think, O my soul! the dreadful day
When this incensèd God
Shall rend the skies and burn the seas,
And fling his wrath abroad."

The preacher himself "raised the tune" and "sang alone for half a line," after which "a voice or two near him took it up," and then gradually, "led slowly by the leader and by the others retarded, the volume was increased and the time delayed." The sermon was long and throughout keyed to the hymn of wrath. "Oh, sinner," the preacher cried, pointing to the roots of the elm, "look, look, while I take off the hatch of hell." He pictured hell so vividly that many years afterwards the boy who heard the sermon still shivered when he looked at the roots of that tree. But he remembered it as "two hours of agony."

In those days there came to the territory to preach to the rough and uneducated, a man of the highest education and refinement, the Rev. Samuel Charles Mazzuchelli, one of the most remarkable men connected with the early church history of Iowa. This man was born in Italy in 1806, was educated in the priesthood of the order of St. Dominic and came to America in 1828, to serve as a missionary. After coming he had to learn not only the dialects of the Indians, but even the language of the white men of the country. He came to Dubuque in 1835, where one Father Fitzmaurice had started to build a church before the Methodists "raised" their meeting house without spirits, but he died of cholera before he could carry out his work. Father Mazzuchelli completed the church and called it St. Raphael's, the first Catholic church built in the territory.[5] He found many of his own countrymen in the lead mines and they beseeched him to stay among them, but there was work for him in other places. His parish was the whole Mississippi Valley for two hundred or more miles. He went to Davenport where he built a church on ground donated by Antoine Le Claire, to Bloomington and to Burlington, to Iowa City and to Maquoketa to build churches, and in many other places he sojourned to teach his religion to people who were too widely separated to be gathered into churches. He found many who had almost forgotten both God and religion.

The story of Father Mazzuchelli's work in Iowa reads like a romance.[6] He went to many places and he labored unceasingly. He traveled on foot and on horseback, in ox-wagons and on boats. A stranger in a strange land, he slept on the floors of cabins and he ate often the food of savages. In his own land he might have been anyone of many things for he had the gifts of the musician, the sculptor, and the painter, and his talents as an architect are undoubtedly expressed in the old capitol at Iowa City. As a writer he contributed much to the history of the upper Mississippi Valley. His *Memorie Istoriche* was written in Italian after his return to his native country. Its simple and graceful diction could not be lost even in translation. In it he speaks seldom of himself and then always in the third person. He is always the missionary.

[5] Newhall's *A Glimpse of Iowa in 1846*, p. 77.

[6] See *Memoirs of Father Samuel Charles Mazzuchelli*, translated out of the Italian by Sister Mary Bendicta Kennedy, O. S. D., Santa Clara Convent, Sinsinawa, Wisconsin, published by W. F. Hall Printing Co., Chicago, 1915.

He is nothing, his church is everything. When a bishopric was bestowed on Dubuque, founded on his labors, he might have been the first bishop there, but he shunned even church offices and the honor fell to Mathias Loras, who came up from St. Louis.

In Father Mazzuchelli's writings we find much information about the Protestant as well as the Catholic churches. He is not a sympathetic observer and yet he speaks kindly of them. Writing of 1837, he says "There is no corner, however remote, that a settler has reached, where a minister of some sect has not made his voice heard. . . The axe that hews down the trees and clears the road for the emigrants cannot boast of always breaking the profound silence of wild nature." He speaks many times of the Methodists and the Baptists, but he also mentions the Presbyterians. He says that on week days many of their preachers farmed or traded. To his Italian ears their preaching was "loud and boisterous." "Generally speaking," he says, "the ministers are well versed in the letter of the English translation of the Bible and possess great facility in speaking acquired by constant practice; but apart from this they possess very little erudition." In preaching they passed "from the grave to the gay with utmost facility and quickness." They made their audiences laugh or weep at will. They used "loud cries, prayers, exclamations, sobs, frenzies, trembling sweats, contortions," and many oratorical devices. They played on the whole gamut of human feelings and their influence over their auditors was prodigious. Those who came to listen "often broke out into violent weeping, cries and ejaculations, so as to drown the preacher's voice." In 1837 he looked in on a revival meeting which was in progress in Burlington. The meeting lasted for eight days, almost continuously, another taking up the task when one had become exhausted. At last filled with fright and frenzy the auditors rushed from place to place, now leaping into the air and then falling on the floor. He saw a woman "lying on a bench like one dead," and bodily so rigid that she could not be placed in a carriage. The scenes which he describes were not unusual in those days. In some of the great religious camp meetings the ground was often literally covered with prostrated men and women under convictions of sin and in a frightful state of fear of future punishments.

But there were also religious reactions. Disbelief was often as violent as belief. Irreligion was prevalent in Iowa Territory and crass atheism even was flaunted in many places. In 1839 Abner Kneeland came to the territory and started a movement that gave much concern to the promoters of religion.[7] Kneeland began in Boston as a Universalist minister. He became so liberal that his church cast him out. He then styled himself a pantheist and his enemies called him a pagan. He was finally arrested for blasphemy and thrown into prison. That stirred Boston. Ralph Waldo Emerson and many others protested such a procedure. Released from prison, Kneeland formed a colony to find freedom in the west. In Van Buren County they made a settlement, not far from Farmington, to which they gave the name of Salubria, meaning health. Their own conception of freedom was seriously marred by excluding orthodox preachers from their settlement. For a time they prospered and their doctrines spread to other places. Kneeland himself became enough of a political factor to split the Democratic party into "church" and "infidel" factions in 1840 and again in 1842, when he ran for the territorial legislature. Perhaps his political activities contributed to his undoing. In any event, Salubria had no health in it. Parents who named their child Voltaire Paine [8] saw their son grow up a Methodist.

Another New England influence was destined to prove itself much more lasting. In 1836, three families and four unmarried men came to Iowa from Providence, Rhode Island, and made a settlement nine miles north of Fort Madison. Their place was called The Haystack, but the name was changed in the following year to Denmark. During their first winter in Iowa eighteen persons are accounted for as living and sleeping in a single cabin, eighteen by twenty feet, and with a puncheon floor, a hearth of clay, and a chimney of sod. Other

[7] See "Abner Kneeland: His Relations to Early Iowa History," in *Annals of Iowa*, Third Series, Vol. VI, p. 340.

[8] Voltaire Paine Twombley, who became state treasurer.

New England families followed them. In 1838 Asa Turner and Julius Reed came across the river to help them organize a Congregational church, according to New England traditions. Father Turner, as he was called later, remained among them. He was a product of the Yale Theological school, a learned and good man who soon took all Iowa to his heart. Writing to the mission board of his church he said of the new country that "it was so beautiful there might be an unwillingness to exchange it for the Paradise above." But it was in need of salvation. He beseeched them to send preachers into it. They were sent, or they came until six laborers were in the field. They founded Denmark Academy in 1843, the pioneer of academic education in the territory. But more needed to be done. Irreligion and infidelity flourished all around them. There was Mormonism on one side and Kneelandism on the other.[9] The question was whether *The Book of Mormons* or *The Age of Reason* instead of the Bible should become the textbook of the people. "Twelve men is the least number that will supply this territory in any tolerable degree," Father Turner wrote again to the missionary society of his church. When he received no response, he wrote that "If the churches of the east love the cause of Zion and the prosperity of our common country, and men cannot be obtained from other sources, those now settled in New England had better leave their flocks and come and aid in laying the moral and intellectual foundations of this great state."

It was in the Andover Theological Seminary that the Macedonian call was at last heard. There twelve young men of the class of 1843, many of whom had already been assured comfortable New England parishes, volunteered to enter the missionary work of Iowa. These men ultimately constituted the "Iowa Band."[10] They adopted as their slogan, "Each to found a church, all a college," in the simple faith of the Christian mother who said, "Child, if God make thee a good Christian, and a good scholar, thou hast all that thy mother asked for thee."

[9] Magoun's *Asa Turner and His Times*, p. 220.

[10] See *The Iowa Band*, by Ephraim Adams; also *The Pilgrims of Iowa*, by Truman O. Douglas.

They came to do a hard but a great work. The stories of their hardships as well as their achievements are parts of the history of Iowa. One of the twelve lived in a garret in which he could not stand upright; one succeeded in getting only three members of his church after many efforts; one preached a whole summer in a room over a jail; one founded his church in a bar-room; one spent ten years to get his church going, and William Salter, by reason of many services one of the most distinguished men of early Iowa, traveled up and down the Maquoketa River and its branches and over the prairies and through the thick woods, "preaching and teaching."

But they succeeded, each in his own way and in his own field, and the college of which they dreamed is now called Grinnell. They scattered their ideas of education, which were even more potent than their theology, throughout Iowa. It never became the mass, but it did serve as the leaven. They were the most potent expression of the Yankees whose coming had been foreseen by John C. Calhoun when he warned George W. Jones in congress that they would vote him out of office and make Iowa over into an abolition state. The "Iowa Band" has been praised and also over-praised. They did not do it all, but they did much in Iowa. Among other things they did was to give a new impetus to education, to citizenship a new meaning, and to manhood a new dignity.

# CHAPTER XXXIII

## Iowa in Her First Literary Garb

The first book on Iowa was written by Lieutenant Albert M. Lea and printed by Henry S. Tanner in Philadelphia in 1836. Its title was: *Notes on the Wisconsin Territory; Particularly with Reference to the Iowa District or Black Hawk Purchase.* It was a small book, consisting of only fifty-three pages and a map. Lieutenant Lea wrote his book from personal studies and observations. He accompanied the United States Dragoons on their famous expedition through Iowa and southern Minnesota in 1835. Much of the matter in his book was intended as information for immigrants. It was his purpose to write later a book for "the general reader," but such overwhelming misfortunes overtook his first volume that he never wrote the second one. He realized nothing from the copies that were sent to the west for they were lost in the wreckage of a boat on the Ohio. Financially his undertaking was disastrous, but historically it is one of the most precious remnants of early Iowa.[1]

Lieutenant Lea's book helped to popularize the name Iowa, and we are indebted largely to him for its application to the territory two years later. But the name was already in use in connection with the judicial district of which the Black Hawk Purchase was part. "The district under review," he said in his book, "has been often called 'Scott's Purchase,' and it is sometimes called the 'Black Hawk Purchase,' but from the extent and beauty of the Iowa River which runs centrally through the district, and gives character to most of it, the name of that stream being both euphonious and appropriate has been given to the district itself." The "Iowa"

[1] Of Lea's books only a few copies are extant, held by libraries and private collectors, probably not more than a dozen in all.

River of which he spoke and which he laid down on his map, was the present Cedar River, while the present Iowa was called the Bison. That the district derived its name from the river was hardly correct. The name had come into use through association judicially with Iowa County, Wisconsin Territory.

What is now most to be prized in Lieutenant Lea's *Notes* are the splendid descriptions of the virginal prairies and of the lives and characters of their first settlers. In the employment of the government he had traversed many parts of the United States, but most of all the new trans-Mississippi country fascinated and enchanted him. To him the Iowa country was "one grand rolling prairie, along one side of which flows the mightiest river in the world, and through which many navigable streams pursue their devious way towards the ocean." The prairies were "gay and beautiful, being clothed in grass, foliage and flowers." In the very arrangements of nature he saw something of a special Providence for "no part of the district is probably more than three miles from good timber." So impressed was he with it that he wrote that "all in all, for convenience of navigation, water, fuel, and timber; for richness of soil; for beauty of appearance; and for pleasantness of climate, it surpasses any portion of the United States with which I am acquainted."

He described the climate, which has baffled many others, minutely and correctly. To him the winters were "generally dry, cold, and bracing." Spring was "a succession of rains, blows, and chills," while summer produced "rapid vegetation, and yet it is seldom oppressively hot." But autumn was to him the supreme season of all. From August to December he found here "almost one continuous succession of bright, clear, delightful sunny days." The brilliance of the late flowers and of the foliage on the trees moved him so deeply that in his rhapsodic descriptions he makes even the mighty Mississippi River linger on its way "as if in regret at leaving so delightful a region." It was the same beauty that a few years later made Father Turner hesitate to exchange the prairies for Paradise itself.

But even more we value his descriptions of the first settlers and their habitations, for it is with the men and women of Iowa that this history deals. He speaks of the "neat hewed log cabins" of the first settlers, "with their fields stretching far into the prairies." He visited the people who lived in those cabins and he wrote that "the character of this population is such as is rarely to be found in our newly acquired territories." He tells us that "with very few exceptions, there is not a more orderly, industrious, active, painstaking population west of the Alleghenies, than is this of the Iowa district. . . . For intelligence . . . they are not surpassed, as a body, by an equal number of citizens of any country in the world." This is indeed high praise of the pioneers who laid the foundations of Iowa. It pleases us because it is what we want to think of them. But after due allowances have been made for the writer who was so enraptured of the prairies and its folks, the fact remains that only a substantial and upright people could have moved him to write in such praise.

A few years later there appeared another book on Iowa, one made up of sketches written by John B. Newhall, who hailed from Massachusetts. He came to see the west and to write letters about it. After the manner of older days he dedicated his book to an official patron, Augustus Caesar Dodge, then delegate in congress and perhaps the most stately and pompous person in the territory. The author deemed his sketches worth while "if happily they serve to beguile a leisure hour" in the life of so busy and important a personage. Of himself the author boasts that he did not do as so many others were then doing, gather his information from "the gossip of saloons," nor had he viewed, as those others had done, the country "from the promenade decks of river steamers." He speaks of himself as one who had lived among the people, swimming their creeks, penetrating their forests, descending into their mines and eating the bread of their cornfields. He visited the Indians in their villages and talked with them. He interviewed Keokuk in his "summer home" and he talked with Black Hawk in his cabin. He is curious, industrious, and painstaking. For the historian his book is a treasure house. It contains facts and figures as well as fancies and folklore. It is at once informative and inspirational.

Mr. Newhall saw everything in pictures. "The long blue wagons" of the movers, with their white tops look to him like boats at sea, and as he rides over the prairies he sees them "decorated with all that is lovely and captivating both in fragrance and color." He describes "the rich profusion of red" which "is relieved by the yellow-flowered honeysuckle." He raves over the "sweet jessamine," the "crimson wild rose," and the "blue violets." He is as prodigal with adjectives as nature is with blossoms. In the very wildness of primeval nature he sees an orderliness which he likens to "the extensive parks of noblemen." Nothing is ordinary to him. When he saw the prairies on fire in autumn it was "with a noise like thunder." But if he is extravagant he is also delightful for it is the extravagance of truth.

The things he found to eat on the prairies were quite as wonderful as the things he saw. The wild strawberries crimson the land, the wild grapes hang temptingly on their vines, the wild apples are tart and the wild plums are luscious. The nuts on the trees and bushes are crammed full of delicious meats. Quail rise everywhere out of the grass and always in coveys; prairie chickens, pheasants, and grouse abound, wild turkeys strut in the clearings and ducks and geese come from the north or the south to be shot and eaten. On the banks of the Wapsipinicon he sees deer in herds, and honey made by wild bees from wild flowers flows out of the hollows of the trees. For those who like the fat of the land there are raccoons, opossums, and bears.

He observed carefully and minutely when he entered the cabins of the pioneers and he tells us how they worked and slept and amused themselves. He says the settlers in the land were more than contented with their lots. They were happy in them. To strangers they were hospitable and generous. They had plenty to eat and they were beginning to prosper. The settlers had from six to twelve horses in their primitive stables. The horse was universal. He was the *alter ego* of the pioneer. Even the women could ride horses well and that without either saddles or bridles. Cattle also were numerous. They roamed at random over the prairies. The tinkle of the cow-bell was heard in every clearing. Every master knew the sound of his own bells. Whether it was of wheat or corn, the prairie farms with little effort on the part of the farmer produced forty, fifty, or even sixty bushels on an acre. He even reduced products to prices. The usual price of butter was twelve cents a pound, but in certain seasons it went up to thirty-six cents. Beef and bacon were worth fourteen cents a pound. Eggs were cheap and housewives gathered only so many as they needed for food.[2]

There came also to the west George Catlin. He was an artist out of whom they tried to make a lawyer. Idling away his time and wasting his talents in a Philadelphia law office, he was attracted by the picturesque garb of a band of Indians. He wanted to paint them, not in the streets of civilization, but in their own wild surroundings. With pencil and with brush he followed them. For eight years he lived among them and that as one of them. He lingered with them on the prairies and he mingled with them in the mountains. He wrote letters which were printed in the New York *Commercial Advertiser* and later he made books out of his letters and his notes and pictures. Catlin was a painter and he wrote like a painter. He put colors into his words. His skies are gorgeous and his prairies are splashed with flowers. He spent, fortunately, much time in the Iowa country. He mused on the bluff in which they had buried Sergeant Floyd a generation before, and he visited the grave of Julien Dubuque on the banks of the Mississippi. The historic Indians of Iowa were still living. He painted Black Hawk in the Jefferson Barracks and Keokuk on the prairies by the winding rivers. To gratify the chief's vanity he painted Keokuk also on horseback. The Indians were nature's noblemen to him. He describes them "rather like statues from some master hand than like beings of a race called degenerate and debased." He made group pictures of warriors going to war, and in the hunt and the

[2] John B. Newhall's *A Glimpse of Iowa in 1846; or the Emigrant's Guide*, and *Sketches of Iowa.*

dance, and of squaws and papooses at work or in play. In his writings he praised them for kindness and consideration, for their hospitality and their generosity. As he was permitted to look into the hearts of the red men he denounced the deeds of the white men toward them. But his conclusions were not always sound, for he was sentimental and temperamental. He wrote the truth, but very extravagantly. As a writer his language is florid. He philosophizes, apostrophizes, and rhapsodizes. He writes what he feels and he feels what he writes. He records even the tears he sheds. He wears his heart upon his sleeve and he carries his pen in his eye. To him the prairie scenery is "soul melting." He says "the tongue must be silent that would speak, and the hand palsied that would write." It is impossible to give utterance to the prairies! They are to him "a place where a Divine would confess that he never had fancied Paradise." But nevertheless he writes as one in a "sweet delirium," hearing the while the "soft tones of sweet music" and seeing as in a poet's fine frenzy a "thousand thousand velvet covered hills . . . tossing and leaping down . . . to the river's edge!"[3]

Lieutenant Lea, Newhall, and Catlin all tell us the same story about the primitive Iowa country out of which pioneer constitution makers are about to create a state. But we shall find that they are not so patient nor so perfect in their work as nature was in hers.

[3] See *Letters and Notes on the Customs, Manners and Condition of the North American Indians*, by George Catlin, London, 1841.

# PART IV

## The First State Constitution (1846-1857)

# CHAPTER XXXIV

## Making a Constitution and a State

The first constitutional convention in Iowa was convened at Iowa City, October seventh, 1844. It was presided over by Shepherd Leffler of Des Moines County. George S. Hampton of Johnson County acted as secretary. Of the seventy-two men who sat in the convention, forty-one were farmers and only ten were lawyers. Six were listed as doctors, four as merchants, three as millers and millwrights, three as mechanics, two as miners, and one each as printer, surveyor, and civil engineer. All ranks and classes were fairly represented, farming being the predominant calling. Forty-four of the members were natives of northern states, twenty-five of southern states, and three were of foreign birth. Nearly all were men in the prime of life, few being over fifty years of age.[1]

With the exception of the professional men who sat in the convention, few were educated above the ordinary standards of reading, writing, and arithmetic, and some were probably deficient in even these respects. They were men of the frontier and most of them were the sons of frontiersmen. They knew something about American history, but few of them knew much about laws and constitutions. They had opinions and a great deal of native commonsense. Politically, more than two-thirds of them were Democrats and the remainder were Whigs. The Whigs were at that time worshiping Henry Clay and the Democrats were still thinking in the language of Andrew Jackson, the first president who had gone to Washington from the west, the man who had smashed the social as well as the political traditions of the gentlemen of

[1] Data compiled by Theodore S. Parvin, published in Shambaugh's *The Debates of the Iowa Constitutional Conventions of 1844 and 1846.* Seventy-three men were elected, but one was absent.

Virginia and the scholars of New England who had dominated the presidency for a generation. From Jackson they had imbibed some radicalism, hatred of banks and of all precedents. Self dependent and individualistic in their lives and thoughts, they had an aversion to corporate efforts. They were lovers of freedom, they were restive under restraint, and did not want a great deal of government over themselves, and above all, they wanted those who administered that government to be their servants.

The debates with which the time of the convention was occupied were often trivial.[2] The question whether the meetings should be opened with prayer was both seriously and humorously discussed. One member defined prayer as "a moral precept," and said that "by enforcing this moral duty, we violate or infringe our natural rights." He then proceeded to argue that if men could be made to listen to prayers, then other religious duties might be enforced, even to making every member of the convention "go upon his knees five times a day," and if that were done he said, "we may retrograde step by step, until we get back to the policy and customs of our forefathers, on the eastern side of the Atlantic, where tyrants wield despotic sway, and liberty never had a name." One man replied that he would regret to have it said that Iowa had "so far traveled out of Christendom as to deny the duty of prayer." One member insisted that the public was paying for their time and to have prayers every day would "cost $200 or $300" for the sessions. Another suggested that those who believed in praying could have the use of the hall to meet half an hour earlier and the president could or "would attend to preserve order." One cried out, "In the name of heaven, don't force men to hear prayers!"

[2] The journals of the proceedings of the constitutional conventions of 1844 and 1846 are extant, but they are meager records. The debates, however, were well reported in the Iowa City newspapers of that day, the *Iowa Standard* and the *Capitol Reporter*, the former a Whig organ and the latter Democratic, so that both sides are represented. These reports, together with various newspaper comments, have been collected and edited by Dr. Benj. F. Shambaugh of the University of Iowa and printed under the auspices of the State Historical Society, as *The Debates of the Iowa Constitutional Conventions of 1844 and 1846.*

He said "praying would not change the purposes of Deity, nor the views of the members of the convention," while another uttered a warning that the time "would soon come when men of proper moral and religious sentiments alone would hold the offices." In the end the resolution to have prayer was indefinitely postponed by a vote of forty-four to twenty-six. This vote and the debates throw some light on the attitude of many of the settlers toward religion. It was a period of skepticism in the west.

The most animated debates were called out by the question of permitting banks of issue in the new state. The settlers hated such banks and, following in the footsteps of President Jackson, they had abolished the Miners' Bank at Dubuque, which had been incorporated by the first Wisconsin legislature. Much of the paper money of the time was notoriously bad. But instead of providing good currency, they decided to have none at all. Stephen Hempstead, a future governor of the state and eminent as a lawyer, told the convention that all banks of issue were founded in error and that all additions to the currency depreciated the value of money, while they increased the values of property. Another speaker said that banks had been a curse to every country that had tolerated them and that they had been especially "oppressive on the laboring classes." One member thought every man should issue his own notes and sell them for what they might be worth, and before sitting down, he expressed the hope that no "whiggery" would be put into the constitution. One gifted orator appealed to the delegates to put "their feet upon the neck of the common enemy of mankind," while another with a like gift declared that banking was "an untameable viper," and while some "had proposed to make a pen for it, and chain it so it could do no injury," he thought it better "to cut its head off." One phrase-maker declared that "a bank of earth is the best bank, and the best share is a ploughshare," and another would take all banking and "do it up in a rag, and tie it with a string." Of course there were men who defended banking against such attacks, but they were in the minority, mostly Whigs.

When they came to fix the salaries of the state officers we

get a glimpse of the parsimoniousness of the settlers in public affairs. One member said he was willing to pay a fair price for public services, but not a cent for dignity. Another said he did not want the new state officers to become "gentlemen of leisure, walking about the streets, talking with their friends, with plenty of money in their pockets." Another thought that if the state had even a hundred thousand population it "would not have to pay $700 for having its accounts kept." Another thought that $150 a year would be ample pay for such work, and he added that he "did not want to support government officers at high salaries, to ride about in their coaches and support gold spectacles," nor did he "want them paid for giving wine parties, and electioneering the legislature," but on the contrary, he said that "they should walk from their residences to their offices, as other citizens." Such arguments prevailed, for the salary of the governor was fixed at one thousand dollars a year, that of the auditor at four hundred, and of the treasurer at three hundred, while members of the assembly were allowed only two dollars a day.

But the historic question of the convention was that of boundaries for the new state. All accepted the Mississippi and Missouri east and west, but there were many differences over the northern limits of the state. Many wanted to stop on the forty-second parallel of latitude, while others, among them Ralph P. Lowe, another future governor, wanted to include within the boundaries the Falls of St. Anthony, which "would add wealth and power" to the state. Robert Lucas objected to such boundaries, for they would include a large tract of broken and valueless lands, including the lands of the Sioux Indians, "the title to which would hardly ever be extinguished." The Lucas northern line was finally adopted. This line started in the Missouri River, at the mouth of the Bix Sioux, ran direct to the mouth of the Watonwan, where it falls into the St. Peter's, and down the latter to the Mississippi, including about sixty thousand square miles.

There was much good matter in the constitution as framed, but it cannot be said that it was a great, a broad-visioned, or far-seeing document. It was sorely marred and warped by the prejudices of its makers. Financially and economically they proposed to put the future state into a straight jacket. Zealous in guarding what they called their natural liberties, they locked up the future, and denied to those who would come after them the liberty to develop the resources of the state. To begin with, the convention was too large. It was almost tantamount to a mass meeting transacting a particular and somewhat technical piece of business. Men's vagaries were substituted for fundamental principles.

The new constitution was presented to congress in December 1844, by Augustus C. Dodge, then territorial delegate. On the sixth of February, 1845, the chairman of the committee on territories in the lower house of congress introduced a bill for the joint admission of Iowa and Florida, one a free and the other a slave state, so that the balance between the two factions, or sections, should not be disturbed. The boundaries of the proposed states were objected to. Many southern congressmen wanted to divide Florida so as to make another slave state out of the territory. And to make more free states possible, northern congressmen wanted to reduce the area of Iowa. Florida was not divided, but the Iowa boundaries were materially altered. The changes were based on Nicollet's geological surveys. The meridian seventeen degrees and thirty minutes west of Washington was fixed as the western line, instead of the Missouri River, and for the northern line the parallel of latitude of the mouth of the Blue Earth River. This made an elongated state north and south, extending three hundred miles along the Mississippi with an average width of about one hundred and sixty miles. In shutting the state from the Missouri River it was argued there would result "a homogeneity of character and interest highly conducive to their well being both morally and politically." It was seriously stated that if the Missouri slope were included, because of the resulting "different course of trade," it would "estrange one portion of the people from the other."

With these changed boundaries congress enabled the state to be admitted on the vote of the people. The bill was passed on the third of March and the election was set for the first

Monday in April. When the news of the changed and curtailed boundaries reached Iowa there was a loud outcry against the action of congress. In anticipation of this dissatisfaction, Mr. Dodge addressed a letter to the people of the territory imploring them to accept what congress had given them. He said he had been opposed to the Nicollet boundaries, but further study had reconciled him to them. He regretted the loss of some fertile lands along the Missouri, but

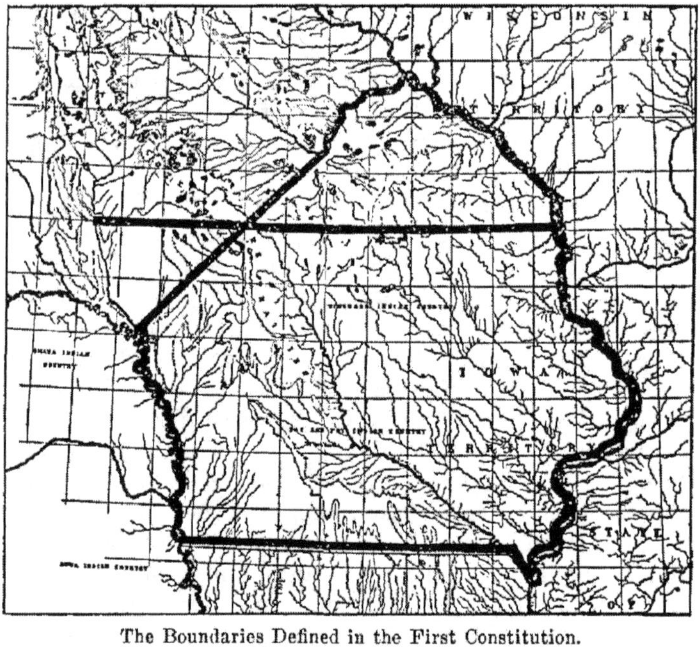

The Boundaries Defined in the First Constitution.

while that was a loss, the state was also rid of "a large extent of land forming the dividing ridge of the waters running into the Mississippi and Missouri Rivers, called the 'Hills of the Prairie'," which, he stated, were "barren and sterile." In conclusion he said: "Whatever your decision on the first Monday in April may be, we will not be able hereafter under any circumstances, to obtain one square mile more for our state than is contained in the boundaries adopted by the act of congress admitting Iowa into the Union."

But Mr. Dodge's surrender to the action of congress did not meet with the approval of the people at home. The Whigs were already minded to vote against the constitution for political reasons, and because of its restrictive clauses. In that emergency, three Democrats came forward and made a determined attack on the mutilated boundaries. They were Theodore S. Parvin, Enoch W. Eastman, and Frederick D.

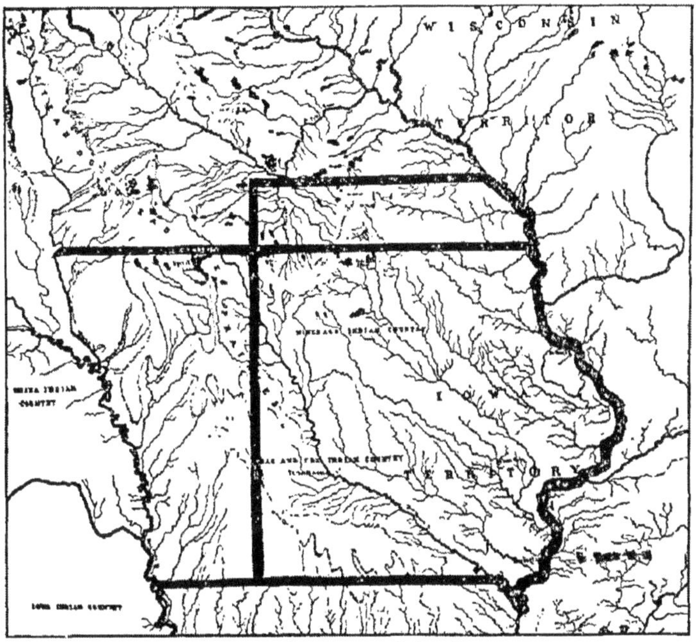

The Boundaries Proposed by Congress.

Mills, and Shepherd Leffler, who had presided over the constitutional convention, joined them in their opposition.[3] They devoted to the cause their abilities and their influence among the people, and it was due largely to them that statehood on the terms of congress was rejected by a majority of nine hundred and ninety-six votes. It was a great service worthily rendered at a critical time. Without it, Iowa might have been something different geographically. Of the three men, Mills died in the Mexican War, Eastman wrote the famous inscrip-

[3] Gue's *History of Iowa*, Vol. I, p. 218.

tion on the Iowa stone in the Washington monument in the national capital, "Iowa, the affections of her people, like the rivers of her borders, flow to an inseparable Union,"[4]—a motto that must have been born out of this historic controversy and which proved prophetic of the state's history in the Civil War—and Parvin lived for another generation and a half, in many ways one of the most useful citizens of the state.

In spite of this victory the question was resubmitted to the people by a resolution which the assembly passed over the veto of Governor Chambers. The proviso that the adoption of the constitution would not carry with it the congressional boundaries did not save the document, although it reduced the majority against it to four hundred and twenty-one. Twice rejected, the eighth, which was the last territorial assembly, created a new constitutional convention, composed of only thirty-two delegates, who were elected in April and who met at Iowa City on May fourth, 1846. The constitution which they drew up was mainly modelled on that of 1844, retaining all the restrictive clauses, wholly excluding banks of issue and all private corporations. But the boundary question was solved for them in Washington where the committee on territories, at the head of which was Stephen A. Douglas, proposed the boundaries as they exist today, the Missouri and Big Sioux Rivers on the west and the parallel of latitude forty-three thirty on the north. These were adopted by the constitution-makers of 1846 and by the people of the state. Congress accepted the new constitution, and on the twenty-eighth of December, 1846, the bill was approved by the president of the United States, and Iowa became a state.

[4] For lack of room on the stone the motto was abbreviated to, "Iowa, her affections, like the rivers of her borders, flow to an inseparable Union."

# CHAPTER XXXV

## The State Government and Politics

On the twentieth of August, 1846, four months before the final admission of the state into the Union, the people of Iowa held their first state election, and on the thirtieth of November, nearly thirty days before the act of admission was approved, Ansel Briggs was inaugurated as the first governor of the state. Briggs was a primitive statesman who hailed from Jackson County. He was a native of Vermont. He came to the Territory of Iowa in 1839 and became one of the early settlers of the town of Andrew, Jackson County. He operated stage coaches and mail routes. He was elected sheriff of his county and he served in one of the territorial assemblies. He was a man of meager education, but of sterling integrity. Those who knew him described him as "a kindly, inoffensive, certainly unaspiring man." He lacked what may be called a public equipment. In securing the office he did not have to compete with abler men, for the abler men of the state did not seek the governorship with its paltry salary. They were willing to be sent to Washington, but they held the state offices in the contempt that the constitution makers had placed on them. But if Ansel Briggs was less than a great governor, he was still a good one.

In the same first state election two congressmen were elected, S. Clinton Hastings of Bloomington, or Muscatine, and Shepherd Leffler of Burlington. They were in Washington when the state was admitted and on the following day, that is on December twenty-ninth, they took their seats as congressmen. But for two years the new state remained without representation in the United States senate, due to petty political strife at home. The constitution provided for the election of senators and judges of the supreme court by the two houses of the general assembly. The first assembly was composed of fifty-eight members, nineteen senators and thirty-nine representatives in the lower house. Of the senators elected eight were Whigs and eleven Democrats, and of the representatives, twenty were Whigs and nineteen Democrats. On the face of the returns the Democrats had thirty votes on joint ballot. The Democratic caucus placed in nomination for senators Augustus C. Dodge and Thomas S. Wilson of Dubuque. The members from Lee County were Democrats who had been elected on an independent or settlers ticket and they refused to vote for the caucus nominees. The Whigs, who were only two votes short of a majority on joint ballot, could not agree among themselves much better than the Democrats. The result was an interminable deadlock, on account of which much needed state business was neglected. After the adjournment of the assembly one of the Lee County members died and the vacancy was filled by a special election. Believing his party had a majority, Governor Briggs summoned the assembly in an extraordinary session, but they were again blocked. A Democratic member from one of the western counties had removed his residence, and the Whigs, who had control of the organization of the lower house, declared his seat vacant. When the Second General Assembly was elected in 1848, the Democrats secured control of both houses and they proceeded to elect Augustus C. Dodge and George W. Jones United States senators, Jones having defeated Wilson in the Democratic caucus.

The two senators from Iowa attracted immediate attention in Washington, where both were already well known, each having served as delegate in congress, Jones from the territories of Michigan and Wisconsin, with Iowa attached to them, and Dodge from Iowa Territory. Jones drew the long term and Dodge the short one, whereupon the latter hastened back to Iowa and secured an election for the full term to follow. The affiliations of the new senators were largely with southern men. It is related that Dodge left a Washington boarding house because Wilmot of Pennsylvania, and other abolitionists "messed" there.[1] They belonged to the first Iowa, which

[1] Parish's *George Wallace Jones*, p. 184.

was largely southern in its population and political complexion. George W. Jones was born in Vincennes, Indiana, and at the age of six was taken by his parents to St. Genevieve, Missouri Territory, where Augustus C. Dodge was born in 1812, a son of Henry Dodge, who was a senator from the state of Wisconsin when the son went to Washington as a senator from Iowa. Jones had been a resident of Wisconsin, but had removed to Dubuque when he was made surveyor general of Iowa, an office he was about to lose through the election of the Whig president, Zachary Taylor, a loss that led him to seek the senatorship, for he was born and bred an office holder at a time when certain men made public business their life work.

The first assembly having failed to elect judges of the supreme court as well as United States senators, Governor Briggs had appointed Joseph Williams chief justice of that court and George Greene and John F. Kinney associate judges. These men were duly elected to these offices by the second assembly. As judges they were held in high esteem by the lawyers who practiced before them as well as by the people. Judge Greene added historical distinction to his office by editing and publishing the decisions of the court during the first eight years of its existence. The four volumes in which the decisions were printed are known as *Greene's Reports*. Greene, who was a native of England, came to Iowa in 1838. He lived for a time at Dubuque, where he was editor of the *Miners' Express*, one of the early newspapers of Iowa. He was an early settler in Linn County and one of the founders of the city of Cedar Rapids. He represented the counties of Linn and Jones in the Third Territorial Assembly. He was a man of multitudinous activities in both private and public life. He was either the promoter or the organizer of nearly all the public and private enterprises of early Cedar Rapids, where his memory is still revered.

Under the constitution of 1846 governors were limited to one term of four years, and so in 1850 Stephen Hempstead of Dubuque was elected to succeed Ansel Briggs. Hempstead was a native of Connecticut, but he seems to have shared in the then prevailing southern sympathies, for he approved a bill to exclude free negroes from the state of Iowa. He was a lawyer by profession, a studious man of strong convictions and unchanging views. He had served in many territorial legislatures and had helped to make the constitution of 1844, speaking in the convention as an opponent of banking institutions. To him the first constitution remained the ultimate expression of all political wisdom, the charter and the shibboleth of the liberties of the people. He spent much of his time in defending an instrument of which the people had already grown tired. He thwarted with vetoes and with lectures all efforts to revise or even to amend the constitution, as Briggs had done before him. A good man and an able administrator of the office of governor, he was nevertheless the official expression of Iowa's provincialism and economic isolation under which the people were every year growing more restless and resentful. The state was rapidly filling up with new people with new ideas, but he held stubbornly to the old. He sat unchanged in the midst of changes that were of the most momentous importance to the future. His administration was one of the great turning points in the history of Iowa, morally, intellectually, and politically.

The first presidential election in which the people of Iowa took part was that of 1848, when Lewis Cass, the Democratic candidate, was defeated by Zachary Taylor, the Whig, and when Martin Van Buren was the Free Soil candidate. In Iowa, Cass received a small plurality over Taylor, 12,092 votes being cast for him and 11,144 for the Whig candidate, while Van Buren received 1,126 votes. A political incident of some historical interest in that election concerned the Mormons who at that time were in control of Pottawattamie County, where they had made temporary settlements while on their way to Salt Lake City. The Democrats learning that the Mormons would vote for Zachary Taylor had the organization of the county delayed.[2] The Mormons then upon petition were annexed to Monroe County, constituting a township of that county. They cast 527 votes for Taylor and only 42 for Cass, but by theft of the returns their votes were not counted.

[2] Gue's *History of Iowa*, Vol. I, p. 251.

In the presidential election of 1852, Franklin Pierce, the Democratic candidate, polled 17,762 votes in Iowa, Winfield Scott, the Whig candidate, 15,856, and John P. Hale, the Free Soil candidate, 1,606. Nationally the Democrats controlled the state by a slender majority and the growth of the Free Soil sentiment showed increasing dissatisfaction over the lack of vitality in the policies of the Whigs.

In state politics the Whigs were laying increased stress on the revision of the constitution, especially with reference to its restrictions on banking and the organization of corporations both for profit and for the development of the resources of the state. The liquor question was periodically injected, but both the Democrats and the Whigs sought to avoid it until the almost matured threats of advocates of prohibition forced both parties to recognize the question, as we shall see later, in the historic campaign of 1854. In the realm of national politics the question of slavery was one of increasing importance. National banking laws, the tariff, internal improvements, the Mexican war, and the Oregon question, relating to the northwestern boundary of the United States, were all matters that figured in the platforms of the two parties in Iowa. The differences between the Whigs and the Democrats over the Mexican war were acute. The former called the war one of usurpation at the behest of the slave oligarchy of the south, while the latter viewed it as a somewhat peaceful annexation of desirable territory which was thereby redeemed from Spanish-American misrule.

# CHAPTER XXXVI

## MANY HIGH AIMS AND DEFEATED HOPES

Iowa began her career as a state with a population of 102,388, but without money in her treasury or an income in sight. It was necessary to sell bonds to the amount of $55,000 to pay the expenses of the new government. Her people were rich in prospects but poor in money. There was no national currency and no provision had been made for a state currency. The one bank of issue, the Miners Bank of Dubuque, was voted out of existence in 1845. It had been denounced as a viper sucking the blood of the people. Census returns in 1848 showed that of gold and silver and bank notes, the latter issued in other states, only $183,426 could be found in Iowa. The bonds and securities held by the people amounted to only $106,357. At one time the per capita circulation was placed at $1.11.[1] Light taxes were levied, but they were poorly paid. Interest rates often ran as high as forty per cent. But the people got along. Most of them lived on farms and they had plenty to eat, and it was not necessary to have many clothes, at least not expensive ones.

The situation was perhaps most deplorable with respect to education. It was estimated that hardly one-sixth of the children were provided with schools. The building of school houses was still discretionary and the people used more discretion than money. The first state assembly created the office of superintendent of public instruction. Ostensibly it was done to improve educational conditions, but some charged that it was done to give an office to Charles Mason, then detached, an eminent and respected man who had been chief justice of the territory. So widespread was this belief that when an unknown man, James Harlan, a Whig, announced himself as

[1] Gue's *History of Iowa*, Vol. I, p. 253.

a candidate, he defeated Mason at the polls. Harlan had come to Iowa from Indiana in 1846 to assume charge of a school in Iowa City that had failed to materialize. The politicians in power sought to cheat him of his office and when they could not do that they had the whole election voided on the grounds of irregularities or errors in the published notices of the election. A second election was then held in which Thomas Benton, Jr., a nephew of the Missouri senator of that name, was pitted against Harlan, who was again elected, but again thrown out of office by the rejection of certain ballots on which his name had been slightly misspelled, while like discrepancies in other places were not counted against his competitor. Never defeated but deeply disgusted, Mr. Harlan retired temporarily from politics. His day had not yet come.

By the extension of the state to the Missouri River, Iowa City had ceased to be centrally located. Bearing in mind how Iowa City had been created by the fiat of a legislature, the First General Assembly proceeded to create another commission of three men to create another capital city, the same to be placed near the geographical center of the new state. The three men, dressed in almost unlimited authority, immediately went about that business. Seemingly without much consideration, they decided on a tract of land in Jasper County, between the present towns of Monroe and Prairie City. There at some distance from the geographical center of the state and on a virgin prairie, they platted what they intended to make the capital of the state and attached to it the name of Monroe City, for no stated good reason. They hastened the surveys so that in October, 1847, they began to sell lots for which they had plenary powers. Four hundred or more lots were sold for an average price of about fourteen dollars each. The commissioners had so much faith in the future of their own city that one of them bought thirty-eight of the lots on his own account. Nor did they fail to realize the potential values of the surrounding prairie. The whole affair soon grew into a public scandal and when the second assembly met they ousted the commissioners and vacated Monroe City, ordering all moneys which had been paid for lots to be refunded, except those which had been paid by the commissioners on their own account. And so the stakes of the surveyors were permitted to rot in the ground and afterwards fields of wheat and corn flourished where the hopes of a state capital had perished.

Out of the agitations of the Sons of Temperance and of the Catholic Total Abstinence societies, the first assembly evolved and enacted a local option liquor law. When the counties submitted this question to their voters all of them voted "dry" except Keokuk County. But as no adequate machinery had been provided to enforce the law, liquors continued to be sold in Iowa. The next assembly therefore repealed the law and substituted for it a system of county licenses. The licenses were not hard to get, nor did they cost much, some no more than $75 a year. Drunkenness was not abated and the friends of true temperance were not satisfied. So the assembly of 1851 embarked on still another experiment, based on the virtuous statement that the state thereafter would "take no share in the profits of retailing liquors." But "the traffic in those commodities as articles of merchandise" was not prohibited, provided they were not consumed on the premises where sold. The men who were addicted to the use of liquors were slightly inconvenienced, but they were in nowise deprived of their liberties. Thus the three futile liquor experiments were making the issue an overwhelming one, but that is another story. These efforts and experiments were serious enough to the men of that day, but to those who look back upon them they are tinged with comedy — and some of them with pathos.

But the greatest problem that the early law-makers had to deal with was that of transportation. They were still thinking of river highways, although railroads had already crossed the Allegheny Mountains. In any event water was cheap. And so was land. And they were willing to exchange land for water transportation. In response to territorial memorials on that subject, congress in 1846 gave to the state every alternate section of land lying for five miles on either side of the Des Moines River, and other sections in lieu of those which had already been sold to settlers, the state to use these lands, or the proceeds of their sales, for the improvement of the river for navigation. The first assembly accepted this grant and memorialized congress for similar grants to improve the Iowa and Cedar rivers. A land grant was also asked for the construction of a military highway from Keokuk via the Raccoon Fork to a point on the Missouri River opposite the mouth of the Platte. This was to be considered part of a national highway to Oregon.

To improve the Des Moines River, as stipulated in the act of congress, the first assembly provided for the election of a board of public works. For a dozen years the Des Moines River had been used, first for keel boats propelled by strong men with poles.[2] In 1837 the first steamboat ascended the river as far as Iowaville, a trip made historic by the presence of Keokuk and his associated chiefs on their return from Washington where they had negotiated the Second Black Hawk Purchase. In 1843 the steamboat *Agatha*, the counterpart of the *Ripple* on the Iowa and of the *Maid of Iowa* on the Cedar, ascended the Des Moines as far as the Raccoon Fork, carrying Captain James Allen and his soldiers from Fort Sandford to the new Fort Des Moines. Allen called it Fort Raccoon, but the adjutant general who forwarded his report said, "Fort Iowa would be a very good name; but Raccoon would be shocking; at least in very bad taste." General Winfield Scott thought so too, and named it Fort Des Moines.

The new board of public works, duly elected, seems to have had no definite plans except to sell the lands in the grant and to spend the moneys on the river. After they had spent about one hundred and fifty thousand dollars they had to abandon the plans which they did not have, and the next assembly abandoned the board, creating new administrators for the trust funds. These new men wisely employed an engineer, Samuel R. Curtis, who came to Iowa from West Point, via Ohio. This eminent engineer, after he had made many surveys, announced that the improvement of the river was mathematically not only possible but certain. He turned prophet

[2] See article on "Early Steamboating on the Des Moines," by Tacitus Hussey, printed in *Annals of Iowa*, Third Series, Vol. IV, p. 380.

and almost poet. He pictured the country tributary to the river as "a thousand miles extent." He said "the trade of Council Bluffs," of "the great valley of Nebraska" and of "the upper branches of the Missouri" could all be diverted to the Des Moines. When the pictured improvement was completed, the Missouri would be abandoned because of its tortuous channel and all the freight would be hauled overland to the Des Moines. Railroads, he admitted, might be built, but they would be mere feeders to the great river highway. When these prophecies were published, "the public mind was exhilarated" and some kind official in Washington added to the joy of the times by ruling that the land grant extended to the state's boundary, and not merely to the mouth of the Raccoon as some had contended, thus adding many millions to the moneys that could be spent. Under this "exhilaration" Ottumwa grew rapidly and Eddyville prospered, while at Pella, in Marion County, where Hollanders had laid out a city far removed from the river, they organized a company to build a New Amsterdam which was to be the river port of the parent city. They were dikers and canalists and for their purposes they found a lake, which was called Prairie Lake, which was to be connected with the river by a diked canal, making a safe harbor for the boats of the future! Fortunes were wasted, for pathos is born when serious men begin to dream.

For an engineer, Curtis was the most magnificent dreamer of those days. To him the valley of the Des Moines was the wonder land of the continent — he followed in the footsteps of Baron Lahontan. In his third and last report he spoke of veins of coal eight feet deep from which fuel could be taken at a cost of two and one-half cents a bushel, eighty pounds. He espied the gypsum of Fort Dodge, and he spoke of the Red Rocks in Marion County as "noted landmarks that have stood for ages as silent and gloomy sentinels, guarding the clear bright river that flows at its base." He predicted that these "silent and gloomy" masterpieces of creation would soon "be rent by the blast and broken by the workmen; and their fragments . . . removed and erected into mansions which will adorn the cities of the Mississippi, and the villages and hills of the surrounding country.''[3]

The Curtis plans included a canal ten miles long at the lower end of the river, where the banks were too low for dams, and a series of dams for the rest of the distance to Fort Des Moines. Much work was started and when money did not come in fast enough from the sale of lands, bonds were sold to anticipate the funds. That was sensible enough, too, but to the men of that day bonds were bonds and spelled bondage. If they were not unconstitutional, they were at least undemocratic. A furore followed. Those who had recourse to bonds were ousted and the men who replaced them were discreet enough to pay their way by issuing nothing more offensive than certificates of indebtedness. They also simplified their own labors by letting the work to contractors. But they blundered by increasing the price of the lands to two dollars and a half an acre instead of the traditional dollar and a quarter which was the sacred price of the squatters. But still nothing prospered and the contractors finally went into bankruptcy, probably without any self impoverishment.

When all these things had happened it was 1853, for while the tide in the river waited, time did not. The fourth assembly came to the conclusion that everything had been wrong, a conclusion not hard to arrive at, and so they began all over again. This time they created a board of four, two elected by the assembly and two by the people, each two to watch the other two. These four men found a contractor ''who had acquired considerable notoriety'' and they employed him after he had incorporated himself and his associates into the Des Moines River Navigation and Railroad Company. That sounded big. The new corporation assumed all the debts, which were many, and agreed to complete the proposed improvements in four years more. As compensation they were generously given all the unsold lands in the grant, all the tolls, water rentals and privileges for forty-one years with an option of some kind for thirty-four years more. So the work

3 Report of September first, 1849, printed in *Senate Journal* of the Third General Assembly, Appendix B, p. 87.

went merrily on — or at least the money was spent that way. After the company had converted many of the remaining lands into cash they proceeded to get into trouble, one of the stockholders insisting on an accounting, and then it was found that no contract existed for the governor had failed to sign it. And there they were!

Then some one found an honest man, Edward Manning of Keosauqua, and having tried everything else they thought they would try him. He was not only honest but he was a qualified business man. When he had made an investigation he reported that after spending the proceeds of half a million acres the state had as assets available "three stone masonry locks and two dams" completed and various other things not completed, including some floating debts. The Manning report showed that instead of improving they had "obstructed the river, causing loss to boatmen and shippers." [4] To add to the general gloom, some one in Washington reversed all former opinions and held that the grant extended only to the mouth of the Raccoon and not to the state boundary. And then in final disgust and despair the state washed its hands of the whole undertaking by transferring what was left of the grant to a corporation known as the Keokuk, Fort Des Moines and Minnesota Railroad Company — but that, and the litigation that followed,[5] again is another story for the steam engine was thundering its way to Iowa City. The state had spent ten years and a million dollars to learn that politicians are not transformed into business men by being elected to offices with big names.

And while they were experimenting along the Des Moines River another set of men believed that they had solved the eternal question of transportation by constructing a plank road from Burlington to Mount Pleasant, a distance of thirty miles. James W. Grimes was president of these hopeful men and he put four thousand dollars of his own money into it.[6] On the eighteenth of December this planked highway was completed and James Harlan, then living in Mount Pleasant,

[4] See Report of Manning to Grimes, 1858.

[5] For an account of this litigation, see *Annals of Iowa*, Third Series, Vol. I, article by Colonel C. H. Gatch.

[6] Salter's *Life of James W. Grimes*, p. 26.

delivered the dedicatory address in which he likened the achievement to breaking of the blockade of a beleaguered city. But the planks in that highway were not worn out by traffic paying tolls; they rotted in the mud of Iowa.

But some wise things also were done in those days. One of the wisest was the passage of a homestead law, exempting the home of the head of a family from sale for debts. The author of this bill was Lemuel B. Patterson of Iowa City, whose name deserves to be remembered.[7] The farmers were poor in money, interest rates were exorbitant, and the right of a man with a family to the shelter of a roof seemed superior to all else. But the next assembly, the third, put a lower value on human rights when the color of the human being was black instead of white, for it enacted a law that blacks and mulattoes, should not be permitted to settle in free Iowa.

The same assembly fastened on Iowa another southern idea, the county judge system, which appeared in the Code of 1851, the first of the state codes. This system was at once the apotheosis of autocracy and the antithesis of democracy. It took all power out of the hands of the people and centered it in one man who was designated the county judge. The judge was the executive and the judicial officer of the county. He had all the powers that were afterwards lodged in supervisors, probate judges, and auditors. What he bound was bound and what he loosed was loosed. It might have worked well if all county judges had been good and wise and just men, but men neither good nor wise nor just were more often elected to such offices. The system was an incubus on early Iowa, but it took ten years to get rid of it, for the judges were intrenched in power.

But the young state was going to school and the rates in the school of experience are often high. And while the lessons learned were valuable ones, still they did not prove permanent ones, for each generation insists on going to the same school, and so human government remains forever experimental. The new hopes and the new dreams recur forever, and as forever men pursue them. It is not alone in fairy lore that the pot of gold lies at the end of the rainbow!

[7] Gue's *History of Iowa*, Vol. I, p. 258.

# CHAPTER XXXVII

## The Last of the Indians in Iowa

The Sacs and Foxes were so reluctant to leave their Iowa lands in 1845, that it was necessary to give them a "military escort" to their new homes in Kansas. The chief Poweshiek led the remnant of the Foxes and Keokuk went forth with his band of Sacs. He did not long survive the ordeal. His last years lacked the nobility of his earlier life. Idleness and luxuries purchased with annuities had weakened him in all respects. He died some time in 1848. No official report of his death was made, for the agent, John Beach, had resigned and his successor had not yet reached the scene. This led to many rumors, some to the effect that he had been poisoned by a member of his own tribe, and others that he had been stabbed by a son of Black Hawk. The probabilities are that he died suddenly of one of the many diseases then prevalent among his people in their new and somewhat unwholesome surroundings.[1] He was succeeded, at least nominally, by his son Wungisa, familiarly known as Moses Keokuk, a name given him after his conversion to the Christian religion. He had his father's gifts of oratory and he is said to have been his superior in both intellect and morals.[2]

With the advent of statehood the doom of the remaining tribes in Iowa was sealed. On the thirteenth of October, 1846, a treaty was made with the Winnebagoes by the terms

[1] See *Early Days in Kansas*, by Charles R. Green, published at Olathe, 1912, p. 12. Mr. Green spent much time among the Sacs and Foxes. He says he was unable to find any confirmation among them of a violent death for the noted chief. In 1883 the remains were carried to Keokuk, Iowa, where they were reinterred in Rand Park, where a suitable monument was erected to his memory.

[2] See article on Keokuk in Bulletin 30, *Handbook of American Indians*, American Bureau of Ethnology.

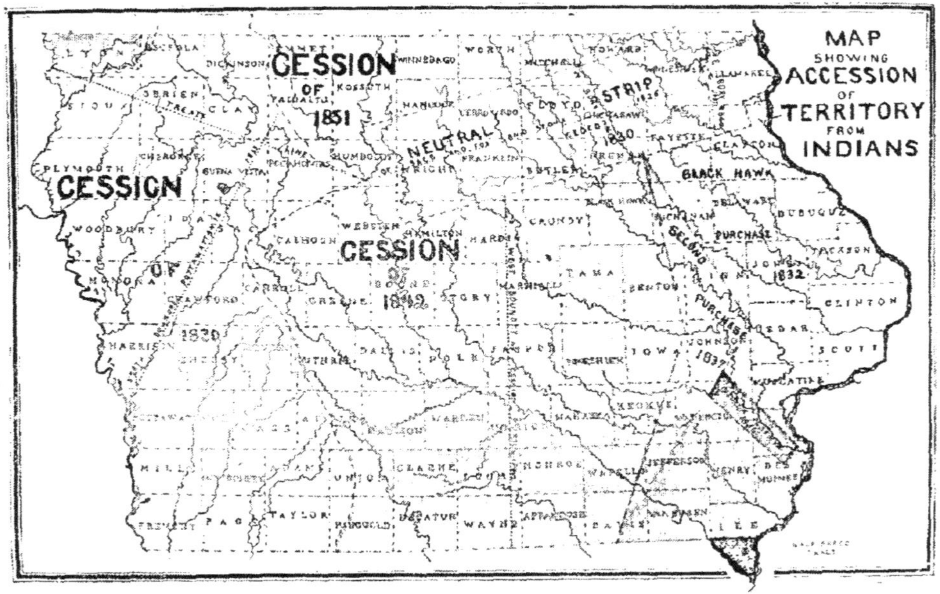
MAP
SHOWING
ACCESSION
OF
TERRITORY
FROM
INDIANS
CESSION
OF
1851
NEUTRAL
STRIP
1830
BLACK HAWK
PURCHASE
SECOND
PURCHASE
1832
1837
CESSION
OF
1842
CESSION
OF
1830
LYON
OSCEOLA
DICKINSON
EMMET
WINNEBAGO
WORTH
MITCHELL
HOWARD
ALLAMAKEE
SIOUX
OBRIEN
CLAY
KOSSUTH
HANCOCK
FLOYD
FAYETTE
CLAYTON
PLYMOUTH
CHEROKEE
BUENA VISTA
HUMBOLDT
WRIGHT
FRANKLIN
BUTLER
DUBUQUE
WOODBURY
WEBSTER
HAMILTON
HARDIN
GRUNDY
BUCHANAN
DELAWARE
JACKSON
CALHOUN
TAMA
BENTON
CLINTON
MONONA
CRAWFORD
CARROLL
GREENE
BOONE
STORY
MARSHALL
CEDAR
HARRISON
POLK
JASPER
IOWA
JOHNSON
SCOTT
MUSCATINE
KEOKUK
MAHASKA
WARREN
JEFFERSON
HENRY
DES MOINES
MILLS
ADAMS
UNION
CLARKE
MONROE
WAPELLO
FREMONT
PAGE
TAYLOR
RINGGOLD
DECATUR
WAYNE
APPANOOSE
DAVIS
VAN BUREN
LEE

of which they surrendered their reservation in Iowa in exchange for another in Minnesota. Fort Atkinson thereupon became useless, and in 1849 its lands and buildings were sold by the government. The sojourn of these Indians in Iowa had not been long. All attempts to civilize them had failed. Nor had such attempts been wisely made. They were more subject and amenable to the practices of the whiskey vendors and of the unscrupulous traders of all kinds. Their influence on the future state was not great, but they left the region which they occupied enriched with a varied and musical nomenclature. Four of the counties in northeastern Iowa still bear their names, Allamakee, Winnebago, Chickasaw, and Winneshiek, and cities and towns almost without number.

Under treaties made June fifth and seventeenth, 1846, the Pottawattomie, and their associated Chippewa and Ottawa, agreed to give up their lands along the Missouri, which they had occupied for about a decade. They were more peaceful than the Winnebagoes and their women were spoken of as the most modest and reserved among the Indian tribes in Iowa. Fort Croghan, near the site of the city of Council Bluffs, erected to protect them against the Sioux raiders from the north, was never of much consequence as a military place. But it derived some distinction by being afterwards, in part, occupied by one of the most famous of the missionaries among the Indians, Father Pierre Jean de Smet, a Belgian who came up the Missouri River from St. Louis. If he did not leave many converts, he left many letters which still rank as literature.[3] He thought well of the Pottawattomies. "The Ioways, the Sauks and the Otoes," he wrote, "are beggars compared to these." But he also said of them that they changed their wives "as often as the gentlemen of St. Louis change their coats." He denounced the traders and whiskey vendors among them with all the hatred of a just and God-fearing man. He described whiskey barrels as cannon with which the red men were being exterminated. On a day when the annuities were to be paid he saw eight barrels of whiskey

[3] *Father Pierre Jean de Smet's Life and Letters* have been printed in four volumes, New York, Francis P. Harper, 1905.

rolled out of a boat and when the Indians had consumed their contents they had also lost their moneys. He saw a squaw offering to exchange her papoose for a bottle of whiskey, while the men traded their blankets, their guns, and their horses for the same stuff. "Detestable business!" he cried out, but in vain. In his letters we read also of other things, of George Catlin, the artist, wandering along the banks of the Missouri, and of John James Audubon passing through the country studying its bird life. Father de Smet himself lingered in that region until he "heard with a feeling of pleasure, the tinkling of the cowbells" in the neighboring settlements—bucolic pictures of a beautiful region saddened by the sorrows of the departing tribes as they crossed the river into the more arid west!

After the Winnebagoes and the Pottawattomies had given up their reservations, only the Sioux remained in Iowa. They were represented mostly by marauding bands. To protect the settlers who were encroaching upon their lands the government in 1850 established on the Des Moines River what was first called Fort Clarke and later Fort Dodge, in honor of the two Dodges, father and son who were at that time serving in the United States senate, one from Wisconsin and one from Iowa. No fort and no city in Iowa was ever more honorably or more worthily named. This fort was the last to be established in the Iowa country, with the exception of the temporary ones that were erected after the Spirit Lake and Minnesota massacres of a later period. But it was not long maintained, for in 1851, on the twenty-third of July, a treaty was made by the government with the Sioux—which was not completed until in 1852—under the terms of which they agreed to vacate their lands in Iowa in the following year. In this treaty the Sisseton, the Wahpeton, the Mdewakanton, and the Wahpekuta bands concurred. In 1853, Fort Dodge was in consequence abandoned as a military establishment.

It was in 1852 that the Sioux fought their last battle on Iowa soil with their historic enemies, the Sacs and Foxes, and for the Sioux it was a bloody affair. The Sioux came down the Des Moines River to hunt, and the Sacs and Foxes, probably mostly of the latter tribe, came from Tama County on a like mission. They were at Clear Lake when they heard of the presence of their enemies and they immediately set out to meet them. The chief, Petokape, was shot by a Sioux squaw. The Sacs and Foxes lost four warriors and two chiefs and the Sioux sixteen in all, including women and children, and one of them was taken prisoner. The Sioux dead were left unburied and their bleaching skeletons were found by the early settlers in that region.[4]

With the departure of the Sacs and Foxes, Fort Des Moines was abandoned in 1846, after an existence of only three years, leaving around it a trading post and a few log cabins destined to be the beginnings of the future capital city and metropolis of the state. But though the Sacs and Foxes at that time ceased to exist as tribes in Iowa, many bands of them, especially of the Foxes, remained in places where the eyes of the government could not see them. They were peaceful and harmless, and the white settlers had no reason to complain of their presence, in fact many of them protected the wanderers. Gradually others who had gone to Kansas returned, finding that country not to their liking and suffering homesickness for their Iowa lands. Some fled back to escape the consequences of new tribal wars. The men returned first, soon to be followed by the squaws and papooses. In the winter of 1856-1857 there were eighty wikiups on the Iowa and four on the Cedar, sheltering about eighty persons.[5] One of the returning chiefs, Mamanwanika, brought with him $730 saved from annuities which had been paid in Kansas. They took counsel among themselves and also with their white friends and decided to buy a piece of land in Tama County on the Iowa River. In these efforts they were strongly befriended by their white neighbors, who had taken pity on the homeless and homesick ones. But they were not citizens of Iowa, not even legal residents. They were outlaws who had absented themselves from the reservations to which they had been assigned

[4] See *Ten Years on the Iowa Frontier*, relating the pioneer experiences of William H. Ingham in the fifties.

[5] See "Meskwaki and Meskwaki People of Today," in *The Iowa Journal of History and Politics*, April, 1906.

by the government. To cure these defects the general assembly of Iowa in 1856 did so considerate a thing as to pass a law to permit them again to live in Iowa and to become landholders. The one man who most befriended them was Josiah B. Grinnell, who was then a state senator. Their first purchase was of only eighty acres, the deed of which was taken in trust by the governor of the state. When this news reached Kansas, many others hastened back to Iowa and gradually more lands were purchased until they acquired a tract of about three thousand acres. For these lands they paid eighty-six thousand dollars, many times as much as the government in 1804 had paid them for more than fifty millions of acres. But in spite of the willingness of Iowa people to have them live among them, the government in Washington remained obdurate and for many years treated them as outlaws, refusing to pay them their annuities unless they would go to the reservations assigned to them.[6] This refusal worked untold hardships on them, for they were not adepts at agriculture and there was not enough hunting and fishing on their three thousand acres. During those years they lived by begging and retrograded rapidly.

Such is the origin of the present Tama County Indians, who, in the midst of a teeming civilization, have maintained in Iowa a bit of savage life. They do not live on a reservation, but on their own lands, lands for which they themselves have paid. They are familiarly known as Musquakies, but they prefer to be called Meskwaki and their place of habitation as Meskwakia. There are among them remnants of the Sacs and the Iowas and other tribes, but for the most part they are the descendants of the Indians who by the white men were called Foxes, one of the two tribes which for a hundred years claimed as their domain two-thirds of what is now the state of Iowa.

[6] Their annuities were restored in 1867 when an Iowa man, James Harlan, was secretary of the interior.

# CHAPTER XXXVIII

## The Trail of the Mormons

In the summer of 1846, following almost in the wake of the departing Sacs and Foxes, the Mormons from Nauvoo, Illinois, passed through Iowa on their way to Salt Lake City. They did more than pass through. They opened a great highway from river to river in southern Iowa over which immigration continued to move until the coming of the railroads, two decades later, and along which many settlements sprang up.

Mormonism was at that time still in its infancy. It was in 1827, according to the story of that religion, that the angel permitted Joseph Smith to place his hands on the golden plates and on "the urim and thummin with which to translate" the inscriptions on the plates. Smith himself was a semi-literate, a man of no high moral conceptions, who had attained some fame as one who could locate wells and hidden treasures by means of witch hazels. His revelations found favor with many. Their pretensions and practices made them unwelcome neighbors to those who did not share in their religion, and as a result of that they were driven out of their native New York, and later out of Missouri. They received a welcome in Illinois where they built the city of Nauvoo, on the Mississippi, nearly opposite Keokuk. In 1839 and 1840 many of them made settlements on the Iowa side of the river, where Governor Lucas assured them they would not be molested in the usual pursuits of American citizens. They acquired at that time part of the sites of Keokuk, of Nashville, and of Montrose.[1] But as Nauvoo prospered, most of them left their Iowa possessions and crossed the river. In Illinois

[1] The account of Mormon migration is based on the *History of Utah*, by Hubert H. Bancroft, published in 1890, which was compiled from original Mormon sources.

their prosperity made them both proud and insolent, at least to their non-Mormon neighbors. In 1844 Joseph Smith had himself announced as a candidate for president, which aroused some political hatreds against them. Rumors, many of them no doubt false ones, were set afloat about their religious practices. More and more they became a people apart. Much outlawry along the Mississippi was by many believed to be of Mormon origin. When the aged George Davenport was assaulted at home on Rock Island, July fourth, 1845, from the effects of which he died, one of the perpetrators of that crime was traced to Nauvoo. If the Mormons did not harbor such men they at least made Nauvoo their refuge. The crisis came when the Mormons destroyed the plant of the Nauvoo *Expositor,* a paper that pretended to expose the secrets of the new religion and its evil practices. For this destruction Joseph Smith, his brother Hyrum and others were arrested and confined in a jail in Carthage. The jail was attacked by a hostile mob and both of the Smiths killed. Brigham Young, a wiser leader, became the head of the church, but the hatred was not abated. Unable to defend themselves and denied the protection for which they sought, they finally, on the first of October, 1845, signed an agreement to leave Illinois as soon as they could dispose of their property. That they were fairly treated cannot be said to be true, but they themselves had done much to provoke the wrath from which they had to flee. Their virtues of industry and thrift were belittled and their faults were magnified. The Mormons rapidly sold for little or nothing their houses and their lands and those effects which they could not take with them. It amounted to despoliation and robbery. In these processes a city which had boasted almost twenty thousand people was dismantled, and eventually sacked and burned in part. It was a tragedy, and still but few sympathized with the persecuted people.

In addition to other sufferings, they were forced out in the middle of winter. It was on the tenth of February that the first contingent crossed the Mississippi River. They made their initial camp in Iowa on Sugar Creek, Lee County, almost in sight of Nauvoo. Seven days later the vanguard started on their western journey, of unknown destiny. The fear of the Gentile mobs was behind them and the hope of a new Zion was before them. From the cold of winter they entered the rain storms of an Iowa spring. They floundered around in the softened prairies and suffered all the hardships of pioneer traveling. They were not molested on their journey through Iowa, but they feared attacks from both Indians and white men and so they made their camps in the forms of hollow squares or circles, with the wagons and guards on the outside. Nights and mornings they were called to prayers. But their leaders, to cheer their followers, also provided amusements. They had brass and stringed instruments to make music. They had singing and dancing. They tried to forget their hardships and their homelessness.

It was not until July that the advance guard reached the Missouri River, where they established a camp which they called Kanesville, but which is now known as Council Bluffs. But the last of the Mormons did not leave Nauvoo until September, and the last suffered more at the hands of the mobs than the first, if that were possible. By the middle of July, it is estimated, fifteen thousand persons, with three thousand wagons, thirty thousand head of cattle and horses and mules and sheep were on the Iowa trail which was three hundred miles long. The trail ran through the counties of Lee, Van Buren, Davis, Appanoose, and Wayne, thence northwestward through the counties of Decatur, Clark, and Union, and thence westward through Adair, Cass, and Pottawattamie.

Along their route many of their camps became towns of the future. Two of the stopping places became settlements, Garden Grove and Mount Pisgah, on two branches of the Grand River. At Garden Grove, which they reached in the planting season, April twenty-seventh, they stopped to plant crops so that those who would follow them later in the year could reap the harvest. Hundreds of men were set to work. Some made logs for cabins and rails for fences. Others broke the prairie and planted the crops. The same processes were repeated at Mount Pisgah, so that in both places "industrious settlements sprung up as if by magic." At the latter place a temporary tabernacle was erected. Not only those who followed them that year, but for many years afterwards their followers were thankful for these places of rest. For years they were the abiding places of the sick and the weary. That they suffered and died on the way is amply proved by the cemeteries in which they left their dead. At Mount Pisgah they buried four hundred. The whole trail was spoken of as a cemetery, and for many years it could be followed by the graves that marked it. Many of them, as a matter of history, traveled without the shelter of even wagons. They had nothing but "wheelbarrows or the two wheeled trundle, in which was dragged along a bundle of clothing and a sack of meal—all of this world's goods that the owner possessed." The handcarts had wooden axles and wooden wheels with light iron bands. They were furnished by the church, twenty carts to every one hundred persons. In each one hundred pounds of freight was expected to be carried. It was all pathetic, and much of it was heroic. Before cold weather set in most of them were gathered in the Winter Quarters, on the site of the present city of Omaha. It was there at least they found an expression of sympathy, uttered by a Pottawattomie chief, Pied Riche, who told them that his people also had been driven from their lodges. "We must help one another, and the Great Spirit will help us both." was the Indian's assurance. The red man and the white man on the Missouri were brothers in suffering and in sympathy.

It was while they were on this journey through Iowa that Captain Allen came among them to recruit the Mormon Battalion for the Mexican War. The idea for this organization seems to have come to President Polk while some Mormon elders were in Washington on business connected with their migration and settlement in the far west. The president is said to have had in mind sending a thousand of the Mormon men to California by sea and another thousand by land to help hold the Pacific coast against the Mexicans. Nothing came of that, except the five hundred men recruited by Captain Allen for which the Mormons received $20,000 in bounties, money which they sorely needed.

Many of the Mormons remained in Kanesville, or Council Bluffs, and at other places along their route through Iowa until 1854 when all the faithful were summoned to Salt Lake City. But all of them did not respond to the call of Zion. Some had lapsed in the faith and others refused to give up a land in which they had fared well for the hazards of a journey across the plains and mountains. In the largest of these disaffections Joseph Smith, Jr., and his mother, Emma Smith, the son and widow of the founder of the religion, were concerned. They did not accept Brigham Young's leadership and they repudiated the practices of polygamy. They found many followers and remaining in Iowa they founded the town of Lamoni in Decatur County, under the name and auspices of the Church of the Latter Day Saints. They claim for themselves that they are the true Mormons, and in that faith they have maintained not only their churches, but have carried on a large missionary movement, reinforced with a substantial publishing house. They are a prosperous people and are highly respected.

While the Mormons lived at Kanesville they established two newspapers, one of them edited by Orson Hyde. These were the earliest papers printed in that part of the state. Polygamy was practiced in Kanesville, and to protect them in such practices it is said they had influence enough in Iowa legislation to have a law enacted which still remains on the statute books, that no action for adultery can be brought except on the complaint of the aggrieved wife or husband.[2] That law effectually safeguarded polygamy, for no faithful Mormon wife ever felt aggrieved when her husband contracted other marriages.

[2] D. C. Bloomer in *Annals of Iowa*, Third Series, Vol. II, p. 599.

# CHAPTER XXXIX

## Historic Colonists from Europe

In the month of August, 1847, a band of immigrants who used Keokuk for their Iowa starting point, crossed the Mormon Trail somewhere in Lee County on their way to Marion County, following closely the historic route of the Dragoons in 1835. They were the Hollanders who founded in that year the town of Pella. They are historically important because they constituted the first large body of foreigners to enter the new state. They were ultra-Protestants of the Calvinistic faith. They were Separatists. They were sturdy men and women who had been left over from the days of the Dutch Republic which had boasted of its religious toleration and freedom. The readjustments in Europe after the Napoleonic wars had imposed upon them kings whom they did not like politically, and an established church which they abhorred spiritually. Their persistent non-conformity brought them under governmental disfavor. Their meetings were prohibited, except in small companies, and for disobedience many of them had suffered arrests, so far had the spirit of freedom declined in a land to which the Pilgrims had fled for refuge. It was the usual arrogance of a king and his ministers entrusted with new powers. Finding the conditions in their home land intolerable, thousands fled from it, the majority of them to America.

Those of them who came to Iowa in 1847—many more that year went to Michigan—crossed the Atlantic in four small sailing vessels. They landed in Baltimore, crossed the mountains, and reached the Ohio River, down which they floated to the Mississippi. They spent some time in St. Louis, from which city they sent out spies in various directions to look up a suitable location for a settlement. Both Texas and

Missouri invited them, and held out flattering inducements, but the existence of slavery in those states deterred them. They were tendered the city of Nauvoo, which the Mormons had just vacated, but they preferred to live in their own houses. Iowa, free and new, was their eventual choice, and a Baptist missionary and circuit rider, the Rev. M. J. Post, with whom one of their committees fell in at Fairfield, directed them to the beautiful lands in Marion County. They bought up the claims of the squatters and resold them to themselves by lot, each man paying for the tract that he drew. They were well-to-do people, most of them well educated, and all of them of approved moral character. Among them were farmers, merchants, craftsmen of all kinds, teachers, and even artists and poets. The president of the colony was the Rev. Henry P. Scholte, who was also their minister. They called him "dominie," from the Latin word *dominus,* master. They named their town Pella, from the Hebrew, meaning place of refuge. With little love left for their native land and with high hopes in their adopted country, they hastened to identify themselves with it. The transformation must have been sudden. The ever present John B. Newhall, Iowa's pioneer reporter, wrote in one of his "sketches:" "To tell you this would be like telling you fiction. Just two months ago I halted about sunset at a lone cabin on the ridge road about midway between Oskaloosa and the Raccoon Forks . . . Again today I find myself dashing along this beautiful road. I did not dream, neither was I in a trance, for my eyes beheld the same beautiful earth in its rich garniture of green—yet I discovered a new race of beings." The Indians were gone, and he saw two hundred white men in foreign costumes standing with uplifted hands before an American official, taking their first oath of citizenship in America, "eschewing all allegiance to foreign powers and potentates." Mr. Newhall properly described them as "Protestants who had left their native land much like the Puritans of old"—they were in fact a remnant of the Puritans of Holland.

They found much to do and much to learn in their new land. They were unused to prairies. They were wholly unlike the Americans who had emigrated from one frontier to another. But they were willing to learn the new ways and they were willing to work. During the first winter most of them were compelled to live in improvised houses, dug-outs covered with straw or hay, or houses built entirely of straw, on account of which Pella was long known as Straw Town. They suffered severe hardships and many were afflicted with diseases, including homesickness, but they endured all things, and labor and thrift soon made them prosperous. They were individualists. Each man worked for himself and relied on himself. They held nothing in common except their religious beliefs—and they were not always agreed upon even those. They built churches and schools, and within a half dozen years they helped to found one of the pioneer colleges of Iowa, Central College, which they then proudly called Central University.

Three years later, or in 1850, a band of colonists of an entirely different race and character, Hungarian exiles, reached Iowa and following, probably, the old Mormon Trail to Decatur County, founded the imaginary town of New Buda, named after the Hungarian capital, Budapest. They were men who had fought with Louis Kossuth to free their country from the Austrian yoke. The defeated revolutionists had fled to all parts of Europe, but so strong was the arm of the Hapsburgs that many of them did not feel safe until they touched American soil, which, so President Taylor assured them, was "the natural asylum of the oppressed of every clime." The leader of the Decatur colony was Count Ladislaus Ujházy. In Hungary he had been known as the Count of Comorn, which was one of the last places to be given up by the revolutionists.

They selected a beautiful site on the open prairies upon which they laid out for themselves great estates with castles to be. New Buda they planned along the same ambitious lines—a city of parks and public buildings. They did everything in a regal way. But instead of putting their hands to the plow, as the Hollanders in Marion County had done, they dreamed of vineyards growing, and of Tokay wines in rich goblets. They thought of everything that makes men rich and happy—of everything except doing the work that creates everything. They did not come to labor so much as to dream. Their colony was a romance; it never became a reality. It was a conception of medieval Europe on the prairies of modern America. It was fine, but it was not real.

When they woke up they found themselves living in log cabins and not in castles, and the man who had dreamed of being an American count found himself an American postmaster, distributing intermittent mails. As they did not get along well, Iowa wanted to play the rôle of a generous host, and so a legislature memorialized congress to make a grant of lands to the Hungarians, but congress paid no heed to the request. The asylum promised them by the president of the United States was one that must be reared by the labors of the oppressed. The New Buda was never built. It was a prairie in 1850 and it remained a cornfield. The Count of Comorn and his immediate followers drifted to Texas where he prospered until he rode into San Antonio "behind six white mules, all perfectly matched," while they were still plowing with oxen in Decatur County. It is not opera comique; it is grand opera. But the Hungarians who remained in Iowa learned to labor after the Iowa manner. They prospered and became honored citizens of the state. Among these was one, Ladislaus Madarász, who at one time had in his keeping the crown of St. Stephen—which no one now wears—but who in Decatur County was proud to be a prosperous pioneer, a farmer who was esteemed as a "prince of courtiers." Another one was Francis Varga, who became a public man of some note. Isaac Hainer became a professor of languages in the University of Missouri. Another one, George Pomutz, became a noted lieutenant-colonel in the Civil War. The American pioneers smiled at the efforts of the Hungarian exiles, but Iowa history cherishes them as the makers of a romantic episode in its pages.[1]

A third colony was still more different, and much more

[1] See "The Hungarian Patriots in Iowa," in *The Iowa Journal of History and Politics*, October, 1913.

serious. These colonists came from Germany by way of New York state to build the Amana settlements in Iowa County, a community that has survived its own isolation. Their history has been two centuries in its making. The story begins in Hessia, Germany, in 1714, when Eberhard Ludwig Gruber and Johann Friedrich Rock, one a Lutheran clergyman and the other the son of another Lutheran clergyman, drew a new inspiration out of the foundations of the Mystics and Pietists of that day, with which they sought to confound the Christian formality of that era. They held fast to the Bible, but they believed that God could then as well as of old inspire men to speak and to declare His word and will, and hence they were called Inspirationalists. With their deaths the sect declined, but a century later, in 1817, new life was infused into it by Michael Krausert and later by Barbara Heinemann, through whom, it was believed, God spoke again His word and will. The story of the inspired woman who lived so long, many of her years in Iowa, and who so greatly influenced her people reads like a romance. She learned neither to read nor to write, for at the age of eight she tended a spinning wheel to make a living and she grew up *eine ganz geringe und ungelehrte Magd,* which is to say a very humble and unlettered maid.[2]

Krausert's powers declined and Barbara Heinemann's were eclipsed in a marriage, but the light shone in her again and for many years. In the meantime a new man arose among them, Christian Metz, who was not only believed to be inspired, but who was a man of great executive abilities, an organizer and leader who left his stamp on all his followers. In the meantime also wherever they sojourned in Germany they fell under the displeasure of the clergy and the rulers. They were a peculiar people; they wanted to educate their children in their own faiths, and they would not make oaths and they would not serve in a military capacity, deeming wars no better than wholesale murders. The orders finally were

[2] See "A Brief History of the Amana Society," in *The Iowa Journal of History and Politics,* April, 1904; also Perkins and Wick's *History of the Amana Society;* and *Amana: The Community of True Inspiration,* by Bertha M. H. Shambaugh.

"either back into the fold of the church, or out of the country." After tarrying in the province of Hessen, they soon looked elsewhere. As early as 1826 there existed what is called "a hidden prophecy" in which God is believed to have said: "I found my dwelling in the depth and my path leads through great waters. I prepare for Me a place in the wilderness and establish for Me a dwelling, where there was none," the fulfillment of which was in America. On October 26, 1842, the advance guard reached New York. They purchased the Seneca Indian Reservation, near Buffalo, New York, and there they established three communities which they called Eben-ezer. When more lands could not be had except at high prices and when the growth of Buffalo began to encroach upon their isolation, they came to Iowa, where they built the first Amana in 1855 and where they have built seven other villages scattered over a tract of twenty-six thousand acres of land, each set in its own rural simplicity but all bound together in one bond of Christian faith. The name Amana is biblical, meaning, believe faithfully.

They practice communism, that is they hold all things in common. Each man does his bit of labor and he receives what he needs, the surplus going into the communal funds. But communism is not an article in their creed; it is merely a means they use to reach their religious aims and aspirations. They have found it necessary to maintain their isolation. They work for no honors and for no pecuniary profits; they strive to worship God according to their inspiration. They are brought up in authority and obedience, but they consider themselves free, each in his proper sphere. They live in houses that are owned by the community, which is The Community of the True Inspiration. They eat in communal kitchens and they drink from communal wells. They do not paint their houses because it is cheaper not to do so. They have no ornamental shade trees around their houses for did not Christ curse the barren fig tree? But they have fruit trees that bear and they sit under vines on which the grapes hang in white or purple clusters. They wear plain clothes without vanity. They have no ornaments except the flowers with which God ornamented the earth when He made it in six days. They ask nothing except the right to live in peace and worship in their wide flung valley embowered in wooded hills. They still abhor war and they do not willingly participate in politics, but they are ready to render unto Caesar the things that are Caesar's, and so they pay their taxes promptly and have served in the wars with their means and as noncombatants. They have prospered, but they have not multiplied rapidly, for while they bless marriages they do not encourage them unduly. They break no laws for they need no laws. They have an oasis of quiet in a multitude of turmoils. Visitors wonder and they must wonder themselves over what they have achieved and how it is going to endure, this religious experiment that harks back to the early days when the Christians had all things in common. Christian Metz is dead, but still remembered, and Barbara Heinemann, who died in 1883 at Amana at the age of eighty-eight, is believed to have been the last endowed with the gift of inspiration.

The last of the four historic Iowa colonies was still different and still more *sui generis,* that is after its own kind. It was French and the expression of a pure socialism. In France, in 1840, a political dreamer and writer of fiction published what he called a *Voyage en Icarie.* It was the story of a journey in an ideal land, a land in which every one had what he wanted and that without strife and with the minimum of labor. The people there lived each for all and all for each. Etienne Cabet, the author of the dream, succeeded in eliminating from the human problem everything except human nature itself. He believed in what he had written and others also began to believe in it. They tried their experiment in France, but the conditions there were too old and so they also dreamed of the New World and of the virgin prairies thereof. They came to Nauvoo and lived in other people's houses, or in what were left of them after the furious mobs had driven out the Mormons. They planted vines without fig trees, but they soon found that the little foxes of dissension destroyed the vines under which they sought their repose. They could not agree one with the other; they had not been able to eliminate human nature. Why should some be more than others even if they did not have more than others? But that is not our story. We have to do with the fact that they were split up and that while many went to Texas a few came to Iowa and established in Adams County, east of the present town of Corning, a colony which they called Icaria. This was in 1858. They bought three thousand acres of land, holding it in common and holding all other things in common, except their husbands and wives and children, for they maintained the traditions of a beautiful French family life. They were Christians, but each could worship in his own way. Religion was incidental; socialism was fundamental. It was just the other way at Amana. In the center of their community they had a theater and a dance hall, neither of which they had in Amana. They believed in the social life for they were Frenchmen and Frenchwomen. They wore plain clothes, however, and they ate plain foods. But they were not willing to crucify human nature, as they were doing at Amana, and so differences arose among them. Their children left them, allured by the pleasures and the opportunities of a world teeming outside of Icaria. No checks that could be imposed on human nature or on the nature of children could be made effective. They went into a lingering decline, their dreams dissipated and their ideals unrealized. Before the first generation of them had expired, February 16, 1895, the colony of which only twenty-one members remained was legally disbanded, with enough left for each, but with nothing left of each for all. It remained for one of the last survivors to write their pathetic story.[3] Out of their experiment there came to Iowa from Nauvoo, one man worth while — A. Picquenard, who became an architect, and the designer of the state house that crowns with its golden dome the east hill of Des Moines.

[3] *Annals of Iowa*, Third Series, Vol. VI, p. 107.

# CHAPTER XL

## Geography and Population

But while the coming of a few European colonists makes picturesque incidents in her history, Iowa was not greatly affected by them. We shall see that it was American immigration from the older states that created and determined the character of the new state.

Iowa when admitted as a state had forty-four organized counties. The First General Assembly added seven counties which were carved out of what had been the Winnebago and Pottawattomie reservations, Allamakee and Winnebago out of the former, and Fremont, Page, Pottawattamie, Ringgold, and Taylor out of the latter. That gave the state fifty-one counties. In 1851 the Third General Assembly, anticipating the vacation of the Sioux lands, divided the remainder of the state into forty-nine counties, making one hundred in all. Two years later the assembly made some changes, both in names and in boundaries, among other things combining a county which had been named Yell with one that bore the name of Risely, making what is now Webster County. That left the ninety-nine counties substantially as we now have them.[1] An attempt was made to make the later counties of nearly uniform area, that is of sixteen civil townships, each township being six miles square. But the rule was often de-

[1] At various times attempts have been made to create the one hundredth county, largely for sentimental reasons. In 1870 the Thirteenth General Assembly divided Kossuth County, naming the northern half Crocker, but as it had an area of only 408 square miles, instead of the 432 required by the constitution as a minimum, the supreme court held the act invalid. In 1874 and in 1876 assemblies divided Pottawattamie County, naming the new counties Belknap and Grimes respectively, but both propositions were voted down by the people to whom they were submitted.

parted from, necessarily so in making the border counties, and Kossuth survived all alterations as a double county.

The new counties were named almost at random. Phineas M. Casady, an eminent citizen of Des Moines at that time, was chairman of the legislative committee that had charge of the making and naming of the counties. The extreme northwestern county was given the name of Buncombe,[2] which was later changed to Lyon, in honor of the general who fell leading the First Iowa Infantry in the battle of Wilson's Creek in the Civil War. Many of the names were naturally taken from the battles and heroes of the Mexican War which was still fresh in the minds of men, including the names of Mills and Guthrie, two of Iowa's own heroes in that conflict. Irish patriots and Hungarian revolutionists, and American statesmen and politicians of current fame were remembered, and that somewhat indiscriminately. The Indians also were commemorated, though too sparingly, and the names bestowed on counties were not always those of Indians associated with Iowa history.

By the federal census of 1850 Iowa had a population of 192,214. Although the territory and the state had existed only seventeen years, one-fourth of the population was Iowa born. One-sixth, approximately, of it was of southern birth and probably another sixth was of southern extraction. Another sixth was from New England and the old middle states. Two-sixths of the people had come from the states of Indiana, Ohio, Illinois, Michigan, and Wisconsin. The population was nearly ninety per cent American. But little direct foreign immigration had come to the state, but many men of foreign birth had entered Iowa after residing in the older states of the east.

In 1849 the newly settled people were greatly disturbed by the discovery of gold in California in 1848. The pioneer peoples were adventurers by inheritance from migrating ancestors, and the gold fields of the Pacific greatly tempted their

[2] According to Casady this name was derived from a general in the Revolution. See abstract of address in *Annals of Iowa*, Vol. II, p. 197. Others said it was a name of derision derived from the lobbyists, whose talk was called "buncombe." A county in North Carolina of this name, supports Mr. Casady's interpretation.

restless spirits. Whole communities were depopulated almost as rapidly as they had been settled. Later many disappointed ones returned to find in the soil of Iowa the gold that they had failed to find in the diggings of California.

Two years later a calamity befell the state that retarded the growth of population much more seriously than the gold fever. That was the excessive rainfall of 1851, perhaps the wettest year in the annals of the state. The rainfall for that year stands recorded at seventy-five inches. No doubt tradition exaggerated the floods and there is a manifest unreliability in many of the accounts in the newspapers of that period. But when all allowances have been made, the situation was serious enough. The rains began to descend early in May, after the first seedings had been completed. But little corn had been planted. It seems to have rained almost incessantly until the middle of July. The weather is described as "one storm after another." The Des Moines River at one time stood twenty-two and one-half feet above ordinary water and it was literally miles in width. Fields where wheat and corn should have been growing became lakes of water. Cabins and fences were swept away in the floods and the rivers were filled with debris and with dead animals. The homeless people had to hunt for food, so little was grown. At Fort Des Moines the situation was so serious that a committee was sent down the river to bring up provisions from St. Louis. The pilot of their boat had hard work to find the proper channel of the stream. But in due time they succeeded in having a boatload of food brought to those who were almost on famine rations.[3]

The floods were bad enough, but worse followed them. The last half of the summer was as excessively hot as the first half had been excessively wet. When the rivers went down they left pools of water in the low places which rapidly grew stagnant under the blazing August suns. The odors of decaying vegetable and animal matter, including fish, filled the air. The people were ill-fed and many lacked wholly the seasonable foods. They fell easy victims to many diseases that men and women are heir to in new lands, especially chills and

[3] Gue's *History of Iowa*, Vol. I, p. 266.

fevers which were then called ague. On top of it all there came a scourge of Asiatic cholera, a disease that was prevalent for a generation. The fears and the sufferings must have been great. There were few skilled doctors in the state and they had neither the knowledge nor the medicines with which to combat such a scourge. The newspapers of that day are filled with many gruesome accounts of the situation. We read that many persons in robust health were attacked suddenly by the disease and died within a few hours, while others were literally shrivelled up, suffering indescribable pains. Whole families were wiped out. The sick could not be properly attended and the dead could hardly be given burial.

Many in Iowa became discouraged that year and fled the state never to return. Those who remained spent a hard winter. Wheat which had often sold as low as ten and twenty cents per bushel went up to a dollar and corn was hardly to be had for any price. It was the year of the Gethsemane. But the sunshine of the year that followed was so beneficent that the gloom was soon dispelled. It was a fat year that followed a lean one. New hopes came into the hearts of all men and a new tide of immigration set in, the most marvelous in the history of the state.

Many causes contributed to this unprecedented immigration, from revolutions in Europe to the building of railroads from Chicago to the Mississippi River, and from famines in Ireland to cholera in Ohio. In a decade the population of the state was more than trebled, increasing from 192,214 in 1850 to 674,913 in 1860, according to federal enumerations. The bulk of this new population came into the state in the two or three years following 1852.

The newspapers of that time literally teem with references to the unprecedented immigration. "For miles and miles," said the Iowa City *Reporter*, "day after day, the prairies of Illinois are lined with cattle and wagons, pushing on towards our prosperous state." At a point beyond Peoria, the paper was informed that "during a single month seventeen hundred and forty-three wagons had passed, and all for Iowa." The Chicago *Press* made record of the fact that "most of the passenger trains came in last week with two locomotives,'' which, it said, will ''be understood when it is known that twelve thousand passengers arrived from the east over the Michigan Southern road, during the last week.'' They came also by the rivers, the Mississippi and the Missouri, landing their human freight on both sides of the state. The movement of the population was toward the interior. The Oskaloosa *Times* said: ''From early morning till night-fall, the covered wagons are passing through this place. . . We should think that at least a thousand persons pass through Oskaloosa every week.'' A paper at Burlington reported that, ''20,000 immigrants have passed through the city within the last twenty days, and they are still crossing at the rate of 600 to 700 a day.'' The ferries at Dubuque were just as busy. ''Daily — yes, hourly — immigrants are arriving in this and neighboring counties from Ohio, Kentucky, Indiana and Illinois,'' said one paper, while the Dubuque *Reporter* said: ''Day by day the endless procession moves on — a mighty army of invasion. . . They come by hundreds and by thousands from the hills and valleys of New England . . . gathering fresh accessions as they sweep across the intermediate country, from the no less thrifty and hardy population of New York, Ohio, and Indiana.'' In Keokuk the *Whig* newspaper exclaimed that ''by the side of this exodus, that of Israelites becomes an insignificant item, and the greater migrations of later times are hardly mentioned.'' The *Dispatch*, another Keokuk newspaper, was informed that from the county of Richmond, Ohio, one thousand persons were coming to Iowa.[4]

During a single year four millions of acres of land were transferred to settlers — to do ''a land office business'' became a phrase of the times. Men stood in line at many of the offices until they froze their feet. Eventually numbers were issued by the land offices and those who drew them had in many cases time to go and put in their crops and return before the officials could reach their numbers in making trans-

[4] These quotations were cited by N. Howe Parker in his book *Iowa as It Is in 1856*, which he called ''a gazetteer for citizens and a handbook for immigrants.''

fers. The tide of this immigration was at its height in 1854 and continued through 1856.

For the source of this immigration we must turn to the census of 1860, from which it appears that the New England population of Iowa during the decade preceding increased from 5,535 to 25,040; that of the eastern and middle states, from 24,516 to 103,170, and that of the Northwest Territory states, from 59,098 to 193,915, of which Ohio contributed over one hundred thousand. In comparison with these increases from northern states those from southern states fell far behind, increasing only from 30,954 in 1850 to 54,006 in 1860.

There was also a great increase in the Iowa born population, from 50,380 in 1850 to 191,148 in 1860. The whole population of the state in 1860 was 674,913, of which 568,832 were American born and 106,081 foreign born. But the latter constituted less than one-sixth of all, so that Iowa remained eighty-five per cent American. Of foreign born, two-thirds were German or Irish. In 1850 there were 7,152 Germans in the state and 4,885 Irish, but by 1860 these two elements had increased to 38,555 and 28,072 respectively. The quotas in the state's population from other countries were not large ones, 16,643 British, exclusive of Ireland; 11,814 Scandinavians, almost equally divided between Swedes and Norwegians, with a mere sprinkling of Danes. Of Austrians, Hollanders, and Frenchmen there were less than three thousand each.

The changing character of the population of the state is soon to exercise a powerful influence in the remaking of Iowa, and that is why it is necessary to consider the course of it. Iowa became a northern state, and it remained an American state. Its population, broadly speaking, was typically western with a New England alloy. The alloy was a small per cent of the total, but it was influential, by reason of character and education, far beyond its numerical quantity. The two currents, southern and northern, Puritan and Cavalier, will remain clearly discernible; intermingled, and finally blended.

## CHAPTER XLI

### Living and Working in Pioneer Times

Those who think that pioneer times were days of romance have not read the whole story. They were, on the contrary, for the most part days of hardships, of drudgeries, and of sufferings. If we may think of those early men and women as going about with empires in their brains, they themselves were often only too glad to have shelter for their bodies and food for their stomachs. There were among them some men, and more women, who saw the natural beauties of their surroundings and who dreamed of the future, but for the most part they were very practical and very unromantic men and women. Their romances were of the future, and few lived long enough to realize them.

Before we proceed with events of this history — and there are great events impending — we must pause a while to see how the pioneers lived, what they did, what they ate, how they slept even, and of what things were their thoughts. We must visit with them in their cabins and in their fields. And that is the real history of them.

To begin with, let us look at them on their way to Iowa. Most of them came in movers' wagons. The word mover had a distinct meaning in those days. The pioneers were all movers. Fortunately for the historian, there was among them one who came to take notes and to write. He was John B. Newhall, a reporter on horseback. He was habitually extravagant in the use of words. To him everything of the prairies was "gorgeous with beauty," and "vocal with harmonies." He was an on-looker where men were laying the foundations of a state. To him, as we have already seen, the scenery was "almost divine" and of "unequalled grandeur and loveliness," but to the road-weary movers prairie sunsets and groves were merely stopping times and camping places. Mr. Newhall has left us a description of one of these camps. It is the end of a perfect day on the prairies. The tired oxen have been unyoked and are browsing under the trees. A camp fire is burning. "The old lady"—who is the mother of the family—is "busy frying prairie chicken which the unerring rifle of her boy has brought down." One girl is milking a brindle cow, and a taller one with swarthy arms, is nailing a coffee mill to a tree which her little brother has blazed with his hatchet. "The old man"—he is the father of the family—is shaving himself before "a six penny looking glass" which he has fastened to a tree. A decrepit man, the grandsire of all, is resting in a rush bottomed chair watching curiously the varied activities of the camp. They eat heartily. When it grows dark they go to bed. Some sleep in the wagon and others under the trees—under the wagon when it rains. They are up and off again early in the morning so they may rest during the heat of the day.[1]

When they reach the end of their journey it is not to rest. There is more work to be done. The first thing they do may be to build a "quick house" by setting two rows of posts about six inches apart and filling the space between with grass or hay, and with a roof of the same materials. Before winter came upon them they built a cabin of logs. When the trees had been felled and the logs cut the right length, fourteen and eighteen feet were usual, the neighbors came and helped "raise" the house—with food and generally whiskey as their sole reward. The logs were notched where they came together and the crevices left between them were "chinked" with mud and later with mortar. Cabins were made seven or eight feet high. Some had thatched roofs and others were shingled with clapboards laid two feet to the weather. These clapboards were made with a frow, or froe, driven and wrenched through the wood. A log cabin had one door, one window, and one chimney. The window had panes of oiled paper. The first chimneys were built outside the cabins, of sticks plastered over with mud. The fireplace was wide enough to take six- or even

[1] Newhall's *A Glimpse of Iowa in 1846*, p. 13.

eight-foot logs. There was an abundance of wood to burn and they needed big fires to keep the cabins warm. The door was hung on wooden hinges and it was fastened with a wooden latch. A string passed through a hole served to lift the latch from the outside. At night the latch string was pulled in and then the door was locked. Pioneer hospitality was expressed in the phrase "the latch string hangs outside." The phrase still survives and it may yet express the hospitality of the west. In those days the hospitality was real. In every cabin there was always room for one more, though he were a stranger. There were no dressing rooms, but neither was there mock modesty. When bedtime came, says one writer, the men were asked to step outside until the women had disposed of themselves in their proper beds, and then the men came in and found their places to sleep, perhaps on skins on the floor. The permanent beds were fastened against the walls, often one above the other. The smaller children were placed in the upper beds "to keep the prowling wolves from carrying them off during the night."[2] In one room they lived and slept. When an additional room was added by a "lean to" or an attic, a family was luxuriously provided for. The privacies of life were not always observed, nor were the refinements cultivated.

That such cabins were general and that they were long used, we learn, among other things, from the diaries of two Quaker missionaries, Robert Lindsey and Benjamin Seebohm, who came all the way from England to visit the Iowa settlements.[2a] They have left us a glimpse of Iowa in 1850. In that year they found Burlington "a busy and thriving place." After visiting at Salem and Mount Pleasant, going northward, they "entered upon a prairie, nearly twenty miles over without a single house or inhabitant upon it." Settlers were still shunning the open prairies. In mid-winter they reached the "Oakley meeting," later known as Springdale, Cedar

[2] Carroll's *Pioneer Life in and Around Cedar Rapids*, p. 17; Carroll cites "heap good" and "right smart" as phrases in use in 1838.

[2a] Jones's "The Quakers in Iowa in 1850," based on the *Journal* of Robert Lindsey, in *The Iowa Journal of History and Politics*, Vol. XII, No. 2.

County. At Iowa City they were surprised to find "a handsome statehouse, several places of worship, some stores, and probably about 1,000 inhabitants." At Marengo they found "eight houses and a log court house." They speak continually of log cabins as their lodging places. In one cabin they were two of fourteen men, women, and children who slept in one room, some lying on the floor in front of a blazing fire which they had to keep burning all night to keep from freezing. The cabin was only fourteen by eighteen feet, but they found in it "genuine hospitality" and they made record of the fact that they "felt at home." They went as far as the Three Rivers country south of Fort Des Moines. On their return they passed through Pella, where the Hollanders lived, whose "houses and outbuildings" were "much superior to those of the other settlers and gave evidence that they have brought with them the industry and management of their mother country." They were pleased to find that the minister had "a study room" in which they were well received. Oskaloosa was then a village of five hundred people, many of them Quakers, all living in log cabins. Such diaries are worth more than many histories.

Log cabins were to the pioneers what tepees and wikiups had been to the Indians. But cabins were not the only things they had to build. Fences also were soon needed. At first all livestock ran at large. Owners marked their animals, some with branding irons, but more by trimming or slitting the ears in distinctive ways. Their cabins were built out of logs, fences were built out of rails. The rails were cut ten or twelve feet long and laid with overlapping ends, making zig-zag fences. The top rail, or rails were called riders and were laid in the forks of crossed sticks with ends secured in the ground. A good fence was hog-tight, horse-high, and bull-strong. Thousands of miles of such fences were built from oak and walnut trees. Rail-splitting was an occupation, but most of it was done in winter months when no work could be done on the farms. It was hard work, described by one of the pioneers as "sweating, slapping yellow jackets, fearing snakes, dodging 'pizen' vines, and 'talking Spanish' to the oxen" that were used to transport the rails.[3] But their weather-beaten and vine-covered fences outlasted those who made them.

It was all hard manual labor. Even the plows used in those days were veritable man-killers. Only the shares were of iron, the mould boards being of wood on which neither the clay soils nor the black loams would scour. There were no mowing or reaping machines in the state and the grass and grain were cut with scythes and cradles. In the absence of threshing machines, horses and cattle were used to tread out the grain even as it was done in Bible times, and the winds of heaven were utilized to winnow the grain from the chaff and the straw. The flail was still in much use and wielding that was a strong man's work. When no mills were accessible grain was ground into flour between flat stones and sometimes it was ground in coffee mills. Much corn was eaten after it had been parched, and rye similarly treated was a substitute for coffee. Green corn was dried and when cooked with beans made succotash which was relished by the pioneers as much as by the aborigines. To sweeten their foods they filched honey from the bee-trees and later they made molasses from cane which was grown like corn. The staple meat of the pioneers was pork, fresh and fresh-salted for winter use and pickled or smoked for summer use. They had plenty of wild meat, too, but quail and prairie chicken surfeited them while the appetite for pork lasted. "Corn bread with pork and rye coffee," says one of the early chroniclers, "formed the prairie bill of fare, with an occasional dish of mustard greens." Another authoritative chronicler varies this bill of fare by adding hominy or samp, venison, dried pumpkin and wild game and a few additional vegetables. "Wheat bread, tea, coffee and fruit were luxuries" reserved for "company" occasions. The common hominy was boiled corn from which the hulls had been removed with hot lye, hence called "lye hominy." What was called "true hominy" was made by "pounding" corn. For this purpose a mortar-like hole was made in the top of a stump, the corn placed in it and beaten with a maul. When it was

[3] See the "Reminiscences of George C. Duffield," in the *Annals of Iowa*, Third Series, Vol. VII, p. 358.

sufficiently crushed the bran was floated off in water "and the delicious grain boiled like rice."

There was an abundance of venison. Hundreds and thousands of deer roamed over the prairies and ravaged the growing crops of the farmers. Fences could not keep them out while succulent grain and corn were on one side and wild prairie grass was on the other. From planting time to harvest time the farmers had to protect their crops not only against deer, but against "bears, raccoons, squirrels, blue-jays and wood-peckers," and the recorder may have forgotten the rabbits. The wild life of the prairies fills one with astonishment. A boy who came to Linn county in 1839 counted twenty-seven deer grazing where Twentieth street now crosses First avenue in Cedar Rapids.[4] He was a good hunter who came home with two hundred prairie chickens in his wagon. That was "a good shooting." Hundreds of trees in the timber were loaded with honey, and all of it was honey with the tang of wild flowers. Locating bee trees was the occupation of many. Wild plums were preserved and a tart butter was made from wild crabapples, while wild cherries steeped in brandy made a tonic. One can almost persuade himself there was romance in pioneer life. Life was free and so were men!

Most of the clothing was home-made. Every farmer kept a flock of sheep. In earliest times the carding, the spinning, and the weaving were all done by the women. There was a spinning wheel in every home. Often there were two, a large one for wool and a smaller one for flax, while one loom might serve many families. Linsey, or linsey-woolsey, was made of linen and woolen yarns, the wool serving as the filling. Men rested betimes, but the women did not. They wove the cloth and knitted the stockings. When they could not make new cloth fast enough they patched the old. Even then they could hardly keep their families out of nakedness. One woman said she had often sent her children into the woods on the approach of strangers, because they did not have clothes enough to make their bodies presentable. When they first began to buy cotton goods they came in plain colors and they dyed them to suit

[4] Carroll's *Pioneer Life in and Around Cedar Rapids*, p. 41.

their tastes, using walnut bark and hulls, sumac, madder, indigo, and other native materials. The resulting colors were often hideous.

The pioneers also made their own furniture and they had need of but little. Their tables were made out of hewn logs and for seats they had stools or benches made out of the same materials. The lights on their tables were grease dips at first and after that tallow candles made with their own hands. But they did not have much use for lamps for they went to bed when it was dark and they arose with the earliest dawn.

When they had enough of everything else they still had but little money. Prices for labor and for products were low. In 1846, in the vicinity of Fort Des Moines, corn was worth twenty-two cents a bushel and wheat, fifty-six. Hogs were quoted at $1.50 a hundred pounds and sheep at $1 and $1.25 a head, "neat cattle" at $8 to $10, and horses, $30 to $50. Prices of provisions in the principal towns of the state were summarized as follows: Refined sugar, sixteen cents a pound, brown sugar from eight to ten cents, coffee from ten to sixteen cents, tea from $1 to $1.25, lard seven to eight cents, butter from ten to twelve cents, eggs, five to ten cents a dozen, potatoes sixteen cents a bushel, and fresh meat in the butchers' shops from four to six cents.

Wearing apparel was cheap. A man could buy a pair of thick boots for from $1.87 to $2.25, and a pair of "brogans" for as little as $1.12, while women paid for leather shoes from eighty-seven cents to one dollar a pair, and for morocco or "kid dress slippers," they could spend as much as $1.37. Unbleached sheeting was as low as ten cents a yard, and bleached, twelve cents, and printed calicoes were worth from ten to twenty cents.

Common labor was paid for at less than one dollar a day — fifty cents with board; stone cutters and brick layers were paid from $1.25 to $2 a day; blacksmiths, wagon-makers, and carpenters and joiners from $1.25 to $1.50. What was called "respectable board and lodging" could be obtained in any of the towns for from $1.50 to $2 a week, and the washing was probably thrown in. An estimate of the cost of making a start on a farm was as low as $400, which included eighty acres of land at a dollar and a quarter an acre, a double log cabin for $70, "a good yoke of oxen, a horse, a cow, twelve sheep, poultry, pigs, etc., likewise farm wagon, plough and farming utensils generally, with thirty weeks' provisions laid in, until a small crop is raised for subsistence."[5]

There were no meat packing houses. Hogs were killed on the farm and carried while in a frozen state to the river ports in wagons. The livestock was scrubby. A four-year-old steer that dressed into four hundred pounds of edible meat was considered a good animal, and hogs at three years growth did not weigh more than two hundred pounds. They could run like rabbits and jump like deer. They were the razorbacks of tradition. But they fitted their environment for they had to hunt for their food and the phrase-makers coined "Root hog or die." They used their tusks in the hunt and their molars to crack nuts. They produced more bacon than lard. Cattle ran at large. Fences at first were built to keep them out, not to keep them in. The cow bell was part of the music of the prairies and every pioneer farmer knew the sound of his own bells. Boys on horseback, without saddles, brought the cows home at milking time and when a dog was added, the picture was complete.

Such were the lives and such the labors of the pioneers. All that they got out of life and labor would nowadays not be considered much. They not only labored to live, but they lived to labor. They were glad to get along. At the end of their years they had few riches to count over. They toiled hard in hard times and what they achieved went to make life better for others who lived in the better times — even unto this present day.

[5] Newhall's *A Glimpse of Iowa in 1846*, pp. 45, 47, 59-61.

# CHAPTER XLII

## Social and Educational Conditions

The social life of the pioneers was a meager one. They did not have much time to go visiting and the distances apart were too long. A cabin filled with children and a yard filled with livestock kept both the men and women at home. Even the children had but little time for play. Boys often did the work of men. There is at least one account of two boys, one nine years old and the other ten, who broke prairie sod with two yoke of oxen attached to a plow that they could not lift or drag out of its furrow.[1] At seven girls knew how to help their mothers, especially in the care of younger children. Babies were the only dolls with which they played.

They worked hard, but they varied the monotony of life with a little play. They had sports and games and social "doings" of primitive kinds. The "circular wolf hunt" was a most wonderful sport as well as full of excitement for the boys. With horses and dogs, they formed a circle, "miles around," and gradually pressed in, driving the wolves before them. As the circle narrowed and the animals tried to break through they were killed by the dogs. In the way of public entertainments the spelling school was long popular. The spelling was incidental to the long sleigh rides. The "corn huskings" were afternoons and evenings of social pleasure that were always looked forward to. The finding of a red ear meant kisses all around. Eating and drinking and dancing closed the festivities. The women had their "quilting bees" and their "paring bees," and the men their "log rollings" and "house raisings." Many of these gatherings were accompanied by drinking, and the universal liquor was whiskey, which was as copious as water. In those days a gallon cost only thirty cents.

[1] Carroll's *Pioneer Life in and Around Cedar Rapids,* p. 38.

Neither boys nor girls had much schooling in the territory or the early state for there were few schools at that time. Nor did many care to go when schools were built for them. The rifle on the boy's shoulder was a lighter burden than schoolbooks under his arm. Book learning was not held in high esteem among the native westerners. The fashion of books came with the Yankees from the east, especially with the New Englanders. Among boys the contests were physical, not mental. Every boy was bound to believe, says one of the early writers, that he "could lick all creation" until convinced to the contrary. Their fighting instincts were those of young savages. It was not a bad instinct. Girls also prided themselves on athletic accomplishments. At the first state fair, held at Fairfield in 1854, eleven girls from different parts of the state rode for a prize of one hundred and fifty dollars, probably on bareback horses. The spectators, dissatisfied with the decision of the judges, made up a purse of one hundred and forty dollars and six months' tuition in the Fairfield Female Academy for a defeated favorite. Women and girls were still called females in law and society.

But if there were no schools there were mothers who were school teachers. One pioneer boy, George C. Duffield of the Chequest Creek Settlement in Van Buren County, in his later years wrote: "I wish the picture of an ideal frontier mother might be painted on canvas."[2] He then described her as sitting in the only rocking chair in the cabin, holding the baby in her right arm. It is evening in his description. The numerous family is ranged in a semi-circle in front of a blazing fire which the father of the group keeps going. But the mother is the light and the warmth of that semi-circle. "The left hand holds an old, worn, blue-back Webster's spelling book. The other holds a greasy, flickering tallow candle." As she rocks to and fro she gives out the words for the children to spell, words of one syllable for the little ones and larger words for the older children. They spell until bedtime. She talks to them between the words, telling

[2] See "Youthtime in Frontier Iowa," by George C. Duffield in the *Annals of Iowa*, Third Series, Vol. VII, p. 347.

them the meanings and pronunciations of the words. It is a primitive education, but it is an effective one. "Wonders," said the grateful son in his old age, "were accomplished in nearly every cabin."

The cry for school teachers, like the cry for missionaries, was most heard in the New England states. One may read in the files of a Cincinnati paper of those times that one day the governor of Vermont passed through that city "with thirteen young ladies designed for school teachers" in the west, probably Iowa. Few of the teachers ever returned; most of them remained to wed, and in that manner they served the future as well as they might have done in their school rooms. They made homes in eastern ways for western men. And when their children grew up those eastern mothers demanded schools for them.

There was room in the west for the surplus of women in the east. Early Iowa "was overstocked with bachelors," young men who were making hazards of new fortunes. Fastidious ladies may have looked with disdain on rough western men at first, but they soon saw the worth of sturdy manhood in them. We read in the early accounts that the coming of a family with grown-up daughters created a sensation in a whole settlement.[3] The young men who had lived isolated lives were at first "somewhat crude in conversation, a little clumsy in manner, and as timid and modest as a young girl." It was better they were that way for out of their timidity and modesty might come that beautiful respect of men for women which in itself constitutes a race culture. Courtships followed as a matter of course, but the young men were so timid that they did not know how to bring them to a culmination. Our writer says that they "sort of stayed around," growing more and more "reluctant to depart," until some rude and obtrusive member of the family revealed to them the fact that they were in love and when they found that out there was soon a wedding. Setting up a new home was an easy matter in those days. Wealth was not required and dowries were not dreamed of. All that was needed were willing hands and loving hearts—two hearts and four hands could make a

[3] Carroll's *Pioneer Life in and Around Cedar Rapids*, p. 35.

home in any part of Iowa in those days. Diamond rings were unknown, orange blossoms unseen, and wedding bells unheard. It was love and labor and labor and love—and the children who were born of those early marriages helped to make the state under Grimes and to save the nation under Lincoln.

Many pioneer courtships and marriages were not only simple but crude. There were more Audreys and Phoebes than Celias and Rosalinds in the timber of Iowa. Along the lower Des Moines in what they called the "Hairy Nation" because barbers and razors were not much in vogue, they had some indigenous customs and phrases. There, as in other parts of the world, when a girl was of marriagable age she bound up her hair and lengthened her skirts. Then the gossips said that the girls "had set to." The young men who lingered longer in their presence were spoken of as "setting to." When they were engaged to marry they were "bespoke." Marriages were often celebrated by those who were not invited to them. They came to enact the orgies of the charivari, which was a rustic serenade with tin pans and cow bells. It was rustic rowdyism that could not be appeased except with food and drink for the celebrants. Sometimes it was even worse in its manifestations so that for the timid and modest a wedding might be an ordeal to be passed through.

However, the graces of social life were not wholly unknown. A Chicago newspaper man who visited Davenport in 1840, has left a record of some social distinctions.[4] He spoke of the Le Claire house, a hotel, as one without an equal in either Illinois or Missouri, outwardly, inwardly and even as to furniture. He found "all the youth and beauty of the place" congregated there "at a social ball." He found also "so many ladies educated with all the refinements of our eastern and southern cities." He did not dare to "individualize," he wrote, "but aggregately" he said of the company "that no town the size of Davenport in the Union" could "produce their superiors" whether to "speak of their mental or external accomplishments."

Perhaps the most usual expression of the social intercourse

[4] Reprinted in the Davenport *Sun*, October 24, 1840.

of the pioneers was dancing, which was a somewhat universal pastime. The man who could "scrape a fiddle" was everywhere in demand. In 1854 the chief justice of the state was Joseph Williams, who liked fiddling at least next to the law. He did not think it beneath his dignity to play for dances. One night when he was so engaged, at Tipton, he was surprised to see on the floor a man whom he had just sentenced to the penitentiary for horse stealing. Upon inquiry of the sheriff, who was one of the dancers, he learned that as there was no jail in which to deposit him, and as the sheriff wanted to dance, he had brought his prisoner with him.[5] Why should a sheriff, or even a horse thief be deprived of dancing?

Among men gambling was a prevalent social pastime. It was as universal as dancing. The game of poker had recently been invented somewhere in the southwest and its fascination for men spread rapidly. Horse racing was very prevalent and there was even some cock fighting. Sunday was a favorite day for all such rough sports and when drinking was added the desecration of the church day became flagrant. At best the social recreations of the people were not very refined, and at their worst they were almost barbaric. They were crude and rough times and in many places the rowdy and the bully were the heroes in them.

But many were addicted to better pursuits. Mr. Newhall relates that upon one occasion when he had invoked the hospitality of a farmer—hospitality was one of the outstanding virtues of the period—after supper his host invited him to accompany him to the lyceum. He wondered at the invitation, but he went. The lyceum was held in a horse mill, that is a grist mill operated by horse power. There a number of farmers gathered and debated the question, "Shall the United States bank be rechartered?" The young man who made the best speech was dressed in "a jeans hunting shirt, belted around with a leathern girdle, in corduroy leggings and cowhide brogans." He said things and said them in a way that charmed the reporter more than things he had heard in the Boston Odeon or the Broadway Tabernacle. Such debating

[5] Peter A. Dey in *Annals of Iowa*, Third Series, Vol. VII, p. 82.

societies were not unusual. In those primitive lyceums the future law-makers of the state and nation were being trained.

An intellectual hunger became indigenous to the prairies. Many mothers felt it for their children. They remembered better days and they coveted better ways. Mothers told later how they were thrilled by the sight of books, books that were so rare in those days. What was there in books that thrilled them, or why were they pleased when they saw their children taking an interest in them? Did they see in them the power of the future? And so it was that book agents, for the most part the colporteurs of the religious societies, were well received among many of the pioneers. The books they purchased were mostly on religious subjects, and the religion of them was apt to be either mawkish or terrible. But there were exceptions. Some were literary, like John Bunyan's *Pilgrim's Progress.* But the poorest book that was left in a pioneer's cabin in those days was like a little literary candle lighted never to go out again. Those flickering lights sometimes became great mental illuminations. A book is never wholly worthless, and every bit of light creates a longing for more light.

It was out of these aspirations that the first colleges were founded in the state. But higher learning became the handmaiden of religion. The church people and they alone had the faith in which colleges could be founded. Seminaries and academies for science and for literature and for both men and women had been projected in legislative enactments, but little came of them. The ends and aims remained unrealized until they were vitalized out of the Christian creeds. What men and women believed was more than what legislatures enacted. At that time even the primary needs had not been met. Around 1850 there were still but few schools in the state, and the average school year consisted of only three months and nine days, on an average. An enumeration showed there were then 1,733 teachers in the state and they received all told $87,000 a year—about twenty dollars a month for the three months and nine days! Voices were indeed crying in the wilderness and God-conscious fathers and mothers who loved their children and the future of the state when they heard those cries founded the colleges.

The New Englanders led the van. When they founded the academy at Denmark, which Theodore S. Parvin, a reliable recorder of educational progress, called the mother of all denominational colleges in Iowa, Denmark counted only three log cabins. Their little school was declared "open to every religious denomination" and they hoped to see it grow into a college, which it did, and the first offspring of that mother of colleges was Grinnell College, which was organized on paper at Davenport in 1846, and in reality two years later. That was New England Congregationalism. But other denominations were not far behind in time or spirit. The Baptists had an academy in Burlington and in 1853 they founded Central College at Pella, among the Hollanders who held higher learning in great esteem. But they called it Central University in those days of hope and expectation. An Iowa Conference college was proposed in 1852 and established at Mt. Vernon in 1857 as Cornell College by the Methodists. The Disciples of Christ founded their college at Oskaloosa in 1855, which is now Drake University of Des Moines. In the same year the United Brethren established Western College, six miles south of Cedar Rapids. In 1852 an eastern man, Daniel Coe, who never saw Iowa, gave $1,000 to found a Presbyterian college in Cedar Rapids, of which half was enough to buy eighty acres of land, and in 1856 the Presbyterians established their first realized college at Hopkinton.

These were the beginnings of the denominational colleges. They did not grow like Jonah's gourd, but on the contrary, they were kept alive feebly through the sacrifices of their devotees. Those who taught in them received hardly their subsistence, and those who were taught in them lived on a few dollars a week, but dreaming of intellectual affluence. There is no tribute too great that can be paid to the founders of these colleges. They were those who lighted the little candles that became great illuminations.

# CHAPTER XLIII

## An Interlude the Reader May Skip

Perhaps some reader of this history is asking whether a courtship in the "Hairy Nation," a pioneer mother "spelling" her children in front of a fireplace, a judge fiddling for a dance in Tipton, a colporteur wandering through the settlements, or even the beginnings of a college in a three-cabined village is an event of historical consequence? Many persons when they think of history think of greater things, of events that bulk like battles in some Armageddon. And others think of names and of dates, of lists of men who held offices and of summaries of speeches delivered on great occasions, or of laws enacted. To them, one and all, we want to say that this is a history of the people of Iowa, and the simple incidents we have recounted are really more vital to an understanding of what the people were and what they did than summaries or climaxes. If you want to know about a people you must visit with them in their homes, go with them to their schools and to their places of amusement and of worship, not merely frequent the halls where they make their laws or where orators deliver their speeches. One can learn more from Eumaeus, the swineherd, about ancient Ithaca than from the princes and suitors in the palace of Ulysses. Ruth gleaning in the fields of Boaz means humanly more to us than the Queen of Sheba before the throne of Solomon.

Habitually, we exaggerate and exalt the past. The old historians wrote in heroic terms. We think of the ancient Hebrews as talking with God, and of the Greeks and Romans as demi-gods. But they were just human beings like the rest of mankind. Iowa in pioneer times had the same kind of men and women. God's presence was not more on the hills of Judea than on the prairies of Iowa where men and women in prayer dedicated a college to the cause of education and religion. And the men who advanced in the face of concealed guns at Bellevue had the same kind of courage that is still boasted of in Greeks and Romans. All courage is alike when it becomes the willingness to die in order that others may live. We think of the days of Queen Elizabeth in England and call them spacious, and yet those who have looked into the actual human conditions of those days have found them miserable indeed. But the present is ever kind to the past, and time is the great gilder of human faces and amplifier of human virtues. But if by some magic power we could transform ourselves into the past we think of as heroic, would we not in the next moment pray to be re-transformed into our own selves, living in our own time, nor find it dull by comparison?

History is not a catalogue of names and it is not a chronological arrangement of dates. Nor is it even a mere record of events. Names and dates and events belong to history, but history itself is something more. The whys and the wherefores, the causes and the effects, the antecedents and the consequences are of much more importance. The aim and the purpose in this history is to reflect and to reproduce as far as that is possible to do, the lives of the people who have lived in Iowa and to make a record of those things which have either a curious human interest or a permanent human value.

The writer realizes that he is omitting many of the things that other writers of other histories have deemed important and to which they have given much space in their books. He is not burdening these pages with many names or dates. It does not matter much to him, because he believes it does not matter much to others, who was elected to this or that office in this or that year. Today there is hardly one in a thousand who knows the names of the present state officers, and so why should they care who held offices eighty years ago? Not even the lawyers know what laws have been enacted unless they look them up in the books. Such things may be facts, but facts do not make history, though there can be no history without facts.

But this does not mean that the things omitted have no

values. They may have many values. The records of them should be kept, and that in all their details—but they should be kept in their proper places. They simply do not fall within the scope or the purpose of this particular history. There are many kinds of history that may and that ought to be written. One may write a history of legislation, of farming, of banking, of taxation, of road making, or of factory building. But this is a general history for the general reader and the general reader is the average man who wants to know something about Iowa but who does not care to know everything in detail.

And while avoiding mere moralization and philosophies, yet it should be one of the purposes of all history to make the past serve the present and the future. Each generation must live its own life and serve its own ends; must make, as it will make, its own mistakes and learn its own lessons as it seldom learns them, but it would be human hopelessness if each generation could not glean something from the generation that preceded it and from all the generations that have lived in this earth of ours. The accumulations and the accretions from one generation to another, and from one age to another, may be small, yet is it not by these infinitesimal quantities that progress is marked and mankind advanced? If each generation had to begin all over again would not all efforts be futile, and if none could take thought to better himself and his fellows out of the experiences of others, what better would men be than birds that build their nests in trees, or animals that burrow in the ground, the same yesterday, today, and forever?

But also, as we grow older even if not wiser, men learn to know and to realize that progress is not all, nor is it always made by the sudden and the spectacular scaling of some mountain peak, though it be achieved and accomplished with the cries of Eureka or Excelsior, but rather that it is made little by little and most often along the well beaten paths that others have trod before them. The mountain peaks of human desire and aspiration forever tower over us and above us. Men travel around them horizontally, not up perpendicularly, and they may be and must be satisfied if each encirclement finds them a little higher up than they were when they passed that way before. And as it is with men, even so it is with nations, which are only organized aggregations of men. The circuits of the nations are wider and the mountains to be scaled are higher, but the processes are very much the same. Men build states and they create nations, and they mend them and they break them. When one reads history it seems men are forever doing over again what others did before them, sometimes with a little added intelligence and sometimes with only greater stupidity. As no ultimate solution of their problems seems possible, so there will be no end of efforts and, let it be hoped, no end of development. And as there is no perfection in this earth, so there is no end of human service.

The men and women who came to Iowa in what is here a long ago, but which is really only one of the yesterdays of the world, thought to do in a new land what they had not been able to do in an older. They hoped and worked. They dreamed and they were disillusioned. They succeeded and they failed. The things they did one year they undid in the next. The laws they enacted today they repealed tomorrow. Many of the foundations they laid in hope they tore out in despair. They built and they rebuilt—their houses and their government alike. Their work was experimental and it was transitory. That is the human way. Perhaps it is the divine way also. With all the accumulated experiences that have been recorded and moralized over, no one has yet been wise enough to chart a perfect way or to steer a perfect course into the port of human welfare and happiness.

But what the men and the women of the past did here, and what they tried to do here, is worth writing about and may it be worth reading about in these pages. Iowa was not made rich or great or proud in a day. The lines of those who have labored in this field are long. Each one in those lines did something and each one left something of himself. The living owe a debt to the dead, and it may be the dead have a message for the living. If not, the living still owe a debt and a tribute of gratitude to the departed.

# PART V

## The Remaking of the State

(1854-1859)

# CHAPTER XLIV

## Iowa Becomes a National Factor

In order to understand what is about to happen in both the state and the nation we must for a few moments look back in American history. Iowa from now on is to be a national factor and, for a few years at least, national questions are to affect the course of her history more than local ones.

To begin with, those who framed the constitution of the United States restricted the area of slavery and believed in its gradual extinction. But such hopes had not been realized. Industrial inventions like the cotton gin had made slave labor immensely profitable and, as a result, slave holders sought to carry their institution into the new territories. By the Ordinance of 1787, slavery was excluded from the Northwest Territory out of which the states of Ohio, Indiana, Illinois, Michigan, and Wisconsin were carved, but no such restrictions were placed on the territory acquired from France. The slave holders who could not cross the Ohio were free to take their human property across the Mississippi. They appropriated Louisiana, Arkansas, and Missouri, but the last of these appropriations brought on a bitter debate in congress in the course of which rebellion and even secession were suggested. Henry Clay, then near the zenith of his power, came forward with the first of a series of great compromises the effect of which was not to settle the differences between the two factions, but to postpone such a settlement. The Missouri Compromise, as it is called, admitted the state of Missouri with slavery, but prohibited slavery thereafter in all other territory lying north of the parallel of latitude thirty-six degrees and thirty minutes, which corresponds with the southern boundary of Missouri. This compromise bears the date of February twenty-eighth, 1821.

A prolonged peace followed this settlement. The states of Missouri, Arkansas, and Louisiana, all set up out of the territory of the Louisiana Purchase, offered the slave owners ample room for the expansion of their institution. But the hatred of slavery did not die out in the hearts of men. In the presidential campaign of 1844 James K. Polk defeated Henry Clay for president by carrying the states of New York and Pennsylvania "by a handful of votes."

Then came the Mexican War and its resulting additions to slave territory. In 1848 David Wilmot, a free soil Democrat from the state of Pennsylvania, moved an amendment to an appropriation bill to the effect "that as an express and fundamental condition to the acquisition of any territory from the republic of Mexico by the United States . . . neither slavery nor involuntary servitude shall ever exist in any part of the said territory." The amendment brought forth prolonged and bitter debate. Abraham Lincoln, who was at that time a congressman from the state of Illinois, afterwards said that he had voted for the proviso "in forty different ways." But the congressmen from Iowa voted against it. They were attacked at home for doing so, but they were nevertheless reelected. The proviso was easily defeated. Out of these conditions the Free Soil party was born, which polled enough votes in the presidential election of 1848 with Martin Van Buren as its candidate for president to defeat Lewis Cass and elect General Taylor, the Whig candidate.

In the next year, 1849, California, a part of the territory acquired in the Mexican War, applied for admission as a state. This brought forth another bitter slavery debate. Once more Henry Clay came forward as the peace maker. The result was the Compromise of 1850. California was admitted without slavery. Utah and Arizona were organized as territories with no restrictions as to slavery. As a sop to the contending factions, the sale of slaves in the District of Columbia, under the shadows of the national capitol, was prohibited, and the capture and return of fugitive slaves in free territory was legalized. The latter provision became known as the fugitive slave law. With something to please everyone, the compromise still solved nothing. But for a time it was regarded as another finality. The people wanted peace on the vexed issue. In 1852 the Free Soil party almost disappeared.

But the fugitive slave law proved to be the fly in the sweet ointment of compromised peace. It could not be enforced, or at least its enforcement in the free states was violently resisted. In many northern states this national law was outlawed by public sentiment. The famous Underground Railways were organized. These were routes through free states leading from slavery to freedom in Canada. Iowa had its share of such routes, and men of the highest position acted as conductors for slaves who ran away from their masters. To make matters worse, federal marshals were empowered by congress to enter free states to seize slaves. Many men, tired of compromising, became abolitionists. They believed in abolishing slavery altogether and forever.

And then Iowa entered into the great national debates in Washington. When congress met in December of 1853, President Pierce congratulated the country on its "repose and security." Everything was quiet on the Potomac, on the Mississippi, and on the Rio Grande. But it was only a surface manifest of peace. With the organization of congress, Senator Dodge of Iowa was advanced to the chairmanship of the committee on public lands. He was entitled to that position. He had lived on the public domain in the west. He was an advocate of homestead rights and of preëmptions for which the settlers were then clamoring. On the fourteenth of December he introduced a bill for the organization of Nebraska as a territory, including what is now the state of Kansas. The Nebraska bill was another Pandora box of evils. In the course of congressional business the bill was referred to the committee on territories of which Stephen A. Douglas of Illinois, was chairman. On the twenty-third of January, Douglas offered a substitute for the bill, which Dodge accepted, and which became known as the Kansas-Nebraska bill. It divided Nebraska Territory into two parts, named Kansas and Nebraska. In composing this bill Senator Douglas assumed that the Compromise of 1850 had repealed the Missouri Compromise in so far as it prohibited slavery north of thirty-six thirty. The question of slavery in the proposed territories was therefore to be left to the determination of the settlers. This became the famous doctrine of squatter sovereignty. It was the modern doctrine of self determination. The country was at once thrown into a new uproar. The peace proclaimed by President Pierce vanished.

Senator Dodge not only accepted the substitute for his own bill, but he espoused it openly and actively. Senator Jones, his Iowa colleague, who was a member of the committee of which Douglas was chairman, did likewise. In defense of squatter sovereignty, Senator Dodge made one of his most notable speeches during the prolonged debates in congress. He defended the new sovereignty with all the ability he possessed. To those who sneered at it he replied that the people of the west had long practiced it. They had defined and determined their own rights. He cited his father, Henry Dodge, then a senator from Wisconsin, as one who had upheld and defended the rights of the settlers. He insisted that it was the right of the settlers in the territories to say whether they should live with slavery or without it. He himself believed, as he hoped, that they would choose to be free, but that was for them to determine, not for congress. In the course of his speech he paid his respects to the abolitionists in bitter terms. He called them "intolerant, proscriptive, and bigoted." They were the great trouble makers in the land. In closing his address he said that he believed that if anything of him were to survive in the memories of the people, it would be the part he was taking in the advocacy of this bill.

The protracted debates did not end until the third of March, the last day of congress. It was eleven o'clock at night when Senator Douglas arose to make the closing speech in favor of the measure. He spoke for five hours in fervent advocacy of it. He kept the tired senators awake with his eloquence. In the absence of the vice-president, Senator Dodge of Iowa presided over that momentous session of the senate. It was five o'clock of the morning of March fourth, 1854, when the vote on the Kansas-Nebraska bill was recorded. Thirty-seven senators voted for it and only fourteen against it. Among the former were Augustus C. Dodge and George W. Jones of Iowa. But Henry Dodge, the senator from Wisconsin, had not been swayed by the eloquence of his son, and voted against the bill. The shouts of slavery triumphant filled the morning air of the national capital. "They celebrate a present victory," said Senator Chase to Senator Sumner, as they wended homeward, "but those echoes which they awake will never rest until slavery itself shall die."

The new state of Iowa had disappointed the friends of freedom in the nation. Horace Greeley in the New York *Tribune* wrote bitterly: "What gain had freedom from the admission of Iowa into the Union? . . . . Are Alabama and Mississippi more devoted to the despotic ideas of American pan-slavism?"[1] And Von Holst set it down that Iowa was "a veritable hotbed of dough faces."[2]

But Senator Dodge of Iowa gloried in what they had done. He boasted that Iowa was "the only free state which never for a moment gave way to the Wilmot Proviso." He also boasted that "My colleague and I voted for every one of the compromise measures, including the fugitive slave law, the late Senator Sturgeon of Pennsylvania and ourselves being the only three senators from the entire non-slave holding section of the United States who voted for it."[3] But in Iowa the senator's boastings were to find no echoes. There the stage had already been set for a fight to a finish on these issues.

[1] *New York Tribune*, March 29, 1854.

[2] Von Holst's *The Constitutional and Political History of the United States*, Vol. V, p. 278.

[3] Quoted in Salter's *Life of James W. Grimes*, p. 114.

# CHAPTER XLV

## A Political Revolution in Iowa

There was much indignation in Iowa when it became known that the two senators had voted for the Kansas-Nebraska bill. It was moral indignation that soon found political expression. The provincial indifference and even lethargy which had been somewhat habitual was swept away. There was a new birth of public sentiment. The two senators were denounced. And yet it cannot be said that they had misrepresented those who had elected them. If they had failed in anything, it was in not keeping abreast with the tremendous changes that had been and were still taking place in Iowa, largely due to the new immigration.

The right man for the time had already been found and had already been nominated by the Whigs for governor. He was James W. Grimes of Burlington. He was favorably identified with the public life of the state. Born on a New Hampshire farm in 1816, he had been reared and nurtured in the best New England surroundings and traditions. He was educated at Dartmouth. In 1836, before he was of age, he came to Iowa Territory to be admitted to the bar as a lawyer. He attracted immediate attention in Burlington, then the capital, for he was a superior man, physically, mentally, and morally. He stood for things which all good men coveted. Two years after his arrival he was solicitor of Burlington and in the same year he was elected to the First Territorial Legislature, in which he served as chairman of the judiciary committee. He served also in the sixth legislature and he was tendered the nomination for congress before he was old enough to qualify for such service. He served in the Fourth General Assembly of the new state. He was listed as a farmer, since he devoted much time to horticulture and stock breeding along scientific lines. But he was the leading lawyer of the state. Mr. Grimes received and accepted the nomination at about the time that Senator Dodge was defending squatter sovereignty in the United States senate. The Democrats nominated Curtis Bates of Polk County, as their candidate for governor. He was a lawyer by profession and occasionally an editor. He had helped to make the constitutions of 1844 and 1846. He was saturated with their doctrines. He was a forceful speaker and he continued to believe in the invincibility of his party and its doctrines. It was said of him that he was over-confident.

Mr. Grimes, on the contrary, believed that he had only a fighting chance to win the election. He realized that success depended on himself. The Whigs had won minor elections, but no state victories. They were not even united. There were Seward Whigs who wanted to fight slavery anywhere and at any time, and there were Silver Gray Whigs who wanted to let the bothersome question of slavery alone. The doctrine of squatter sovereignty, however, seemed to unite them. In their platform they denounced it as a "proposition totally unreasonable and absurd on its face, conceived in bad faith and promoted by an ignoble and most unworthy ambition for party and personal preferment." For once the party had dared to speak bravely, for it had found a brave leader. On state issues the platform was just as definite, the basic plank being for the revision of the already obsolete constitution, a document that fitted the young and growing state like a suit of grave clothes.

There were corresponding divisions in the Democratic party. Those who were for slavery out and out were called hunkers. Some of them were free soilers who were opposed to the extension of slavery. On state issues they were opposed to the revision of the constitution. On this issue they lost the votes of many business men who felt the need of banks and other corporations for the development of the state. It was to these business men, and the free soilers, that Mr. Grimes looked for the votes necessary to convert a minority into a majority.

Finding it necessary to be absent from the state, Mr. Grimes issued an address to the people that must still be regarded as a notable and historic document. It has the charm of scholarship and the potentiality of popularity. He discussed state issues boldly. Banks, schools, internal improvements, homestead laws under which foreign-born settlers should have the same rights as those native born, all these things he presented lucidly and convincingly. But it is significant that he devoted two-thirds of the address to the issue of slavery as it was then presented. He stood upon the inviolability of the Missouri Compromise, and he declared that "with the blessing of God" he would "war and war continually against the abandonment to slavery of a single foot of soil now consecrated to freedom." He was not, however, an abolitionist. He was still "content that the slave-holders of the south" should "possess their slaves."

Late in May Mr. Grimes found himself free to devote his time to the campaign. He entered upon a speaking tour that he carried on until the eve of the election. He took his own conveyance and traveled from east to west and from south to north, speaking wherever he could gather the people to hear him, and they heard him gladly for he brought them eloquence of speech and courage of utterance. Iowa had never before heard either that kind of a man or that kind of a doctrine. "It is monstrous hard work that I have undertaken," he wrote to Mrs. Grimes in one of his many letters to her—and her letters that pursued him all over the state were a constant inspiration to him.[1] Confidence in his victory he soon acquired. He himself felt that he was making an impression on the minds and hearts of the people. To Mrs. Grimes he became even boastful. In one of his letters he wrote that he felt that he had "already done more good to the cause of humanity and liberal ideas than has ever been done by all the speeches made in the state, and by many sermons." He talked the same things in all places, in settlements that were "entirely southern," of which there were

[1] This and other quotations from Grimes's letters are taken from Salter's *Life of James W. Grimes.*

many in Iowa, and in abolition communities, of which there were not many. The candor, the sincerity, and the earnestness of the man aroused the people's confidence in him.

But it had a contrary effect on many politicians, those who are habitually afraid of the truth, and who habitually think that political campaigns should be made to deceive the people, rather than to enlighten them. The Burlington *Hawk-Eye*, then the leading Whig paper of the state, partially deserted him. It believed that he was going too far in his opposition to slavery. One of his associates on the state ticket withdrew in fear, if not in disgust, while Mr. Grimes himself spoke of the congressional candidates of his own party as so many "dead weights" in the campaign. They feared that Mr. Grimes would carry them down to defeat. But by so much as he dared to speak the truth he grew strong in that most historic campaign.

The election that year was held on the third of August. When the votes were counted Mr. Grimes had a majority of 2,486, out of a total of 43,594 votes. But it was a personal victory, largely. The Democrats elected all their other state candidates, with one exception. For the general assembly they elected a majority in the senate, but the Whigs had a large majority in the lower house, giving them a majority of ten on joint ballot, thus assuring the election of a Whig United States senator and Whig judges of the supreme court.

To Senator Dodge more than to Curtis Bates, the defeated candidate for governor, it was a staggering blow politically. It had taken the people of Iowa just five months to vote him out of his high office, after making his defense of squatter sovereignty. President Pierce was not unmindful of his services, and as soon as his term expired sent him as minister to Spain, an office that the retiring senator gladly accepted. There was no consolation left for him in Iowa.

His victory made Mr. Grimes a man of national significance. From Ohio, Salmon P. Chase wrote him that it was "the best battle for freedom yet fought." He said that the nation would look to Iowa for "the suggestions which shall shape the new movement." The "dough faces" of Iowa had suddenly become the national leaders! The Burlington *Hawk-Eye* lost its timidity and had the good grace to suggest that Mr. Grimes was fit to be considered as a candidate for the presidency of the United States. He might have made himself such a factor, but he was in no sense an office seeker.

There was an immediate movement to send the victor to the United States senate. Many said he had earned such an election and many more believed that he could serve best in the senate. These suggestions must have held out some temptations to him, for in Washington he would meet men of his own intellectual caliber. But whatever the temptations may have been he put them all aside. He said that he had sought the governorship in good faith and that he had been elected to carry out the many reforms that were needed. On the ninth of December, when he was inducted into the office of governor, he delivered another memorable address, virtually outlining the policies of the new party which was about to be created to combat the spread of slavery.

When the general assembly met, James Harlan was elected to the United States senate, on the fifth of January, 1855. It was the first national aspect of Mr. Grimes's victory. Harlan was a more radical opponent of slavery than Mr. Grimes; he was even tainted with abolitionism. The new senator was a native of Illinois, born August twenty-sixth, 1820. He was reared in Indiana and educated in Asbury University at Greencastle. He came to Iowa in 1846 as a tentative educator. He attracted first political attention when he was twice elected state superintendent of instruction and as often cheated out of the office by the politicians. After those defeats he went to Mount Pleasant as the head of Wesleyan University.

Within a year Iowa had developed and elected to office two men who were destined to become great national leaders, James W. Grimes and James Harlan.

George W. Jones

Augustus C. Dodge

James W. Grimes

James Harlan

# CHAPTER XLVI

## How the State was Re-made

When James W. Grimes assumed the office of governor in 1854, he had in mind a definite program of progressive legislation. Iowa had ceased to be a series of frontier settlements with provincial wants and aspirations; she had become a state with new industrial and economic needs. He was hampered in the senate where the Democrats held a majority of one. "The locofocos do not intend that anything shall be done this session," he wrote on the seventh of January, 1855, "and imagine that they will hold the Whigs and anti-Nebraska men responsible for the failure to do the necessary legislation."[1] In that juncture it was one of the Democrats, William F. Coolbaugh, a senator from Burlington, who solved the riddle. He was a business man of the highest type. He believed in the business policies of the new governor, even if he did not endorse his political views. He placed business above politics, and the state above his party. He held the balance of power in the senate, and he used that power for the good of the state. He made Governor Grimes's program possible, and the state is still indebted to him for it.[2]

The revision of the constitution, or rather the making of a new constitution for the state, was the basic fact in the new movement. Until that was done the corporation and banking laws that were needed could not be passed. But it required time to revise the constitution. The people, however, were

[1] See Salter's *Life of James W. Grimes*, p. 65. According to Mr. Grimes there were only ten real Whigs in the general assembly; "the other forty-five are known as anti-Nebraska men, Republicans, and woolly-heads." The locofocos were Democrats.

[2] Peter A. Dey, in *Annals of Iowa*, Third Series, Vol. VIII, p. 83. Mr. Dey, who then lived in Iowa City, recalls that Governor Grimes and Mr. Coolbaugh occupied the same room in what was then the Clinton House.

ready and eager to do it. When the question was submitted to them in 1856, they gave a majority of 18,628 in its favor. In December of that year thirty-two delegates to a constitutional convention were elected, and these delegates met at Iowa City on the nineteenth of January, 1857, to frame what is still the constitution of the state.[2a] When a law creating a state bank, with branches in the principal centers, was submitted in 1858, only 3,697 votes were cast against it, and 41,588 votes for it, showing how completely the people had outgrown the old notions. The best men in the state were summoned to directorships in these banks. The paper money which was issued circulated at par and when the banks went out of business under the operations of the national banking laws of the Civil War, they met all their obligations in full.

With the new constitution came a new capital. As the territory had outgrown Burlington in 1839, so the state had outgrown Iowa City in 1855. The trend of population had been up the Des Moines River. On the twenty-fifth of January, 1855, a law was passed designating the city of Des Moines as the capital. The site for the state house was selected by three commissioners. The sightly hill on the east side of the river seemed so far away from the village which lay nestled in the fork of the Raccoon that many protests were made against the location, and it was even charged that the commissioners had been under some undue influences, but nothing came of the protests. The site was not changed. A temporary state house was erected, three stories in height and of brick. In the autumn and early winter of 1857 the state government was transferred from the banks of the Iowa to the banks of the Des Moines. There were no railroads at that time west of Iowa City and so the state's property was carried in wagons and sleds, the safe of the treasury department, though it was at that time nearly empty, requiring ten yoke of oxen to draw it over the snow. Governor Grimes followed the capital to Des Moines, but only to deliver his valedictory address.

[2a] Under section 3, article X, the revision of the constitution has been voted on "in each tenth year," since 1870. In 1920 for the first time it was answered affirmatively, providing for such revision.

To compensate Iowa City for its loss, it was made the permanent seat of the State University, and the old capitol building, which was erected in 1840, was turned over to the uses of learning. Iowa City ceased to be the state capital, but it became the educational center of the state. The loss was not greater than the gain. The State University needed Iowa City as much as the city needed the university, which at that time was literally scattered over the state and not doing effective work anywhere. Unfortunately, the influence of Governor Grimes was not helpful to the school. State universities were western conceptions, and Mr. Grimes was an eastern man. He believed in the denominational colleges which were then struggling for a mere existence. He believed that they "should be encouraged and not depressed." He thought they would be sufficient for all "who wish to enter the professions of law, physics and divinity," but the state, he said in his first inaugural address, has a greater need of "educated farmers and mechanics, engineers, architects, chemists, metallurgists and geologists," and, therefore, he recommended that the resources of the university should be used to develop a "practical polytechnic school," instead of a scholastic or professional one.

Fortunately, his ideas in this matter did not prevail. But acting, perhaps, on his suggestions, R. A. Richardson, a member of the lower house from Fayette County, introduced a bill for the creation of an industrial college. It was defeated on its first appearance, but in 1858 the idea was revived and out of it the college at Ames was born. The story reads like a fairy tale. On a winter's night three young men, of whom Richardson was one, and Benjamin F. Gue of Scott County, and Ed. Wright of Cedar County, the other two, met in a miserable lodging room. All three were "pioneer prairie farmers." They had come to Iowa in the same year, 1852. They were abolitionists, prohibitionists, and liberals in religion. They talked over the hardships of farming in those primitive days. They wished for something better for others, for the children of the farms. Why could not education be made to serve agriculture also? Lighten its labors and increase its production through scientific knowledge and methods? Before they went to bed they formulated a bill for the creation of an agricultural and mechanical college, and pledged themselves to see it through. When they introduced their bill — it was the next day — it was referred to a committee that reported it back for indefinite postponement. There were no funds for such a chimerical and visionary enterprise! Mr. Gue, acting as spokesman for the trio, protested and threatened to make an appeal to the people — the people at least did not believe in education for the few, but for the many, for the sons of farmers and of mechanics as well as for the sons of the professional classes and the rich! That brought men who had almost sneered at the idea to their senses. The bill was passed with a paltry $10,000 in the way of an appropriation. But that was enough for a beginning. A site in Story County, near the town of Ames, was selected — but it took ten years to build the college, although in the meantime the Morrill Bill was passed in congress and signed by President Lincoln, through which the college received a grant of half a million acres of land, a grant so munificent that an effort was made, under the leadership of ex-Governor Kirkwood, to unite the beginning which had been made at Ames with the university at Iowa City. But the school at Ames survived.

On the subject of common schools, Governor Grimes thought more clearly than he did on higher education. He made what he called an adequate common school system a part of his state program. He held the common school to be the most essential of all. He said it was cheaper to build school houses out of taxes than it was to build asylums and poor houses. He insisted that property must be made to pay for its own protection against crime and ignorance. Schools must be supported not out of rates paid by parents and guardians, but out of taxes paid by property. The working out of the adequate system he had in mind was entrusted to a commission of three men, Horace Mann of Ohio, Amos Dean of Iowa City, and the attorney general of the state as legal adviser. The connection of Mr. Mann with this work was merely nominal, most of the credit belongs to Amos Dean.[3] But as a matter of fact, also,

[3] Parvin's *History of the Early Schools and Education in Iowa*, 1830-59.

no perfected system was devised at that time. The one vital idea that came out of the movement was that schools should be provided for all children, and that they should be supported out of taxes.

The moral leaven in the new movement took the form of a prohibitory liquor law which was modeled on the Maine law. The attempts to regulate the evils of drinking had all proved failures. In the campaign of 1854 both political parties gave modified support to prohibitory legislation. The bill was introduced by Amos Witter of Scott County. Only eight votes were cast against it in the upper house and only eleven in the lower, and the people approved it by a majority of 2,910. When the law was considered in the supreme court, two justices sustained its validity, but one, Justice George G. Wright, dissented on the ground that it had been invalidated by its submission to the people, the people constituting no constitutional part of the legislative machinery of the state.

The law, which went into effect in 1855, soon became unpopular, and it was also hard to enforce. To allay the discontent and more especially to meet the views of the Germans, who were then coming into the state in large numbers, and not to retard what was then considered a desirable immigration, the law was modified in 1857, and again in 1858, so that it permitted "the manufacture of beer, cider from apples or wine from grapes, currants, or other fruits grown in this state." These changes were known as the wine and beer clauses. But even in that form the law was not popular, and in their next platform the Democrats said that it had "vexed and harassed the citizens, burdened the counties with expense and litigation, and proved wholly useless in the suppression of intemperance." But the law was permitted to remain on the statute books, nowhere and at no time wholly enforced, and all the time in many places wholly ignored for years.

But in many ways the finest thing in the re-making of Iowa under Governor Grimes was the creation of institutions for the care of defectives. Up to that time not even the insane had been adequately provided for. If violent, such unfortunates were confined in county jails, and if harmless, they were permitted to roam at large. The governor made the building of the first asylum for the insane, at Mt. Pleasant, his personal care and concern. But so obtuse to these finer things were many of the politicians of that time that the taxes levied for them were bitterly assailed and those who favored them had all manner of wrongful motives attributed to them. The blind, the deaf, the dumb, and the feeble-minded also shared in the forward movement.

A mere enumeration of the things commenced under Governor Grimes during his three years in office can leave no doubt that he was the creator of modern Iowa. Business and politics, education and the humanities, all received from his administration a new stamp and a new impetus. His was the most comprehensive and creative mind of that period in Iowa, and his superiority was later recognized nationally. Nor does all of his influence appear in the records. It has been said of him by one who knew him well, and who himself had the fineness of intellect to understand him, that Mr. Grimes "labored for results, not for distinction."[4] While he was a statesman he was also a politician. He knew the influential men of his party in every county of the state. He corresponded with them, and while asking them for their opinions he was at the same time imbuing them with his own. He helped to shape their opinions and he furnished them with ideas. His invisible mental and moral influence was upon every new law and upon the new constitution — he sought none of the credit for himself; he coveted it all for the good of the state and the welfare of the people. The three years during which he was governor have no parallel in the history of the state in progressive transformations and achievements — and the stamp of James W. Grimes was on every act.

[4] Peter A. Dey in *Annals of Iowa*, Third Series, Vol. VIII, p. 83.

# CHAPTER XLVII

## The Building of the Railroads

Before there were railroads in Iowa the state was covered with a network of stage coach lines. In a directory printed in 1856 the principal routes were listed as follows: Davenport to Council Bluffs, Burlington to Council Bluffs, Burlington to Centerville, Burlington to Keokuk, Davenport to Cedar Rapids, Davenport to Dubuque, Dubuque to Cedar Falls, Dubuque to Iowa City, Cedar Rapids to Cedar Falls, Keokuk to Iowa City, Keokuk to Keosauqua, Bonaparte to Birmingham, Ottumwa to Chariton, Oskaloosa to Council Bluffs, Fairfield to Keosauqua, and Muscatine to Burlington. Over these routes stages were operated with much regularity. Merchandise was transported in wagons over the same routes. Farmers hauled their products to the markets, generally to the nearest river points. Hogs were for a time driven from southwestern Iowa to St. Joseph on the Missouri, and later from northwestern Iowa to Yankton on the same river. Fifteen miles was a day's journey for hogs on the hoof and food had to be provided for them at designated stations on the route.

From very early time, the hopes of the settlers were centered on railroads. The first legislature in which Iowa participated, the one held at Belmont in 1836, chartered a road from that town to Dubuque — and double tracked it on paper. In the First Legislative Assembly of the Territory of Iowa, James W. Grimes introduced a memorial to congress for a land grant to aid in the building of a railroad. Even at that time John Plumbe, Jr., at Dubuque was dreaming of a trans-continental road. In the same city, Lucius H. Langworthy worked out a plan for a road to Keokuk, via Iowa City, traversing what was then the settled part of the state. His plans included wooden rails faced with iron, and he estimated that such a road could be built for $10,000 a mile. In 1848 he was made president of a board of directors to build his proposed road. In 1849 upon a report of its engineers the general assembly of the state memorialized congress for a land grant to build it,[1] and two years later the general assembly voted for it the right of way.[2]

But the growth of Chicago as a railroad center in the early fifties upset for a time all north and south plans. Men began to realize that the traffic of Iowa would be eastward and not southward. To make a connection with a Chicago road then building to the Mississippi, the Davenport & Iowa City Railroad Company was organized at Iowa City in 1850, October fourteenth, with James P. Carlton as president. That was the beginning of the first realized railroad in Iowa.[3] In the next year a survey of this line was made, and in 1853 the data and prospects were sold to the Mississippi & Missouri River Railroad Company of Chicago, a corporation that bound itself to complete the line to Iowa City by January first, 1856, and to build thereafter branch lines both north and south. On these stipulations bonds were voted and stock subscribed. Work on this line was commenced at once. Peter A. Dey who had made the Illinois surveys for the company, came to Iowa to do a similar work on this side of the river. His principal assistant was a young engineer named Grenville M. Dodge, who was destined to win many distinctions in the new state, while Mr. Dey, no less prominent in public life, became a man of many services and an exemplar of the state's best citizenship. The first railroad thus brought to Iowa two of its finest men.

In 1854 the first locomotive engine was ferried across the river at Davenport, where thousands went to view it as one of the curiosities of the times. By hard work, in which the people of Iowa City assisted, the road was completed on the date specified, January 1, 1856, and the first train from Chicago entered the Iowa capital on the third of January. It

1 *Laws of Iowa*, Second General Assembly, p. 171.

2 *Laws of Iowa*, Third General Assembly, p. 129.

3 Shambaugh's *Iowa City; a Contribution to the Early History of Iowa*, p. 104.

carried many prominent guests, for whom a banquet was given in the capitol building. The usual speeches were made, for another new era had dawned. The road from Davenport to Iowa City was sixty-seven miles long. It was bonded for $14,925 per mile — probably its total cost.[4] But it was far from a completed railroad. It had many steep grades and it curved around many hills. The ties were laid on the frozen ground, and when the spring thaws came, rails and rolling stock sank in the mud, suspending operations.[5]

The building of the first road aroused widespread interest. Every town talked of railroads. Innumerable projects were floated, and many promoters soon appeared on the scene. One of these promoters was a man named H. P. Adams, who came from the east to build the long talked of line from Lyons to Iowa City.[6] He set surveyors to work and he issued proclamations. He invited towns to bid for his favors. So eager were the people to have railroads that they did not stop to examine the promoter's credentials, nor his abilities to perform his contracts. Stock subscriptions were made, subsidies and bonds were voted with alacrity. Adams was a fugitive from justice. A lawyer, who was also a congressman, and who is known in Iowa railroad history as General Ney, came from Pennsylvania to apprehend Adams. But after he had talked with the persuasive promoter, who showed him the kingdoms of graft, the attorney waived his right to arrest him, and he remained as the orator in extraordinary for the promoter's schemes. Ney made speeches that literally talked the money out of the pockets of the people. He told them that while Caesar had crossed the Rubicon to destroy the liberties of Rome, H. P. Adams had crossed the Mississippi to make the Iowa wilderness blossom like the rose. He talked of a suspension bridge across the river a mile long, a bridge from which the locomotives would "laugh" at the steamboats below. Hundreds of men were set to work on the grades and cutting timber for ties. But when all possible subscriptions and bonds had been converted into cash or negotiable paper,

[4] Larrabee's *The Railroad Question*, p. 320.

[5] Wm. J. Haddock's *The Prairies of Iowa*, p. 14.

[6] Oral relation by Peter A. Dey to the author.

the promoters decamped, leaving unpaid debts, stranded workmen, and indignant settlers. It was Iowa's first experience on the dark side of railroad promotions.

But swindlers were not the only ones who discouraged railroad building. There were men who thought that they could prove that they could not be successfully operated in Iowa. Some argued that their operation would be fraught with dangers. Had not a bridge in Illinois gone down under the weight of a train, killing and injuring many? It did not occur to them that the remedy was to make bridges stronger, not to stop railroad building. And was it not dangerous to run trains at high speed through towns and over country crossings? How could collisions be avoided? To meet this objection, Governor Grimes proposed that the speed of trains should be regulated not only through towns, but over country crossings.

But it remained for a Muscatine lawyer to evolve the strangest of all objections to railroads. He admitted that railroads might be successfully operated in some places, but Iowa was not one of them.[7] This state, in his opinion, was destined to be an agricultural one, and the products of the farms could not be carried on railroads. "Livestock," he said, "cannot be taken to an eastern market because the distance is too great to carry them on cars, and flour cannot be carried such a distance on railroads without shaking the barrels to pieces, unless the barrels are strong and heavy as pork barrels, and that would be so expensive as to make it unprofitable." How ridiculous such arguments seem now, but they must have seemed less so then, for in those days teamsters and stage coach men opposed the building of railroads on the ground that it would take the bread out of their mouths, and the farmers would be deprived of their markets for horses! How often since the fate and the doom of the horse have been sounded!

But neither swindlers nor pessimists could stop the progress of the railroads. The Iowa City road was soon augmented by a branch line to Muscatine. On January twenty-sixth, 1856,

[7] Hiram Price in *Annals of Iowa*, Third Series, Vol. I, p. 592.

a line was projected from Clinton to the Missouri River by way of Cedar Rapids. Work was at once commenced on it, being completed to De Witt in 1858 and to Cedar Rapids in 1859, a distance of about eighty-three miles. This road is remarkable because it was constructed without legislative aid or local subsidies.[8] Railroads were profitable too, it was soon demonstrated. In the first six months of its operation the Davenport-Iowa City line showed earnings of $184,193, or $2,749 per mile, or at the rate of $5,500 per mile a year.[9]

But the people were determined not to wait the building of roads by corporate capital or private enterprise. They had plenty of land and they were willing to exchange it for roads. The land belonged to the government and they were generous with it. In response to memorials and petitions and largely through the persistent efforts of a congressman, James Thorington, by an act approved on the fifteenth of May, congress made four land grants to the state of Iowa to be used for the building of railroads. Governor Grimes was at once urged to convene the Fifth General Assembly in extraordinary session to re-grant these lands to corporations to build the roads, which he did. The legislature was convened on July second and in a short session made four re-grants for as many railroads across the state from east to west, one from Burlington to a point on the Missouri River, opposite the mouth of the Platte; one from Davenport to Council Bluffs by way of Iowa City and Fort Des Moines; one from Lyons to Maquoketa and thence to the Missouri as nearly as practicable on the forty-second parallel, and one from Dubuque to Sioux City. To each of these lines was given the alternate sections of land designated by odd numbers lying within six miles of the roads. For lands already taken by settlers the companies were to be indemnified. These grants were equivalent in the aggregate to a strip twenty-four miles wide from the Mississippi to the Missouri. To compensate the government, the price of the remaining lands was advanced from $1.25 to $2.50 an acre. It was a gift of 3,840 acres for each mile of road to be built

[8] Larrabee's *The Railroad Question*, p. 328.

[9] *Ibid.*, p. 328.

and at the government's fixed price of $2.50 an acre it amounted in money to $9,600 a mile. This stupendous transaction "occupied the attention of the general assembly less than ten days, and so far as known, no member pecuniarily profited or attempted to profit by its action." [10]

But munificent as these gifts were, the companies did not make haste in the building of the roads. They hesitated long, coveting the lands, but afraid that the lines could not be operated at a profit. They built no faster than settlements were made, and often they did not keep pace with them. The panic of 1857 also hampered their operations. And after the panic came the Civil War. In consequence the first of the four railroads did not reach the Missouri River until 1867. In 1859 less than five hundred miles of railroads were in operation in the state, credited as follows: The Des Moines Valley line, forty miles; Keokuk and Mt. Pleasant, thirty miles; Burlington and Missouri River, seventy-five miles; Muscatine and Oskaloosa, forty miles; Muscatine and Tipton, thirteen miles; Davenport and Iowa City, sixty-seven miles; Dubuque and Pacific, forty-two miles; and Dubuque and Western, thirty-five miles.[11]

[10] Peter A. Dey in *Annals of Iowa*, Third Series, Vol. VII, p. 86.

[11] *Annals of Iowa*, Third Series, Vol. III, p. 600.

# CHAPTER XLVIII

## A New Element and a New Frontier

The issues over which the Civil War was fought began to take definite form during the administration of Governor Grimes. It was he who prepared the state to do her part to maintain the union of the states and to rid the nation of slavery. But before we proceed to consider the development of those issues, we must make another survey of the state, so that we may know what Iowa was before the Civil War, and what were the social and economic conditions of her people, both of which were greatly affected by the immigration of the decade by which the population of the state was trebled from 1850 to 1860.

The treaties made with the Sioux Indians in 1851 and 1852, and the final division of the state into counties as they now exist, in 1851, threw the whole state open for settlers. But for many years the movement of population into the northern and northwestern counties was retarded. It was still a faraway country which the Sioux had only nominally vacated.

But there was ample room for the new comers in the older parts of the state. In truth, the first settlers had left untouched the best land resources of the state. They made their farms as they built their towns, largely along the rivers. They had shunned the open and the upland prairies, deeming them not only unfitted for human habitations, but for cultivation even. It is hard now to comprehend the aversions which they had for such lands. North of Mount Pleasant, the Quaker missionaries who made a tour of the state in 1850 had noted a prairie "twenty miles over" without a human habitation on it. Two years later others found a stretch of such untenanted lands in Linn County, thirty miles from northwest to southeast, lands of unparalleled fertility awaiting only the magic of the plow to convert them into fields of wheat and corn. The earliest settlers were literally "timber folks." Their origin and their traditions all had to do with wooded lands. They were men who believed that where trees would not or did not grow, men could not live and prosper. As farmers these timber men were neither industrious nor enterprising. They cultivated patches rather than farms. They made livings in easy ways, and they were much addicted to hunting and trapping and fishing.[1]

The immigrants who came during the fifties were men and women of a different kind. They came from the hard working and thrifty classes of New England, New York and Pennsylvania, and from trans-Allegheny states where they had become transplanted easterners. They became the "prairie farmers" of Iowa, a distinct element in the population and development of the state. They were the men who gave the final character to Iowa as a state. To them hunting and trapping and fishing were incidental occupations. Those among them who settled in the towns became traders and manufacturers. They did all things diligently and well. We are told that they came "deliberately and intelligently to make homes for themselves and their children on the beautiful prairies of Iowa."[2] On the prairies of Linn County the name of one of the townships perpetuates the fact that many of them came from the far away state of Maine.

There were foreign admixtures in the new immigration, but compared with the whole these were slight. This foreign element was two-thirds either German or Irish, and the Germans were at least twice as numerous as the Irish. An increasing Scandinavian influx also is noticeable. At first these foreigners were addicted to town life, especially in the cities along the Mississippi, but later they became more widely scattered and more distinctly rural. The status of the foreigner for a few years was affected by Know Nothingism, a name given to the doctrines of what was called the American party

[1] F. I. Herriott in *Annals of Iowa*, Third Series, Vol. VIII, p. 186.

[2] Dr. George E. Crawford's recollections of Iowa in the fifties, printed in the Cedar Rapids *Republican*, August 21, 1920.

which had its origin in native fears of foreign influences in America. It was the period of the first enormous tides of immigration. One of the predominant ideas of this party was to exclude immigrants from suffrage until after a residence of twenty or more years. In one of the elections the party was successful in nine states, but its own excesses proved its undoing and the prejudices which it aroused retarded rather than aided the processes of Americanization. In Iowa the movement at no time had much strength for such far-seeing men as Governor Grimes were opposed to it, neither were the foreigners numerous enough in the state to make them a menace to even the most timid Americans.

Nor was the new American immigration wholly homogeneous. There were two rather distinct currents. One came from the Atlantic seaboard states and the other from the trans-Allegheny states. The mental collisions between these two elements are described as often "earnest and amusing." [3] The easterners laid more stress on family connections and traditions, while the westerners made no fetiches of such things. The former talked a great deal of culture, and the latter more of achievements. To the westerners a man was what he did, and to the easterners he did what he was. But these social differences were never serious. The elements were easily blended into one type, but we are assured that "our standpoint is nearer that of the New Englander, developed by liberal surroundings." This was probably due to the fact that the New Englanders, few as they were comparatively with the whole, were more tenacious of their "notions" and were better prepared to promulgate their ideas through their educational systems. It was in the fifties that Iowa ceased to be either southern or nativistically western, and became more like a transplanted east with a New England aspect.

The likeness of the new Iowa to the old east was noticeable in 1854, when a cultured woman came to Iowa to lecture on "temperance and woman's rights,"— where does not the missionary spirit venture? [4] After the manner of the times she wrote a series of letters which were printed in the New

[3] Peter A. Dey, in *Annals of Iowa*, Third Series, Vol. VII, p. 85.

[4] Mrs. Frances D. Gage; see Parker's *Iowa As It Is in 1856*.

York *Tribune*, then a Whig household paper in the west, as "Sketches on Iowa." She was well received by the people. She wrote of them as a "strong, earnest, energetic, right-thinking and right-feeling people." She praised them for recognizing at that early date "all grog shops as nuisances" and for holding "the vendor of ardent spirits liable for his own transgressions;" for their sense of justice in securing the property rights of the wife and making her the joint guardian of her children, and for their humaneness in securing "the homestead to the family" by a claim superior to that of all creditors. To her Iowa was no longer "way out west." She said it was "half past one" here, and she advised eastern merchants not to bring their old goods to Iowa, and "faded belles" no longer to "flatter themselves that last year's fashions will answer." In Oskaloosa she went to hear Mr. Grimes "talk to the dear people." To her "the men looked just like men elsewhere, only they were a little more civil and genteel, and did not make quite so general a spittoon of the court house." When she went to church, "The ladies rustled rich brocades, or flitted in lawns as natural as life." The women wore pretty bonnets beneath which glowed their rosy cheeks and sparkling eyes. "To sum it all up," she declared, "this is the most beautiful country I have ever seen. . ."

And greater genius touched Iowa in the fifties. Fredrika Bremer, the Swedish novelist, sojourned in Keokuk and shook hands with "refined people . . . well-bred and well-dressed ladies and gentlemen, the aristocracy of Keokuk," and liked their "frank and friendly manner."[5] And a little later there lived in the same city a "young man idling about his brother's job printing office . . . setting type a little, making pretense by reading law a little, writing himself down as an 'antiquarian' in a bran-new first directory the ambitious young city ever had, swapping yarns in a drawling way with other fellows" — that was Mark Twain in embryo.[6] He lived at the "old Billings house" and gazed

[5] Bremer's *The Homes of the New World*, Vol. II, pp. 81-83.

[6] Sam M. Clark in *Annals of Iowa*, Third Series, Vol. II, p. 401.

at the Mississippi which he was to immortalize in literature. But the people among whom he sojourned did not know him — neither did he know himself then.

The movement of population into the unsettled portions of the state during this decade was most pronounced up the valley of the Des Moines River — which became one of the factors in determining the location of the final capital. Some followed the Mormon trail, and some penetrated deeper into northeastern Iowa where the Winnebagoes had but recently vacated their lands along the Turkey and the Volga rivers. The first settlers there were largely New Englanders, but later there was a veritable rush of Norwegians. It was in 1854 that the settlements at Waterloo, Fort Dodge and Sioux City took definite form. At that time a line drawn through those three centers had north of it very few white inhabitants, and not many south of it for many miles. They were frontier towns. Fort Dodge, which was a sort of gate way to the country of the Sioux, was abandoned as a fort in 1853, when the garrison was removed to Fort Ridgely, in Minnesota. William Williams, who had been a sutler at the fort, remained in the place and became the virtual founder of the city. The removal of the soldiers was not wholly unprotested, for many feared that the days of Indian troubles were not over, fears that were to be tragically realized later.

The Indians soon found occasion to make trouble. In 1854 a band of Sioux went as far east as the Clear Lake region to attack encampments of Sacs and Foxes who were still lingering in the state. By mistake they killed and scalped a Winnebago, an event that threatened to precipitate an inter-tribal war. The white men also became involved through a minor incident that continues to be remembered as the Grindstone War. A Sioux warrior in pursuit of a gaudy rooster which he coveted for his next meal upset a grindstone belonging to James Dickerson, breaking it. With a piece of the broken stone Dickerson in his turn pursued the Indian and felled him to the ground. It was an injury for which reparations were demanded. Dickerson refused, but his wife settled with the red men for six dollars in money and some quilts. While these disturbances occurred many settlers fled from the country, but the more determined soon rallied and drove out the Indians. Governor Hempstead sent Dubuque militiamen to the scene, but before they could reach it the dangers were over. As soon as Governor Grimes came into office he reiterated the demands on the war department in Washington for protection on the frontier. When no heed was paid to these requests he made Major William Williams at Fort Dodge an executive agent to watch the Indians and to act in an emergency.

From Clear Lake to the Missouri there were still but few settlers in northern Iowa. The most noted character among these, perhaps, was James Dickerson, who was called "Jimmy." He was a true man, fearless and venturesome, honest and hospitable. He had come to Iowa in 1834. When too many settled around him he moved on for he was one who hovered on the frontiers and hated close-up neighbors. His occasional occupation was that of capturing elk and buffalo calves for the markets. He was at Clear Lake as early as 1851 and in the following years probably went as far west as the Des Moines and Little Sioux rivers.

A pioneer of a different kind was Henry Lott, a fellow as despicable as Dickerson was noble. Probably as early as 1846 he was at the mouth of the Boone River carrying on an illicit trade with the Indians. He gathered around him a band of desperadoes who plundered both races. For the theft of some ponies he was driven out of the country by a wandering Sioux chief, named Sidominadota. Lott left his family behind. One of his children, and later his wife, died of neglect, for which he vowed vengeance. In 1853 he returned, passing through Fort Dodge with an ox-wagon in which he carried, among other things, three barrels of whiskey. He established himself in Humboldt County near a creek which still bears his bloody name. He soon came into contact again with Sidominadota, but without being recognized by him. Lott and his son misled the old chief in an elk hunt, waylaid and murdered him. In the night time, disguised as Indians, they went to his lodge and killed all the inmates except a girl who hid herself in the grass and a boy who recovered from the blows under which he had fallen. These children carried the news of the outrage to a band of Indians led by Inkpaduta. The crimes were laid to Lott who saved himself by leaving the country, going, it was believed, to California where he was in due time hanged by a vigilance committee.[7]

In the same year, 1854 — an historic year in Iowa — a man of still another type came to this region, William H. Ingham of New York, a descendant of the Schuylers, an eastern man who had felt the lure of the west — and the more he saw of it the more it allured him.[8] He wanted to see the wilderness of primeval nature. Let us journey with him, briefly. He did not have far to go to reach the open prairies. A few miles east of the present city of Grinnell he stopped at what was called the Travelers' Rest. There he heard about "a preacher and others" who were "about to found a city and a college" on the prairies. If he had waited to meet the preacher, Josiah B. Grinnell, he might have gone no farther, for they were men of like spirit. But he passed on. At the Raccoon Forks he found a small settlement and a large field of ripening grain. He thought it "an ideal site for a town." In Dallas County he found a few squatters on the site of Adel. From there to the Missouri River he encountered no white men. On the river he found Kanesville, still a Mormon town, and below it the trader Peter A. Sarpy. While he tarried with him he saw cowboys ride their ponies pell mell through the store — and saloon. On his return trip, Mr. Ingham struck far northward, crossing the Des Moines River north of Fort Dodge, and then to Cedar Rapids by way of Clear Lake. On the entire journey from Council Bluffs to Clear Lake he "did not see a white habitation," but in many places game was so plentiful, including turkeys, "that it was not even sport to shoot them."

The venturesome explorer was so pleased with the country he had seen that it lured him back in the face of winter, still in 1854. This time he was accompanied by one D. E. Stine.

[7] Gue's *History of Iowa*, Vol. I, p. 291.

[8] *Ten Years on the Iowa Frontier*, an account of William H. Ingham's life in Iowa edited by his son, Harvey Ingham. Unfortunately this valuable booklet is not paged.

On hardy horses they rode from Cedar Rapids to Fort Dodge in five days, with good weather on the journey though it was in November. They were sheltered there in the old Wahkonsa House, so named after a Sioux chief of some note. Still they pressed northward. They found a hunter's cabin in the forks of the river, and four settlers in Humboldt County on the site of what is now Dakota City. Among them were two Germans, Christian Hackman and August Zahlton. Where Algona now stands embowered in beauty of trees and fields, they found two brothers, Asa C. Call and Ambrose A. Call, the former accompanied by his wife — they were spending their honeymoon there. They had reached the place some time in July.

By 1856, however, a new northwestern frontier had been created, with Fort Dodge as a point of radiation. The settlements, small and widely separated, extended up four streams, the two branches of the Des Moines, Lizard Creek and the Little Sioux River. George Granger's settlement was in Emmet County near the state line and beyond him was Springfield in Minnesota. In Palo Alto County, West Bend came into being in 1854, and in 1856 seven families from Illinois formed the "Irish Colony" in the same county which survives as Emmetsburg. In the valley of the Little Sioux apostate Mormons from Kanesville founded Smithland in Woodbury County in 1851. There were settlements at Pilot Rock and Milford in Cherokee County, at Sioux Rapids in Buena Vista, and at Peterson and Gillett's Grove in Clay.

In July, 1856, the first settlers reached the lakes in Dickinson County. They were Rowland Gardner and his son-in-law, Harvey Luce, and their families, nine persons in all. They built a cabin on the southeast shore of West Okoboji lake. Gardner was a typical pioneer. He had "moved" from New England by successive stages, spending one year at Clear Lake, which pleased him until he heard more glowing reports of Spirit Lake.

They had not been long in the new wilderness when they heard the discharge of fire-arms, announcing the arrival of others. These proved to be four young men, Dr. Isaac H. Harriott, Bertell E. Snyder and William and Carl Granger, who had come from Red Wing, Minnesota. They liked the country so well that they determined to spend the winter there, hunting and fishing, all except William Granger who soon returned to his family in Minnesota. They built a cabin on the north side of the strait separating the two Okoboji lakes. Opposite them James H. Mattock soon thereafter made a home for his wife and many children. A little later three other families built two more cabins, three miles away, on the east side of East Okoboji. One was occupied by Joel Howe and his son-in-law, Alvin Noble, and their families, and the other one by the J. M. Thatcher family. A sixth cabin was erected on the southwest shore of Spirit Lake, six miles distant from the Gardner cabin. In these six cabins were housed about forty persons in all, most of them children.

These lake settlements were the outposts of civilization. The red men who roamed through the country seemed to be on friendly terms with the white men, but they must have felt some resentments toward those who were invading what had been for many generations the favored hunting and fishing places for bands of Sioux. To them the largest of the lakes was known as Minnewaukon, meaning spirit water. Many myths and legends were woven about this lake. It was believed that it was one of the abodes of the Great Spirit, and because of that the waters of the lake were never at rest. The larger of the other two lakes was Minnetonka, meaning the great or deep water, and the lesser one they called Okoboji, signifying place of rest.

For the first white settlers the lakes and their surroundings must have held many fascinations. There were beautiful groves interspersed with fine prairies. Fish abounded in the water, and game in the timber. For those who lived in a state of nature it was hardly less than an earthly paradise. And it must have seemed more so as the summer began to wane and the autumn to deepen, and the green of the grass and the trees was turned into scarlet and gold and into russet and brown under the haze of the Indian's own summer. But little did those who were allured and fascinated by such beauties dream that in them lurked an evil spirit which was to destroy them and all their hopes.

## CHAPTER XLIX

### The Spirit Lake Massacre

The winter of 1856 and 1857 was one of unusual severity. Late in November snow fell for four days. It was only the first of many such storms. The weather was so severe that the snow remained until in March and even April. There were banks of snow fifteen and twenty feet deep.[1] All the settlers in northern Iowa suffered, but those around the lakes most of all, for they were the farthest from the sources of supply. Toward spring almost famine conditions prevailed. In February two men, Luce and Thatcher, volunteered to go east to bring needed provisions. They had to go to Hampton, Shell Rock, Cedar Falls and Waterloo before they could get what they wanted. Four men returned with them, Robert Clark, Jonathan Howe, Enoch Ryan, and Asa Burtch. Near the mouth of Cylinder Creek, in Palo Alto County, their oxen gave out. Thatcher and Burtch then remained to guard their stores while the others proceeded to the lakes on foot, which they reached on the sixth of March.

But the Indians suffered more than the settlers for they had less to do with. Many of them were in starving conditions. Some may have blamed the white men for both the severity of the weather and the scarcity of game. Toward spring many roving bands set out to find food in the settlements. One of these was under the leadership of Inkpaduta, or the Scarlet Point. He was known even among his own people as a bad Indian. His followers were the renegades of the Sioux. Among them were thieves and murderers. The leader himself was charged with having encompassed the death of his own father. In his personal appearance he was most

[1] Carpenter's "Major William Williams," in *Annals of Iowa*, Third Series, Vol. II, p. 152.

repulsive, the coarseness and brutality of his countenance being aggravated by deep marks of smallpox. He was reputed to be the brother of Sidominadota, the chief who was murdered by Henry Lott in 1854. On the assumption of this relationship the massacres of 1857 have been accounted for as an Indian's revenge. But this theory is rejected by most modern writers.[2] They hold that Inkpaduta was not capable of such noble feelings. They say he was a Wahpekuta, while Sidominadota was a Sisseton Sioux. Those who reject the relationship and the theory of blood revenge, explain the atrocities committed by the villainous nature of the Scarlet Chief and by the inciting incidents that preceded his arrival at the lakes. Cruelty and murder were habitual to this Indian.

The exact movements of Inkpaduta's band are matters of dispute among writers.[3] They were first reported in force at Smithland, where they met with much resistance. For a time they were even disarmed. At Correctionville they beat one settler into unconsciousness. They tarried at Pilot Rock and the Milford colony without doing much damage. Passing through portions of Buena Vista and O'Brien counties, they plundered many isolated cabins. At Peterson they showed the uglier side of their natures. They made prisoners of women and girls, afterwards releasing them. At Gillett's Grove one of the Indians was killed and beheaded. Fearing savage vengeance for this act, the settlers fled and reached Sioux Rapids from which they attempted to summon aid from Fort Dodge.

On Saturday evening, the seventh of March, Inkpaduta's band reached the Gardner cabin on Lake Okoboji. They celebrated their arrival with a war dance. But this does not seem to have excited any alarm, neither did the fact that they pitched their first camp on the trail communicating with the

[2] For these two theories see "Inkpadutah's Revenge," by Harvey Ingham, in the *Midland Monthly*, Vol. IV, and *The Spirit Lake Massacre*, by Thomas Teakle, pp. 74 to 77.

[3] No Iowa subject has been more written about. Mrs. Abbie Gardner Sharp's *History of the Spirit Lake Massacre* is basic material; Thomas Teakle's *The Spirit Lake Massacre*, is an authoritative work, based on all the extant information on this historic episode in Iowa history.

other cabins. On the next morning while the Gardners were at breakfast, an Indian entered to ask for food. A place was made for him at the family table. Later others came, including women and children, and they also were given food. During the morning Dr. Harriott and one of his companions came to leave letters for Gardner to take to Fort Dodge on a trip he had intended to make to procure provisions. But it was not until in the afternoon of the day that the Indians aroused any suspicions. Fearing mischief from them, Luce and Clark set out by a concealed way to warn and, perhaps, to summon the other settlers. They did not reach the other cabins, neither did they return — they were shot on the way.

The inmates of the Gardner cabin heard the discharge of the fire-arms and began to fear the worst, especially Mrs. Luce, whose husband was involved. Toward evening a number of the Indians were seen approaching the cabin. Instead of barring the door, they were still received kindly. They demanded all the flour in the house. While Gardner was stooping over the barrel to give them what they wanted, he was shot in the back and fell dead on the floor. Then the women were seized and beaten to death, and scalped before the eyes of the terrified children. The little ones were seized next and beaten to death against the posts and trees, all except a fourteen year old girl, Abbie, of whom they made a prisoner.

At probably about the same time, similar scenes were being enacted at the Mattock and Granger cabins. What happened there are matters of conjecture. The position of the bodies when found indicated that the Mattocks had fled toward their neighbors for help and that three of the young men had gone out to render it, while one remained in the cabin, presumably to defend their own home. Dr. Harriott was found with his hand fastened in death on his broken gun which he must have used as a club in his own last defense. In reports made to the governor of the state it was stated that many Indians had been killed in this encounter. This was incorrect. Abbie Gardner's testimony was to the effect that only one red man was wounded and none killed. Having murdered twenty, and taken one prisoner, the Indians celebrated their first day of carnage with a scalp dance. Abbie Gardner, in scant clothing for the cold weather, was compelled to witness these fiendish orgies in which the scalps of her own dear ones were carried on poles.

After dancing nearly through the night the Indians started early in the morning toward the cabins on East Okoboji, where they killed all the inmates excepting Mrs. Thatcher and Mrs. Noble who were added to their list of prisoners. On the thirteenth of March, the work around the lakes was completed at the Marble cabin, where the man was killed and the woman taken as a captive. In all, the dead then numbered thirty-two.[4]

The first news of the massacre was carried to the outside world by Morris Markham, a trapper, who made himself one of the heroes of Iowa history by the thought he took of others in that emergency. He had spent the winter in one of the cabins, but had been absent in search of a yoke of strayed oxen. He returned on Monday night, the second day of the tragic events. In the Gardner cabin he stumbled on the scenes of death and desolation. On his way to the other cabins, he was arrested by the barking of a dog, and then saw the Indians sitting in a council. He slipped past them unobserved, but only to find in the other cabins like death and destruction. He spent part of the night pacing up and down in a ravine to keep from freezing to death, and in the early light he set out for the nearest settlement, which was at Granger's Point on the Des Moines. Having told his story there, two trappers volunteered to go to Fort Dodge to summon aid, while Markham himself and George Granger went to Springfield to warn the settlers. This act saved the lives of many, if not of all in that settlement. Some fled, but others barricaded themselves in one of the cabins to await the coming of Inkpaduta's men. Messengers were dispatched to the nearest Indian agency and thence to Fort Ridgely. The Indians came in due time, but they were met with such strong resistance that they soon departed, probably surmising that aid had been summoned from the fort. As soon as the Indians had left, the survivors loaded

[4] The names of the dead have been inscribed on the monument which the state has erected near the site of the Gardner cabin.

their children and wounded in a sled and, with the able-bodied on foot, fled toward the settlements in Iowa.

At Fort Ridgely within a few hours of the receipt of the news, Captain Bernard E. Bee with forty-eight men set out for Springfield and Spirit Lake. They reached Springfield after the settlers had taken flight. They started in pursuit of the Indians who were hastening northwestward. At one time the scouts were in close contact with the red men, while they were concealed in a deep ravine. It is well that they did not discover the presence of the enemy, for if an attack had been made the four captive women would have been killed, under orders to that effect given by Inkpaduta. The pursuit was soon abandoned by Captain Bee because of lack of provisions and proper equipment.

The first authentic news of the massacres was carried to Fort Dodge by the two trappers from Granger's Point. It was confirmed by three men from Newton, Iowa, who had reached the lakes a few days after the tragedy and had returned in haste to summon aid. Mass meetings were held both in Fort Dodge and at Webster City, and volunteers for a relief expedition were called for. So many offered themselves that a selective draft had to be used, only the fittest being accepted. Ninety-one approved men were organized into three companies, A and B from Fort Dodge, and C from Webster City, with C. B. Richards, John F. Duncombe and Johnson C. Johnson as captains. Major William Williams, who held the executive commission from Governor Grimes, was elected battalion commander. He was sixty-five years of age but he stood the ordeals through which they passed and was the soul of the expedition. The provisions and equipment were inadequate for such a journey, but they were the best to be had in frontier settlements. On the twenty-fourth, all being in readiness, the men started for the lakes.

The story of this expedition is a chapter of glory in the history of Iowa. Nothing finer was ever undertaken by men at any time or anywhere. Their march has forever given historic interest to every mile of ground over which they passed. One may still follow their route up the valley of the Des Moines.

In an automobile it is now the trip of a few hours from Fort Dodge through Dakota City and Humboldt to Emmetsburg and beyond.[5] Every mile is now a scene of rural beauty, with fine homes in spacious grounds. Returning, one may cross the Iowa divide, which separates the waters of the Mississippi from those of the Missouri, and passing the lakes, follow the course of the Little Sioux through Sioux Rapids to Pilot Rock. But it was different three and sixty years ago when the relief expedition marched up the Des Moines. The snow was then four feet deep on the level and in the ravines it reached into the tree tops.

On their first day out they were able to cover only six miles by floundering through the snow banks. When night came each man wrapped himself up in his blanket and slept on the ground under the open skies. At the end of the second day they were able to reach Dakota City. All day they had tramped back and forth to beat down the snow so that oxen might pull their loads through it. To make matters worse a thaw set in which converted much of the snow into slush. At Dakota City some were accommodated in the cabins of the settlers, and the others slept out of doors again. On the third day they struggled to reach what was known as McKnight's Point. That day the men, pulling and tugging on long ropes, had literally dragged not only the loads but the oxen through the drifts. Unable to reach their longed for destination, and suffering from snow blindness and exhaustion, they were compelled to spend the night where there was not a tree to shelter them or to afford fuel for fire. They slept on the snow and so closely together, to keep warm, that "when one turned all had to do likewise." Their evening and morning meals consisted of crackers and raw ham. Conditions grew so much worse that on the fifth day out Major Williams offered every man his liberty to go back. Every man remained in the ranks, except two men, who were sent home because of their age and infirmities. From time to time additions were made to the

[5] The author of this history, in company with Lieutenant-Governor Ernest R. Moore, Senator W. G. Haskell, and Almon S. Reed, made this trip in the summer of 1920.

little army by settlers who volunteered to accompany them, so that at last they counted one hundred and twenty-five, and among their accretions were Cyrus C. Carpenter, then a surveyor, later a governor, and the brave Morris Markham, and also Thatcher and Asa Burtch whose provisions had been commandeered for the expedition. At last they reached the Irish settlement where they found many refugees assembled.

The story is too long to be retold here in detail, although every mile calls upon one to record what happened to these brave and enduring men. After they had passed the Irish settlement they met on the prairies the forlorn refugees from Springfield — in the distance each group mistook the other for Indians and prepared to defend. The refugees presented a sorry sight. They were almost out of food, and all their blankets and clothing were wet or frozen. To do for them was for the relief expedition reward enough for all that they had suffered on the way. With them was Morris Markham, but instead of seeking safety or even rest, he enlisted in the expedition and returned with them over the dreary miles he had just traveled. When they reached Granger's Point, a horseman from Captain Bee's command arrived with the news that the pursuit of the Indians had been given up.

There was, therefore, nothing further to do except to return to Fort Dodge. Before starting back a detail was made up to go to the lakes to bury the dead. Among those who volunteered for this duty was Captain Johnson who was placed in command. After they had performed these sad rites, differences came up as to the best way to return. Some wanted to go by the known and beaten way of Granger's Point, while others wanted to go by a more direct route. Among the latter were Captain Johnson and William Burkholder, a private, who perished on the prairies, being caught in a blinding blizzard. It was not until ten years later that their remains were found.

But in indescribable ways the sufferings of the four captive women were even greater. Carrying packs by day and sleeping on the ground by night, it took them six weeks to reach the Big Sioux River. The burdens they had borne over the intervening miles were heavy. Abbie Gardner's portion, for a fourteen-year-old girl, consisted of "eight bars of lead, one pint of lead-balls, one tepee cover made of the heaviest, thickest cloth, one blanket, one bed comforter, one iron bar three feet long and half an inch thick . . . one gun, one piece of wood several inches wide and four feet long to keep the pack in shape." The other women carried more. They were often without food and when it rained they had no shelter. While crossing the Little Sioux on drift wood, Mrs. Thatcher, who had been ailing, was tripped, by an Indian, into the water. She was able to keep herself afloat and reached the shore, but other Indians with clubs and poles pushed her back into the water and finally one of them shot her through the head. The Indian women hailed this murder of a captive with "loud shouts of joy." A little later Mrs. Marble was ransomed through the intervention of two Christianized Indians. Before the efforts to rescue the remaining captives were successful, Mrs. Noble was killed by Roaring Cloud, Inkpaduta's son, with whose commands she had refused to comply. Three civilized Indians finally succeeded in ransoming Abbie Gardner in June after more than three months of captivity, the price being "two horses, twelve blankets, two kegs of powder, twenty pounds of tobacco, thirty-two yards of squaw cloth, thirty-seven yards of calico and ribbon, and other small articles." She was taken to St. Paul, where attentions and many gifts were heaped upon her and a state dinner given in her honor, after which she went down the Mississippi to rejoin her sister Eliza in Iowa.

# CHAPTER L

## Crimes and Counter Crimes

The Indians at Spirit Lake were not the only law-breakers and murderers in Iowa at that time. It may almost be said that around 1857 crime was rampant in the state. The Battle of Bellevue and its warnings to the lawless had been forgotten. The great influx of new population brought with it all kinds of evil-doers also. Where the people labored and accumulated there thieves congregated and plundered. As in the earlier time, horse stealing was the most prevalent crime. Above almost every other form of property the horse had a monetary value. Good horses were then worth from $100 to $150 a head. They were the power in front of the plow and the means of transportation. The thief rode away on his stolen property. Thieves coöperated with each other. They had routes over which they operated and taverns in which they were harbored. Brown, the outlaw of Bellevue, kept a tavern and the first settler on the site of Cedar Rapids, Osgood Shepherd, had a house of like repute. The timber sheltered them and they secreted themselves in the roughest places. They congregated at the Red Rocks in Marion County and at the Palisades in Linn County. The thief passed the horse to the next man on the route while he himself returned to his home where he was found the next morning sleeping like an innocent man. Many of the horses were taken to Illinois where there was a good market for them. Out of such a state of society murders became naturally more and more frequent in occurence. The man who steals may also kill. In the space of ten years fifteen murders were committed in the two counties of Jackson and Clinton.[1] It is said that only one of

[1] Gue's *History of Iowa*, Vol. I, p. 336.

these murderers was ever brought to justice. The criminals employed the best lawyers because they had the most money with which to pay them. Constables and even sheriffs were often either friendly with or afraid of the criminals and many judges were weak and easily intimidated. Legal quibbles and technicalities prevailed and changes of venue were easily obtained. Witnesses against criminals found it convenient to be away or not to tell the whole truth. Men naturally valued their own lives and they paid for the protection of their properties and families in such ways.

But what none dared to do alone they were finally forced to do *en masse,* and so the Vigilance Committee came into existence. They were stern oath bound men, who rode in masks in the night time or who operated bare-faced in broad daylight as they became more conscious of their power and more insolent in its exercise. Seven hundred men in the counties of Jackson, Jones, Clinton, Scott, Cedar, and Johnson are said to have coöperated.[2] A proclamation was published in the Jackson *Sentinel,* to the effect that the criminal laws of the state would be enforced by them "to the very letter" where "legal officers neglect their duty." They promised to "be governed by the penal laws of the state so far as it is convenient." "Legal officers" were warned to commence no proceedings against members of the committee, and the "unjust death of any member of the committee" would be avenged. Those who spied on their doings would be shot forthwith. The Vigilantes, or Regulators, as they became known, set up virtually a new government. They observed some of the forms of usual governments. In the moonlight in the woods or by the light of torch fires they held courts of their own, presided over by a judge and with jurymen standing up, for it did not take them long to hear the evidence or to reach verdicts. The witnesses for the defense were not present, or they were not heard, for they did not dare to speak lest they themselves would be suspected, and the verdicts were always "guilty." In the fourteen years, from 1846 to 1860, "at least forty-five lynchings, affecting more

[2] Gue's *History of Iowa,* Vol. I, p. 338.

than seventy victims occurred."[3] The greatest number of these happened in 1857. It is believed that the panic and the hard times influenced both the thieves and those who were determined to defend their property.

The little town of Andrew in Jackson County, from which the state drew her first governor, Ansel Briggs, figures in the history of that period as a center of crime.[4] There on the eleventh of April, 1857, they hanged Alexander Gifford, for the fifteenth murder committed in Jackson County, without a single legal execution. Having lost faith in the courts, the people took the law into their own hands. Gifford confessed he had murdered one John Engles for the sum of $150, paid by two men, fugitives from justice in the state of New York. Engles knew of their connection with a certain crime and so they wanted him put out of the way. On the twenty-ninth of May they hanged one William P. Barger from the same tree, north of the town. Barger had committed his crime of murder three years before. After three convictions he had secured another change of venue and was taken to De Witt in Clinton County. The "people" decided to make an end of court technicalities. So they went to De Witt, headed by a postmaster, and took him from the jail. The accounts state that "Their movements were open, calm, and deliberate." They brought their victim back to Andrew in the same way, to "the seat of Lynch justice chosen by the self-styled Vigilance Committee," says the same account, where "Men, women, and children looked on the spectacle and winced not." After Barger had been buried, "some of the 'refined spirits' of the mob dug up his body, placed it upright in a buggy, and drove it to Cobb's Hotel, leaving a paper in the hand of the corpse calling for dinner and horse feed."[5] It was following that gruesome performance that the committee printed its proclamation in the Jackson paper.

Jones and Clinton counties also appear in the annals of

[3] Black's "Lynchings in Iowa," in *The Iowa Journal of History and Politics*, Vol. X, No. 2, p. 157.

[4] *Ibid.*, p. 187.

[5] Reprinted in the *Cedar Valley Times*, Cedar Rapids, June 11, 1857, from the Maquoketa *Excelsior*.

lynching that year, but Cedar County was most afflicted. In that county they hanged Alonzo Page on June eighteenth, Jacob A. Warner on the twenty-fifth of the same month, and shot Peter Conklin on the twenty-seventh. In July, on the third, they hanged Alonzo Gleason and Edwin Soper, near Lowden, and on the fifth an unnamed horse thief near Tipton, and a man named Kelso on the fourteenth and another named Keith on the twenty-first. But they were doing the same things in many other places during the same months. In Montezuma, Poweshiek County, on July fourteenth, they hanged William B. Thomas, alias "Comequick," who had been a terror to settlers in those parts. His crime was a double murder.' At the Nine Mile House, now Leighton in Mahaska County, nine miles from Oskaloosa and nine miles from Pella, he fell in with a Mr. and Mrs. Casteel, who were looking for a farm, for which they had a thousand dollars with them. "Comequick" led them to a secluded place in the timber of Poweshiek County, made way with them and took their belongings. The woman's brother trailed the criminal to his lair, but the lawyers exhausted his money and his patience until he appealed to the people who responded promptly. The mob "built a fire beneath the prisoner to add to his torture and aid in forcing a confession" from him.[6] Mob law was brutalizing the people.

Even in counties so far removed as Palo Alto, where the first settlements were not made until in 1855 and 1856, the horse thieves carried on their nefarious trade. Operating in a prairie country, they made use of caves or "underground stables" in which to conceal their stolen animals in day time. A number of such hiding places were found later.[7] And they had members of the Vigilance Committees up there also. In Cedar Falls in 1858 they had a "round up" of the thieves, when several of them were hung.

At last it began to dawn on the people that the Regulators themselves needed regulating. Lynching had become a mania and almost a pastime. Innocent men were no longer safe.

6 Parker's *History of Poweshiek County*, pp. 62, 63, and 66.

7 McCarty's *History of Palo Alto County*, pp. 52-53.

The whisper of suspicion might grow into a lynching bee. Members used the committees to punish their enemies. In Cedar County one "Regulator" named William Corry in such a way brought about the lynching of Alonzo Page. Having quarreled with his neighbor, Corry circulated the report that Page was connected with the horse thieves. He was notified by a committee to leave the country which he refused to do, conscious of his innocence, and thereupon they went to his house and shot him to death. But Page did not die in vain. What the courts could not do after repeated attempts to bring the Regulators to bay, was accomplished by an old man, Canada McCullough, a highly respected pioneer of Cedar County. He knew Page and he knew he was innocent and so he denounced those who had murdered him. A committee waited on him and told him either to keep still or to leave the country. He refused to do either. He lived on his own land and he believed in freedom of a man to tell the truth. The Vigilance Committee then proceeded in a body to his house. He saw them coming and loaded his rifles and with a drawn gun awaited them in the door of his log castle. He was known as a "dead shot" as well as a just and fearless man. Because of that, no man dared to raise his own gun. They were willing to kill others, but not to be killed by others. McCullough defied the whole mob and called them murderers to boot. They dispersed, and it is said that it was the last appearance of the organized regulators in those parts.[8] The power of one just man had triumphed over many hundreds who realized that there was no longer justice in the processes they followed. And so gradually the courts reassumed their sway. The people had learned that unorganized justice, however righteous in its first conceptions, is a menace to the people themselves.

But other men in those days who stole thousands instead of horses, and who robbed the future instead of log stables, fared better. They were men who plundered whole counties. When the Third General Assembly in 1851 divided the rest of the state into counties, many of them were without residents.

[8] Gue's *History of Iowa*, Vol. I, p. 350.

It did not take schemers long to see the opportunity that was afforded them. A few men would acquire so-called residence in one of the unsettled counties. They built a few shacks, or even one would do. Then they proceeded to set up a county organization on paper. They pretended to elect county officers. They were willing to hold two or even three offices each, if there were not enough men to go around. Of course they kept all their records in legal form for they were educated scoundrels. Then they passed resolutions to build bridges and court houses and to drain swamps. They let contracts for such *quasi* improvements, issued warrants in payment or issued bonds which were sold to "innocent" purchasers. They had certain processes of make-believe to give validity to their work. A ditching machine dragged across a swamp left the trace of the performance of a contract, even if it did not carry off the surplus waters. A few pilings driven by the sides of a stream with a brush fire over them left the remnants of a bridge which had not been built, and charred foundations of a cabin were the visible evidences of a court house that had once stood there. All cases were not so flagrant, but all were bad enough.

A blank book maker for one of these bogus county organizations who went out to collect his bill has left some record of his experiences.[9] He found himself on an open prairie. His map told him he was in the right place. He was looking for a court house. He stopped at a double log cabin to inquire his whereabouts. "Wall, stranger," said the lone inmate, "I reckon you're about thar." Surprised at the court house, he told his story and showed his bill. The lone inmate listened and after while said, "Wall, stranger, let's have a meeting of the board." The meeting was forthwith held, the lonely man constituting the whole board. In due form he received the bill and allowed it, and drew a warrant for its payment. Later the same man acted as county treasurer and paid the bill which he himself had received, allowed, and for which he had drawn a warrant. The creditor was glad to get his money in any way. County warrants in "stupendous amounts" were

[9] Charles Aldrich in *Annals of Iowa*, Third Series, Vol. X, p. 47.

thus drawn and debts piled up for *bona fide* settlers to pay. Of course there was resistance to such debts, successful in some cases and unsuccessful in many others. The foundations of fortunes were laid in such frauds.

The formation of banks outside of the state in which they were forbidden to issue money, was another form of fraud. What the constitution of Iowa forbade, the venal legislatures of the territory of Nebraska permitted to be done. Neither assets nor honesty were requisites for a charter to organize a bank that could issue paper money.

The mushroom towns of Fontanelle and Florence figured conspicuously in such transactions. No one knew what bills they issued were worth. Often they became wholly worthless over night. Every business man subscribed for a "bank detector," but the publishers could not keep up with the changes. Men hated to hold the bills over night for fear they would be worthless in the morning.

When the panic of 1857 struck the country nearly all of this money became worthless and the hard times were doubly aggravated. There was universal financial chaos, until the Iowa State Bank and its branches were organized. They were hard times indeed. Even real estate became valueless. The necessities of life were not to be had. In the newer portions of Iowa families lived on wild game and salt and a little flour ground in coffee mills. They cut up their grain sacks to make clothing, and for taxes, which had to be paid, they sold muskrat skins.[10] On top of it all came crop failures over two-thirds of the state in the summer of 1858, when it rained almost incessantly, and there were frosts in every month of the year. Men wondered what had brought more plagues than had afflicted Egypt in a new land so favored and in which they had labored so hard.

[10] Gue's *History of Iowa*, Vol. I, p. 354.

# CHAPTER LI

## THE COURSE OF POLITICS

All representatives from Iowa in congress up to 1855 were Democrats, with one exception. In 1848, on the face of the returns Daniel F. Miller, a Whig, received a majority in the First congressional district. But by throwing out the votes cast by the Mormons at Kanesville, his opponent, William Thompson, was declared elected. When Miller contested the seat, the house of representatives declared it vacant, on June twenty-ninth, 1850. In a special election then held Miller was elected by a majority of two hundred and fifty-seven votes.[1] In the election of 1854, James Thornington was elected to congress from the same district, being carried through on the Grimes tidal wave of that year. Although the party was not then in actual existence, he has been styled the first Republican congressman from Iowa.[2] Thornington devoted himself largely to getting the railroad land grant made by congress. In 1855 the Whigs elected for the first time the judges of the supreme court, George G. Wright chief justice, and William G. Woodward and Norman W. Isbell associate justices. Isbell was a noted jurist of his time, and Wright became famous in Iowa for many things. He was an orator, a raconteur, and he became a United States senator. The election of James Harlan as United States senator to succeed Augustus C. Dodge has already been recorded.

In 1855 the Democrats made a strenuous effort to reverse the Whig majority of 1854, in the election for minor state officers, but the Whigs surprised them as well as themselves by almost doubling their majorities of two years before. But if that election was fatal to Democratic hopes, it was not less

[1] Gue's *History of Iowa*, Vol. I, p. 259.

[2] *Ibid.*, p. 283.

so to the Whig party. The Whigs were not able to grasp the new issues. They had compromised so often that they had lost all political courage. As a party, they had been weighed in the balance and found wanting. The victories that had been won in Iowa in their name were victories founded in the moral courage of James W. Grimes, and Mr. Grimes found that he was no longer in harmony with what had been his party. As early as 1855 he wrote approving a movement "to wipe their hands of Whiggery."[3] It could not do the work he had in mind. The new alignments that were necessary to do that work were then impending.

It was the passage of the Kansas-Nebraska bill which brought the new alignments about. In the face of new issues men felt free to act along new lines. There were Whigs who believed in slavery. They were called "silver grays." Eventually they went to the Democrats, who believed in slavery. There were free soil Democrats, and these eventually united with the free soil Whigs to form the organization called the Republican party. Governor Grimes became one of the guiding minds in the new organization. "I am sanguine," he wrote to Salmon P. Chase of Ohio, on May twelfth, 1855, "that we shall organize a party that will carry the elections in most of the northern states in 1856, and in all of them in 1860."[4] In Ripon, Wisconsin, a free soil Whig and a free soil Democrat unitedly issued a call for an anti-slavery meeting to be held at Jackson, Michigan, and that place has been called the birthplace of the Republican party. In Iowa it was not until the third of January, 1856, that a similar call was issued, for a meeting to be held at Iowa City on February twenty-second, Washington's birthday, "for the purpose of organizing a Republican party, to make common cause with a similar party already formed in several other states of the Union." This call was signed by "Many Citizens," and was printed in many newspapers. It was probably written by Mr. Grimes. The terseness and the impersonality of the language are his.

The call acted like magic. Men were ready; they had been

[3] Salter's *Life of James W. Grimes,* p. 63.

[4] *Ibid.*, p. 70.

waiting to be called for the new duties. On the appointed day so many came to the meeting that it had to be held in the hall of representatives in the state capitol. Philip Velie of Muscatine was made chairman and J. T. Lane, N. M. Hubbard, J. B. Stewart, and C. C. Nourse acted as secretaries. Thirty-nine counties were represented and each county was given a member on the committee on resolutions. The result was thirty-nine articles of political faith. Every man came with his "ism." But out of the multiplicity they wisely evolved simplicity. The party was organized "to maintain the liberties of the people, the sovereignty of the states and the perpetuity of the Union." Was not that enough—and what could have been more then? Or what can ever be more? Freedom and that alone was declared national. They were not abolitionists. Slavery was declared to be "a local institution, beyond their reach and above their authority." But they did not propose to let it spread to new territories. Of the meeting itself the Muscatine *Journal* said, "It was the largest, most intelligent and enthusiastic ever convened in the state." That, of course, was friendly newspaper praise. The newcomers of Iowa were much in evidence, for the same paper said that many of the best speeches were made by men "who had not resided within our borders over two years." Among these new men, Samuel J. Kirkwood was, perhaps, most prominent. Politically, he had always been a Democrat. He came to the meeting on a chance invitation from a man who had known him in Ohio. When called upon to speak, he acquitted himself so well that he was later made a member of a committee to draw up an address to the people, J. B. Grinnell and William M. Stone being associated with him.

Before adjourning that day the new Republicans selected delegates to help organize a national party and to nominate candidates for president and vice-president. They also placed in nomination a full state ticket which was headed by Elijah Sells for secretary of state. Then they gave nine cheers and went home to await results. The response of the people was instant. The new party swept the state. It elected majorities in both houses of the general assembly, the two congressmen from the state, who were Samuel R. Curtis and Timothy Davis, and the four presidential electors who subsequently cast their votes for John C. Frémont. The majorities ranged around eight thousand, in spite of the fact that nearly nine thousand irreconcilable Whigs voted that year for Millard Fillmore, the Whig candidate for president.

To celebrate their victory—the election was held in September—the Republicans invited Abraham Lincoln to speak at a mass meeting in Burlington. "It would be very pleasant to shake hands with the Fremonters of Iowa," Mr. Lincoln wrote in reply, "who have led the van so splendidly, in this great charge which we hope and believe will end in a most glorious victory — all thanks, all honor to Iowa! But Iowa is out of danger, and it is no time for us, when the battle still rages, to pay holy-day visits to Iowa—I am sure you will excuse me for remaining in Illinois, where much hard work is still to be done."

Under the new state constitution an election for governor was to be held in 1857. Governor Grimes did not seek re-election, and so Ralph P. Lowe of Keokuk, a judge of the district court, was nominated and Oran Faville of Mitchell County for lieutenant-governor, which was a new office. The Democrats named as their candidates for the same offices Ben M. Samuels and George Gillaspy. The Republicans made much capital out of the new constitution and the projected state bank, but the election turned largely on national issues. They blamed the Democrats for the disturbances in Kansas and they denounced the Dred Scott decision by which slaves were reduced to mere chattels, calling it the "last and most alarming of those bold innovations upon the rights of the free states." The Democrats replied that it was a dangerous thing to impugn the decisions of the supreme court of the United States, and they deplored alike the activities of the "black Republicans" of the north and the "fire eaters" of secession in the south. The election, which was held in October, resulted in Republican majorities of about twenty-four hundred, majorities so small that they alarmed the Republicans and encouraged the Democrats in the belief that the new party was something merely ephemeral.

Ralph P. Lowe was the first Republican governor of the

state, and he was also the first to be inducted into that office in Des Moines. His administration fell on evil days in Iowa, for the panic of 1857 was then in full effect. When the general assembly met, also for the first time in Des Moines, the retiring governor, James W. Grimes, was promptly elected to the United States senate to succeed George W. Jones, who received scant consideration at the hands of his own party. Jones was no longer popular, not even among Democrats. He had continued to affiliate with the men of the south in congress. He voted to force on the people of Kansas the Le Compton constitution, a document framed by slavery men who had usurped the government of that state. He paid no heed to a resolution of the Iowa legislature asking him to vote against that infamous instrument. The sentiments of his constituents might change, but Senator Jones did not change with them. But if he were incapable of change, his party was capable of regrets. He was blamed for their losses in politics. "The negro question," said one Democrat,[5] "with which we have legitimately nothing under the heavens to do, has cost us two governors, two United States senators, four congressmen, the whole of the supreme bench, and both houses of the legislature for three successive sessions . . . we have nothing left us but our party platform and political honor." And the newspaper paragraphers questioned even the remnants of political honor!

But it was hardly true that Iowa had nothing to do with the negro question. She had not only a human interest in it, but a territorial, and possibly an economic interest. If slavery could be introduced into Kansas and into Nebraska, it could at least be debated and voted on in Iowa. Men did not think calmly on that question in those disturbed times. If they had so thought on it there might have been no Civil War. Calm thinking in the south would have convinced men there that slavery would become an impossible human institution. The very trend of world civilization was against it. But instead of calm thinking there came the tramp of John Brown's crusaders, who, as we shall see, had much to do with Iowa.

[5] Henry Clay Dean.

# CHAPTER LII

## JOHN BROWN IN IOWA

Iowa soon became involved in the negro question over which armed men were fighting in Kansas. Anti-slavery and pro-slavery men were being rushed into that territory, each in an attempt to out-vote the other. The south sent its guerillas, and the north its fanatics. Societies were formed in far off New England to encourage and to aid the emigration of free men to the afflicted territory and they supplied arms for those who were willing to fight as well as to vote. For free men, Iowa was the highway to Kansas, and her soil became a recruiting ground. The state was also a highway for fugitive slaves who were conducted along what were called Underground Railways which led to Canada, where slave laws passed in Washington were not effective. An esteemed citizen of Burlington, Edwin James, who was also a noted scientist, was arrested in Illinois in 1855, while acting as a guide for fleeing slaves.[1] He was defended by David Rorer and Marcellus M. Crocker, and liberated under a decision by Judge Ralph P. Lowe, who refused to recognize the validity of such an inhuman law. Governor Grimes then wished himself a private citizen so that he might act as "a law breaker," in protest against the fugitive slave law.[2] Men refused to be calm in those troubled days, while the rights of Iowa men in Kansas were being outraged.

The Rev. Pardee Butler who had gone to Kansas from

[1] Edwin James was a noted scientist and humanitarian who lived for many years in Burlington. He was a member of Long's Expedition in 1819 and he was one of the first men, if not the first man to scale Pike's Peak. James Peak was named after him. He was an authority in botany, and he was versed in many Indian dialects, translating portions of the Bible into many of them.

[2] Salter's *Life of James W. Grimes*, p. 83.

Posten's Grove, Iowa, was captured by guerrillas, his face painted black in derision, and he was then set adrift upon an old raft on the Missouri, with the warning that he would be shot if he dared to return to Kansas. When Iowa men in that territory appealed to Governor Grimes for protection, the governor addressed a letter to the president on the subject. He called attention to the fact that free men had not only been deprived of the right of suffrage by armed ruffians, but that they had been driven out of their homes. An army raised in Missouri was at that time marching into Kansas with the avowed purpose of driving out all those who had gone there from free states. Another armed force had placed itself on the immigrant route from Iowa, "to prevent at the point of the bayonet any further emigration from this state." Had Iowa men no more rights on American soil? The governor informed the president, August twenty-eighth, 1856, that if the national government did not protect the citizens of Iowa in their rights, then it would become the right and the duty of the state "to interpose to arrest the progress of the evils." In support of this extraordinary position the governor cited the Virginia Resolutions written by Madison in 1798. The governor did not carry out such a policy, but when Richard J. Hinton and a band of crusaders had marched through Iowa in 1856, he permitted them to take from the arsenal in Iowa City 1,500 muskets to be used in the Kansas warfare.[3] The governor did not turn over the muskets, but he left the key to the arsenal on his desk where Hinton could find it.

While Iowa was confronted with such questions, John Brown was passing back and forth through the state. He first came to Iowa on his Kansas missions in September of 1857. Three of his sons had become settlers of the territory and he was going there to help them defend their American liberties. He was going to do for his sons what the government of the United States had neglected to do. Brown was then still unknown to fame. He had not yet caught the imagination of a nation. But when he returned from the

3 See Richard J. Hinton's *John Brown and His Men.*

wars in Kansas, he was heralded as the hero of Ossawatomie.

After his first exploits he went east to appeal for help among the New England sympathizers. He received not only bestowals of sympathy, but the materials with which to continue his warfare. He had an order on a quantity of rifles and powder, which had been placed on deposit in Tabor, Iowa, by one of the eastern societies. Tabor was a New England settlement on the banks of the Missouri, in proximity to Kansas. It became not only a miniature armory, but a hospital as well, where the wounded and sick in the cause of human freedom were cared for. The rifles in question had been stored in the cellar of the home of a Congregational minister, the Rev. John Todd. But Tabor had more than rifles. Its woodsheds even "were temporized for bed rooms, where the sick and dying were cared for."[4] We are told that "every place where a bed could be put or a blanket thrown down was at once occupied."

Brown took with him to Tabor on that trip a man by the name of Hugh Forbes as the drill master for his army. This man was a soldier of fortune who had fought under Garibaldi in Italy. Brown was a dreamer and Forbes was a mercenary. Eventually they quarreled over money matters. Forbes then went down the Missouri River into the "enemy's" country, and Brown fearing that he would betray him, changed his plans. Instead of striking his decisive blow in Kansas, he decided to strike it somewhere in the east. He went into Kansas, but soon returned with thirteen men of his own kind. These were the beginnings of his famous band. When he reached the Quaker settlements in Cedar County, he was financially stranded. He had hoped to sell his mules and his wagon, but money was a scarce thing in Iowa at that time.

But in Springdale, Cedar County, he found what was better than money, friendship and sympathy, first at the hands of John H. Painter, and later from many others. A farmer, William Maxson, living three miles northeast of the village, agreed to house his men, taking the mules and wagon in payment. Work was provided for the men on neighboring farms,

[4] Todd's *Early Settlement and Growth of Western Iowa*, p. 121.

and what time they did not spend in laboring they devoted to drilling with arms under Aaron D. Stephens. A motley company it must have appeared to the on-lookers, who were peaceful Quakers. The scene is historic now. Among them were "poets, orators, scholars, and Kansas war heroes." They were "eager, curious, restless men," and "a veritable band of crusaders." But they were orderly and well behaved and so deeply devoted to some hidden ideal that they won the friendship of all who came in contact with them. Young men of the neighborhood were drawn to them, conspicuously, Edwin and Barclay Coppoc, the sons of a Quaker widow. While the men tarried on the Maxson farm, Brown went east to confer with his friends. When he returned, he had money and he took his band to Chatham, Canada, where he organized them into a miniature government. He drew up a plan for a provisional government for the United States which has been called "a piece of insanity in the literal sense of the word."[5] When they reëntered the United States each man went his own way, to await the great summons.

Then once more Brown passed through Iowa on his way to Kansas. This time he did what he had not done before. He invaded the state of Missouri with two bands of raiders. One slave owner was killed and some horses were taken, a theft that Brown justified on the ground of unpaid wages to black workers. With this booty and a band of slaves, including women and children, he returned to Tabor. He himself was now a fugitive from justice and he had in his keeping stolen property. When the people of Tabor realized this they withdrew from him their support and sympathies. This treatment so enraged Brown that he forsook and almost cursed the place, going eastward. In spite of what had happened, he was well received at Grinnell by the founder of that town, Josiah B. Grinnell, who was then a state senator. He was assigned to the best bedroom in his host's house and on the following Sunday he was invited to speak in the Congregational church. In his address he alluded to a mysterious mission on which he

[5] Von Holst's *The Constitutional and Political History of the United States*, Vol. V, p. 78.

was bent. "Some one has to fail," he said, that others may succeed. "It is a question," he declared, "whether a dead man is a failure when living ones climb over him easier to scale the wall."[6] While in that place he was described as a man who stood erect in spite of his accumulated years. He wore "a full long beard, almost white, with hair parted and standing up, suggesting Andrew Jackson as pictured." He was even likened to Michael Angelo's conception of Moses. He was restless, alert and watchful, for he knew that a price had been placed on his head in Missouri for what he had done there. He knew that he was being tracked and followed, but he boasted that he could "shoot sixty times a minute." It is believed that while in the Grinnell home Brown wrote parts of his Harper's Ferry Proclamation.

At Springdale, among his good Quaker friends, he was also still well received. The slaves he had with him, with the connivance of Mr. Grinnell, William Penn Clarke, an abolitionist of Iowa City, and railroad officials, were secreted in a freight car on the Rock Island railroad at West Liberty, which was attached to a passenger train and hurried to Chicago on the way to Canada. It was now February of the fatal year of 1859. Before Brown left he saw Edwin and Barclay Coppoc, and they promised to join him when summoned. He had two other Iowa men under his command, Stewart Taylor and Jeremiah Anderson, the four constituting a fifth of his final band. In July, the Coppoc boys were summoned to Chambersburg, Pennsylvania. On the sixteenth of October Brown and his men struck the blow at Harper's Ferry — with a score of men he defied the governments of the state of Virginia and of the United States of America, a challenge so stupendous that its echoes were heard around the world. In Boston Ralph Waldo Emerson succumbed to the spirit that prompted the deed and in France Victor Hugo wrote the event into literary rhapsodies. Two of the Iowa men fell fighting at the ferry, Edwin Coppoc was hanged on a gallows in Virginia, not regretting the part he had played, and Barclay Coppoc, who was not at the ferry, but had been left to guard the camp, found his way

[6] Grinnell's *Reminiscences of Forty Years*, p. 214.

back to Iowa as a fugitive from justice. Later when an officer came from Virginia with extradition papers, Governor Kirkwood refused to honor them because of inaccuracies, and by the time the papers had been corrected, Coppoc had made his escape. Coppoc afterwards died an accidental death in the opening of the Civil War.

There is another Iowa aftermath that may be related here. While at Springdale, John Brown revealed his plans, at least in part, to a few trusted friends, among whom was John Varney, a Quaker who shuddered at the possible consequences of the attack on Harper's Ferry. He took counsel on the matter with two discreet young men, Benjamin F. and David J. Gue, who also were Quakers born. These two men prepared letters which they sent to the secretary of war in Washington, apprising him of the intended attack. One of the letters was mailed at Big Rock, Iowa, and the other was sent to the postmaster at Cincinnati to be forwarded by him. The letters were not signed. Another similar letter was mailed to the secretary of war from Wheatland, Iowa, by A. L. Smith.[7]

In the congressional investigations that followed the tragedy at Harper's Ferry, John B. Floyd, the secretary of war, admitted that he had received warnings, in which Harper's Ferry had been designated as the place of attack. But he had paid no heed to them. The letters were anonymous and he said the things predicted had seemed to him preposterous. What might have happened, and what might not have happened had the secretary thus apprised acted according to these advices? It was John Brown at Harper's Ferry who set the nation aflame.

David J. Gue became a famous artist and Benjamin F. Gue, a law-maker, a lieutenant governor, and historian of his state. But all the time they kept their secret of the writing of those letters. It was not until twenty-eight years after the event that Mr. Gue, the historian, told the story of the letters in the pages of an Iowa Magazine, *The Midland Monthly.*

[7] *The Midland Monthly*, February, 1897.

# CHAPTER LIII

## Just Before the War

The slavery question was only one of many that troubled the politicians and statesmen of that time. The Maine liquor law and the Massachusetts suffrage law [1] alike plagued the Republicans. Taxes to pay for the humane institutions were called burdensome. The state was rife with scandals. One had to do with the location of the new capitol and another with the construction of the hospital at Mount Pleasant; the school funds had been mismanaged and one superintendent of public instruction was a defaulter; [2] the land claimants along the river had a quarrel with the Des Moines Navigation Company; in Poweshiek County, Josiah B. Grinnell, the friend of John Brown, was defeated for reëlection to the state senate, and in Des Moines County, Fitz Henry Warren, one of the most brilliant men of that era, failed of election because the politicians had placed a foreign-born candidate on the same ticket. Denials and defenses would no longer serve and so the Republicans proceeded to investigate their own administration and to formulate needed reforms, while over all hung the specter of the panic of 1857, which had filled the state with the wreckage of business, public and private.

In the midst of such turmoil the governor, Ralph P. Lowe, good and amiable and honest, sat bewildered. He was not strong enough to cope with things as they were. When the time for nominating a candidate for the high office in 1859 drew near, it was felt that his leadership would not be sufficient, and so he was prevailed upon to step aside, though he coveted a second term. The political consideration is said to

[1] The Massachusetts law was one that restricted suffrage, especially as affecting men of foreign birth.

[2] James D. Eads, who was reported to be $46,403.81 short in his accountings of the school fund.

have been the promise of a seat on the bench of the supreme court. In any event, he received a nomination for such an office. When the convention was held, on the twenty-second day of June, Samuel J. Kirkwood was nominated for governor. Practically by all he was regarded as the one man who could lead that year. He seemed to belong to the people. He was virile and vigorous, a man who was not afraid and one who both dared and knew how to fight a campaign, for it was a fight that confronted the politicians. For lieutenant governor the party nominated Nicholas J. Rusch, a Scott County man of German antecedents.

But if the Republicans were in some despair, the Democrats were in high hopes. Having been out of offices for four years, they had nothing to defend, and everything to attack. They were ready to capitalize every form of discontent, whether it grew out of taxes or morals. They still believed that Iowa was normally a Democratic state. The national organization of the party was interested in redeeming Iowa. They deemed it a necessary preliminary to the presidential election of 1860. President Buchanan expressed his interest in the campaign, and it was believed, by Republicans at least, that a fund of $30,000 would be provided by eastern men who wanted to stop the Republican drift which in the name of morals was unsettling the financial and industrial conditions of the country. Business was more than morals to them! As Kirkwood had seemed the one man for the Republicans to nominate, so the Democrats thought of only one, Augustus C. Dodge, who was at that time wending his way homeward from his mission in Madrid.

And thus at a most critical time the two great parties stood arrayed against each other under their strongest leaders. The contrast between the two men was hardly less than the contrast in the two platforms. Kirkwood, like Lincoln, was a man of the common people. He came from them and he adhered to them. He was a plain, blunt, out-speaking man. He had fearlessness, and as a politician also adroitness. He had the ruggedness of his times and of the west, though he had been born on a Maryland farm in 1813. As a boy and a young man he had done a little of everything in poor and humble surroundings, but he had managed to acquire a fair education, including some Latin and Greek. He came to Ohio, on his westward course, in 1835, where he began by working on farms in summer and teaching school in winter. He was twenty-eight years old when he took up the study of law, which he afterwards practiced with considerable success. He became a prosecuting attorney and he was a member of the constitutional convention of Ohio in 1850. In 1853 he came to Iowa City to associate himself with his brother-in-law, Ezekiel Clark, who himself was a man of parts and achievements in the state, in various enterprises at Coralville on the Iowa River. He became a farmer, a miller, and a merchant. Politically he had always been a Democrat, but he became a free soiler and in 1856, almost by chance, he helped to organize the Republican party. In the same year he was elected to the state senate. In that body, in 1858, he attracted national attention as the author of a resolution denouncing the Dred Scott decision as "not binding in law or in conscience," and declaring that Iowa would not tolerate slavery within her borders "in any form or under any pretext, for any time, however short, be the consequences what they may." This resolution, it is believed, moved Robert Toombs of Georgia to make an attack upon the state of Iowa in the United States senate, which brought from Senator Grimes not only a reply but a notable defense of his state.

Who and what Augustus C. Dodge was is already known. He had been part of Iowa and her government, territorial and state, for two decades and more. He had been part of everything that Iowa had been. He knew her people and the people knew him. He had power and prestige. He came back to them from Madrid, not from a mill on the Iowa River. He wore the toga of a diplomat, and his opponent the dusty blouse of a miller. After the manner of that time — a manner glorified by Lincoln and Douglas in Illinois — a series of joint debates was arranged. The two men would be pitted against each other on the same platform. Curiosity and interest were at once aroused. The Democrats believed, and many Republicans almost feared, that the advantages would be on the side of Mr. Dodge. A trained and skillful speaker polished by four years of European culture, how could an ungainly man taken from a mill, a farm and a store, a homely man in ill-fitting clothes and one addicted to uncultivated speech, stand up against his antagonist? Fortunately for Mr. Kirkwood and unfortunately for Mr. Dodge, an obscure and unnamed Democratic editor blundered by referring to the Republican as the "plow handle" ticket, alluding to the fact that both Mr. Kirkwood and Mr. Rusch were farmers. The Republican editors were not slow to seize the phrase and to make the most of it, well knowing that the majority of the voters of the state were farmers. What had been uttered in derision, they converted into a slogan.

What followed was a campaign of virulence, almost of violence. The personalities of the candidates were not spared. Everything was laid bare and everything was imputed to them. Mr. Dodge was a man who had subsisted on the public and tabulated statements were made to show to what extent he had drawn on the public treasuries. His mental equipment had been tainted with the notions of the effete monarchies of Europe. Mr. Kirkwood was pictured as a "renegade from the dark lantern fraternity, still tainted with the vices of Know-Nothingism.[2] The two United States senators, who with others interested themselves in the campaign [3] were also

[2] Indianola *Weekly Iowa Visitor,* July 7, 1859.

[3] A list of the men who supported Kirkwood, more or less actively, as speakers and writers in that notable campaign, reads like a roster of men famous in Iowa affairs not only then but later: Senators Harlan and Grimes, Messrs. Samuel F. Miller, Fitz Henry Warren, Timothy Davis, James Thorington, Francis Springer, Hiram Price, James B. Howell, Clark Dunham, John Teesdale, John Mahin, Adison H. Saunders, A. B. F. Hildreth, William H. Seevers, James F. Wilson, Josiah B. Grinnell, F. W. Palmer, Charles Aldrich, Jacob Rich, Judge William Smythe, Eliphalet Price, Reuben Noble, Samuel R. Curtis, William Vandever, Charles C. Nourse, John A. Kasson, Grenville M. Dodge, Caleb Baldwin, Ed Wright, C. C. Carpenter, Henry O'Connor, Jacob Butler, Joseph M. Beck, John W. Noble, J. W. Rankin, Henry Strong, George B. McCrary, Hawkins Taylor, Moses McCoid, R. L. B. Clarke, James W. McDill, George G. Wright, Henry P. Scholte, James B.

attacked. Senator Grimes was charged with being the owner of a beer garden in Burlington,[4] and Senator Harlan taunted with being "the mighty Ajax of the Maine law."[5] And had he not been seen drinking in a Des Moines saloon during the state convention?[6] A Methodist minister, a Mr. Jocelyn, added to the flames by declaring that he would rather vote for an ultra slavery man than vote for Nicholas J. Rusch, who had been instrumental in modifying the prohibitory law of 1855. That brought Senator Harlan, who was a Methodist, and whose term would soon expire, into danger, for the Rusch men said they would vote against Harlan, if the Methodists voted against him. And so it went in a campaign on which everything was staked by the two contending parties.

The first of the joint debates between the two candidates was held in Oskaloosa in the presence of a vast concourse of people. The candidates talked in the afternoon and again in the evening. They did not handle each other tenderly. They contended with spurs on and they fought with verbal lances and broad swords. They asked each other questions that neither dared to avoid. Mr. Dodge said he would help enforce any law of the land, or any decision of the courts, while Mr. Kirkwood said he would help violate the fugitive slave law anywhere or at any time for he did not recognize human beings as chattels. The most spectacular of the joint debates was the closing one at Washington, Iowa. There the Democrats met their candidate and brought him into town in a carriage drawn by four splendid horses, deeming that honor fit for a man who had returned from the court of Spain. Later in the day the Republicans shrewdly "rigged up a hay rack," and on that, drawn by a yoke of oxen, they paraded their candidate through the town. The contrast was so strik-

Weaver, N. D. Carpenter, N. M. Hubbard, A. W. Hubbard, H. Clay Caldwell, William Penn Clarke, Coker F. Clarkson, John H. Gear, William B. Allison—compiled in a footnote by F. I. Herriott for his series of articles on "Iowa and the First Nomination of Lincoln," *Annals of Iowa*, Vol. VIII, p. 217.

[4] Dubuque *Herald*, July 21, 1859.

[5] *Iowa Weekly Reporter*, June 8, 1859.

[6] Dubuque *Herald*, September 14, 1859.

ing that the victory was almost won before the speaking began.

When the election was held, on the eleventh of October, Mr. Kirkwood received a majority of 3,170 votes. The victory was a substantial, but not wholly satisfactory, one to the Republicans. The truth is that many timid voters still shrank from the radicalism of the abolitionists and feared the impending conflict. Five days later John Brown made his attack at Harper's Ferry. When the news of this tragedy reached Iowa, his prophetic words at Grinnell and his revelations at Springdale were easily recalled. On the second of December, Brown and the Iowa boy, Edwin Coppoc, were hanged. In Davenport a German language paper, *Der Demokrat*, inverted its column rules and appeared in newspaper mourning over the tragedy. In many places flags were half-masted. When congress met again, Senator Grimes wrote home, "We have done nothing in the senate but discuss 'John Brown,' 'the irrepressible conflict,' and 'the impending crisis.'"[7] In the same letter he said that "the members on both sides" sat "mostly armed with deadly weapons," and their friends were similarly armed in the galleries. An unwise word spoken in the senate might have brought on the war in that august body. The national capital was filled with talk about the dissolution of the Union. When Governor Kirkwood delivered his inaugural address, on the eleventh of January, 1860, he deplored and even condemned what John Brown had done, in so far as it was rebellion against the government, but he praised "the unflinching courage and calm cheerfulness with which he met the consequences of his failure." His address was so outspoken that many members of the assembly opposed its printing as a public document.

For the presidential election in 1860 the Republicans held their state convention on January eighteenth, and the Democrats on February twenty-second. The Democrats selected delegates favorable to the candidacy of Stephen A. Douglas, but the Republicans were divided in their opinions. There was perhaps more Seward than Lincoln sentiment in the state. So far as the records show Lincoln had made but two speeches

[7] Salter's *Life of James W. Grimes*, p. 121.

in Iowa, in Council Bluffs and Burlington. His appearance in the western city was without political consideration or consequence.[8] On the ninth of October, 1858, Lincoln spoke in the Illinois campaign at Oquawka, and by invitation on the evening of the same day he made an address in Grimes Hall, Burlington. A brief announcement was sufficient to fill the hall. On the eleventh of that month the *Hawkeye* lauded his speech highly, but without attempting to make a synopsis of it. The paper spoke of it as a speech "replete with sound argument, clear, concise and vigorous, earnest, impassioned and eloquent," but it might have said as much of many other speeches. No ado was made over his presence in the city, and Mr. Lincoln came modestly to fulfill his engagement. It is related that he entered the old Barrett House with a small package in his hand. It was wrapped in a newspaper. He handed it to the clerk at the desk and asked him to take good care of it. He also confided to him the fact that it contained his "boiled shirt." It was all the baggage he carried.[9] The man puzzled the people of Iowa, who were his neighbors, as he puzzled others.

Iowa was entitled to eight votes in the memorable Chicago convention. But so many were eager to serve as delegates that to accommodate all, thirty-two delegates were selected, giving to each one-fourth of one vote, a fractional arrangement that amused the big gathering in the Chicago "Wigwam," as the convention hall was called. The thirty-two men included the men of leadership in the party of the state. It was an aggregation of the state's best public talent. Among them were abolitionists and moderates, that is, men who were still content to treat slavery as a rightful institution within its proper territorial restrictions. That they were influential in the Chicago convention, or that they played an important part in selecting the candidates is hardly true. John A. Kasson as a member of a sub-committee that drafted the historic platform, perhaps, exerted the most influence.

8 Lincoln came up the Missouri on a steamer to rest and was induced to speak; see *Annals of Iowa*, Third Series, Vol. IV, p. 462.

9 *Annals of Iowa*, Third Series, Vol. VIII, p. 455.

He attracted the attention of Horace Greeley and other leaders.[10] On the first ballot for president, Iowa cast two votes for Lincoln, two for Seward and one for each of four other candidates, Cameron, Chase, Bates, and McLean. No other state in the convention showed such an infinitesimal division. On the second ballot four of the candidates received votes, and on the third, when Lincoln's nomination had seemed a foregone conclusion, Lincoln received five and one-half votes, Seward, two votes and Chase one-half of one vote.[11]

In the democratic national convention, held at Charleston, fifty-seven ballots were taken without effecting a nomination. An adjournment was then taken to Baltimore, where Stephen A. Douglas, Lincoln's opponent in the great senatorial contest in Illinois, was nominated. The radical slavery men then seceded and in a convention held in Charleston again, W. C. Breckinridge of Kentucky received the nomination. A third party was organized under the name of the Union party, which placed John Bell in nomination as the fourth candidate. The Republicans opposed the extension of slavery; the Breckinridge Democrats held it as a divine institution; the Douglas Democrats relegated the question to the people, and the Union party held the constitution both supreme and sufficient for all the national troubles. In Iowa the radical proslavery Democrats held a convention of their own, and endorsed Breckinridge. They upheld the Dred Scott decision, denied that either congress or the people could restrict slavery, adhering to the right that American citizens could settle in the territory of the United States "with whatever property they legally possess," including slaves.

During the summer and autumn of 1860 politics was the principal business of the people. Both of the great parties

10 "John A. Kasson . . . with Horace Greeley, formed the sub-committee which drafted the platform of that famous convention."—Gue's *History of Iowa*, Vol. II, p. 42.

11 The detailed record of how the Iowa delegates voted is not extant. Alvin Saunders and C. C. Nourse were known as Lincoln leaders; Governor Kirkwood voted for Lincoln although he had Chase prejudices; Senator Harlan supported Seward; William B. Allison supported Chase; John A. Kasson, by reason of a Missouri residence, favored Bates.

organized numerous marching clubs. Rallies, processions, picnics, and barbecues were the order of the day all over the state. Newspapers and speakers were often abusive and vituperative in their discussions and in a few places personal violence was resorted to. Lincoln made no speeches in Iowa, but Douglas made two, one at Iowa City, on October, ninth, and one at Cedar Rapids on the following day. In both places he made the significant utterance, in reply to the threats of secession: "I tell you people of Iowa today that whoever is elected president, must be inaugurated, and after he is inaugurated, he must be supported in the exercise of all his just powers." He had made concessions to the slave oligarchy of the south, but he remained a Union man. In the election Iowa cast 70,118 votes for Lincoln, 55,639 for Douglas, 1,034 for Breckinridge, and 1,763 for Bell. Douglas kept his word. He was present at the inauguration of Lincoln, and dying, soon afterwards, he said: "Tell my children to obey the laws and uphold the constitution," words that were afterwards inscribed on his monument. They are noble words still, the foundation of all government and the keystone of the arch of the Union.

# PART VI

## The Civil War and After

## 1860-1867

# CHAPTER LIV

## THE CALL TO ARMS

On the twentieth of December, 1860, within six weeks after the election of Abraham Lincoln, the first act of secession was passed, by the state of South Carolina. By a legislative declaration that state ceased to be part of the United States. James Buchanan of Pennsylvania, was president. He himself was a loyal man, and he did not believe that a state had a right to secede. But he did not know what to do to prevent it. At least, he did nothing. "Mr. Buchanan, it is said, about equally divides his time between praying and crying," Senator Grimes wrote from Washington to Mrs. Grimes, who was in Burlington.

When Andrew Jackson was president, they talked of secession in South Carolina, but they subsided when he threatened to hang them higher than Haman. If Andrew Jackson had been president in 1860, instead of James Buchanan — but there is the eternal "if" in history!

While the president wept and prayed, his cabinet was going to pieces. Many of them were southern men. They were going back home to help organize the rebellion. When Secretary Cobb resigned, to quote Senator Grimes again, he wrote, "saying that he was going home to Georgia, to assist in dissolving the Union, and breaking up the government; and Buchanan replied to the letter, and *complimented Mr. Cobb*, as you have seen."[1] But one member of the cabinet did not resign at that time — he was the secretary of war. He remained in Washington and used the power of his office to dismantle the north and to equip the south for the impending war. He is said to have caused a hundred and fifteen thou-

[1] Salter's *Life of James W. Grimes*, p. 132.

sand rifles, to speak of no other materials, to be transferred to the south.[2]

Abraham Lincoln looked on from Springfield, Illinois. He knew what it meant, but he had no power to prevent it. Of all men, he was the least warlike. He yet hoped for peace. His appeals were still to the better natures of men. Governor Kirkwood went to Springfield to talk over the situation with him. They met on the street, and they had a long conference in the room of a hotel.[3] More must have been said of peace than of war for, after the conference, the governor wrote to Senator Grimes suggesting the Missouri Compromise as another settlement of differences. "The restoration of the Missouri Compromise line," the senator wrote back, "has been offered to the disunionists and contemptuously rejected."[4] When the governor wrote again to the senator, he said, "Whatever comes, and at all hazards, the Union must be honored — the law must be enforced." To Mr. Grimes, Iowa had "a peculiar interest in this question." If one state could close to her the mouth of the Mississippi, others could close to her all the avenues of trade. "If she will not agree to this, it becomes her people to insist that the constitution of the country shall be upheld, that the laws of the land shall be enforced, and that this pretended right of a state to destroy our national existence shall be sternly and emphatically rebuked." He said he believed that the people of Iowa "would risk all things and endure all things" for the honor of the national flag and for the preservation of the national Union. Governor Kirkwood wondered what he should do in the meantime. "Shall I tender the aid of the state to Mr. Buchanan?" he asked. He was ready to pledge the last fighting man and the last dollar. In a characteristic postscript the governor asked if any arms could be obtained in Washington. The senator replied, "no," and the governor then issued orders to have all the arms of the state collected and repaired. But there were not many to be found. Most of them had been carried to Kansas.

[2] Rhodes's *History of the United States*, Vol. III, pp. 353-355.

[3] Byers's *Iowa in War Times*, p. 32.

[4] Salter's *Life of James W. Grimes*, p. 133.

Iowa at that time did not have even an organized militia. Military preparations had been made legislative jests.[5] Even in that very year, 1860, when Governor Lowe had asked for a law to organize the militia, the committee on military affairs had replied that they were unanimously opposed to it. But, fortunately, there were in the state many volunteer companies. They were social as much as military organizations. They were made up of what were called parade soldiers. The men wore gaudy uniforms, and they called their companies by pretty names, such as Blues, Greys, Guards, Rifles, or Zouaves. There were four such companies in Davenport alone, largely officered by men who had been trained in Germany. As the war clouds deepened, these play-soldiers wanted to become real soldiers. Early in January they began tendering their services to the governor, and the Dubuque Greys tendered theirs to the secretary of war, who must have laughed at them. Priority in making such tenders is claimed for the Burlington Rifles, of which C. L. Matthies, a German-American, was captain, but the records in the governor's office show that the first letter of acknowledgment was written to Captain H. R. Cowles, who had tendered the Washington Light Guards.[6]

One state after another seceded, until eleven had severed, so far as they could sever, the ties that bound them to the Union. But South Carolina kept herself in the van, beginning the war by firing on Fort Sumter, which was still flying the Stars and Stripes in the harbor of Charleston. That was done on the fourteenth of April. Two days later, Major Robert Anderson was compelled to surrender the fort, saluting the flag with fifty guns before hauling it down, and then marching the garrison out with flying flags and beating drums.

On the same day, President Lincoln issued a call for seventy-five thousand volunteers to put down what was still regarded as a mere insurrection. Iowa's allotment of troops was one regiment, of ten companies of seventy-eight men each, "for immediate service." They were to be enlisted for nine

5 *House Journal*, 1856-1857, pp. 183, 184, 429, 454, 458.

6 Byers's *Iowa in War Times*, pp. 39-40.

months — seventy-five thousand men in nine months were to crush the rebellion!

There was at that time a telegraph wire as far as Davenport, but not to Iowa City, to which the news was carried by a messenger. The governor immediately issued a call for the First Iowa Regiment of infantry. The responses were so many that he was embarrassed to find places for all who wanted to serve their country. The governor was overwhelmed — and his faith in Iowa was vindicated.

A tidal wave of patriotism swept over the state. War meetings became the order of the day. To save the Union became the religion of the people. For the time being partisan differences were forgotten. "Ten days ago," Governor Kirkwood wrote to President Lincoln, "there were two parties in Iowa. Now, there is only one, and that one for the constitution and the Union unconditionally." At one place the Republicans and Democrats spliced their flag poles and from the combined height floated the Stars and Stripes. A church conference which was holding its sessions resolved to "stand still and see the salvation of God." In Iowa City a call was issued "for a general rally of all citizens . . . who formerly served in European armies . . . who know well their duty to God and their adopted country." The concluding words on this flaming poster were: "Rally, ye sons of Germany, Bohemia, and France!" Money also was offered. Bankers telegraphed the governor to draw on them. The town of Brighton sent $1,250 to the governor as an offering, and the colony at Amana, where men did not believe in war, sent $1,000, with a promise of more. Within a week twenty-one companies were tendered to the governor.

The call for troops was issued on the seventeenth of April, and by the eighth of May the ten companies of the First regiment were all in Keokuk, the place of rendezvous. Of the companies accepted by the governor for this regiment, two came from Burlington, two from Muscatine, two from Dubuque, and one each from the counties of Linn, Johnson, Henry, and Scott. Patriotic demonstrations, banquets, flag presentations, speeches and music marked their going forth.

On the eleventh of May, in the court house at Keokuk, the men elected their own regimental officers, John F. Bates of Dubuque colonel, William H. Merritt of Linn lieutenant colonel, and Asbury M. Porter of Henry major.

Those for whom there was no room in the First regiment were not only disappointed, but many of them became resentful. They blamed and criticised the governor. To keep the peace among the zealous patriots, the governor, without authority from the war department, created the Second regiment, and followed it with the Third, summoning them to assemble at Keokuk. He literally begged the war department to accept these willing men. "I am overwhelmed with applications," he wrote. "I can raise ten thousand men in this state in twenty days." To satisfy the clamorous ones on the Missouri, he authorized the creation of the Fourth regiment at Council Bluffs. But while men were willing to serve, neither the national nor the state government could supply them with arms. "For God's sake, send us arms," was the governor's appeal, "we have the men to use them." [7]

The state treasury was so empty and so poor that the governor wanted to avoid the expense of an extraordinary session of the general assembly, but when it was assembled, on the fifteenth of May, R. D. Kellogg, a Democrat, moved a resolution that "the faith, credit and resources of the state of Iowa, both in men and money" be pledged to the national government. The resolution was passed by a unanimous vote.

[7] Byers's *Iowa in War Times*, p. 46.

# CHAPTER LV

## The First Glory of the War

The spirit of the people was right in 1861, but everything else was wrong. There was plenty of patriotism, but no materials with which to begin a war. The treasury of Iowa was empty. There were more taxes delinquent than taxes paid. The people were poor. Following a panic they had passed through a series of bad crop years. The national government was in no better condition. What arms it had possessed had been transferred to the South. In a military sense, President Lincoln had inherited a bankrupt country.

How poverty-stricken the state was at that time is revealed in the records of the First Iowa. Fortunately, there was a young man in one of the companies of that regiment who had the writing habit, and a pen touched by much of the magic of genius. He kept a diary which later he expanded into a volume in which vivacity and veracity are conspicuous.[1] He complains bitterly of the unpreparedness; of all the deficiencies, and later of the inefficiencies of those who were placed in command of the regiments and the companies in camps and on the fields of battle. The men were drilled with wooden sticks and often under men with wooden heads. They had no uniforms. The women made the clothes in which they marched away to help put down the rebellion. They made the clothes "the way they wanted them," not as the government wanted them later. For the Burlington Zouaves, who constituted Company E in the regiment, they selected a cloth of azure gray — probably the only kind they could get in sufficient quantities. It was of an open weave, fluffy and fuzzy.

[1] Eugene F. Ware, whose later *nom de plume* was "Ironquill." He was a member of the Burlington Zouaves before the war and entered the service as a member of Company E of the First Iowa Infantry.

Out of this material the women made coats in the form of hunting frocks "of the Daniel Boone type." They fitted "closely at the neck, wrists and waists, but they had ample width everywhere else." The trousers were of "heavy buckskin type and color." They trimmed these coats and trousers with strips of "flannel of a beautiful Venetian red," and on the hats, which were of the black felt hunting pattern, they fastened a "brilliant red cockade." That is what the women "wanted" for their young heroes. They did not realize that the red stripes and cockades would later make excellent targets for the guns of the enemy.

On the seventh of May, thus dressed up, the Zouaves were ready to proceed down the Mississippi to Keokuk, the place of rendezvous. The band played for them the music of "The Girl I Left Behind Me," which has been played for soldiers ever since. It brought tears to all eyes. On the boat they sang "Dixie Land" before that stirring tune had been made the peculiar property of the Confederacy. On the way down the river they were cheered, but not by all the people. One-third, it is estimated by the diarist, of the people were secession in their sentiments. They were southern people, or people who had come in contact with southern sentiments. In Keokuk the secessionists tried to win the war by selling poisoned pies to the hungry Union boys, and the saloon-keepers "doped" their beer and whiskey. That soon led to riots in which glasses and plates and heads were smashed. They were riotous times. After long waiting they were supplied with arms — muskets that were stamped "U. S. A. 1829." They dated back to the Black Hawk War. They could "out-kick . . . a government mule." Being girl-sick, the boys called these muskets, "Hannah," or "Mary Jane," or "Silver Sue."

Anxious to go to the front, the regiment was detained in Keokuk week after week. Their camp life was miserable. There was no order, there was no discipline. Neglect and incompetence were everywhere. The officers spent more time in the saloons than on the drill grounds. The guard houses were filled with men who were not guarded. The men sent out details to bring in their officers. The diarist says that "Rations were wasted. . . Twenty per cent of the men went on the sick list. . . Officers were most inefficient, and did not know how to take care of their men." They did not know how to take care of themselves. When the regimental officers were selected, in the court house at Keokuk, by popular vote, politics and geography were satisfied, "but the soldiers of the regiment were not." Still they were detained, until they wondered why they had been enlisted and for what, and until they feared "that the war would end before any one knew that the First Iowa were enlisted." But when they feared the war was over, it had not yet commenced.

Finally, after they had spent fifty of their ninety days in camps in Iowa, they received orders, on the thirteenth of June, to embark on a Mississippi River steamer which would carry them into the enemy's country. At last they were going to have a chance to fight! They were disembarked at Hannibal, Missouri. They were transferred to freight cars in which they rode to Macon City, and from there to Renick, near Boonville on the Missouri. There they realized they were among the enemy. They saw the remnants of a skirmish which had been fought, in the form of guerrilla horsemen riding madly away. They saw also their real commander, General Nathaniel B. Lyon, of the regular army. He was a little wiry man, not at all an impressive soldier. Other troops joined them until they numbered about three thousand. They learned there that General Jackson's army had been partially whipped; that it was in retreat, and that they would go in pursuit of it. On the third of July they started. They liked marching. They sang "The Happy Land of Canaan" as they marched. It was sung to the tune of old "John Brown," who was then mouldering in his grave. "See those Iowa greyhounds stretch out when they sing 'The Happy Land of Canaan,'" said General Lyon. "There goes that tam 'Happy Land of Canaan,'" said General Sigel. It was their boast that they could out-march anything on two legs. The diarist says that their officers "got to attaching the name of their state to their commands." They said, "Forward, Iowa," and "Halt, Iowa," which pleased them, for they liked still to be reminded of Iowa. They were proud of their state.

At Clinton, Missouri, they received accessions to their numbers, the First and Second Kansas regiments, and some regulars, until they numbered over six thousand. After that they marched like an army. Sometimes it rained all day, and at other times it rained all night. They were often wet and covered with mud. They began to realize that army life was duty and drudgery. On the twelfth of July they marched forty-six miles. It took men to do that. On the night of the nineteenth of July, a cyclonic storm blew down their tents and they "were all as wet as drowned rats." In the morning they could not make fires for there was nothing dry enough to burn. They had "a sack of flour . . . and a quart of salt; no meat, no coffee, 'no nothing.'" They ate their dough raw "and poured onto it a round of still whiskey." The wonder is they did not all go on the sick list and die.

After marching in that way for many days, they began to hear of the enemy in front of them. They were eager to fight them, though they knew that they were outnumbered. On the twentieth of July their three months were up. They could lay down their arms. But they did not want to return without having been in a fight. They began to demand "a fight or a discharge." They preferred a fight for they did not want to go home empty handed. They wanted their sweethearts to receive them back as heroes. On the ninth of August they reached Springfield. At sundown the bugles blew and while they were standing in line, General Lyon rode past on a dapple gray horse and told them, "Men, we are going to have a fight. . . We will march out in short time. . . Don't shoot until you get your orders. . . Don't get scared. . . It is no part of a soldier's duty to get scared." It was all so matter of fact. They liked better what "Irish" Sweeney said to his cavalrymen, "Stay together, boys, and we'll saber hell out of them!" That sounded more like what they wanted to do.

That night they slept on their arms, four thousand of the six thousand, General Sigel having marched the other two thousand to the rear. The plan of battle was to crush the enemy between them, but General Sigel's force was routed and his guns were taken and turned on the men under General

Lyon. The soldiers slept well, though it was on the eve of their first battle. When they were awakened there was "just . . . a slight flush of dawn in the east." They ate a bite and they marched a bit, crouching along the ground at the last. When they "got close the firing began on both sides. . . How long it lasted? . . . It might have been an hour. . . It seemed like a week. . . It was probably twenty minutes." They pushed forward, and they were swept backward. "No man deserted. . . No man broke ranks or ran." They saw their comrades falling around them. Some were wounded and some were dead. It did not seem to make any difference. Their lips became parched. They heard each other speak in strange and husky voices. Some voices seemed to come from the grave. "Have you any water in your canteen?" — they heard that often. While bullets were flying around them they held their canteens to the lips of others who were powerless to help themselves. The bonds of comradeship had never been so strong before. They picked up some guns which a Louisiana company had left in flight. They were marked "U. S. A." They were new guns. They were not like the muskets marked "U. S. A., 1829," with which they were fighting. Some Iowa men recognized an "Ottumwa man" who had gone south and become a Texas cavalry leader. They "got him." But when they saw a real Texas ranger in the act of rescuing a flag which had been dropped, some one cried out, "Don't shoot!" They were in the presence of a brave man doing a brave act — and their instinct told them not to kill him for doing it. That was fine. It was chivalry. One is glad that Iowa men felt that way; it is one of the things in the war that still can bring the glow of pride to Iowa cheeks.

At last there came the final charge. The battle was not over, but it was stopped. No one knew then who had won the victory — and it is still disputed. But it was a Union victory, none the less. Four thousand men had held their own against many times their number. It was proved that the men of the north, from the farms and shops and stores, could and would fight. At that time that needed sorely to be proved.

The rout at Bull Run had thrown the whole country into doubt. But the commander, General Lyon, was among the dead. He fell near the Iowa lines. The tradition is that when a bullet found him he was giving some command to the Iowa regiment. General Sturgis, who took over the command, in his report mentioned "particularly the First Iowa which fought like veterans." In his report, General Schofield said, "Captain Totten's Battery in the center, supported by the First Iowa and regulars, was the main point of attack." But it is not necessary to believe that the men of Iowa fought better or more than others, where all did so well. Out of four thousand and three hundred engaged, seven hundred and twenty-one were listed as casualties, and two hundred and twenty-three of them were dead. The casualties of the Iowa regiment were one hundred and sixty, twenty of whom were dead — they could not go home as heroes, but their mothers and sisters and sweethearts were never to be ashamed of what they had done. For those twenty men, and for all the others, there ought to be a monument on Wilson's Creek, for they were the first offerings of Iowa in the Civil War.

The little battle in Missouri fell at an opportune time. The news of it thrilled the country — so shortly after the disaster at Bull Run. Courage flowed back into the hearts of men as they read the news of it. President Lincoln ordered a proclamation of thanks to be read before all the regiments in the service. "Remember Wilson's Creek" and the "immortal First Iowa," Governor Kirkwood repeated to those who followed them in the service.

The First Iowa was marched to St. Louis to be mustered out. Their enlistments had expired. They had fought their one battle on their own time. It was patriotism and pride, not mere duty. At St. Louis the loyal people erected triumphal arches for them to march under, and the school children scattered flowers in their paths. The regiment was disbanded, and Governor Kirkwood would not permit it to be reorganized. Theirs was a completed record. So let it stand in history. But six hundred of its men immediately reënlisted in other regiments which were then forming.

# CHAPTER LVI

## The Reaction and the Recoil

When the veteranized boys of the First Iowa came home from Wilson's Creek they found the war, in which they had been so anxious to participate, was not over. It had not yet commenced in all its seriousness. During their absence, enlistments had been the order of the day. Of infantry, ten regiments had been completed, or were then being completed; of cavalry, four, and two batteries.

They found something else, too — the evidences of discord, and of disloyalty even. The men of Iowa were no longer of one mind. In fact, they had never been of one mind. The first effusions and enthusiasms of patriotism had soon subsided. The resolution pledging the resources of the state to the nation had been passed by a unanimous vote, but when the question was on voting $800,000 in bonds to make good that pledge, twenty-four men showed up in the extraordinary session of the general assembly to cast their votes against it. They said the bonds were unconstitutional. That the state could not contract so large an indebtedness under its constitution except "to repel invasion, suppress insurrection, or defend the state in war." Iowa had not been invaded or attacked, and there were no insurrections within her borders. When the bonds were offered for sale, no purchasers appeared. Governor Kirkwood begged the people of the state to purchase their own bonds, but the people were poor and those who had money were timid. By the last of July only sixteen thousand dollars worth of them had been sold, and three months later, the sales had reached only eighty thousand dollars. To supply the new regiments with the barest necessities, the governor borrowed money, often on his own credit, or on the credit of his friends — and there were some who said he had no right to do that in the name of the state.

The reverses that came to the Union army during the first year, such as the defeat at Bull Run, aroused the discontented and the disloyal. They dared to come out into the open. Iowa had a large southern element. Their sympathies were naturally with the south. Some of them deplored and others denounced the war. At the town of Ossian some one hoisted a Confederate flag. In Marion County a convention grieved because they saw their "beloved country distracted at home, and disgraced abroad."[1] They saw "commerce paralyzed . . . coasts blockaded . . . states invaded and dismembered." They blamed President Lincoln for it all, and not those who had passed the resolutions of secession, or those who had fired on Fort Sumter. The bitter name of copperhead came suddenly into vogue — it was the name of a snake that lies concealed in the grass to strike its victim.[2] But if this subtle influence deterred some from enlisting, it made others more determined to fight to the bitter end. The sense of duty more than the feeling of enthusiasm began to draw men into the service of their country.

To troubles within were added troubles from without. In the southern counties there was the daily fear of raids by guerrilla bands from Missouri, and from the western and northern borders came the complaint that "citizens are almost daily being shot down . . . by Indians." Caleb Baldwin, who sent this message from Council Bluffs, feared that the northwestern counties would be depopulated. The government had withdrawn or weakened its garrisons in the Indian country and the red men roamed at will. The governor replied by making Mr. Baldwin a staff officer, with authority to protect the frontiers. But he could not supply him with arms. The Fourth Iowa had its origin in this western fear. The governor sent Ezekiel Clark to Washington to procure arms, and Mr. Baldwin sent Grenville M. Dodge, who had been a railroad surveyor, on the same mission. Young Dodge scored. He knew how to do things, and how to get what he

[1] Byers's *Iowa in War Times*, p. 50.

[2] Some have derived the opprobrious term from the Indian head on a copper coin, which was worn as an emblem by the disloyalists.

wanted. He got arms enough to equip a regiment, and the governor authorized him to create in Council Bluffs the Fourth Iowa Infantry, believing that it would have a good effect on the border.

To protect the southern border companies of Home Guards were organized in all of the counties of the southern tier. Cyrus Bussey was placed in command of southeastern Iowa. A serious situation soon confronted him.[3] A guerrilla chief, called General Martin Green, was so encouraged by the news of Bull Run that he planned an invasion of Iowa. He probably counted on the moral support and the aid of the southern sympathizers in that part of the state. He advanced on Athens, a town on the Des Moines River, opposite the little town of Croton on the Iowa side. They boasted that they would take breakfast in Athens, dine in Farmington, and sup in Keokuk. Athens was held at that time by a force of three hundred Home Guard troops under Colonel David Moore. Bussey learned through a spy of the proposed invasion. He had men, but not any arms. Through a railroad official he learned that a supply of arms was at that time in transit — they were the arms that Dodge had coaxed out of Washington. He did not wait for permission. He forced open the cars and supplied his men with the rifles which they needed. From Keokuk he rushed up a few companies of the Sixth Iowa, which were detained there for lack of transportation. General Green came up and opened fire on Athens, but the place was too well defended for him to take it. A few stray cannon balls sped across the Des Moines and fell near Croton — and that was as near as the Civil War ever came to Iowa. Bussey was at first criticised by Baldwin and Dodge for taking their arms, and he was mildly reprimanded by the governor, but when they learned to what good use he had put them, he was commended. General Frémont at St. Louis admired the act so much that he induced Bussey to enter the service, which he did by organizing the Third Iowa Cavalry, which became one of the crack horse regiments of the war.

[3] General Cyrus Bussey's "The Battle of Athens," in *Annals of Iowa,* Third Series, Vol. V, p. 81.

As fast as the Iowa regiments were organized, often with little or no training, they were sent to the front, which was by way of the Mississippi. But they were not called upon to participate in any great battles during 1861, a year in which no great battles were fought. On the seventeenth of September, five hundred men of the Third Iowa fell into an ambush to which the name of the Battle of Blue Mills has been given. The colonel of the regiment, Nelson G. Williams, was under military arrest for some blunders at Shelbina. The lieutenant colonel, John Scott, and the men were eager to wipe out the disgrace by some heroic action. Coming in contact with the enemy's forces, they proceeded into action, without waiting for reinforcements which had been promised. They found themselves in a trap out of which they fought their way gallantly, but with a loss of seventy, nine of whom were killed.

On the seventh of December a greater disaster befell the Seventh Iowa, at Belmont, which is described as General Grant's first battle, and it almost proved to be his last, also. The general had been ordered to go from Cairo to Columbus to menace the Confederates who were establishing themselves in force. On the way down they saw a detachment of the enemy at Belmont. The men clamored for a fight and General Grant yielded against his own better judgment. He had no authority to bring on a battle. At first they won an easy victory, but while celebrating it the Confederates made a counter attack and almost overwhelmed them. The Seventh Iowa, one of the regiments engaged, lost two hundred and twenty-seven men, fifty-four of whom were among the dead.

The fruits of the first war enthusiasm had been the ten regiments of infantry, the four regiments of cavalry, and the three batteries already noted. But in September the governor had to make an appeal for more men. "It is the cause of the government, of home, of country, of freedom, of humanity, of God himself," he told the people of Iowa. The response was made, but not with the alacrity of the earlier enlistments. The men who offered themselves were older, and they were animated more by a sense of duty than the feeling of enthusiasm. Four more regiments of infantry were soon in being, and the

Fourth Cavalry was completed. The Fifteenth and the Sixteenth regiments of infantry were recruited during the winter months, and the Seventeenth and Eighteenth were projected but not filled until the following spring and summer. These twenty-four units, eighteen infantry, four cavalry, and two batteries, constituted the state's offerings for the first year of the war. The state had been called upon to furnish 19,316 men and it offered 21,937. The Seventeenth and Eighteenth regiments were free-will offerings. "They were offered to the nation out of the generosity of our people, and were accepted by special order of the secretary of war."[4]

In the midst of these momentous events, Governor Kirkwood was reëlected. He did not seek a renomination, and he did little to bring about his own reëlection, except to discharge his multitudinous duties as war-governor. But he was not unopposed in his own party. At times he must have felt overwhelmed by criticism. His critics enumerated the things that had been left undone and pointed out the errors in the things that had been done. When the convention of his party met on the thirty-first of July, four candidates appeared to contest his right to a renomination. They were men of parts, too. Samuel F. Miller, who became a justice of the supreme court of the United States; Elijah Sells, a popular politician; Fitz Henry Warren, who had organized the First Cavalry; and Samuel A. Rice, a man of sterling character who later won high distinction as an officer. Governor Kirkwood was easily renominated. The platform was a piece of patriotism. The war was its one theme and victory for the Union its one aspiration and hope. John R. Needham of Keokuk County was named for lieutenant governor. The Democrats named for the same offices, Charles Mason and Maturin L. Fisher. Their platform disapproved of the war and they expressed the belief that a Union formed in peace "can never be perpetuated by force of arms." They proposed a national conference to formulate a peace. Mason withdrew from the ticket and William H. Merritt of the First Regiment was named in his stead. A band of pacifists formed a third party which

[4] Ingersoll's *Iowa and the Rebellion*, p. 308.

they named after the Union, nominating Nathaniel B. Baker, who had been a Democratic governor in New Hampshire, as their candidate. He declined and became a supporter of Governor Kirkwood, and later his adjutant general to help win an enduring peace by fighting for it.

Governor Kirkwood made but two speeches of any moment in his own behalf, one at Des Moines and one at Davenport. First of all he replied to his critics. He admitted his own failures. But they were not his failures in fact. He admitted the men in the regiments had not been properly cared for, "but that is your fault, not mine," he told the people. "I had no money to do it," he said in sorrow. He told them that the uniforms in which the immortalized First Regiment had fought the Battle of Wilson's Creek had not yet been paid for. The same was true of the uniforms of the Second and Third regiments. The men in the service had not received their pittances of thirteen dollars a month. There was no money to pay them with. The bonds of the state had been discredited outside and no buyers of them had appeared in Iowa. Many men were willing to risk their lives, but few their money. And yet men might lose their lives, but they could not lose their money as long as the state and the nation endured. The governor told his audience in Des Moines that he had borrowed money to the extent of his abilities on his own credit and on the credit of his relatives and friends. "The bank of this city," Des Moines, he related pathetically, "holds my protested notes for $6,000." He had done for the state and for the soldiers he loved what he had never done in his private business, permitted his notes to go to protest! Instead of finding fault with him, their executive, he asked them to find fault with themselves. He asked that the people should uphold the hands of those who were their servants and who were doing all that they could, often more than they could. And then forgetting his own burdens and forgiving his critics, he paid a matchless tribute to the men who had so freely offered their lives for their country, and he appealed to all to fall in line with those who were marching to the music of patriotism.

# CHAPTER LVII

## The Realities of War

If the first year of the war had closed in gloom, the second year opened in despair. "In God's name, can't something be done with our army?" Governor Kirkwood wrote to Senator Grimes on the eighth day of January, 1862. But something was even then impending.

General Grant was still at Cairo. He had nothing to remember except the disaster at Belmont. But he was looking ahead. He looked on the Confederate line which stretched from Columbus on the Mississippi to Nashville on the Tennessee. He believed he could break the line by attacking in two places, Fort Henry and Fort Donelson, the one on the Tennessee and the other on the Cumberland. He begged his superior officer for permission to try. He was put off. Who was General Grant? But when at last a grudged permission was given him, he took Fort Henry in a single day and then moved toward Donelson, which was the stronger place.

He had in his little army three Iowa regiments, the Seventh, Twelfth, and Fourteenth. He went to St. Louis to get more troops for his undertaking. He found there the Second Iowa languishing in disgrace. While guarding McDowell's Medical College, used as a federal prison, some property had disappeared, for the theft of which the regiment was held responsible. Colonel Tuttle and Governor Kirkwood protested such unjust treatment. General Grant coveted the stalwart Iowans and the men were eager to follow him to the front to vindicate their good name. The regiment was marched through St. Louis to the boat with its banner furled, and without the tap of a drum or the note of a bugle or a fife — it was in disgrace.

Colonel Tuttle accepted for himself and his men what others had declined — the honor of leading the assault to be made on the fort, supported by the three other Iowa regiments and one from Indiana, Lauman's brigade. The colonel led his men. Three color bearers, Doolittle, Page and Churcher, were shot down and the fourth, Voltaire P. Twombley, was wounded but he carried the flag to its goal. Fort Donelson was taken in a sacrificial assault, one of the most heroic of the whole war. Halleck, the unrelenting, had the grace to telegraph to Adjutant General Baker in Des Moines that "The Second Iowa proved themselves the bravest of the brave. They had the honor of leading the column that entered Fort Donelson." The regiment paid the price. Of six hundred and thirty men engaged, it lost one hundred and ninety-seven, of whom thirty-three were dead and the others wounded. General Buckner made the "immediate and unconditional surrender" which General Grant had demanded of him, fifteen thousand men and sixty cannon fell into Union hands and the Confederate line was compelled to fall back almost a hundred miles. The victory in which the Second Iowa had led made Grant a major general, and Tuttle a brigadier general.

The news of the victory reached Des Moines on the following day. The legislature was in session. The editor of the *Register*, Frank W. Palmer, carried the news to the speaker of the house, Rush Clark, who sprang to his feet in the middle of a roll call, shouting, "Grant has taken Fort Donelson." Scenes of indescribable joy followed.[1] Pandemonium raged, which soon spread to the whole city. Men celebrated the victory until they did not know what they were doing. To them the fall of Donelson was the beginning of the end of the war. Governor Kirkwood and other officials went to the scene of the victory, to look after the state's wounded. They brought back with them the flag which had been carried in the terrible assault — and the flag remains one of the state's proudest memories.

But other Iowa regiments were soon to add to the glory of the state. Brigadier General Curtis had been placed in command of the Army of the Southwest, operating in Missouri.

[1] Charles Aldrich in *The Iowa Historical Record*, January, 1892, p. 215.

He had with him two Iowa infantry regiments, the Fourth, commanded by Colonel Grenville M. Dodge, and the Ninth, commanded by William Vandever. Curtis and Vandever had both resigned their seats in congress to enter the army. The Third Iowa Cavalry and the First and Third Iowa batteries were also with this army. Dodge and Vandever were placed in command of brigades, turning their own regiments over to the lieutenant colonels. On the sixth and seventh days of March the Army of the Southwest met the enemy in vastly superior numbers at Pea Ridge. On the first day they almost lost the battle, but they hung on tenaciously. Dodge had three horses shot under him and a fourth crippled, while he himself was wounded. It was his first trial and he proved himself a fighting man of whom generals are made. The victory was completed on the second day. The Iowa regiments and batteries counted over five hundred losses, one-third of all that were incurred. It was an Iowa commanded battle. The victory made Curtis a major-general and Dodge a brigadier-general. Iowa rejoiced again, and so did the nation. The gloom was becoming a glow of glory.

A wave of optimism then swept over the country. Many felt that the war would soon be over. So much did this spirit of confidence fill the land that the recruiting offices were closed on the third of April. It was believed that no more enlistments would be necessary, that the men under arms could finish the war and do it speedily.

But, alas, for such premature hopes! Three days later the Battle of Shiloh was fought and that to the verge of disaster. General Grant, who had been absent, reached the scene on the second day when a victory was wrested from a defeat. But the victory meant no more than that the army had been able to save itself with enormous losses that represented nothing gained. Of the forty thousand men who had been attacked in their camp, ten thousand had been killed or wounded or were missing — one-fourth of all engaged! And of these losses, one-fourth fell to the eleven Iowa regiments which had been caught in that slaughter pen. Pittsburgh Landing had not been selected as a battlefield, but as temporary camp for an army which General Grant intended to use against Corinth. While the regiments were still assembling, and before any intrenchments had been made, the Confederates came in force to attack them. Confusion reigned supreme. Men fought like tigers, but commanders did not always command. When the news of the disaster was published, the wildest rumors were set afloat. The brunt of the criticism fell on General Grant. He was attacked in congress. Senator Harlan of Iowa said that he did not think he was "fit to command a great army in the field."[3]

For the troops from Iowa, who were so heavily engaged, Shiloh was a veritable trial by fire. Three whole regiments, the Eighth, Twelfth, and Fourteenth, were literally wiped out. In attempting to protect a battery they had overstayed, and as a result they were surrounded and cut off. Some of them fought their way out. The Third which was also involved, but not so deeply as others, succeeded in extricating itself. The bulk of the men in the three regiments became prisoners of war. The Fifteenth and Sixteenth were new regiments; they came from Iowa to be led into battle. They were made over into veterans in a single day. These two regiments were thrown into a brigade with the Eleventh and Thirteenth Iowa, of whom Marcellus M. Crocker became the commander, following the death of Colonel Hare of the Eleventh. Crocker fought the brigade so well that it took his name and the organization was kept intact until the end of the war, although General Crocker himself did not remain in command.

Iowa had in the spring of 1862 fifteen infantry regiments in the service, the First having been disbanded. Eleven of these participated at Shiloh, two at Pea Ridge, and the other two, the Fifth and Tenth, took an honorable part in the campaign under General Pope against New Madrid and Island No. 10, the town being taken on the fourteenth of March, but the island, which was an engineering feat, requiring twenty-three days in its reduction.

But the war was not over. The disasters were so many that

[3] Brigham's *James Harlan*, p. 173. Later Senator Harlan made amends to General Grant by defending his course as president in the San Domingo affair.

the recruiting offices which had been closed in April were reopened in June. President Lincoln still believed that another one hundred and fifty thousand men would be enough, but he was prevailed upon to call for 300,000, and a little later he called for 300,000 more to replace the losses in old regiments. To fill the state's allotments, Governor Kirkwood, on the ninth of July, issued a call for more men. The responses at first were slow. The men of Iowa were in the harvest fields. The draft was talked of. It was still considered almost a disgrace to be drafted. The loyalists dreaded it and the disloyalists said they would resist it to the bitter end. But when the harvests were over the men of Iowa again began to volunteer. No draft was necessary to command their services. They offered them freely. But the men who enlisted were older and they went about it in quieter ways. The tide of enlistments soon ran so high that the governor and the adjutant general were at a loss how to care for them. The governor boasted that he could put twenty regiments in the field in a week, if the government could provide the clothing and the arms for them. Men enlisted not singly, but in whole companies. In many communities only the old men and the boys were left, and the boys had to be restrained from literally "lying" their way into the regiments.

But the old men could not be restrained. They formed a regiment of their own, which became the Thirty-seventh, called the Graybeard regiment. All the men in this organization were over forty-five years of age and some of them were sixty. They boasted that they had given more than thirteen hundred sons and grandsons to the armies of the nation — and now they were not only offering themselves, but they were insisting that they should be accepted. The war department yielded to their importunities and the Graybeards were mustered into the service. The regiment was unique. There was none other like it in the whole nation. It was the highest expression of the patriotism of the people of Iowa in 1862. They served well until the end of the war, although they were never called upon to participate in battles, and they were mustered out with the special thanks of their government.

Out of these overwhelming offers of men, twenty-two new regiments of infantry were organized which were numbered from nineteen to forty, inclusively. The Forty-first regiment also was organized, but it consisted of only a single battalion, composed mostly of three companies left over from the Fourteenth which went to pieces in the Battle of Shiloh. The Forty-second and Forty-third regiments were projected, but were never completed.[5]

The state was also called upon to make additional provisions for guarding the northern and southern borders. Insurrections and guerrilla raids were still feared along the Missouri state line. In September, 1862, under an act of the legislature, the governor created the Southern Border Brigade, made up of one company from each county in the southern tier of counties. In the north the long feared Indian outbreak came in that year. In what are known as the New Ulm massacres, the Sioux killed over six hundred settlers and laid waste all of southwestern Minnesota. Iowa, fortunately, was not touched. Governor Kirkwood sent S. R. Ingham to organize the Iowa settlers. He had the coöperation of A. W. Hubbard, a staff officer. The Northern Border Brigade was organized with A. W. Sawyers in command. A chain of what were called block houses — some of which were of sod — was erected stretching across the frontier from Sioux City to Chain Lakes. But no Indians ever came to molest them — after the Minnesota massacres they were severely punished by the federal troops.

Politically, the year 1862 was quite as important as it was militarily. Many in the north felt that the war had been a failure. They clamored for peace. Any kind of a peace would do. The emancipation proclamation of the president gave new hopes to some, but many others looked on it with misgivings. They spoke of being willing to fight for the Union, but not for the "niggers." The drafts talked of were also unpopular. And so for one reason and another the political pendulum swung the other way. The great states of

[5] Briggs's "The Enlistment of Iowa Troops During the Civil War," in *The Iowa Journal of History and Politics*, Vol. XV, No. 3, p. 359.

Pennsylvania, New York, New Jersey, and even Ohio and Indiana fell by the wayside, and Illinois, the state of Lincoln and of Grant, sent to the United States senate a man who had been a spokesman for the infamous Lecompton constitution of Kansas days.

But the new trans-Mississippi River states helped to save the Union politically. Iowa and Minnesota and Kansas and Washington and Oregon sent solid Republican delegations to congress, but even then President Lincoln had a working majority of only twenty-two votes in the lower house of congress — a narrow margin to carry through the great war measures. Six of those twenty-two votes were from Iowa. Up to 1860, Iowa had only two congressmen, but by the census of 1860, following the immigration of the preceding decade, the state was given six members in the lower house. In the first election to fill these places, the Republicans elected James F. Wilson, Hiram Price, William B. Allison, Josiah B. Grinnell, John A. Kasson, and A. W. Hubbard, all Lincoln true and tried men, and a galaxy of statesmen that has never been excelled from the state. With these six men added to the two United States senators, Harlan and Grimes, Iowa became one of the states on which President Lincoln leaned heavily — and the state never failed nor faltered. Harlan stood in close relations to the president. Grimes was at the head of the naval committee, where he brought to bear a master mind on one of the great departments of the government. He was one of the first to insist on an adequate naval program, and one of the first to advocate the building of iron-clads. He was the brains of the navy and the inspiration of every naval commander. If to these Iowa men in Washington is added Samuel F. Miller, who was called to a place on the bench of the supreme court of the nation by President Lincoln, the Iowa equation of power and influence in national affairs is still more multiplied.

The appointment of Miller to the bench of the supreme court was one of the political surprises of the state and nation. It was the destiny of a lawyer from a frontier town to become the judicial successor of Marshall and Story, with whom he was most often compared. He was born in Kentucky in 1816, of German ancestry. He studied medicine and for a short time practiced it. But he turned to the law which was more to his liking, receiving his degree in that profession at the somewhat advanced age of thirty. He came to Keokuk in 1850. His abilities were so conspicuous that it was said the politicians who feared him conspired to put him on a shelf in the supreme court. Well recommended for the place, President Lincoln hesitated, for he had never heard of him. He was no sooner on the bench than he became one of its dominating influences, specializing in constitutional questions that arose in connection with the war and reconstruction.

After the disasters of the spring months, the achievements of the Union armies during 1862 were nowhere highly decisive. The Iowa regiments remained largely inactive. In September the Fifth, Tenth, Sixteenth, and Seventeenth took conspicuous parts in the battle of Iuka, where the Fifth, especially, and its colonel, C. L. Matthies, fought themselves into enduring fame. "The glorious Fifth," so reads General Rosecrans's report, "under the brave and distinguished Matthies," fought "with valor and determination seldom equalled, never excelled in the most veteran soldiers," while the Seventeenth is described as standing "like a rock holding the center." The Fifth lost nearly half of the men it had in that engagement. Iuka made Matthies a brigadier-general. On the third and fourth days of October, thirteen of the Iowa regiments participated in the battles of Corinth, and The Hatchie, where the Third Iowa was sent on a desperate and mistaken mission which cost the lives of sixty officers and men in a few moments of fighting. Of the regiments raised in 1862, only two, the Nineteenth and Twentieth, came under any serious fire in that year, and that was at Prairie Grove in Missouri, where the First Iowa Cavalry also won new laurels.

In September, 1862, there was held a meeting of the governors of the loyal states, at Altoona, Pennsylvania, the meeting being called at the instance of Governor Curtin of that state. It was held to consider the state of the Union and to advise with the president about a more vigorous prosecution of the war. Before the governors met the president's Emancipation Proclamation was issued. They drew up an address of a commendatory nature which was read to the president when the governors were received at the White House. Governor Kirkwood spoke strongly in opposition to the military policies of General McClellan, but on this he was not supported by all of the other governors. No reports of what was said were made, but Governor Kirkwood, as he afterwards recalled it [6] said to the president that "General McClellan was unfit to command his army, that his army was well clothed, well armed, well disciplined, were fighting in a cause as good as men ever fought for, and fought as bravely as men ever fought, and yet were continually whipped, and . . . people did not think he was a good general who was always whipped."

"You Iowa people then judge generals as you do lawyers, by their success in trying cases," said Mr. Lincoln, smiling.

"Yes, something like that," the Iowa governor replied; "the lawyer who is always losing his cases, especially when he was right and had justice on his side don't get much practice in Iowa. . . Mr. President, our Iowa people fear and I fear that the administration is afraid to remove General McClellan." This remark made the color come into the president's face, after which Mr. Kirkwood explained that he did not mean fear in the ordinary sense, but fear of the effect upon the army.

"Mr. Lincoln was silent for a brief space, and then he said slowly and with emphasis, 'Governor Kirkwood, if I believed our cause would be benefitted by removing General McClellan tomorrow, I would remove him tomorrow. I do not so believe today, but if the time shall come when I shall so believe I will remove him promptly, and not till then.' "

The time did come when the president so believed and so acted. The Iowa governor was simply ahead of time. The man to succeed General McClellan was even at that moment thinking and planning how to take Vicksburg, the achievement that would make him the hero of the nation.

6 Statement of S. J. Kirkwood, over his signature, in *The Iowa Historical Record*, January, 1892.

# CHAPTER LVIII

## In 1863 — A Year of Victories

For the Iowa troops, 1863 began at Vicksburg. In this great undertaking and achievement of the Union armies Iowa had from first to last thirty-two of her fighting units engaged. In the preliminaries, the siege, and the aftermath, the infantry, the cavalry, and the batteries of Iowa were all in action. The whole battle area was strewn with the dead and the wounded and the sick of the state. In no battle and in no victory of the war did the troops of the state bear a greater burden or share in a more glorious renown.

Vicksburg on the Mississippi was regarded as the Gibraltar of the Confederacy in the west. The natural situation of the city was advantageous and it was well defended. In the autumn of 1862, Grant began planning to take this stronghold. His first plans included two frontal attacks, one to be made by his own army and another by an army under General Sherman. There were some serious differences of opinion, the war department preferring General McClernand to General Sherman. Grant's own army was forced to withdraw from the undertaking, his cavalry defeated at Coffeyville and his stores captured at Holly Springs, while General Sherman, left unaware of the fate of Grant's army, marched down the Mississippi into a somewhat disastrous defeat at Chickasaw Bayou, where five Iowa regiments were engaged, and where one of them, the Fourth, fought so valiantly that by a special order of General Grant they were permitted to inscribe on their banner "First at Chickasaw Bayou," an unusual honor.[1] General McClernand, succeeding General Sherman, then fought a brilliant action at Arkansas Post, in which Iowa regiments had a share of the glory.

[1] Byers's *Iowa in War Times*, p. 200.

General Grant then changed his plans. He decided boldly and brilliantly to make the attack from below, where the defenses were weakest. He sent General Sherman with an army down the west bank of the river, and with gunboats he ran past the batteries of the city. Both undertakings were highly successful. Sherman's army was ferried across the river, not only into the enemy's country, but between two enemy forces. They had to defend themselves in the rear and to fight their way to Vicksburg. A series of battles followed in rapid order, Port Gibson, Raymond, Jackson, Champion Hill, and Black River, in all of which Iowa men participated. Time seemed the essence of the coveted victory. General Grant sought to take the city before he might be compelled to fight General Johnston's army in the rear. So on the nineteenth and twenty-second days of May he ordered two stupendous assaults on the works that defended the city, but both proved failures.

In the assault of the twenty-second nearly all the Iowa regiments were engaged, many conspicuously, including the First and Second batteries. It is the proud record of one of the Iowa regiments, the Twenty-second, that it penetrated the works of the enemy more deeply than any other. General Grant in his report said: "No troops succeeded in entering any of the enemy's works with the exception of Sergeant Griffith, of the Twenty-second Iowa Volunteers, and some eleven privates of the same regiment; of these none returned except the sergeant and possibly one man."[2] The man was David Trine. Five of the men were slain within the fort.[3]

[2] Ingersoll's *Iowa and the Rebellion*, p. 477.

[3] The men with Sergeant Joseph M. Griffith in this exploit were: John Robb, Munson L. Clemmons, Alvin Drummond, Hezekiah Drummond, William H. Needham, Ezra L. Anderson, Hugh Sinclair, N. C. Messenger, David Trine, William Griffin, Allen Cloud, David Jordan, and Richard Arthur. The five killed within the fort were: The two Drummonds, Anderson, Arthur, and Griffin. By some the honor of leading this charge is given to N. C. Messenger. See Byers's *Iowa in War Times*, p. 228.

The oral testimony of E. J. C. Bealer, who was a member of company A, is that there were at least eighteen men in the assaulting party and that Robb was among the killed. There was naturally great confusion and no one knew exactly what happened.

The regiment in this assault was led by Colonel William M. Stone, who was soon wounded and carried off the field, being succeeded by Lieutenant Colonel Graham in the command, who led his men to Fort Beauregard, the walls of which were scaled by Sergeant Griffith and his gallant band making ladders of themselves. They planted the flag on its ramparts, but it was a useless though a glorious victory, for the rest of the line could not advance to support them. Another Iowa regiment that penetrated the works of the enemy was the Ninth, whose color-bearer is said to have saved the flag by wrapping it around his body and rolling down hill with it. But in no regiment was there lack of valor.

After that assault, General Grant's army settled down to a siege of the city, in which two Iowa brigadier-generals, Lauman and Herron, held distinct parts of the line. Reduced to starvation and after having endured untold hardships, the gallant defenders of the city surrendered on the fourth of July. Once more the Mississippi flowed unvexed to the sea, and the name and fame of General Grant filled all the land. No greater blow for the final victory had been struck in the war up to that time. It was in some respects the greatest victory of the whole war, and Iowa's share of it was an integral part of the victory. The same wires that carried the news of the fall of Vicksburg carried also the news of the repulse at Gettysburg, making an American Fourth of July of rejoicings such as had not been celebrated since the signing of the Declaration of Independence. A third victory in which five Iowa regiments participated, the successful defense of Helena, which had been attacked by a vastly superior force, passed almost unnoticed, but at any other time it would have seemed an important event in the war.

The fortunes of war, like other human fortunes, are unequal. In the fighting that followed the fall of Vicksburg — and there was a great deal of it — at the siege of Jackson, Mississippi, Jacob G. Lauman, the first colonel of the Seventh Iowa, who had fought his way up to a brigadier-generalship, lost all the honors he had won by obeying the orders of a superior officer, leading his brigade against a strongly fortified place, in which the Third Iowa lost half of the men it had in the engagement. Lauman was relieved of his command, and his military career came to an ending.[4] But while one star went down another arose in spectacular splendor. John M. Corse used the Sixth regiment in a skirmish so brilliantly that it won for him a brigadier-generalship — the main starting point of a career in many ways unexcelled among Iowa commanders.

A season of rest and recuperation followed for the Iowa troops, but in the autumn of the year, late in November, nine of the regiments of the state participated in the campaigns around Chattanooga, where they helped to storm Missionary Ridge and to scale Lookout Mountain. Six of the nine fought with Hooker "above the clouds." "God bless you all," President Lincoln wired to General Grant, for these new victories, victories so significant that the general in command believed they would have ended the war, could the people of the south have known what they meant and could they have made their knowledge effective on their rulers.

At home a series of disturbances marked the year 1863. If the Union reverses of 1862 had encouraged the disloyalists, the successes of 1863 made them resentful. A secret order, known as the Knights of the Golden Circle, gained a great following in the state. Governor Kirkwood, who had many sources of information, some of them secret, estimated their number at 42,000. He wrote to the secretary of war that "paid agents of the rebels" were working in Iowa. At times the situation seemed to him so serious that he feared insurrections. To one man he wrote: "It would be a terrible thing to have civil war with all its horrors in our state, and if it comes I intend it shall be horribly atoned for by those who bring it on."[5] He encouraged the organization of additional Home Guard companies, especially in the southern half of the state.

[4] Byers's *Iowa in War Times*, p. 235; in a footnote the statement is made that General George A. Stone of Iowa, who saw the assault, and who talked with Lauman felt confident that, wisely or not, Lauman "was acting under positive orders."

[5] Byers's *Iowa in War Times*, p. 235.

The most serious or at least sensational of the internal disturbances occurred in Keokuk County and bears the name of "The Skunk River War." There were a great many disloyalists in Keokuk County, and they seemed to be most numerous along the Skunk River, not only in that but in other counties through which that stream flows. Among the settlers along that river was a Tennessee family of the name of Tally, who came to Iowa in 1848.[6] A son of this family, named Cyphert Tally, was a young man of eloquence, but of little education. He became a Baptist minister. Called upon to preach the funeral sermon for a Union soldier, he was objected to on the accusations of disloyalty. He finally delivered his funeral address in a grove. The incident made him a talked of man and he received many invitations to address meetings of the disloyalists.

The climax was reached August first, 1863, when a Democratic mass meeting was held near English River. Tally was the chief speaker. Several hundred of his kind were present, with arms concealed in the straw of their wagons. Loyalists also were present. Altercations and even fist fights followed. Two women who wore butternut badges, which were the emblems of the disloyalists, almost had their clothes torn from their bodies. Threats were made that they would go to South English, a loyalist stronghold, and "clean it out." The citizens of that place hastened to arm themselves. In the afternoon of the same day Tally and his band came. He was warned not to go through the town, but he claimed the right to go where he pleased. The cries of "copperhead" were soon heard. The accidental discharge of a gun started a general firing. Tally standing in the back of a wagon, with a revolver in one hand and a bowie knife in the other, was one of the first men shot down. One of the horses was wounded and that caused a runaway with the body of the dead man in the wagon.

The friends of Tally were then summoned to revenge his death. They came from Wapello, Mahaska, and Poweshiek counties. They constituted the Skunk River Army which has

[6] From an old history of Keokuk County, published about 1880.

been placed at a strength of four thousand men, but consisted probably of less than a thousand, or no more than five hundred. Messengers carried the news of a civil war to Davenport, where Governor Kirkwood was then staying. The governor issued an order for three hundred stand of arms. On second thought he decided to go in person to the scene. He reached Sigourney on Wednesday, the disturbances having commenced on Saturday. Troops followed the governor, composed of Home Guard companies from Muscatine, Washington, and other places, eleven in all. Two cannon also were brought upon the scene. At night the governor made a speech in which he used no soft language. He warned those who were bent on making trouble that they would regret it. In the meantime the "army" was melting away, and only the bitterness and the bickerings remained to disturb the peace of that part of the state. The murderers of Tally were never punished, for they were never disclosed.

Soldiers home on furloughs, and the relatives of those who had died, in many places resented the activities of the disloyalists. In Keokuk they threw the type and presses of the *Constitution-Democrat* into the Mississippi because of its disloyal utterances. In Dubuque similar action was threatened against the *Herald*, then edited by D. A. Mahoney, who was placed under arrest by the federal government.[7] Henry Clay Dean, another radical, and who was charged with the authorship of some of the literature circulated by the Knights of the Golden Circle, was also placed under arrest, while George W. Jones, who had been a United States senator, was held at Fortress Monroe on the evidence of intercepted letters written to Jefferson Davis, expressing his sympathies. None of these men, however, was ever convicted or even tried.

During the year, Iowa added six organized units to its men in the service, the Sixth, Seventh, Eighth, and Ninth cavalry, the Fourth Battery, and a regiment of colored troops. There were at that time not enough blacks in Iowa to complete the regiment, and so four companies from other states were added. According to the records of the war department, Iowa had

[7] Byers's *Iowa in War Times*, p. 266.

filled all its quotas up to June eleventh, 1863, with an excess of 13,897 men.[8] The quotas for 1863 totaled only 12,618 men, leaving the state with a surplus of 1,281 men to its credit, without any new enlistments. But in the autumn came another call for 300,000 men, intended to fill the places of the men whose terms would expire in the following year. Of this number 8,910 men were required from Iowa.

Politically, 1863 was an important year in Iowa. Governor Kirkwood's second term was about to expire, and he refused to be a candidate for reëlection, though he was much urged to do so. For him the office had been one of hard work under severe difficulties. He had endured criticism and abuse. He had accepted them as parts of the burdens of his office. But as he was ready to quit, others were eager to begin. The Republican state convention was held that year at Des Moines on the seventeenth of June. For governor the two leading contestants were Elijah Sells, of many political memories, and Fitz Henry Warren, the cavalry leader. Warren had many kinds of prestige. He was an orator of power. He had been an associate editor of the New York *Tribune*, and he was the author of the famous letters, "On to Richmond," in which he had outlined a vigorous offensive policy. But in the eleventh hour, Colonel William M. Stone came home from Vicksburg with his wounds of the twenty-second of May. On the eve of the convention he captured an audience largely made up of delegates who would vote on the morrow. It was soon apparent that Sells could not be nominated. The contest lay between the two soldier candidates, and Stone captured the nomination because of offenses Warren had given to the supporters of the civilian candidate.

On the eighth of July, the Democrats held their convention in Des Moines. It was only five days after the victories of Vicksburg and Helena, in which Iowa men had participated, but under the leadership of D. A. Mahoney they resolved that the war "for the purpose of carrying out the emancipation proclamation" of the president was outrageous. They de-

[8] Briggs's "The Enlistment of Iowa Troops During the Civil War," in *The Iowa Journal of History and Politics*, Vol. XV, No. 3, p. 364.

nounced also the suspension of the writ of *habeas corpus*, and the substitution of martial law. As their candidate for governor they named Maturin L. Fisher, who refused to accept the nomination on the conditions named in the platform. A committee then named James M. Tuttle, the hero of Donelson, who had just won new laurels at Vicksburg, where he had commanded a brigade. He was persuaded to accept the nomination, but in his letter of acceptance he virtually rejected the platform of his party so far as it referred to the war.

With two noted soldiers as the contestants the discussions in the campaign turned almost wholly on the war. Both men were criticised; Tuttle for repudiating politically what he had achieved in the war, and Stone for deserting his place in the army to seek political preferment. In the election, Stone received 86,122 votes against 47,948 cast for Tuttle. By a special enactment of the general assembly soldiers in the field were permitted to vote, and they cast 16,791 for Stone against 2,904 for Tuttle.

After three years of war, the people were war-weary. They were hoping for the end of it all. But they realized that the battles would have to go on for at least another year. The end, though it seemed in sight, had not yet been reached. The western armies had done more than the eastern ones. Everything was still safe on the Potomac, but nothing had been achieved on the road to Richmond. The victories of Vicksburg and Chattanooga had made the name of General Grant one to conjure with. The command of all the armies was about to be given to him.

# CHAPTER LIX

## THE LAST YEAR OF THE WAR

The Iowa regiments entered the activities of 1864 with the campaign under the ultimate command of General Nathaniel P. Banks to destroy the last trans-Mississippi stronghold of the Confederacy, centering at Shreveport, Louisiana. The Iowa troops were in the armies of General A. J. Smith, which proceeded up the Red River, and under General Frederick Steele, which operated from Little Rock, forming two of the concentrating columns. The undertaking was one of the most disastrous of the war. Smith's column won distinguished victories until it made a junction with General Banks's own column, when one disaster followed another. The battles of the Sabine Cross Roads and Pleasant Hill were inadequately fought. Colonel William T. Shaw of the Fourteenth Iowa was in command of an Iowa brigade, which distinguished itself at Fort de Russey. After the disasters at Pleasant Hill the army had to fall back toward the Mississippi. Colonel Shaw, whose troops had borne the brunt of the fighting, criticised his superior officers in a communication which was printed in the Anamosa *Eureka*, his home paper. His charges included not only incompetence and cowardice, but drunkenness. For this he was dismissed from the service at the instigation of General Banks.[1] His criticisms were justifiable, but they violated army discipline. The misfortunes that befell General Steele's army were tragic. He was called upon to follow plans that should never have been made, and to obey orders that never should have been given. General Samuel A. Rice and General Francis Marion Drake distinguished themselves by doing almost impossible things to redeem the whole undertaking from utter failure. The name of Banks was long execrated among Iowa men.

[1] Ingersoll's *Iowa and the Rebellion*, p. 207.

But the failures in the southwest area of the war were soon forgotten in the brilliant campaigns that followed. General Grant was at last in supreme command, under President Lincoln, with General Sherman in charge in the west and General Sheridan in the Shenandoah Valley. It was a new dispensation and the country was looking for new achievements. In the eastern armies, Iowa was barely represented. Company K, of the Eleventh Pennsylvania, was an Iowa company, under Captain Franklin A. Stratton, in the Army of the Potomac.[2] In Sheridan's army in the Shenandoah Valley were three Iowa regiments, the Twenty-second, the Twenty-fourth, and the Twenty-eighth, which had been transferred from the west to the east by water, receiving a great ovation as they passed through Washington to enter the valley by way of the historic Harper's Ferry.[3]

But it was in Sherman's army that the men from Iowa were destined to play their principal parts in the campaigns of 1864 and 1865. Fifteen Iowa regiments participated in the fighting around Atlanta, and seventeen regiments marched with Sherman to the sea. Some of the regiments were under fire for eighty-one days. Many Iowa commanders won honors in these later campaigns.

The state had entered the war with few men trained to command. But three years of war had brought out both their mettle and their technique. One of the first of these commanders to attract national attention was Grenville M. Dodge, who had recruited the Fourth Iowa at Council Bluffs, and had won his laurels at Pea Ridge in 1862. After the fall of Vicksburg, in preparing for the Chattanooga campaign, General Grant wrote to General Sherman, "Bring Dodge along, he is an officer on whom you can rely in an emergency."[4] The first task placed before him was to rebuild the railroad from Decatur to Nashville, without which the armies would starve. With no tools save axes and picks and shovels, the more than one hundred miles were built. His men fought as

2 Ingersoll's *Iowa and the Rebellion*, p. 709.

3 *Ibid.*, p. 709.

4 Byers's *Iowa in War Times*, p. 423.

well as built. It was one of the astonishing feats of the war. In 1864, General Sherman was able to close so suddenly on Atlanta because the engineering skill and energy of General Dodge threw a bridge across the Chattahoochie in three days, taking the materials from the forests, and over that bridge the Army of the Tennessee passed. Dodge was a corps commander when the Atlanta campaign began. While he was leading a part of his corps, the Sixteenth, to the left, it was his fate or fortune to receive the first onslaughts of the Confederate force that sallied forth from the city to attack the Union army in the rear. Dodge halted his line, left-faced it, and with only 4,500 men "fought a desperate battle with half the rebel army, receiving and repelling the first fierce onslaught — an onslaught that had been intended to destroy the Army of the Tennessee." [5] It was the enemy that encountered the real surprise. Dodge's men captured eight battle flags and the enemy dead were more than five hundred. The manner in which the Iowa commander saved the Union army from disaster was described as "grand and impressive." But a month later, on the nineteenth of August, General Dodge for the third time was wounded, ending his connection with that campaign. When he recovered he was placed in charge of the army in Missouri.

A service as material and a glory even more spectacular fell to another Iowa commander, General John M. Corse, who was a division commander in the same campaign. The Confederate general, Hood, had escaped with a whole army and was marching northward, in October, a diversion that might have halted General Sherman's plans. The critical point to be held was Allatoona Pass, where a lieutenant colonel, Tourtellette, with an Illinois regiment was guarding valuable stores. From Kenesaw Mountain, General Sherman signalled to Corse, who was at Rome, to hold the pass to the last extremity. Corse could not take his whole division, as General Sherman may have intended, but with only about two thousand men, including part of the Thirty-ninth Iowa under Colonel James Redfield, he started on his assigned task,

[5] Byers's *Iowa in War Times*, p. 425.

reaching the pass on October fifth. His celerity had been vital, for on the same day the Confederates invested the place. At 8:15 in the morning the Confederate general, French, informed Corse of the fact, and called upon him to surrender "at once and unconditionally . . . to avoid a needless effusion of blood." He was allowed five minutes to decide what he would do. But General Corse did not wait five minutes to send back the reply: "Your communication demanding surrender of my command I acknowledge receipt of, and respectfully reply that we are prepared for 'the needless effusion of blood' whenever it is agreeable to you."

The repulsed and angered Confederate commander began the attack immediately. His men charged "by regiment and by brigade, and dashed against the works as though mad." After the battle had raged for three hours, General Sherman realizing from the smoke that the place was under attack, signalled: "Hold fort; we are coming."[6] When Sherman received his reply he said, "If Corse is there he will hold out. I know the man." Sherman had asked and Corse had pledged almost more than human courage and endurance could encompass. What followed has been described as "The most terrible combat in which American troops ever took part, and well nigh as terrible as any of which history speaks."[7] Men bayonetted each other over the works, and officers thrust their sabers through officers. Corse himself fell insensible, wounded in the face. Colonel Richard Lowell of the Seventh Illinois commanded until he too was wounded, by which time Corse came back. The battle was not over until two o'clock in the afternoon. Seven hundred and seven officers and men in Corse's command had been wounded or killed, being a third of all engaged. Redfield was among the dead. General Sherman was unstinted in his praise of so heroic a service at so vital a point and time. "Your presence alone saved Allatoona," he told General Corse, and two days after the battle he issued a general order, tendering the thanks of the

[6] Ingersoll's *Iowa and the Rebellion*, p. 721; Sherman's message to Corse was the origin of the gospel hymn, "Hold the Fort for I am Coming."

[7] Ingersoll's *Iowa and the Rebellion*, p. 221.

Samuel J. Kirkwood

Mrs. Annie Wittenmeyer

Grenville M. Dodge

John M. Corse

army to the general and his associates "for their gallant defense of Allatoona," one of the bravest incidents of the whole war, and one that is most often remembered.[8]

With Atlanta fallen, which had been the machine shop of the Confederacy, General Sherman severed his connections and set out on his memorable march to the sea, in which Corse commanded a division, and W. W. Belknap, Vandever, E. W. Rice, Williamson, Wever, and Milo Smith, brigades. The city of Savannah was presented to the nation as a Christmas gift. Then the army marched northward through the Carolinas to coöperate with General Grant pressing southward to Richmond. When Columbia, South Carolina, was reached, Iowa men were the first to hoist the Stars and Stripes over the state house in which the secession had its birth. The city was surrendered to Colonel George A. Stone of the Twenty-fifth Iowa, who was then in command of the Iowa Brigade of the Fifteenth corps. The other Iowa regiments were the Fourth and the Ninth, the Thirtieth and Thirty-first. The capture of the city required no fighting. The mayor and aldermen met Colonel Stone and made the surrender. But it was done to "none but Iowa troops."

But the Stars and Stripes had preceded the surrender. The account is that Crocker's Brigade on the night before the surrender, the sixteenth of February, 1865, went into camp on the Congaree River, opposite Columbia. In the evening General Sherman rode up and talked with General Belknap, the commander of the brigade. Among other things he said it would be an honor to be the first to put the Stars and Stripes over the cradle of secession. Major H. C. MacArthur of the Thirteenth regiment overheard this remark, and accompanied by a squad, with the permission of General Belknap, undertook to achieve the honor which General Sherman had mentioned. Three of the squad were wounded and one was killed, but that did not deter the others. They found two state houses, the old one and one in course of construction. They hoisted flags over both. While they were doing this the city was being surrendered to Colonel Stone. The men of the

[8] William Salter's article on General Corse in *Annals of Iowa*, Third Series, Vol. II, p. 105.

Thirtieth, evidently in some chagrin, took down the flag of the Thirteenth and hoisted their own in its stead, which was the "official" flag to which the city had surrendered. For some time the flag of the Thirteenth was missing, but it was eventually restored to the regiment.[9] But, in any event, both flags were Iowa flags.

The South Carolina capital possesses also an Iowa literary interest. It was in a prison near that city in which an Iowa man, Major S. H. M. Byers, was confined, after he was taken prisoner in the Chattanooga campaign of 1863, and it was there that he composed the famous ballad "The March to the Sea," "which gave its name to the picturesque campaign." The words and the music were carried out of the prison in the hollow of a wooden leg on which Lieutenant Tower, of Ottumwa, walked out when he was exchanged. The song caught the popular fancy of the day and spread rapidly over the land. When Sherman's army reached Columbia, Major Byers made his escape and he met an army singing the song he had composed in prison.[10] In recognition of his services, as well as of his abilities, the major was given a place on General Sherman's staff, completing one of the romantic incidents of the war.

While seventeen Iowa regiments were marching with Sherman, and three were fighting with Sheridan, twelve other regiments were in the far south helping to reduce Mobile, one of the last Confederate strongholds to fall. On the eighth of April, 1865, when the war was almost over, Colonel J. L. Geddes of the Eighth, commanding a brigade, led the assault on the Spanish Fort, one of the two main defenses of Mobile, and on the ninth General Steele, the first colonel of the Eighth Iowa, led the attack on Fort Blakeley from the other side. With General Steele was his *fidus Achates*, Major John F. Lacey, one of the bravest and at the same time most modest of the Iowa men in the war. They entered the fort "with cheers that made the welkin ring."[11]

At the same time cheers made the welkin ring from east to

[9] See *The Capture and Destruction of Columbia, South Carolina, Personal Experiences and Recollections of Major H. C. MacArthur.*

[10] Byers's *Iowa in War Times*, pp. 349-350.

[11] Ingersoll's *Iowa and the Rebellion*, p. 736.

west, and from north to south — for the South too was glad that it was over at last. In a noble spirit of desired reconcilation, General Grant refused to receive the sword of General Lee, and the planters who had been embattled soldiers were told to take their horses and mules home to cultivate the soil. But a like spirit was not yet in all hearts, for in the midst of the rejoicings, Lincoln was shot by a frenzied fanatic, halting and marring the work of peace and reconciliation.

When the war was over the regiments that had fought in the east were reviewed in Washington by General Grant and President Johnson, and the members of his cabinet. On the second day the Iowa regiments which had fought with Sherman passed. Lurton Dunham Ingersoll, the war correspondent whose contributions to history entitle him to a monument on the capitol grounds, has left for posterity vivid glimpses of that scene: Of Major General John M. Corse "as his division wheeled by the grand colonnade of the treasury" . . . receiving a "fine reception"; of Brigadier General E. W. Rice, of the Second, Sixth, Seventh, Tenth, and Thirty-ninth regiments, ". . . with torn banners;" ". . . Belmont, Donelson, Champion Hills, Jackson, Missionary Ridge, and Allatoona shone brightly from the honored folds . . . through a grand storm of cheers; . . ." of Stone's brigade which ". . . soon marched up . . . the Fourth, Ninth, Twenty-fifth, Twenty-sixth, Thirtieth, Thirty-first regiments, their banners blazing with names of great battles from Pea Ridge to Bentonsville; . . ." "of the thinned and honored Seventeenth regiment, and not far behind the Iowa Brigade, commanded by the distinguished W. W. Belknap;" . . . the Eleventh regiment, then the Thirteenth, Fifteenth and Sixteenth — "men who had first met the enemy in the forest by Shiloh Church, and had gone through four years of as gallant warfare as any troops who ever fought."

But the regiments were not all there, the regiments that fought at Mobile, the regiments that had fought so gallantly under Thomas against the hordes of Hood, and the regiments that marched and skirmished and kept guard and maintained order through all the regions that had been devastated by war — they did not march in the Grand Review.

# CHAPTER LX

## By Way of Summing Up

In the form of distinct organizations, Iowa contributed to the war forty regiments of infantry, nine of cavalry, and four batteries. All enlistments except the First regiment had been for three year terms. In 1864, the state furnished to the nation five more regiments of Hundred Day men, who took no part in the war proper, but who nevertheless rendered useful services. These organizations were numbered from forty-four to forty-eight, inclusively, completing the state's forty-eight regiments. The exact number of men enlisted during the war can never be known, for many of the early records were improperly kept and some were lost. Many men were enlisted twice, and a few three times. The records in the adjutant general's office in Des Moines show a total of 79,059 enlistments, including the reënlistments.[1] Reduced to a three-year basis, Iowa's quotas under the various calls of the government aggregated 61,220 men, but the state furnished on the same basis 68,630. About four thousand men were drafted, but when these are deducted, the state still has an excess of volunteers over the quotas called for. The state had not been properly subject to the draft. On estimates of population, two-thirds of the men of military age entered the service, and they constituted above nine per cent of the total population. Of the Iowa soldiers, 12,368 were dead when the war closed, or almost one-fifth of all in the service. Almost as many more were largely, and many wholly, incapacitated.[2]

Four Iowa commanders attained the rank of major general,

[1] For a detailed account and analysis of enlistments from Iowa, see *The Iowa Journal of History and Politics*, Vol. XV, No. 3, article by John E. Briggs.

[2] Byers's *Iowa in War Times*, p. 606.

Samuel R. Curtis, Frederick Steele, Grenville M. Dodge, and Francis J. Herron. Two of these were West Point men, Dodge received some military training in an academy, and Herron was the exception. He was a bank clerk who entered the army by way of the famous Dubuque Greys. The title of major-general by brevet was conferred on thirteen men, the most noted of whom in a military way was John M. Corse, and, with political prestige added, W. W. Belknap.[3] Of the brigadier-generals, the ranking one in point of ability was probably Marcellus M. Crocker, whose career was cut short by disease.

In a military way the three men who stand out most are Generals Dodge, Corse, and Crocker, all men fit to have commanded independent armies. Crocker stayed long enough to make his worth known, but not long enough to realize all that was in him. When the war broke out he was noted as a criminal lawyer in Des Moines. He leaped into fame by asking for a hundred men to accompany him into the service. The men responded, but the capital city was then too far away from railroads and telegraphs to land his contingent in the First regiment. Corse started with a West Point education. He was a fighting, commanding man by instinct, and yet one of the gentlest among men. He had a daring spirit, an heroic soul. Bravado was mingled with bravery in this man of wonderful human energy. With a cheek bone crushed and an ear shot off, he felt that he could "lick all hell yet." He might have been another Sheridan. By one of the earlier historians, one who observed and studied men in action, he was called "the only military prodigy the state . . . furnished in the War of the Rebellion."[4] General Dodge was of other mettle. By common consent he was awarded the premiership among Iowa commanders. He was an en-

[3] The other major generals by brevet were: W. T. Clark, Cyrus Bussey, William Vandever, H. H. Heath, Fitz Henry Warren, James I. Gilbert, James A. Williamson, Jacob G. Lauman, Edward Hatch, W. L. Elliott, and E. W. Rice. The six men who became brigadier generals were: James M. Tuttle, Charles L. Matthies, Marcellus M. Crocker, Samuel A. Rice, John Edwards, and Hugh T. Reid.

[4] Lurton Dunham Ingersoll.

gineer and his mind was highly constructive. He could plan battles as well as fight them. He was supremely an executive — an executing man. He walked in the fellowship of Grant and Sherman. Politically, he was a man too great to be a governor or a congressman, and not ambitious enough to become president.

But not all men who were heroic or who had abilities acquired titles in the war. Fortune favored some more than others. Sometimes it was the fleeting opportunity and sometimes it was the ability to grasp the flitting chance that advanced men in the service. But those who rose to eminence may be deserving of no more praise than those who remained privates during three or four or more years of service. After all, they fought the battles and won the victories. Theirs the unrecorded names, the unheralded memories — but they were none the less the embodiment of the spirit of the nation, and their collective spirits, however well or ill led — and more often ill than well — made the victory possible.

Nor did the men do it all. The women did as much. For every valorous deed done in battle there was a valorous deed done in a home, and for every broken body on a field of carnage there was a broken heart in some home. Without music or acclaim, without epaulettes or stars, the women fought their battles and won their victories. In Iowa they went into the fields to plant and to harvest the crops, not only to feed their own children, but to sustain the armies at the front. In every city and town and neighborhood they maintained an aid society. And how much they did with the little they had to do with! They made the first uniforms, and they mended the last rags in which the heroes came back home.

There were leaders among them as well as there were among men. Many might be named, and all comparisons are odious where all did all that human hands could do and human hearts could prompt. Mrs. Ann E. Harlan, the wife of Senator Harlan, who had a brave spirit in a frail body, was one of the first on the field of Shiloh, where it was said of her she "outranked Halleck."[5] And it is well that women outranked

[5] *Annals of Iowa*, Third Series, Vol. II, p. 490.

men when it came to doing the works of human mercy where human cruelty had reigned. The care of the sick and wounded was not yet a science on battlefields or in camps. By reason of her husband's position, Mrs. Harlan was able to do wonderful things for the care of those who were most in need.

But the supreme genius of mercy among Iowa women was Mrs. Annie Wittenmeyer of Keokuk. She became the great mother of the Iowa men in the war. She was a mother of the human crowd by nature. In Keokuk, to which place she came from Ohio in 1850, she was soon found looking after all the children who had poor homes and no schools. She started day schools and Sunday schools for them. When the war broke out she saw that the boys who had been under her influence were among the first to go to the front. She followed them. She saw what they lacked and what they needed. She made an appeal, and when she returned from the front she found enough on the docks to fill two boat loads. The people were ready enough to give; all they needed was leadership.[6]

Her greatest contribution to human welfare in the war was the diet kitchen, an idea which came to her out of a pathetic incident. In one of the hospitals she visited she heard a sick soldier saying peevishly, "Take it away, I don't want it." And she heard the attendant reply, "Well, that's all there is." The complainant turned out to be her own brother. He had typhoid fever, and all that the attendant could offer him was a piece of pork floating around in its own grease. Out of that she evolved the idea of a diet kitchen for the sick and wounded, a kitchen provided with food fit for the sick, prepared by women. The national government soon saw fit to adopt her idea, and she was placed in charge of the entire service. The secretary of war furnished her with passports strong enough to break down all military barriers and red tape. General Grant praised her and President Lincoln invited her to the White House. When congress voted her a pension it was stated that "although we find many pre-

[6] *Annals of Iowa*, Third Series, Vol. IV, p. 277.

cedents as to the amount, we find no precedents as to the value of her services."

In Iowa her most enduring work was the founding of the home for soldiers' orphans. In going about her work, soldiers dying committed to her their children. To leave little ones unprotected and unprovided for was to many the one great regret in dying. She promised them that she would be a mother to them also. She laid their wishes before a convention of the aid societies, held at Muscatine. The result was the founding of the first of such homes, all of which were finally concentrated in the institution at Davenport, one of the noblest of the state's many charities. It was her influence with Mrs. Stanton, brought to bear upon the secretary of war, that secured for that institution the grounds that had been made historic as the rendezvous of many Iowa regiments.

In the history of the war no one is entitled to a higher place, either from Iowa or the nation. She is fit to sit in the company of senators and generals — and President Lincoln when he talked and communed with her in front of his own home fire, must have found in her the expression of the things which he had in his own heart.

# CHAPTER LXI

## After the War

Iowa was still in her youth when she came out of the war. Her resources were still untouched and her spirit was still abounding. Growth and development were yet her natural processes. And so the wounds were soon healed and the losses soon replaced. There were compensations for all the payments that had been made in the name of patriotism. The state was enriched by what had been spent in blood and treasure. There were empty homes and empty hearts, but glorious memories soon filled the vacant places. Wider visions and deeper purposes came also. Duties nobly done, sufferings heroically borne, and sacrifices patriotically made, all these ennobled the state and her people. Iowa had become a self-conscious entity in the union of states.

"When this war began," Governor Kirkwod said in retiring from office, "ours was a new state, without a history. Today her name stands on one of the proudest pages of our country's history — graven there by the bayonets of our brave soldiers, and that page is all overglowing with the proofs of their heroism and devotion." No eulogy can be added to those words. From Wilson's Creek to Mobile Bay, from Lookout Mountain to the swamps of the Carolinas, and from the valley of the Mississippi to the valley of the Shenandoah, the sons and daughters of Iowa may wander over ground made sacred by the sacrifices of their forefathers.

But the trouble and travail of the war were not all over when the peace was signed. Many problems remained to be solved, and those who had to solve them could not always be agreed. They groped and stumbled about in the dark. Not all the politicians were statesmen. Some looked upon the victories won as merely the spoils of the victors. One wonders what Abraham Lincoln would have done and one wonders if even his fame could have survived the ordeals of peace. Perhaps his infinite influence as a national hero was saved to a people who needed a hero shaped out of the heart of the west by the cruel bullet of the assassin. The fury of a Booth may have been the mercy of a benign Providence. He fell in the hour of triumph, and he died in the love and confidence of all the people. He survives as almost a godlike ideal of manhood. Being dead he has influenced the hearts of the people and shaped the course of a nation, perhaps more than he could have done had he outlived his own achievements.

Two questions most prominently confronted the nation when the war was over: What to do with the states that had been in rebellion, and what to do with the black men who had been freed. Even in Iowa where the negro had not perplexed the people with his presence, and where at most his condition had been only an academic question, the people could not agree on what disposition to make of him. The Republicans among themselves soon quarreled over the question, and the Democrats, politically prostrated at that time, stood discreetly by. The proposition to enfranchise the negro was strongly opposed by some who had been abolitionists. They believed in the principle, but not in the policy. The party had other work to do, and it must not endanger its ascendancy. We shall carry the elections even if we bear the blackman on our shoulders, said others. Duty is more than policy, and right is more than victory.[1] When the roll was called in the first Republican convention after the war the vote stood five hundred and thirteen for negro suffrage, and two hundred and forty-two against it. The minority was not small.

Thereupon many Republicans seceded and formed a new party founded on anti-negro suffrage. Thomas H. Benton, Jr., who had been a Democrat before the war, was nominated by them for governor, and H. H. Trimble, who had remained

[1] One of the principal debates along such lines was by Josiah B. Grinnell, who had been the friend of John Brown, and Hiram Price, who had been a Democrat, the former opposing negro suffrage at that time, and the latter favoring it.

a Democrat, was named for judge of the supreme court. Both were men worthy of consideration politically and in the war both had distinguished themselves as officers of high rank and brilliant services. The Democrats made no nominations of their own, but endorsed the anti-negro nominations, accepting what they called "the chief issue in their platform," namely, the "equality of the white and black races," though the equality was only political. The Republicans won the election with Governor William M. Stone as their candidate for reëlection, but their former majority was literally cut in two. But Iowa would enfranchise the negro.

The other question, the reconstruction and restoration of the states which had been in rebellion, was centered in Washington, where it became an issue between the president who had inherited Lincoln's seat and congress. The breach between them soon became a yawning chasm. In Iowa, as in other states, in 1866, those who supported the president's course called themselves conservatives. They held a convention of their own. They adopted a platform in which they sought to interpret the mind of the dead by declaring that Andrew Johnson's ideas were in harmony "with the declared policy of the late President Lincoln." The regular Republicans, who were not at all radicals, though the others were styled conservatives, both opposed and denounced the course of the president and upheld the purposes of congress. The Democrats still remained discreet. They endorsed the views of the Johnson Republicans, and added to it a demand for the immediate restoration of the states which had been in rebellion, and that without any disqualifications.

In congress the bitterness of the debates over these questions resulted in a physical assault on Josiah B. Grinnell of Iowa, by Lovell H. Rousseau of Kentucky. Rousseau had served with distinction in the Union army, but he took the southern view of race questions. Angry debates over the Freedman's Bureau bill between these two men became personal and also trivial. On the fourteenth of June, 1866, the Kentuckian met Grinnell on the east steps of the capitol and demanded an apology for words that reflected on his good name and on the honor of his state. When Grinnell refused, Rousseau attacked him, using a rattan cane with a metal head. Grinnell did not defend himself and made no attempt even to get away from his antagonist. Investigations followed as a result of which the Kentucky member was reprimanded before the bar of the house.[2] He soon afterwards resigned his seat, and Grinnell was defeated for renomination, largely due to the contempt for a man who had failed to defend himself when attacked.[3] Voluntary martyrdom was not accepted in Iowa as a substitute for the manly art of self defense.

The regular Republicans carried the elections of 1866, electing both their state and congressional candidates by majorities around thirty-five thousand. The president then retaliated by removing from offices all Republicans who had not been loyal to him. Postmasterships became political premiums. In the following year, 1867, the regular Republicans accepted this challenge of the president. In their platform they condemned to the uttermost his policies and commended in the highest terms the "military reconstruction policies of congress." They defied the president and rejected his national leadership. They eulogized congress for its "firmness in resisting the conspiracy to turn over the government to the hands of traitors and their allies." They declared also for equal suffrage, "irrespective of color, race, or religion." This phraseology was adroit, if it was courageous, for it carried with it a condemnation of the lingering prejudices of the era and spirit of Know-nothingism. On this platform they elected Samuel F. Merrill of Clayton county as governor, defeating the veteran, Charles Mason, who had been resurrected from a not inglorious past of politics. But the scene of battle had already been shifted to Washington, where two Iowa men were destined to play important parts, James Harlan who had remained as secretary of the interior, and Senator James W. Grimes.

[2] *Congressional Globe*, 1st Session, 39th Congress, p. 4017.

[3] In his *Reminiscences of Forty Years*, p. 163, Grinnell says he was unarmed and physically inferior to his antagonist. From his deathbed Rousseau sent a frank, if late, apology to the man he had assaulted.

# CHAPTER LXII

## IOWA'S PART IN THE NATION'S TURMOIL

The differences between the president and congress involved the political fortunes and personal peace of two Iowa men conspicuously, Secretary Harlan and Senator Grimes. Harlan's selection as secretary of the interior had been one of the last important appointments of President Lincoln, made on the ninth of March, 1865, five days after his re-inauguration, and one month and five days before his assassination. The relations between the president and senator had long been of a close nature, socially as well as politically.[1] Mr. Harlan seems to have hesitated about accepting the office, but felt impelled to it from a sense of duty. The interior department at that time had a surplus of employees, and many of them were engaged in corrupt practices. Mr. Harlan in accepting expressed the hope that he could "get the pack of thieves now preying on the Govt. under its auspices out of power." He did not deem it his duty to lend his name "to plaster over their corruptions."[2] After the death of President Lincoln, he remained in the cabinet of President Johnson, against the advice of his friends and, perhaps, against his own better judgment, for he was not entirely in harmony with the president's views.

Having his purposes in mind, Secretary Harlan soon entered on a course of wholesale dismissals from office. Among the supernumeraries who fell by the wayside were many newspaper correspondents whose services had been merely nominal, and various protégés of congressmen. Having

[1] Mary Harlan, the daughter of the secretary, subsequently became the wife of Robert T. Lincoln, son of the president, the marriage occurring at the Harlan family residence in Washington, September 24, 1868.

[2] Letter from Harlan to James F. Wilson, March 24, 1865.

access to publicity they became potential enemies of the secretary. They poisoned the public mind. They impugned the motives of the new secretary and made all manner of charges against him, including at last those of common dishonesty. He was charged with putting his own son on the pay rolls of the department, as a messenger, with profiting in the sale of Indian lands, and even with using the coal of the department over which he presided for use in his private home. Some of the charges were so serious that the secretary had to make at least indirect replies to them. But that only brought on new charges and new attacks.

Among the men dismissed from office was Walt Whitman, the poet, whose recently published *Leaves of Grass* had made some stir in literary circles and, perhaps, more in the moral world. Whitman had literally shocked the conventional world, for what is now looked upon as a classic of American literature was then regarded, at least by many, as an outrage in published form. Whitman was a poor man and owed his office to services he had rendered to the sick and wounded in Washington during the war. He did not do much work for the government, but he devoted much of his time to his own manuscripts. It was assumed that Harlan had caused his dismissal because of his writings. One W. D. O'Connor, who is described as a brilliant writer, invented the story that Harlan had personally gone to Whitman's desk, in the night time, had extracted therefrom the poems, placed them under his moral ban, and had dismissed the poet from service. The records show, on the contrary, that Whitman was dismissed for the same reason as others whose services were no longer required. When the poet's claims for reinstatement were pressed, Mr. Harlan said that he saw no reason why the author of the *Leaves of Grass* should be longer pensioned in a department devoted solely to business.[3] This seems to be the basis for the O'Connor story which still survives in literary histories.

In the meantime the seat in the senate given up by Mr. Harlan remained vacant. The general assembly would not

[3] Brigham's *James Harlan*, p. 210.

meet until January, 1866, and Governor Stone made no effort to fill it by appointment. The governor himself coveted it. Former Governor Kirkwood's eyes also were fixed on it, and Mr. Harlan, himself urged him to become a candidate. In this Mr. Grimes joined. Thus encouraged, Mr. Kirkwood announced his senatorial candidacy. Governor Stone was then urged to appoint him, but the governor on one pretext and another delayed doing so; first he waited until after the meeting of the party convention, and then until after the election. Finally, Governor Stone announced himself as a candidate, and so did John A. Kasson, Samuel R. Curtis, Fitz Henry Warren, and A. W. Hubbard. And last of all, Mr. Harlan announced his own candidacy for the seat which he had vacated. His place in the cabinet had become uncomfortable for him, both on account of the attacks made on him, and of his growing differences with the president. Harlan was in fact in deep and in many troubles. He defended the president weakly, but without offending the regular Republicans of his state. The Harlan announcement fell like a bomb in Iowa politics. How could he do such a thing after having urged his friend Kirkwood to become a candidate! "I have no hostility to Harlan," Senator Grimes wrote to Kirkwood, "I advised him not to leave the senate, but when he did leave it and voluntarily pledged himself to you and thus induced you to become a candidate for his succession I think fair play entitles you to the place." A breaking of long time friends followed. Senator Grimes, true to his own pledges, remained loyal to the former governor. Harlan then proposed a compromise with Kirkwood, by which he was to receive the next full term in the senate and the former governor the unexpired term, which was for less than two years. Kirkwood rejected this and the matter went before the Republican caucus of the general assembly, where Harlan proved himself the master politician, securing for himself the full term, and giving to Kirkwood the unexpired term. All this time Harlan remained in the cabinet, a seat that he did not resign until July twenty-seventh, 1866.

The differences between the congress and Johnson reached

their first climax in 1867, when the judiciary committee of the house reported a resolution for impeachment, which was defeated on the floor by a vote of one hundred and eight against fifty. On the fifth of August, 1867, the president removed from office Secretary of War Stanton, appointing General Grant in his stead. The senate refused to confirm, and General Grant refused to hold the office. Stanton returned to his office and was again removed. On the same day, February twenty-fourth, 1868, the impeachment of President Johnson was moved in the house where it carried this time by a vote of one hundred and twenty-seven against forty-seven. Stanton's removal was held to be in violation of a tenure of office act passed by congress March second, 1867, and that with "the intent to violate the constitution of the United States." Under this vote the president then had to be tried before the United States senate as judges, the chief justice of the supreme court presiding. It was one of the most momentous proceedings in American history. James F. Wilson, a congressman from Iowa, was made one of the seven managers of the trial.

Senator James W. Grimes of Iowa now enters as one of the principal actors. At no time had he been in sympathy with the president. He had branded some of his acts as foolish and others as wicked. But he could not persuade himself that he was guilty of the high crimes and misdemeanors for which presidents are impeachable. Above all else, he doubted the policy of impeachments. He did not want to introduce into the United States the methods of the Latin republics, "where the ruler is deposed the moment popular sentiment sets against him." When the senator's attitude drew criticisms he prepared "An Opinion," in which he defended his own views. In this able presentation of the issues he questioned the wisdom of destroying "the harmonious working of the constitution for the sake of getting rid of an unacceptable president." He said also that he was opposed to "an approval of impeachments as a part of the future political machinery." Rather than make such a departure he would bear with the idiosyncracies of an erring executive. He said he was not enough of a partisan to bow to party necessities, nor did he consider the charges against the president sufficiently proved.

The senator took this position against the advice of nearly all his friends, both political and personal. They warned him in vain that it would mean his political undoing. Mr. Coolbaugh, his long time friend, though politically opposed to him, told him he had been the idol of his party and state and this action would make him an outcast. Mr. Grimes thanked him, but replied that no personal considerations, no political honors, nor anything else could swerve him from doing what he believed to be right. But the worry and the stress and the strain of it all brought on a stroke of apoplexy. When the time came to vote on impeachment, he was carried into the senate chamber on a litter. The chief justice excused him from arising to cast his vote, but with uplifted head he voted no, while his colleague, Senator Harlan, who had recently left the president's cabinet, voted yes. Senator Grimes's vote was decisive. The count of the senate stood thirty-five for impeachment and nineteen against it. One vote changed would have given the desired, or necessary, two-thirds.

Senator Grimes had saved the president from impeachment, but he had done it, probably, at the cost of his own life. A storm of abuse and execration burst over him. Political abuse could go no further. When he returned to Iowa, sick man as he was, he was held in disfavor even in Burlington where he had been the most prominent and popular citizen. When congress reassembled he returned to his place, but it had few attractions for him. He was sick and he was weary of it all. He had never been enamoured of public life, or of office holding. He was soon ordered to Europe for rest and recuperation. He traveled with Mrs. Grimes, to whom he had always been finely devoted. He wrote charming letters to the few friends who had remained loyal to him. But the baths of Europe worked in him no cure. Instead, he suffered there a second stroke. Persuaded that he was done with public service he sent to the governor of Iowa his resignation as United States senator.

When he returned to the United States public sentiment

had changed. Those who had voted for impeachment, not those who had voted against it, had to explain their actions. At last, but too late, Mr. Grimes found himself acclaimed a far-seeing statesman. President Johnson had lived out his term of office and no harm had come to the country. The people then knew, as Mr. Grimes had known in a time of clamor, that his impeachment would have been a national blunder.

But the re-honored senator did not live long to enjoy the public's re-approval. He died on the seventh of February, 1873, mourned by a city and a state, both of which he had served for a generation. It was written of him that he had been "A leader more than a follower of opinion, his guiding hand was upon the institutions and laws of a new era in the state of Iowa, and in the nation. He . . . gave early and efficient help in bringing up the country, and President Lincoln and his cabinet, to the great measure of emancipation. The naval victories of the war were organized with his counsel, and under his eye. No senator was more successful in carrying measures which he believed to be right. Never obtruding himself, but with apparent unconsciousness, and keeping out of public sight, he came to be recognized by common consent as one of the triumvirate . . . whose opinions ruled the senate in the era of the nation's transformation. . . The foundation of his character was in a strong sense of justice, truth and moral obligation."[4]

Two political generations after him have passed away, but his premiership in Iowa statecraft has not yet been disputed, if it ever can be disputed.[5]

[4] Salter's *Life of James W. Grimes*, p. 392.

[5] James S. Clarkson relates that one time he asked Judge Nathaniel M. Hubbard, who had a supreme knowledge of Iowa men, whom he esteemed Iowa's greatest men. He replied that Samuel F. Miller and James W. Grimes were "the greatest Iowa men in greatness born." He placed Grimes next to Lincoln in ability. "Grimes" he added, "had the clearest, strongest mental ray among Iowa men." See *Annals of Iowa*, Third Series, Vol. V, p. 477.

# PART VII

## The Years Between

## (1865-1885)

# CHAPTER LXIII

## A Prelude to Things Modern

The twenty years that followed the Civil War in Iowa history may be called the years between. The romance of the pioneer periods was gone, and the realities of progress and prosperity had not yet dawned. It was a period of industrial readjustments, of discontent and unrest. It was all more or less prosaic, and none of it really heroic.

To begin with, it must be taken into consideration that war conditions had made materials dear and money cheap. In 1865 the relation between them stood at two hundred and forty — one hundred representing normal. That is, it took two dollars and forty cents to pay for a dollar's worth of goods. When they began to decline, some years later, they kept on declining until around 1880. Agricultural products not only went down most rapidly, but went lowest of all. We shall see that new lands worked with new machinery outran consumption — the industrial populations of the cities had not yet been organized. The ratio between farmers and artisans, between food producers and food consumers was still adverse to the former.

It was apparent to all that an industrial ailment existed, but no one knew how to diagnose it or to prescribe for it. Quack doctors appeared in rapid succession with many quick remedies, each one regarded as a sure cure for its brief season. The middlemen, the railroads, the banks, the tariff, each one in its turn was held to blame. The period is strewn with the hopes and the wreckage of new ideas expressed in new political parties. Every theory and every experiment was tried at least once. For the student of economics and politics the era is prolific.

That somewhat indefinite thing called politics was much in

evidence, but political principles were at a rather low ebb. The Republican party remained the dominant organization throughout the period, but it maintained its supremacy by first dodging issues and then by compromising them. To carry the next election was ever the next problem. Partisanism was abject, and spoils were the objectives. When everything else failed there was always left the appeal to the passions and the prejudices of the war. The whole Civil War was fought over in each campaign. To this was given the name of waving the bloody shirt. But however easy it was to fan the smouldering embers into flames, the human rights underlying that war were not always exalted.

The material prosperity of the period was low, especially on farms, and, in consequence, little progress was made. The farms were not prosperous, and the cities were stagnant. Corn sometimes sold as low as ten or twelve cents a bushel, and wheat, which was a better barometer — for wheat was cosmopolitan while corn was still provincial — was delivered for as little as thirty-seven cents a bushel. In the cities a dollar a day was a standard wage, and a section man on a railroad received six dollars and sixty cents a week with which to support his family, provided it did not rain, or the worker was not ill. The people of Iowa continued to exist, but they did not live.

Educationally the period was dull. The State University languished and the college at Ames could not find its place in the economic system for which it had been created, nor did it find any lodgment in the hearts of the people. Scientific agriculture was still regarded with the contempt of book-farming, and those who did not despise it were at least suspicious of it. The denominational colleges, perhaps, fared a little better, for the creeds which had given them birth were still regarded as vital and men still lived and died by them. The standards of teaching in the common or public schools were woefully low. The cheapness of the teacher was more considered than the benefits derived. What is now the Teachers' College at Cedar Falls was established on the foundations of an orphanage as a weak expression of a desire for more and better teachers. Education, like everything else, was commonplace.

In the earlier years of the period the "wild west" lingered in Iowa. Its boundaries were somewhat indefinite. Robert Louis Stevenson when he crossed the continent in 1879, even at that late date, thought that it began in the vicinity of Creston. There, he says, he realized he "had come among revolvers," and he confesses he "observed it with some emotion."[1] He saw a conductor kick a red-faced tramp off the train, an altercation in the course of which both men had their hands on their hip pockets.

The "tramp," as he was called, was one of the products of the era, a human resultant of the then prevailing stagnation. Discouraged by industrial conditions, or encouraged by the thought that the world owed him a living, he severed all ordinary human ties and abandoned himself to beggary. He took free passage on railroad trains. He stopped at the back doors of farm houses to ask for food. He slept in lumberyards or in straw stacks along the country highways. Thousands of such men infested the land.

There was a large movement of population into the northwestern quarter of the state, but before that section was fully developed, thousands of people began to leave Iowa. They founded settlements in Kansas, Nebraska, Dakota, and even in far away Oregon. In the fear of depopulation, the general assembly created the office of commissioner of immigration, to re-people Iowa with foreigners. Many communities that had been settled by Americans were re-settled by Europeans. There was also a movement from the farms to the cities, but the cities to which the people migrated were not in Iowa, for the cities of this state still held out few industrial opportunities.

But the prophets of better things also appeared before the period ended. In the rural districts they preached diversified farming, and in the cities, industrial development. The ailments were not so much political as they were industrial. Political doctors were not needed so much as industrial ones. But it took the people a long time to find this out.

[1] Stevenson's *Across the Plains*, p. 24.

# CHAPTER LXIV

## The Course of Politics

During the twenty years of this middle period, seven men sat in the governor's chair, beginning with William M. Stone, who was reëlected in 1865. He was succeeded by Samuel L. Merrill of Clayton County, who served four years. In 1871, and again in 1873, Cyrus C. Carpenter of Webster County was elected, and he was followed by a return of Samuel J. Kirkwood, the war governor, and Joshua G. Newbold who filled out the term. In 1877 John H. Gear of Des Moines County was elected, and again in 1879. The last governor of the period was Buren R. Sherman of Benton County, who also served two terms.

The prestige of the office which Grimes had made great and which Kirkwood had used for a great purpose was in a state of decline. It was not the men who held the office who were to blame, but the times in which they served — not even Kirkwood could re-gild his own fame. The times were ordinary, and the men were not extraordinary. Governor Stone was the remnant of a war governor. He was vigorous, demonstrative, and at times aggressive. Patriotism he had in large measure, and its fires never ceased to burn within him. At times he rattled the saber and waved the flags of the war that was becoming a memory. He was by profession a lawyer; an advocate or a prosecutor.

Governor Merrill also had been a soldier. He was colonel of the Twenty-first Iowa. He was a different man. He gave the state the benefits of his business training at a time when taxes and finances and industrial reconstruction were foremost issues. In making land grants to railroads he was the first to reserve specifically the right of the state to regulate rates.[1]

[1] Wm. H. Fleming, who was private secretary to the governor, in *Annals of Iowa*, Third Series, Vol. V, p. 341.

The spectacular event of his administration was the first great reunion of Iowa soldiers, at Des Moines, on August first, 1870, when President Grant and General Belknap, then secretary of war, and many other noted commanders were present. Twenty thousand Iowa veterans marched in the grand parade. Governor Carpenter had come to Iowa as a surveyor on the frontier. He was a member of the Spirit Lake relief expedition; he entered the Civil War as a captain, and he was a colonel by brevet when he came out of it. He was mild, conservative, and just to all and to all interests. In a time of many troubles he tried to hold the balances even. He coined at least one phrase, to the effect that the excessive freight rate was the skeleton in every corn crib. It fitted his times.

Governor Kirkwood is already well known in this history. His third nomination for governor was brought about in a dramatic manner. General James B. Weaver, a brilliant orator of the time, had fairly won the nomination over his rivals, who included John Russell and John H. Gear. But Weaver was an idealist and a prohibitionist at a time when the more practical politicians were still dodging such issues. They laid plans to defeat him by stampeding the convention. When Audubon County was called its votes were cast for Samuel J. Kirkwood, which caused a great uproar. A delegate asked by what authority the name of Governor Kirkwood was used. A "veteran white haired Republican of imposing form" and stentorian voice — and his voice and form constitute his fame — arose and said it was "By the authority of the great Republican party of the state of Iowa." The man was Dr. S. M. Ballard. The roll call was interrupted by the withdrawals of Russell and Gear from the race, in deference, they said, to the war governor. Though carefully planned this stroke had the magic of impromptu wisdom, and the convention was thrown into great confusion. General Weaver saw his votes melt away, two hundred and sixty-eight being cast for Kirkwood and only two hundred for himself. The coveted and well nigh garnered honor was wrested from him. He felt like Achilles, but he fought like Ulysses in the campaign that followed. He supported the party in the presidential campaign of 1876, but with ever waning zeal, and after that he set himself adrift, becoming the leader of various new movements and parties. He remained for many years the veritable stormy petrel of Iowa politics. But he probably dealt as justly with his party as his party had dealt with him.[2] Kirkwood did not serve out the term allotted him in the lottery of politics. His potent name and personality were used to solve a senatorial contest, as before they had been used to settle the disputed governorship. The lieutenant governor, Joshua G. Newbold of Henry County, was thereby permitted to serve a few months as governor.

John H. Gear, who succeeded him as governor earned the title of "Old Business." He was a business man who had been associated with William F. Coolbaugh in the wholesale grocery trade in Burlington. He was also an adroit politician. It was said of him that he knew every man in politics by his first name. The last of the governors of this period was Buren R. Sherman of Benton County, who was neither great nor inefficient in office. He had a good record as a soldier and he was a diligent executive. The sensational incident of his administration was the ousting of John L. Brown from the office of state auditor, for alleged irregularities in accounting for certain moneys. When Brown refused to vacate his office, the governor called out a company of the state militia to accomplish his desires.

By the census of 1870, and the new apportionment, Iowa was given nine representatives in congress, an increase of three members. The state was divided into as many districts with boundary lines so drawn as to make each one possibly Republican. The Democrats justly complained that the Republicans made the congressional map look like a crazy quilt. But so many new and perplexing issues came up that their political boundaries became ineffective. The first serious break came in 1878, when General James B. Weaver, who had left the Republican party, and Edwin H. Gillette were elected to congress from the Sixth and Seventh districts as exponents of the new doctrines of Greenbackism, with Democratic en-

[2] J. S. Clarkson in *Annals of Iowa*, Third Series, Vol. V, p. 567.

dorsements. In 1882 Thomas Updegraff in the Fourth district was defeated by L. H. Weller, a Greenbacker, and W. P. Hepburn in the Eighth by A. R. Anderson, who was nominated as an independent Republican on an anti-monopoly and anti-corporation platform. Anderson had been a state railroad commissioner. He specialized in the unfairness and excesses of the prevailing railroad rates. The defeat of so strong a man as Colonel Hepburn by a man of ordinary abilities specializing in the grievances of the people, set the politicians to thinking. Many of them hastened to put their houses, as well as fences, in order to meet the new situation. It had its effect even in the United States senate where Senator Wilson of Iowa came forward with a defense of the proposed Interstate Commerce Commission, which had been defeated in that body after having been passed in the lower house. The bill was passed and part of the credit for it has been given to the political reverses in Iowa.[3]

When Governor Merrill received the resignation of Senator Grimes, in August, 1869, it became necessary to elect two United States senators, one to fill out the unexpired term, and one to fill the regular term following. For the short term, James B. Howell, publisher of the Keokuk *Gate City*, was elected by the general assembly, and for the long term, George G. Wright, who had been chief justice of the supreme court of the state. Wright's chief contestant for the office was William B. Allison, who was then serving his fourth term in the lower house where he had become a man of distinction. So confident had the Allison men been of winning the election that they had a banquet prepared to celebrate the event. But in defeat they were gracious, and invited the victors to be their guests at their banquet — and at the same time and place the vanquished laid plans for the next senatorial election.

That next election came in 1872, when Mr. Allison and James F. Wilson appeared to contest with Senator Harlan for his seat. The fight, for such it became in fact, was one of the bitterest in Iowa politics. Mr. Wilson made but little headway, the main contest being between Mr. Harlan and Mr. Allison.

3 Henry Wallace's *Uncle Henry's Own Story*, Vol. III, p. 34.

It was fought out in every legislative district of the state. Men were nominated and elected to the assembly on the direct issue of the senatorship. At times it seemed that there were two Republican parties in the state — an Allison and a Harlan party. Mr. Harlan had many kinds of prestige. He had been many years in the senate and he had been the friend of Lincoln. Mr. Allison was then in his very prime, about forty years of age, a strikingly handsome and vigorous man, but not an orator. He was more apt in national statistics than in figures of speech. The geographical situation favored him, for the northern half of the state had never been represented in the senate. The *State Register* newspaper in Des Moines espoused his cause and that was perhaps the determining fact in his favor. It paraded all of Harlan's past and contrasted it with all of Allison's future. When the general assembly met to put an end to the bitter strife, on the tenth of January, 1873, Mr. Allison received sixty votes in the joint party caucus, Mr. Harlan thirty-eight, and Mr. Wilson twenty-two. Mr. Allison was only one vote short of a majority. On the third ballot five of the Wilson men deserted their candidate, three of them going to Mr. Allison, giving him the necessary majority.

The decision reached in that senatorial caucus retired Mr. Harlan from public life, after serving three terms in the senate and in the cabinets of two presidents. It was the ending of a distinguished career. But the historic contest of 1872-1873 placed the mark of distinction on another man — James S. Clarkson, the editor of the *State Register*. It was his victory almost as much as it was Mr. Allison's. Mr. Clarkson was already a power in state politics and one of the most brilliant editorial writers in the west. He came to Iowa in 1856 as a boy, from Brookville, Indiana. His father, Coker F. Clarkson, hardly less distinguished than his son, founded Melrose Farm in Grundy County, where he practiced and demonstrated the new scientific farming. It was from that farm that he was graduated into agricultural journalism. His two sons, Richard P. and James S., soon drifted to Des Moines where they found employment on the *Register*, the former as type-setter and the latter as reporter and local editor. Frank M. Mills, then the foremost publisher of the state, soon recognized the extraordinary abilities of the young editor. After the war, the Clarksons, father and sons, bought the *Register* and soon made it a great state paper. During the Harlan-Allison contest the family was not agreed, the father adhering to Senator Harlan. As a result of this disagreement he sold his interest in the paper to his sons, remaining, however, as the editor of an agricultural department. James S. Clarkson, who had been chairman of the Iowa State Republican Committee, was advanced to membership on the national committee of the party where he exerted a recognized influence.

But still another senatorial election soon followed. Before his first term was completed, George G. Wright wrote a frank letter in which he said he would not be a candidate for reëlection, having found nothing in Washington that could tempt him to remain there. His decision was in part personal, but there was also a political basis for it. He had not been in agreement with his party on some of the financial questions; he was even suspected of having Greenback leanings. Mr. Harlan again announced his candidacy for the senate. But the general assembly solved the situation by taking Samuel J. Kirkwood out of the governor's chair where he had been placed to keep General Weaver in the background. He was elected to the senate three days after he had been inaugurated as governor, but he did not resign the office of governor until he had served out nearly the full term.

During the twenty years under consideration, Iowa was honored with the tenders of four places in the cabinets of presidents. When President Lincoln made Senator Harlan secretary of the interior, it was the first cabinet appointment that came to the state. President Grant asked James F. Wilson to take the office of secretary of state, but he declined it, largely because it was tendered him after another man had filled the offices in the department. General W. W. Belknap was given the position of secretary of war in the same cabinet. Belknap was compelled to resign in 1876 under a cloud. He had been charged with official misconduct. Tried before the senate, he was acquitted on a verdict of "not guilty on the facts." The facts were that the man was not guilty at all. but he was forced to assume the blame for acts committed by another, one so close to him that he could not do otherwise. When President Hayes made up his cabinet he placed in it George W. McCrary of Keokuk, who as a member of congress had proposed the resolution for a joint commission of fifteen to solve the presidential contest between Rutherford B. Hayes and Samuel J. Tilden. It was that committee that gave the presidency to Mr. Hayes, and he was naturally grateful to the man who had invented the idea. When James A. Garfield became president he selected Samuel J. Kirkwood for secretary of the interior. Mr. Kirkwood, who had resigned the governorship to become senator, thereupon resigned the senatorship to become a cabinet member, Governor Gear appointing James W. McDill of Union County, to succeed him in the senate. But Mr. Kirkwood's term in the cabinet was cut short by the assassination of President Garfield. In six years he had been governor, senator, and member of a cabinet. Frank Hatton, one of the publishers of the Burlington *Hawk-Eye*, and postmaster of that city, became first assistant postmaster general under President Garfield, and served for a time as postmaster general under President Arthur.

After having served in congress, John A. Kasson was, in 1867, elected to the legislature from Polk County to lead the movement for a new state house. It was defeated in 1868, but carried in 1870. Out of the bitter contest a partisan and incompetent commission was selected to have charge of the work. In 1872, a new commission was created, composed of Maturin L. Fisher, Robert S. Finkbine, Peter A. Dey and John G. Foote, with the governor an ex-officio member. These men tore out the defective beginnings which had been made and carried on the work to successful completion, with Mr. Dey as the consulting engineer and Mr. Finkbine as superintendent and Ed. Wright as assistant superintendent of construction.

# CHAPTER LXV

## Railroads and the Wild West in Iowa

None of the four railroads across the state for which land grants were made in 1856 had been completed when the Civil War closed. The first of the projected lines to be completed was what is now the Chicago and Northwestern, which opened its line to Council Bluffs in 1867. The Des Moines Valley Road, which was built out of the remnants of the Des Moines River improvement land grant was completed from Keokuk to the capital city in 1866. It was the first railroad to reach Des Moines, which was then a city of about ten thousand population. The first train to enter the city was a much heralded event. "Hear, oh, ye heavens," so ran a public proclamation printed on large posters, "and give ear, oh, ye earth! Let the glad news sweep over the prairies and around the universe, that the first train on the Valley road will come into Des Moines on the afternoon of the 29th of August, 1866. . . Let us have a perfect roar and rush and thunders of enthusiasm."[1] The event was celebrated not only with noise, but with banquets and speeches. It was the beginning of another "new era." It had taken ten years to build the road, the first shipment of rails from England reaching Keokuk as early as 1856, carried on steam boats up the Mississippi. Rails, though they had to be made on the other side of the ocean, then cost only sixteen dollars a ton.

What is now the Chicago, Rock Island and Pacific Railway, was thirteen years in building from Iowa City to Council Bluffs, delayed by panics, the war, and bankruptcies. In 1865 it was still at Kellogg. The Burlington and Missouri. now the Chicago, Burlington and Quincy had its terminal somewhere west of Ottumwa. Its builders had lost faith

[1] *Annals of Iowa*, Third Series, Vol. VIII, p. 12.

in the then far west. In the autumn of 1866, the president of the road, James F. Joy, was persuaded to look over the proposed extension of the line. Somewhere in the vicinity of the city of Red Oak, he said to his associates, "I'm not in for it," meaning the extension. "This country is uninhabitable," he told them; "where will they get fences, where will they get fuel?" They had halted in the midst of an unbroken prairie. To him the region looked forever impossible for human habitation. He could not visualize the future and he lacked the faith of the settlers who were pushing on ahead of the railroads for which the state had so richly provided. But a young man, Charles E. Perkins, who was a member of the party, and who afterwards became president of the road, was "in for it." He wanted the road built forthwith.[2]

Among the greatest of the Iowa railroad builders was John I. Blair, a somewhat eccentric millionaire of New Jersey. The new state found favor in his eyes. When he came to Iowa what is now the Chicago and Northwestern line had been built as far as Cedar Rapids, under the name of the Chicago, Iowa and Nebraska Railroad. In 1859, the eastern stockholders of this road formed a corporation including John Weare and John F. Ely of Cedar Rapids and G. M. Woodbury of Marshalltown, to extend the line to the Missouri River. In 1860 the state regranted to them the lands of the Iowa Central Air Line, which had contracted to build the line along the forty-second parallel, but had defaulted. In 1861 Blair took control of the construction beyond Marshalltown. The Cedar River was bridged in 1860, and in 1861 forty miles of track were laid in spite of the war. In the following year the road was extended to Marshalltown, in 1865 to Boone, and in 1867 to Council Bluffs. Blair and his associates in 1867 and 1868 acquired the rights of the Iowa Falls and Sioux City Railroad Company, which was one of the four beneficiaries of the act of 1856, but which had been stopped at Iowa Falls. This line was completed to Sioux City in 1870. The land grants of these roads were consolidated under the Iowa Railroad Land Company, of which Blair was the first president, succeeded

[2] *Annals of Iowa*, Third Series, Vol. VIII, p. 375.

by Horace Williams of Clinton and P. E. Hall of Cedar Rapids, and of which Henry V. Ferguson served as secretary from 1868 to 1918 when its affairs were finally closed.[3]

In those days the wild west was in Iowa. In 1865, Boone, then on the frontier, and known as the town of Montana, was described as "simply a stretch of prairie about sixty feet in width." On this town strip were located about one hundred one-story buildings, "about every other one a saloon, gambling house or dance hall."[4] Montana was "the end of the line." Its frontier type of buildings sheltered many who preyed on the men who in the sweat of their faces built the railroads that were the harbingers of civilization. The proprietors provided "plenty of music and whiskey." Fist and gun-fights were usual occurrences in the streets of the village. The "strip" was frequented by "tall, black mustached, rough looking men, with wide sombreros, their pants in their boots, armed *cap-a-pie.*" They jostled each other through the street, looking for trouble and finding plenty of it. Young officers in the uniforms of the United States, coming and going to the army posts of the west, were also present, "sipping wine with straw-haired girls," while Indians decked in blankets and feathers went about stealthily looking for fire-water and dogs to convert into feasts.

All the feats that now seem impossible, even when seen in the motion picture shows, were then performed in Iowa. On one occasion an Indian who had filled himself with fire-water, raised the war whoop and went slashing his way through the village. In an instant the lariat of a cow-boy fell over the shoulders of the infuriated red man and he was "bounced behind a cowboy's pony to the cooler."[5] "Paid off cowboys" came to Montana to spend their moneys and rode their bucking ponies through the dance halls shooting daylight through the roofs, afterwards paying for all the damage with their hard earned dollars. But there were others also in the village. Fine looking young men who had come west to make

[3] Brewer and Wick's *History of Linn County*, p. 232.

[4] Stanton's *When the Wildwood was in Flower*, p. 13.

[5] *Ibid.*, p. 13.

their fortunes, mining engineers and land speculators and well fed capitalists who were ready to invest their moneys in the new opportunities. Our chronicler as he moved about the place, found satisfaction in the fact that "everybody was an American, and the English the only language heard."

Western Iowa was during those years a cattle country. Many of the ranches were of great extent. The cattle when ready for market were driven to the railroad and shipped to Chicago. The mails were carried in relays generally from one county seat town to another. A mail man's outfit consisted usually of a buckboard and horse and a Colt's revolver, for the country was infested with cattle thieves and horse thieves and prowling Indians. Some of the carriers had outfits that looked like battle equipments. Prairie wolves, or coyotes, also infested the country. They were cowardly creatures but they made enough noise to scare the timid tenderfoots. But when roving in packs and hungry, they occasionally attacked human beings, especially if the latter would not stand their ground. The coyotes lived in holes in the ground. Their habitations were cleverly constructed, showing that they were not so stupid as they looked. The animals selected a side hill in which they excavated a hole at an angle of about forty-five degrees, about eight feet deep. Then they made an up-turn of about two feet and at the top of that the lair was constructed with room enough for the young. When water ran into the hole it sank away at the bottom leaving the nest high and dry, and when pursued into their burrows by other animals the coyotes fought them from the vantage of the top.

In winter time the ranchers had to contend with blizzards on the open prairies and in summer time with windstorms and occasionally with a tornado, or "cyclone." In the autumn months prairie fires menaced not only their hay stacks, but often their cattle, for the fires swept with such terrific fury that escape from them was often impossible. At night these fires could be seen for miles, and the crackling and the roaring of the flames sounded like the besoms of destruction.

The railroad trains, when the line was extended westward

from Boone, were somewhat indifferently operated. The country was unsettled and wild game was abundant, especially prairie chickens. Trainmen could not resist the temptation to hunt along the way. Carroll County was a favorite hunting ground. There many trains were stopped and all on board, from engineer to passengers, would tramp over the prairies to shoot chickens, each one invariably bringing back a supply of birds. That trains were delayed did not matter until the officials made drastic rules against hunting on the way.[6] The engines and cattle cars of that day were not large and a train of ten or a dozen cars was heavily loaded. It required two nights and a day to pull a stock train from the Missouri Valley country to Chicago and many cattle perished on the way. When trains were caught in snow drifts and blizzards the fatalities were multiplied. There were no snow fences to protect the cuts and no snow plows to clear the tracks. Traffic was thus frequently tied up, sometimes for weeks at a time.

In 1868 there was brought to the town of Boone a mysterious block of stone. It was large and heavy, weighing five tons; it was conveyed on a wagon drawn by oxen. Its origin was known to have been in the vicinity of Fort Dodge, for which Boone was then the nearest railway station. It was of gypsum, a friable stone that hardened under exposure to the air. Vast deposits of it had been found in Webster County and some of it had been used for building materials. At Boone the stone was placed in a car and started on its way to Chicago, where it was shaped by a German sculptor into the effigy of a human giant. Carefully concealed, it was then shipped to Cardiff, New York, not far from Syracuse, where it was secretly buried deep in the ground. In the following year the owner of the land with guilty knowledge, started to sink a well over the burial place of the gypsum giant. When the workmen struck what had been buried there they were surprised, almost horrified. The human monster was carefully uncovered and hoisted to the surface.

Startling reports soon filled the newspapers and a rush of

[6] Stanton's *When the Wildwood was in Flower*, p. 47.

the curious to the scene followed. The perpetrators of the fraud provided a shelter and charged an admission fee. It was called the "American Goliath," also the "Onondaga Giant" — everything except the gypsum fraud. Scientists came also. Geology and archaeology and biology and even theology were all interested. Inspection and retrospection were applied. Dr. James Hall of New York, who was the first state geologist of Iowa, pronounced it in the name of science, "The most remarkable archaeological discovery ever made in this country and entirely unlike any relic of the past age known to us." In the *Scientific American* a writer declared that it was easier to believe that it was "a veritable petrification" than a statue, for he could not find "a chisel mark upon the entire image." To him it was "the most extraordinary and gigantic wonder ever presented to the eye of man." If once a man, wrote another rhapsodist, "Then he must have lived in the forgotten ages. . . Man with his feeble mind cannot grasp the idea. . . That finely shaped head, was it ever the seat of intellect?" And if a statue, "Where now the intelligence that conceived the subject and grandly wrought its completion? . . . the contour so perfect, and repose so life-like, and the countenance so noble!" And yet the contrivance was hardly a year old and the intellect that conceived it was a fakir! What deceived the scientists most were the marks of erosion by water, which had been carefully retained by the sculptor. The theory of petrification was soon rejected; it was agreed that it was a statue of great age — it probably had some connection with the Phoenicians, who were a sea-faring people! All the time the curious paid to see the widely advertised wonder. P. T. Barnum, then a great showman, wanted to buy it, but to its owners it was worth a fortune that even he could not encompass. But the hoax was not long lived. The Fort Dodge *North West*, then edited by B. F. Gue, in a pamphlet, made a full exposure of the matter, tracing the block of gypsum from Fort Dodge to New York. The shrewd perpetrators, among whom H. B. Martin and George Hull were chief, finally confessed their deception — but for what could they be punished? For their cleverness? And what could the scientists be punished for, their gullibility?[7] From it all, Fort Dodge gypsum gained renown and in 1871 the first mill for its utilization on a commercial basis was built, the beginning of one of the state's important mineral industries.

When the junction between the Union Pacific and Central Pacific railroads was effected, completing transportation to the coast, the Iowa roads made haste to get each its share of the traffic. The present Rock Island entered Council Bluffs in 1869, and the Chicago, Burlington and Quincy a little later. But without such an incentive it took longer to build a line across the northern part of the state. Work on such a road was commenced at McGregor in 1857, with the aid of large local subscriptions. The company failed and a new one, the McGregor Western Railroad Company, in 1864 received from congress the munificent grant of the odd numbered sections for ten miles on each side of the proposed line. But in spite of this, it was not able to build the twenty miles per year required of it. A second company also failed, but the third one, the Chicago, Milwaukee and St. Paul, finally completed the road to Sheldon in 1878.[8] It was the delay in this construction that sent William Larrabee of Clermont, a farmer and a miller, to the state senate in 1867. His first election, in a Democratic district, was a recognition of his abilities as a business man, and in the hope that he would solve their transportation problem.

In making these re-grants it was stipulated that the companies thus benefitted should "at all times be subject to such rules, regulations and rates . . . as may from time to time be enacted and provided for by the general assembly of the state of Iowa." This idea was not new, but it was new as a contractual stipulation. But the assertion of this power over rates on the part of the state filled the railroad promoters with misgivings. They said that financiers would not invest their moneys under such conditions, and to give force to their statements work on some of the lines then under

[7] Gue's *History of Iowa*, Vol. III, p. 39.

[8] Larrabee's *The Railroad Question*, p. 328.

construction was stopped. An effort was made to have the clause repealed in an extraordinary session of the legislature, but Governor Merrill refused to convene the general assembly for such a purpose, and gradually railroad building was resumed.

On January first, 1870, nearly three thousand miles of railroads were in operation in the state, the mileage having been doubled in about two years. For the construction of these, and other lines, subsequently, the state, through gifts from congress, donated 4,069,942 acres of land, one-ninth of all the lands in Iowa. Few of these lands were sold for the minimum price. Many of them were not sold until prices had advanced to eight and even twelve dollars an acre.[9] In addition the roads received county, township, and municipal aid in the form of taxes levied, as well as many private donations. But in spite of this, railroad building and operating were hazardous undertakings. If fortunes were made, fortunes were also lost, often through incompetence and sometimes through dishonesty. The railroads were not in every instance built to serve the people, or even to earn dividends on honest investments.' Many of the promoters were speculators and some of the bankruptcy proceedings were money making devices for promoters who were in effect wreckers.

When these facts became known and when rates were kept high and often made discriminatory, favoring certain communities and certain shippers more than others, discontent soon began to multiply. To quiet these complaints a bill to regulate rates was passed by the lower house of the general assembly in 1870, but it was defeated in the senate. But that defeat multiplied popular discontent until it became an agitation. The railroad troubles in Iowa had commenced.

[9] Larrabee's *The Railroad Question*, p. 329.

# CHAPTER LXVI

## Population after the War

During the war the population of Iowa had remained almost stationary. The census of 1865 showed an increase of only eighty thousand over that of 1860, which was hardly a respectable birth rate over death rate among a young and vigorous people. But the war was hardly over before the rush of immigration set in again. The state census of 1865 gave Iowa a population of 754,732, which was increased to 1,191,000 in 1870, a growth of four hundred and thirty-six thousand in five years, or a yearly increase larger than the whole increase during the war. The following state census, that of 1875, showed a population of 1,350,544, or almost double that of 1865. But the population was excessively rural. In 1870 there were only eight cities in the state with more than five thousand people. These were Davenport, 20,121; Dubuque, 18,432; Burlington, 15,178; Keokuk, 12,761; Des Moines, 12,380; Council Bluffs, 10,021; Iowa City, 7,009; and Cedar Rapids, 6,081.

To increase the population of the state was the passion of the times. Every acre that was not brought under the plow was considered wasted. The land should be made productive. The Creator had made it to help support the world. The landless of America and the oppressed of the world were not only invited but urged to come to Iowa. In 1870 the legislature created a state commission to promote immigration, especially from Europe. A pamphlet on "Iowa the Home for Immigrants," prepared by A. R. Fulton, was translated into many foreign languages and was scattered broadcast. In the same year the state participated in a national conference to encourage immigration. The steamship companies readily coöperated with these efforts. And so did the railroad companies of Iowa which had lands to sell. To sell fertile lands for low prices was a pastime. In all this time no thought was given to the Americanization of the aliens who were invited to come and to make their homes in the state. On the contrary, they were told that here they could live their old lives over again. Nor was there much need for concern over such things at that time. Most of the immigrants came from countries whose people cherished American ideals.

The bulk of the immigrants who came to Iowa during those years were Germans and Scandinavians, and the rest came from England, Scotland, Ireland, Wales, Holland, and Bohemia. The Germans, who had re-peopled the Mississippi River cities and counties before the war, after the war spread over all parts of the state. Of the Scandinavians, there were more Norwegians than Swedes and more Swedes than Danes. These nationalities followed their European latitudes, the Norwegians to the north, the Danes to the south, and the Swedes between them, although there were many overlappings.[1] The Norwegians took possession of many communities, almost of whole counties in northeastern Iowa. The census of 1870 disclosed 5,524 Norwegians in the single county of Winneshiek. The Bohemians, who were the latest comers, made extensive settlements in the counties of Johnson, Linn, Benton, and Tama, with Cedar Rapids as a center. The majority of them settled on farms, but they materially increased the urban populations of Cedar Rapids and Iowa City. Their industry, thrift, and frugality soon enabled them to make material progress. The Hollanders made new settlements in the extreme northwestern part of the state, in Sioux and later in Lyon County. Orange City in Sioux County was an offspring of Pella in Marion County, of a preceding generation. The other European nationalities were intermingled with the rest of the people of the state. But the preponderance of the American element in Iowa remained. Four-fifths of the new settlers were of native stocks from the

[1]George T. Flom's "The Growth of the Scandinavian Factor in the Population of Iowa," in *The Iowa Journal of History and Politics,* Vol. V, p. 267.

older states. No mid-western state remained more American than Iowa.

For a number of years the settlement of western and especially northwestern Iowa was retarded by recurring plagues of grasshoppers that devastated whole counties and depopulated many communities. For a decade these insect pests literally terrorized the people. The first historic flight alighted in 1867. They arrived that year on the eighth of September, "settling over the land like snowflakes." They devoured everything that was green and succulent, and when they could find nothing else to subsist on they attacked the bark of young trees. When cold weather came they hid themselves and perished in heaps. But before dying they had perforated the soil and deposited their eggs in vast quantities. The farmers, forewarned, tried to destroy the eggs in the following spring by frequent plowings and harrowings of the ground, exposing the eggs to the action of the frosts. So numerous were the eggs that after each harrowing the ground looked as if it had been seeded with rice. But all such efforts were vain. The vitality of the eggs was not destroyed. They brought forth a horde of young in due season. All efforts to destroy them were in vain. They flourished and destroyed the crops. The young creatures were wingless, but later in the season they sloughed off their exteriors when two embryonic wings appeared. These wings developed rapidly, enabling them to make short flights within a few days and in ten days they were strong enough for long flights, whereupon they flew away as mysteriously as their ancestors had come in the year before. It was the belief of the time that these plagues had their origin somewhere among the foothills of the Rocky Mountains.[2]

In 1873 the grasshoppers returned in flights that covered the skies like clouds. After they had devoured everything that grew, they became a pest in the homes of the people, which they invaded. Along the railroads they were so thick that trains were stopped, the crushed insects acting like grease

[2] *Annals of Iowa*, Third Series, Vol. IV, p. 256.

upon the rails.[3] In 1873 "the hoppers were a foot thick on the water (of the Des Moines River) and more coming over the banks just like a waterfall."[4] In their flight they obscured the sun and made "a roaring noise like the sound of a waterfall."[5] They often covered twenty miles a day and after them the country looked "as though swept by a prairie fire." In their wake one settler wrote that "naught remained but a wife, two children and a yoke of oxen," and food for none.[6] In some places "hopper dozers" were used to fight the pests. These were bent strips of tin filled with tar into which they were swept and burned.[7] But naught availed, In 1873 the pests ravaged all of western Iowa as far east as Ames. Relief was needed to save the settlers from starvation. The adjutant general of the state was placed in charge of this work, and the legislature in 1874 appropriated $50,000 for seed for the ensuing planting. The last of the historic plagues occurred in 1876, with hatchings in 1877, after which they did not return. They disappeared as suddenly and as mysteriously as they had come.

During these years not only were new settlements halted, but thousands left the ravaged areas. The prices of farm lands went down fifty per cent in many places. Good farms went begging for purchasers. Many did not tarry long enough in the land to dispose of their holdings. But men of faith, and also speculators, profited greatly by these calamities. They bought when others were anxious to sell and the foundations of many substantial land fortunes were laid.

Settlements in the north central counties of the state were long delayed also by vast tracts of land partially under water. These were called sloughs. In some of them the water did not dry up from one year's end to another. They were the dread of travelers as well as the bane of settlers. Some of the sloughs were shallow lakes, but in others the waters were submerged in bottomless mud overgrown with rank grasses and

[3] Stanton's *When the Wildwood was in Flower*, p. 51.

[4] McCarty's *History of Palo Alto County*, p. 51.

[5] *Ibid.*, p. 135.

[6] *Ibid.*, p. 105.

[7] Palo Alto *Reporter*, June 9, 1877.

rushes. The early writers speak of them as being of almost limitless extent.[8] They were the homes of countless muskrats whose houses projected above the waters, giving to the sloughs the appearance of submerged villages. In summer time these places were the haunts of millions of marsh birds. Yellow-headed blackbirds, redwings and marsh wrens were the most numerous among this varied bird life. Ducks and geese in vast flocks visited these sloughs in spring and autumn and many remained to raise their young, using the tops of the muskrat houses for their nesting places. The smaller birds made their nests in the tall grasses and rushes. Pests of mosquitoes were bred in these places, while dragon flies, called "devil's darning needles," were so numerous that they gave a brilliant glow to the scenery.

The sloughs constituted portions of what were known as swamp lands which at one time were deemed so worthless that they were disposed of to speculators at their own prices. One of the most flagrant of these sales was made by the supervisors of Wright County in 1862, who sold eighteen thousand acres of such lands to the American Emigrant Company for the sum of fifteen hundred dollars, or at about eight cents per acre. The voters of the county approved this sale with only one dissenting vote.[9] In many instances such lands were disposed of before *bona fide* settlers had entered them in large numbers, through venal county organizations. The total of such lands granted and certified to the state by the national government amounted to 1,570,000 acres.[10] Later when drainage systems were developed these lands proved to be the most productive in the whole state.

8 Charles Aldrich's "Sloughs of Northern Iowa," in *Annals of Iowa*, Third Series, Vol. V, p. 27.

9 Webster City *Freeman-Tribune*, July 13, 1904.

10 Gue's *History of Iowa*, Vol. III, p. 92.

# CHAPTER LXVII

## The Causes and Growth of Discontent

Farming was the principal occupation of the people of Iowa, and around 1870 the business of farming was not profitable. At the end of a year of hard work and frugal living the most industrious and frugal husbandmen found that they had but little left, hardly enough to pay their debts and taxes. Could the boundless fertility of the soil and the labor they put on it yield them nothing more than a bare living? They had expected much of the railroads, but they thought they were reaping none of the hoped for and longed for benefits. Prices for products were so low that after they had paid the freight rates on them there was little left. They began to think that the railroads were absorbing their profits. But as a matter of fact many of the railroads were not profitable investments. Much of the country through which they ran was still too sparsely settled.

The basic trouble was the reaction after the war. Following a period of expansion there came a period of contraction. Prices fell and business became stagnant. The culmination came in 1873 in the form of a panic which sent all values tumbling down. The blame for it all was variously placed and the remedies proposed were many. The railroads, the banks, the currency, the middlemen, those who bought and sold, each in turn was blamed and legislation was demanded to set things right. The politicians at first temporized and then they compromised, putting off the evil day.

The first offspring of discontent and hope was an organization known as the Patrons of Husbandry, which in the west became known as the Granger movement. It was a secret order which had its origin in the District of Columbia. Each unit in the organization was called a Grange, from which the word granger as applied to farmers was derived. In Iowa the ideas of the grange became contagious around 1870 and by 1872 more than five hundred local societies were in existence and more were being organized every week.[1] Ostensibly these organizations were non-political, but none the less they exerted in time a powerful influence in politics. Their main object was to promote coöperation among the farmers, and the politicians hastened to make their platforms conform with the new ways of thinking.

One of the first ideas evolved was that of direct and collective buying and selling with the consequent elimination of middlemen. Coöperative stores, elevators, and warehouses were established. But these efforts were not uniformly successful. In a few places they did well, but it was not due to coöperation so much as to able individual management of the society's affairs. Membership in a grange and election to office in it did not endow every man with business ability. Men who found that they could do business for others, soon preferred to do business for themselves. Those who remained to manage the coöperative business enterprises were not always men who could compete with those who managed their own business. Nor could the pleas of loyalty to their societies hold the farmers. Gradually they returned to the practice of buying and selling where and to whom it advantaged them most. The result was a gradual dissolution of the coöperative enterprises.

But if their business operations were not wholly successful, their social activities proved boons to the farmers and their families, for women and even children were included in the membership of the granges. The farmers were brought in closer contact with each other, and so were their families. They helped to break the isolation and monotony of farm life. The intellectual as well as the social life was stimulated. The secret rituals of the Patrons of Husbandry were in themselves educational. They were florid and declamatory, but they were of human interest. There was in them also the spirit of brotherhood and sisterhood. The winter meetings were

[1] Gue's *History of Iowa*, Vol. III, p. 57.

debating societies for the men, and for the women social and literary experiences. Budgets of news, songs, essays, and impromptu speeches made up the programs. Hamlin Garland, who as a boy participated in these gatherings, testifies that "Nothing more picturesque, more delightful, more helpful has ever arisen out of American rural life." [2] They were to him "a most grateful relief from the sordid loneliness of the farm." It is the testimony of all who participated in them that they sweetened the social life of the farmers and widened their mental horizon. They were like little colleges formed among the people. They increased self-thinking, self-reliance, and eventually those who participated learned the power of public sentiment in shaping the policies of government.

The influence of the granges can soon be noted in the platforms of the political parties. In 1873 the Republicans found the grace to say that "the producing, commercial and industrial interests of the country should have the best and cheapest modes of transportation possible," and after accounting themselves brave to take so advanced a position, they added that "actual capital invested" in transportation companies should still have "reasonable compensation." Such were then the nice balances of politics. Abuses, excessive rates, and discriminations in charges were denounced. The platform makers ventured even into the realm of morals, denouncing all corruption, and advocating honesty, purity, and economy. The Democrats went farther; they abandoned their own party organization entirely to make room for a new anti-monopoly party, which proclaimed the legislative regulation of all corporations and the making of maximum railroad rates by law.

The election of 1873 was close. For the house fifty Republicans were elected and fifty opposition. It required one hundred and thirty-two ballots to elect John H. Gear speaker. It was a period of financial distress for which many remedies were proposed. One of the remedies was a law that remade the railroad world. Passenger rates were fixed at three and four cents a mile, the higher rates for the poorer roads, and for

[2] Hamlin Garland's *A Son of the Middle Border*, p. 166.

freight purposes the railroads were divided into four classes and schedules of rates to be charged were enacted for each class. All discriminations between communities and between individuals were made unlawful. Rates and services were to be for all alike. This legislation became known as the Granger Law. The author of the bill was Frank T. Campbell, who afterwards became lieutenant governor of the state. At that time he represented Jasper County in the legislature. The law was approved by Governor Carpenter.

The railroads protested what they called confiscatory legislation. They denied the right and the justice of it. But they finally agreed to give the new rates a fair trial, all except the Chicago, Burlington & Quincy Railroad, which secured a temporary injunction against the rates being put into effect. The injunction was dissolved by Judge John F. Dillon of the Federal court, who upheld the right of the legislature to regulate and fix railroad charges. His decision was later sustained in the supreme court of the United States. It was then regarded as an epochal victory for the people.

With the railroad question disposed of, the discontent had to do with the monetary matters of the country. The money of the country consisted of gold, silver, and greenbacks. The greenbacks were notes of the government printed on pieces of paper one side of which was green in color. They were redeemable in gold. As the war progressed more and more of such paper was issued. As the ability of the government to redeem such promises was doubted, the value of the greenbacks fell until it took two and one-half paper dollars to make one gold dollar. Sound finance dictated the redemption and the retirement of the greenbacks. The resumption of specie payments became a mooted question. Many were opposed to it. Others were in favor of issuing more greenbacks. They insisted that the money in which the soldiers had been paid was good enough for the bondholders also. Those who so believed proceeded to organize a new political party which was called the Greenback party.

In 1873, congress did a thing that at the time attracted but little attention — demonetized silver, in conformity with an international agreement to that effect. The supplies of silver were growing so rapidly that the commercial nations of the world despaired of being able to keep it on a par with gold. As a matter of fact, silver as a monetary metal had been little used. In a hundred years the total coinage of silver in the United States had amounted to only eight million dollars. From 1834 to 1873 very little silver had been coined. President Grant approved the demonetization of silver, and in 1875 he approved an act for the resumption of specie payments to begin in 1879. All these were efforts to place the country once more on a sound financial basis.

This legislation brought the greenback issue into prominence. On May tenth, 1876, a state convention of protestors was held in Des Moines at which the Greenback party was formally launched. The resumption of specie payments was denounced as another effort of the financiers to crush the people. It was declared to be the duty of the government "to establish a monetary system based on the faith and the resources of the nation and adapted to the demands of legitimate business." All the resources of the government, not the gold of the few, should constitute the monetary basis. Give the people more money by printing more of it! Make money easy, not hard! Make it responsive to the wants of the people, and not directed by the greed of the financiers!

The Republicans met this new issue by declaring themselves to be in favor of "a currency convertible into coin." But they continued to favor "the gradual resumption of specie payments by continuous and speedy steps in that direction." It was equivocation and cowardice. How could one and the same process be both "gradual" and "speedy," except in a political platform made to face both ways? But it was the year of a national election and the Republicans in Iowa succeeded with a majority of about fifty thousand. In 1877, the discontent being still rampant, the Republicans yielded still more by declaring for the remonetization of silver, to undo what was becoming known as "the crime of 1873," and by advocating that "silver be made with gold a legal tender for the payment of all debts, both public and private." They also advocated the

Samuel F. Miller

John A. Kasson

James S. Clarkson

David B. Henderson

maintenance of the then "present volume of legal tender currency . . . until the wants of trade and commerce demand its further contraction." The Democrats went in for greenbacks without any apologies. The Grange in its state convention entered the domain of politics far enough to favor the repeal of the act to resume specie payments, the remonetization of silver, and the repeal of the national bank act. That year General Weaver formally severed his connection with the Republican party and became the most active of the Greenback leaders.

But there were many who cared more for morals than for railroads or money, and these made the liquor laws of the state their paramount consideration. The prohibitory law of 1855, with the wine and beer amendments of 1857 and 1858, was still on the statute books. During all the intervening years the sales of wine and beer had been legal, but not the sales of the stronger liquors. Nevertheless, the stronger drinks had been sold. Those who were licensed to sell wine and beer sold also whiskey and gin. A minority had repeatedly sought to bring this issue to the front, but the two dominant parties had succeeded in evading their importunities. But year by year the minority grew more insistent. At the meeting of the Woman's Christian Temperance Union, held at Burlington in October, 1878, Mrs. J. Ellen Foster of Clinton, proposed a constitutional amendment on the subject.[3] The idea was soon endorsed by other temperance societies, including the State Temperance Alliance, and the politicians accepted it as a solution of their perpetual dilemma. They would abide by the decision of the people. The Republicans made it part of their platform in 1879, and in 1880 the general assembly passed a joint resolution of submission. The liquor men protested, and the Democrats called it the "most offensive form of sumptuary legislation," but in 1882, the joint resolution was passed the second time, as required by the constitution.

[3] Fellow's *History of Prohibition in Iowa*, p. 4.

# CHAPTER LXVIII

## Issues Settled and Postponed

The panic of 1873 stopped nearly all railroad construction. The roads that were then in operation but barely survived. All the time the people were clamoring for the construction of more lines. The railroad men took advantage of the situation to move for the repeal of the Granger Law, whose rates, they said, were oppressive and retarded the investment of eastern capital in railroad properties. The people were then asked to forget and to forgive; but all were not yet ready to give up what had been gained. An attempt to repeal the law in the general assembly of 1876 was not successful.

The railroad men then had recourse to sympathy and strategy. They presented the companies as facing bankruptcy. The Chicago and Northwestern had a deficit of over six hundred thousand dollars, the Illinois Central nearly three hundred thousand; eleven other roads had deficits and seven had defaulted the interest on their bonds. Under the Granger rates, so they said, no road could earn its dividends. The state was at a standstill in railroad building. The people wanted more roads, but they could not get them. The politicians and newspapers of Iowa were still afraid of the Granger sentiment. The roads then made use of strategy. Charles Aldrich, later the founder of the State Historical Department, then a farmer near Webster City, was sent to New York and other cities where he enlisted the aid of the great newspapers. Among others the New York *Tribune* printed liberal editorial advice to Iowa. "Other states will grow and become rich," said the *Tribune*, while Iowa will languish because her laws repel capital. Immigration will go to other states. These articles were then reprinted in Iowa papers, papers that did not dare to speak out themselves. The propaganda was subtle and successful. Iowa was soon spoken of as "red-hot as with a great prairie fire."[1] The railroad attorneys became a new power in Iowa. They were as wise as serpents and as gentle as doves. They begged for mercy and they promised new railroad lines and more justice in rates.[2]

When the Seventeenth General Assembly of Iowa met in January, 1878, a great peace was made between the railroads and the shippers of the state. It took the form of a repeal of the Granger Law[3] and the substitution therefor of a railroad commission composed of three men to be appointed by the governor. These men were to hear all complaints and to resolve all grievances into blessings. Similar commissions had been created in eastern states, conspicuously in Massachusetts. Even William Larrabee, who had entered the senate as a railroad promoter and who was destined to be a railroad reformer, voted for this repeal.[4] And Frank T. Campbell, the author of the Granger Law, as lieutenant governor, had the honor of presiding over the senate that repealed it. Governor Gear appointed able men to the commission, Cyrus C. Carpenter, the former governor, Peter A. Dey and James W. McDill. But it was the postponement of an issue, not a settlement of it. Eight years of bitter strife resulted in a truce between the contending forces. It was soon found that the commissioners, whose powers were wholly advisory, could accomplish little. They rode on passes and their wages were paid by the railroad companies. Railroad rate abuses were multiplied, not lessened. It was a condition, not a theory that confronted the roads. Their traffic was light, consisting largely of grain. To exist at all they struggled for business, making low rates at competitive points and excessive ones at others. The farmers at the same time were receiving low

[1] Charles Aldrich in *The Iowa Journal of History and Politics*, Vol. III, p. 256.

[2] Thomas F. Withrow represented the Rock Island; John F. Duncombe, the Illinois Central; Nathaniel M. Hubbard and Major E. S. Bailey, the Northwestern; Henry W. Strong, the Milwaukee, or St. Paul; Thomas Potter, a manager, not an attorney, the C. B. and Q.; and John S. Runnells, the Pullman Company.

[3] *Laws of Iowa*, 1878, pp. 67-72.

[4] Larrabee's *The Railroad Question*, p. 335.

prices for their products, a large part of which went to pay the railroad transportation charges. The troubles were more basic — they inhered in the whole industrial system. There was no coördination between the producers and consumers.

The monetary issues were national, but the people of Iowa took a prominent part in their discussion and settlement. The points of attack were two principally, the pending retirement of the greenbacks, and the demonetization of silver. In 1878 the financial world was thrown into some alarm by the introduction of a bill by Congressman Richard P. Bland of Missouri not only for the remonetization of silver but for its free and unlimited coinage at the ratio sixteen to one as compared with gold. Free coinage meant that the government mint should not charge the owner of the silver anything for coining his metal into dollars. Vast quantities of silver were at that time being mined in Colorado and other western states and the price of silver was falling. It was a theory of the times that as the price of silver declined other commodity prices also declined. The Bland bill proposed nothing less than the maintenance of an abitrary value for silver, no matter how much of it might be taken out of the mines or imported into the country. When it looked as if there were votes enough in congress to pass such a bill, Senator Allison of Iowa came forward with an amendment which was intended to limit its evils. This amendment ordered the secretary of the treasury to purchase each month two million dollars' worth of silver for purposes of coinage, and authorized him to purchase, at his discretion, up to four million dollars' worth. The Bland bill so amended was passed by both houses of congress, but was promptly vetoed by President Hayes, on February twenty-eighth, 1878. On the same day the bill was re-passed by both houses of congress over the president's veto, so strong was the silver sentiment. The Allison amendment was a compromise for which the Iowa senator was often blamed afterwards. It did not represent what Senator Allison believed, but it was an effort on his part to ward off a greater evil, that of free and unlimited coinage of silver. The final settlement of financial heresy was postponed until a time when public sentiment could be better educated.

Prohibition, the third of the three paramount issues of that period, was not so easily disposed of. It was in many ways the most vital of all. Before the final passage of the joint resolution, many questions were brought up by those opposed to it. One of these was compensation for those whose property might be outlawed. But all propositions for compensating the brewers and liquor dealers were rejected. The senate passed an interpretative resolution to the effect that the amendment would not forbid the manufacture of liquors for export. This was to protect a distillery which had just been opened in Des Moines. This act was properly denounced by many newspapers not only as inconsistent, but outrageous.

On the second of March, 1882, the senate passed finally the joint resolution for submission of the question to the people. On the thirty-first the governor signed the bill designating June twenty-seventh as the day for the special election. The two months that intervened were almost wholly devoted to discussions of this issue. It was the subject of every editorial page and the theme of many sermons. Tons of literature were scattered over the state. Temperance speakers from all parts of the country came to Iowa to assist in winning the hoped for victory. Party lines were disregarded. It was a nonpartisan election. Many prominent Democrats were for the amendment, and many Republicans of like prominence were opposed to it.

On the eventful election day business was almost suspended. The churches were kept open in many places and continuous prayer meetings were held in them. Bells were rung at intervals to call the faithful to the defense of their homes against the saloons. Bands of children paraded the streets of many cities, carrying banners asking their fathers and brothers to vote for the homes and the schools of the state. In all the history of Iowa there had never been such an election. In fear and trembling the friends of the amendment awaited the counting of the ballots, and indignation and rage filled the enemies of prohibition when the results were made known. A majority of nearly thirty thousand was counted for the amendment — 155,436 having voted for it, and 125,677 against it.

On the twenty-ninth of July Governor Sherman formally declared the amendment a part of the organic law of the state. It was forthwith in force and effect, but no provision had been made for its enforcement. It was observed in many places, but in others it was neither obeyed nor enforced. In many cities the councils licensed the liquor men to violate the law. When the political conventions were held that year, the Republicans disregarded the issue, holding to their theory that it was a non-partisan one, but the Democrats pledged themselves to resist the enforcement of the amendment and to get rid of it as soon as possible. The Republicans carried the state, but by largely reduced majorities.

In the meantime, the amendment itself was declared invalid, within four months after its adoption by the people. The decision to this effect was rendered by Judge Walter I. Hayes of Clinton, in a case brought before him in Scott county.[6] It was a friendly suit to test the question. A saloon keeper who refused to pay for beer he had purchased was sued by a firm of Davenport brewers.

The decision was based on defects in the legislative procedure and record. The joint resolution passed in 1882 was not identical with the one passed in 1880, and the house in the latter case had failed to enter the same in full on its journal. The language of the original resolution was: "No person shall manufacture for sale, sell, or keep for sale, as a beverage, or to be used, any intoxicating liquors whatever, including ale, wine and beer." The resolution as passed the second time omitted the words "or to be used." It was by many believed at the time that the wording was changed by collusion, but this was never proved.

The case was at once taken to the supreme court of the state. The decision of the lower court was sustained by a majority of four against one, Judge J. M. Beck, dissenting. He held that the irregularities were not vital. The legislative intent and purpose were plain. At the request of Governor Sherman, the attorney general sought a rehearing of the case, which was denied in the April term, Judge Beck again

6 Koehler & Lange vs. Hill, 60 Iowa, 543.

dissenting. Storms of protest followed. The four judges were denounced and execrated. None of them was reëlected, while Judge Beck became a popular idol of the temperance people.

In the political campaign of 1883, the Democrats presented Judge Hayes as their candidate for judge of the supreme court. The Republicans followed the logic of the situation. They went before the people with a platform pledging the party to enact a law based on the rejected amendment. Buren R. Sherman was renominated for governor, and Orlando H. Manning of Carroll County was named for lieutenant governor on the strength of his phrase, "A school house on every hill, and no saloon in the valley," which became a state slogan. The Republicans were successful, and in 1884 the legislature enacted statutory prohibition, reviving and amending the prohibitory law of 1855, with the wine and beer clause eliminated, and this went into effect July fourth.

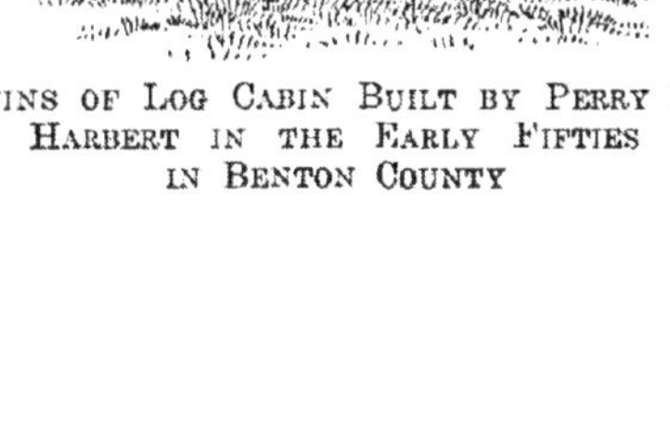

RUINS OF LOG CABIN BUILT BY PERRY M. HARBERT IN THE EARLY FIFTIES IN BENTON COUNTY

# CHAPTER LXIX

## Changing Conditions

The settlement of Iowa was contemporaneous with two great industrial events, the building of the first railroads in the United States, and the invention and development of the mowing and reaping machines. The first railroad was built in 1827, and the first settlements in Iowa were made in 1833. After many experiments, both in England and the United States, it was in 1833 that the basic idea of the modern reaper and mower, namely the sliding sickle in stationary guards, was discovered. The first practical cutting machine is credited to Cyrus McCormick. But after the grass and grain were cut, the problem of taking care of it perplexed the inventors for many more years. At first a man with a rake pulled it from the platform on which it was dropped. It took years to provide the man with a seat on the machine. It took until 1861 to perfect the idea of a self dropper, simply a series of slats that could be raised or lowered. The self raking device was a marvel in its day. The Marsh Harvester, on which two men bound the grain, was the prelude to the self binder. These inventions made the settlement and development of Iowa possible.

A few mowing and reaping machines were in use in the state before the war, but only a few. Up to that time grass was cut with a scythe and grain with a cradle, which was a scythe with a series of slats to catch the grain. Even after the war the introduction of improved machinery was comparatively slow. Farmers were often too poor to buy high-priced machinery, and there were also some lingering prejudices against the new devices. Why not do work as work had always been done? Were not the new processes more wasteful than the old? But when prejudices were once broken down, and poverty was overcome, not only the mower and the reaper but other labor and time-saving devices came rapidly into use. Wheeled plows and cultivators, improved harrows, seeding and planting machines, stalk cutters, hay rakes, all these lessened the labors of the husbandman and multiplied production many fold. The back of the sower and the reaper was no longer bent, and the man with the hoe almost disappeared.

The wonder of human history is not that the reaper was invented in 1833, and not that the self binder was used in the fields of Iowa in 1870, but that the sickle, which was used in the fields of Boaz, the fields in which Ruth gleaned, should have remained in use for forty centuries more. And the wonder is not that the threshing machine and the separator came into use, but that even in Iowa, men should have used oxen to tramp out the grain, and the winds of heaven to winnow it from the straw and the chaff. And then the wonder came—the wonder which still endures—that with the machinery of production multiplied many fold, and transportation augmented beyond all comprehension, there should still be want and hunger anywhere among men.

But relieved of the bulk of his hard labors, the husbandman was not relieved of his problems. It came about that he produced more than he could sell. Production was multiplied far beyond consumption. The world as a whole was still primitive and provincial. The great industrial centers had not yet been organized into high consuming units. The potential purchasing powers of the cities did not keep pace with the potential producing powers of the farms. And so with all his machinery, the estate of the farmer seemed worse than it was before. What did it advantage him to grow more wheat and more corn, when it was cheaper to burn the corn than to sell it and buy coal with the money? He learned to know that he was often imposed upon on the way to the markets and also in the markets themselves; he knew that railroad rates were excessive and he believed that some middle men were no better than highwaymen. He was indignant and impatient; he complained and he became querulous. Then came demagogues who exchanged promises for votes and made matters worse rather than better by the enactment of laws that were not based on any human reason and that recognized no natural laws of either politics or economics. All these things were added to the endless troubles of the world. And the problems, do they not still abide?

Nevertheless an historic emancipation was wrought by labor saving machinery on the farms. And, fortunately, devices as wonderful found their ways into the homes. In Iowa the sewing machine was concurrent with the reaping machine. The McCormick and the Singer were almost contemporaneous. Women were relieved of carding, and the spinning and the weaving were all done by machinery. The sewing machine traveled a mile while the woman with the needle bent her fingers over a yard. Socks and stockings were made in factories, and the click of the knitting needles became a pastime instead of a drudgery. Washing machines, however imperfect at first, took the stoops out of weary backs, and clothes wringers—such simple devices—took the twists out of wrists and fingers. Even the butter in the milk was brought forth without lifting and pressing the dash. Heaven's blessing on the men who came with their thoughts to relieve our mothers and grandmothers of so many of their labors! Lincoln's proclamation of emancipation, for which a million men died or suffered more than death, was meager in its results compared with the emancipations the world owes to the inventors of machinery.

And the man who ran a mower and the woman who ran a sewing machine were no longer content to live in a log cabin. When drudgery ceased, aspirations came. Other men with other ideas made it possible for them to live in better houses. They went to the pineries of the north, felled the trees, and floated them down the rivers to mills that cut them up into studdings, rafters, sidings, and shingles. What is called the rafting of logs began as early as 1845.[1] It reached its height in 1870 to 1890. In some years the Chippewa River district alone sent down 600,000,000 feet of logs and 400,000,000 feet of sawed lumber. In 1865, W. J. Young of Clinton, Iowa,

[1] Captain A. W. Blair in the *Chicago Timberman*, reprinted in Downer's *History of Davenport and Scott County*, p. 434.

added the idea of a steamboat hitched to the stern of a raft to accelerate the industry. The Mississippi towns prospered in the business. Dubuque, Clinton, Davenport, Muscatine, Fort Madison and Keokuk became great milling centers. The pine lumber was light and easily transported over the railroads to all points in Iowa, and it was soft and easily worked up into houses. Native lumber was soon largely supplanted, stone ceased to be used, and brick became discarded material. Log cabins went out of fashion. They were converted into stables, grain, or hog houses. But many of the first pine houses were themselves only makeshifts, of boards upright with battens, and without plastered walls or ceilings. But it was from the forests of the north that Iowa people were eventually re-housed. Families ceased to live in one or two rooms, and however cheap, division walls became civilizing influences, for the refinements of life are born where partitions abound.

For a time pine lumber promised to solve another problem of the farms, that of fencing. The rail fences were still in use during the middle period of which we are writing, but few new ones were being built. What labors were represented in the thousands of miles of rail fences! Some of the early settlers on the prairies tried sod fences, but the rains and the frosts soon dissipated them. Hedges of willows were tried, but they were almost as useless as sod fences. Then some one introduced the osage orange, brought from the southwest, a yellow-rooted, tough-fibered, thorn-bearing shrub that grew into a tree on the least provocation, but if it were semi-annually cut back it formed a dense mass of thorns that restrained cattle and horses, but not always hogs. Those who sold land and osage slips, as early as the fifties, boasted a great deal of these hedges and thousands of miles of them were planted. Forty cents a rod and four years of time were all that were required.[2] A hundred acres could be fenced in at a cost of $250! Even railroads were then thinking of fencing their rights of way in such manner. But the shrubs were neglected and osage orange hedges in time became nuisances that had to be uprooted. In

[2] N. Howe Parker's *Iowa As It Is In 1856*, p. 66.

the seventies came an invention that was destined to revolutionize Iowa agriculture — the twisted and barbed wire fence. But it was not something new. It had been tried two decades before that time. In a book printed in 1856 there is a record to this effect: "More recently, the wire fence has been introduced, and succeeds well where it is properly made." [3] The fact that it did not succeed then may be attributed to the absence of the barb, which is the real restraining power of that fence. In 1859, Samuel Freeman, a blacksmith and a farmer, built a wire fence in Hickory Grove Township, Scott County.[4] In 1861, according to the same account, his son, of a more inventive mind, added barbs to the smooth wires. He may have borrowed his idea from the osage orange hedges. It was a valuable idea that was not patented. Others used revolving disks on the wires for the same purpose. But the value in the idea was not realized until machinery was devised to attach the barbs to the wires, and that on a commercial basis. This invention is credited to a man named Glidden. The result of this invention was a sudden expansion of wire fencing. Only eight tons of barbed wire were sold in 1875, but after that it increased rapidly.

Far-seeing men soon saw the possibilities in barbed wire fences. They took thought to levy tribute on all those who would be in need of them. They bought up all the basic patents, and when the matter was tested in the courts it was held that the Washburn-Moen Company of Worcester, Massachusetts, was in control of the industry. Wire that had been sold for eight and six and even five and a half cents was jumped up six cents, more or less, to eleven and thirteen cents a pound. The farmer's hope of a cheap and serviceable fence went down. There was then in existence in Iowa a State Agricultural Society, which had attached to it an organization of writers on rural topics. "Father" Clarkson, the agricultural editor of the *State Register*, and the dean of the craft, invited them to an "oyster supper" at his home in Des Moines.[5] When

[3] Parker's *Iowa As It Is in 1856*, p. 66.

[4] Gue's *History of Iowa*, Vol. III, p. 102.

[5] Wallace's *Uncle Henry's Own Story*, Vol. III, p. 26.

the editors "got down to nuts and raisins and coffee," Mr. Clarkson proposed the organization of a Farmers' Protective Association, one of whose duties it should be to fight the barbed wire monopoly, or "trust," as it came to be called—one of the first, if not the first, of many such named organizations. He also proposed an incorporation, with directors, to enter into contracts with a Des Moines manufacturer, W. L. Carpenter, to make barbed wire in defiance of patents and court decisions. The undertaking succeeded. Law suits resulted, of course. It was in 1881. The general assembly the following winter appropriated a small amount to defray the costs of the litigation, making the state virtually an intervenor. Albert B. Cummins, then a young and rising attorney in Des Moines, appeared as counsel for the farmers of Iowa, and won his first public recognition, and he also won his case, or at least enough of it to drive the trust to different tactics. They reduced the price of barbed wire to five and one-half cents a pound, a pound being equivalent to a rod of wire. That was intended to kill the Des Moines competition, but as it served the only end the farmers had in view, that is lower prices, they were willing to close their factory.

The use of barbed wire worked a revolution in farming. Up to that time grain growing had been the principal occupation. Cattle were long pastured on the open prairies. In the western parts of the state there were still "miles and miles of unoccupied lands, with not a single tree to break the monotony of the undulating plain."[6] On these vast herds were kept. The settlers who came with barbed wire soon cut up these ranges. Under the newer dispensation, cattle were kept in pastures and fattened on corn in feed lots. Prairies that had simmered under summer suns and that had glistened in coats of snow, began to be dotted with homesteads and with groves—unfortunately, too many planted cottonwoods instead of walnut and hickory trees. The variations were the soft maples, and even Lombardy poplars were tried.

But grain growing received another and more serious setback. A tiny, ill-smelling insect called the chinch bug appeared

[6] Stanton's *When the Wildwood was in Flower*, p. 41.

on the stalks of wheat. The farmers thought it was one of the plagues of ancient Egypt, but it was more likely a warning that they had cropped their soil to the point of exhaustion by growing wheat on it one year after another. The result was soil so weak in nitrogen that the plants no longer had strength to resist the ravages of these insects. Instead of fifty and sixty bushels of wheat per acre, the yield fell to forty, then thirty and twenty. The pests were at their worst in 1879 and 1880, and the years thereabout.[7] Prosperous fields of green would in a few days look as if they had been scorched by an invisible fire. When there was no wheat to devour, the insects attacked the green corn, and they invaded even the homes of the people. What had been the land of hope, became the land of despair. But prices remained low in spite of lowered yields. In 1877 wheat at Winterset, in Madison County, after being hauled thirty miles to market, was worth thirty-seven cents a bushel, and hogs, two cents a pound.[8] The complaint was, and it grew, that stock raising was done "for the benefits of the beef trusts and the railroads."[9] The blame in this world can always be placed on someone else. The sins of others make the whole world groan.

There was groaning enough in those years. Something was wrong in the world, even if God remained in His heaven. The politicians who wanted to hold offices, even if they could not cure the ailments, came forward with platforms and promises and nostrums. Trust them, and prosper. And all they asked in return was an office that paid a few thousand dollars a year, and the sense of a little brief authority. The millennium was in their mouths. There was anti-railroad and anti-monopoly talk, but the men who believed in greenbacks were the most profuse in their promises. Make more money and there will be more prosperity. The substance of things hoped for and the evidence of things unseen were alike in their greenbacks, which were simply pieces of paper with green ink on one side. All that was required was a printing press—how easy the road to

[7] Hamlin Garland's *A Son of the Middle Border*, p. 228.
[8] Wallace's *Uncle Henry's Own Story*, Vol. III, p. 7.
[9] Stanton's *When the Wildwood was in Flower*, p. 51.

wealth seemed to them. While many prophesied, others railed. General Weaver, who was elected to congress to enact the millennium, and to bring from Washington the blessing for which an older man wrestled all night with an angel from heaven—him they called "Jumping Jim," the mockers and unbelievers, and Mr. Gillette, they called "Heifer Calf," because he had actually wept before an audience while telling the tale of a calf that was worth no more than a few farthings, and another of the prophets they stoned with the opprobrious name of "Calamity," though his real name was L. H. Weller, who also made the journey to Washington to see what could be done.

But without hope in the politicians, thousands began to leave Iowa. For them the land of hope was across the Missouri River, or at least across the Big Sioux. In them the ancient and honorable spirit of the movers was revived. If wheat could not be grown in Iowa they would go where wheat could be grown. They were wheat farmers, and they did not want to be any other kind of farmers. Kansas and Nebraska and the Dakotas beckoned to them and the wanderlust of their ancestors was re-expressed in a later "Westward Ho!" By 1881, when it was mostly Dakotaward, the movement had "become an exodus, a stampede . . . Hardly anything else was talked about . . . Every man who could sell out had gone west or was going."[10] Newspapers which did not want to see their subscription lists depleted, and those who loved Iowa, pleaded for the people not to go. They drew woeful pictures of droughts on the plains, and of blizzards in the Dakotas. The Farmers Institutes "pleaded for diversified farming." The mistake had been in growing nothing but wheat in certain sections of the state. With the coming of the chinch bugs and the departure of the wheat growers, the flouring mills began to suffer. Up to that time every town had maintained its own mill, and many towns had more than one mill. But soon the swallows began to build their nests in the smokeless chimneys and refuse and waterplants filled up the ponds that had fed the mill wheels.

There was a depression, but the places that had been vacated

[10] Hamlin Garland's *A Son of the Middle Border*, p. 234.

were soon filled by others, and the others were apt to be foreigners, men who were willing to begin all over again. The racial elements of many communities were wholly changed. It was the Yankees who had moved out. The newcomers were not only willing to begin over, but they adopted new ways and new methods. They made Iowa what nature had made it, a grassland again. They sowed tame grasses and fenced them in with barbed wire. They did not depend on the increase of their herds as expressed in calves, but they milked the cows and began to make butter and cheese. The older settlers had not believed that the clovers could be grown in Iowa, even after what they called "the Indian" had been taken out of the prairies, that is to say the tang of the wild grasses.[11] There were still men who believed that what never had been done, never could be done, and some of them were willing to spend their time to prove it. Strange is the tenacity of prejudice and error, and persistent the atavism of reaction. But the clover grew, the red clover and the white clover, and the milk began to flow into the pails of prosperity. It was a double prosperity, for the clovers enriched the lands that bore them.

With clover and bluegrass came a return of the inventive genius which has so often blessed mankind. Some one thought out what was called a creamery, a central station to which the milk could be brought to be made into butter. In 1876, at the Philadelphia Centennial, Iowa butter had taken the first premium, and that had given a great impetus to the industry and also to the demand. The first creamery in the state was started at Spring Branch, in 1872, by John Stewart of Manchester.[12] The second one was built at Monticello by H. D. Sherman, in the same year—November. Sherman later organized the state dairy commision which became a potent influence in Iowa. Stewart soon had in operation a number of creameries, centering around Strawberry Point—the butter that took the Philadelphia gold premium was made about four and one-half miles southeast of that town. The prize-taking butter was made by W. S. Carrington. That was worth more than making a speech on the hustings or enacting a law in congress.

[11] Wallace's *Uncle Henry's Own Story*, Vol. II, p. 14.

[12] Letter of A. O. Kingsely to Walter L. Cherry, September 17, 1919.

At Delaware, Iowa, the first cheese factory was started as early as 1866 by the Kingsley brothers, who came from Syracuse, New York, and the first cheese maker was a young woman from that eastern city.

But the development of the creamery was hampered by the inconvenience of transporting milk in bulk, nor did any one then have a clear idea of butter fat. These problems came to the mind of an itinerant mechanic, J. G. Cherry, who was then living at Troy Mills on the Wapsipinicon. He was an Englishman by birth and an inventor by nature. He invented an improved submerged pail for milk, and later a can with a floating top that saved the milk from being churned in transportation. He patented his devices and incurred law suits. He was poor and they tempted him with a few thousand dollars in ready money, but his wife said she would rather be poor in money and rich in hope — and so the idea was not sold to buy bread, but saved to build an industry. The next great invention was the separator that took the cream out of the milk. A wealth that had never been dreamed of by the wheat growers poured into the state, and the fertility of the soils that had been exhausted by the grain growers was restored and even multiplied by the butter makers. So successful was this form of diversified farming that it soon became a basis of wild speculations in which promoters filled the state with creameries that failed because they were not built in honesty, nor operated by competent men. The human parasite on industry is as persistent as the chinch bug in wheat, and he infests most where business sense has been weakened by dazzling hopes of riches which have not been earned by labors honestly and adequately rendered. But the dream of getting something for nothing, making bricks without straw, and being rich with nothing more to do, is an ever recurrent one.

Even wiser for the future were the men who sought to advance diversified farming by improving the livestock of the state — cows that would produce more milk and milk richer in the essential butter fats, steers that would carry more beef to the block, and hogs that would yield more pork. Up to the beginning of the period under consideration the primitive breeds were still in vogue. The "line back" cow and the "razor-back" hog were still bred and the "heavy draft horse was practically unknown." [13] We are told that before 1870 a few spotted hogs, then called "Maggies," but now known as Poland Chinas, had been brought to Iowa, and fewer Chester Whites, then new in the west. They were looked on as curiosities at first, but they began to attract attention when they carried more weight to market, and that on less feed than the earlier breeds. In Washington County, which was settled by a progressive people, a series of protracted meetings was held in 1867, the result of which was that fifteen farmers pledged ten dollars each "to finance the momentous project" — for that time — of investing in "a Short Horn bull — then called Durhams." They found the animal that they wanted to improve their stock in a herd in Van Buren County. The Washington committee drove eighty miles overland to make their purchase of a yearling animal.

Two years later, live stock journalism was born in Iowa, when James H. Sanders established the *Western Stock Journal*, at Sigourney, then "a small inland town thirty miles from a railroad." We are told also that at that time there was not a single periodical in existence, either in America or Europe, devoted exclusively to the livestock interests and the principles of breeding.[14] Sanders had been a school teacher and he now became the prophet of a new prosperity. He could write as well as farm. His paper was poorly printed on a hand press. It was simply a beginning, another voice crying in the wilderness. It preached a new gospel and it slowly found a few disciples. In a few years the paper of humble beginnings became part of the *Live Stock Journal* of Chicago. The beginnings of what is now the profession of agricultural journalism were made at about the same time. The *Homestead*, destined to wield influence under Henry Wallace and later under James M. Pierce, had made a feeble beginning in agricultural journalism. In the meantime important work for farming was being rendered by a coterie

[13] H. G. MacMillan in *Farmer and Breeder*, Sioux City, December 15, 1919.

[14] *Ibid.*

of volunteer writers on the weekly press of the state. Coker F. (Father) Clarkson was doing such work for the weekly edition of the *State Register*, L. S. Coffin for the Fort Dodge *Chronicle*, Dr. S. A. Knapp for the Keokuk *Gate City*, Colonel John Scott for the Davenport *Gazette*, E. C. Bennett for the Waverly *Republican*, James Wilson (Tama Jim) for the Traer *Star-Clipper*, or what is now the combined paper, and Henry Wallace for the Winterset *Chronicle*. These men, week by week, preached the gospel of the new farming, farming by diversification and with improved live stock. Their followers multiplied. Short Horns and Holsteins, Poland Chinas, Chester Whites and Berkshires, Norman and Percheron horses followed, and even in the poultry yards, Asiatic fowls strutted like giants on feathered legs by the side of the barnyard breeds that were left from Noah's Ark.

At the same time corresponding changes in ideas and methods were being wrought in the towns and cities. Men began to talk about factories, and towns aspired to be something more than way stations on transcontinental railroads. Many hopes became disasters, for many beginnings were made in error. Iowa did not have the artisans to make watches, but she had the raw materials for packing houses and cereal mills. Iron industries were established in Davenport, furniture factories in Burlington, mill work plants in Clinton and Dubuque, and a dour Scotchman, George Douglas, later assisted by John Stuart, brought to Cedar Rapids the Scotch oatmeal processes which they advertised under the American name of Quaker Oats, founding an international industry.

Such were the men who laid the foundations of a truly greater Iowa, an Iowa not yet wholly realized. They were the newer pioneers, and they did a work as fine and essential as the older pioneers who broke up the prairies and made the first laws and constitutions. They diversified the country around the cities, and they built the cities in the country — live stock men, and dairy men, and factory men — each and all of more true and lasting significance in the state than the politicians who made the speeches or the legislators who made the laws.

# CHAPTER LXX

## Life in the Years Between

Those who can remember so far back have many pleasant memories of the seventies in the last century, and some remembrances that are not so pleasant. They can recall that it was an era of hard work and of small rewards. It was a time of cheapness. The farmers sometimes sold their corn for fifteen cents a bushel or less. Potatoes were worth no more in the markets. Farmers' wives carried their eggs to town and received nine and eight, and often no more than six and five cents a dozen for them in trade. On many farms the eggs were not gathered, and the apples were left to rot in the orchards. In the towns, a dollar a day was standard wage. College graduates who taught school received thirty dollars a month, and often less. High school girls were paid as low as twenty dollars a month for teaching, and shrewd school directors sometimes persuaded them to serve for fifteen. Cheapness was the magic word of the times.

But living also was cheap. It did not cost a great deal to subsist. Two or three dollars would pay for a winter's supply of potatoes for a family, and potatoes filled many voids. In southern Iowa a wagon load of coal could be bought for a dollar and a quarter. In the country, teachers paid two dollars a week for their board, and the room and bed were thrown in. In the college towns students eked out a studious existence on thirty cents a day. There is the record of two young men in a seminary town who lived on "less than fifty cents a day for both!"[1] A man who filled a clerical position nearly all the days of his life boasted that he supported his family on forty-five dollars a month, and his wife spent that income so frugally and so well that the nine or ten children were well reared and entered good careers.

[1] Hamlin Garland's *A Son of the Middle Border*, p. 218.

In the towns the houses had several partitions, but in the country they still had but few. In the towns the houses had lawns, not always well kept, but in the country the front yards were still used, more than occasionally, for pastures for calves and even pigs. If loving hands had planted a flower bed in the spring, it was apt to be overgrown with weeds in mid-summer when the woman of the loving hands spent her time cooking for harvesters. Many of the shade trees were still cottonwoods, and the windbreaks were apt to be of soft maples. Whitewash was used more than paint. The men were practical and the women had almost forgotten to be sentimental. Houses were places in which women worked, and in which men slept. On the farms men worked from sun to sun — and the women could always find something to do after the sun went down. It was the boast in many families that they got up at five in the morning, summer and winter alike, although why they did it no one ever explained satisfactorily. It was a state of mind, a rural hall mark of diligence and thrift. There were exceptions, but the rule holds good.

There were few luxuries in the homes, hardly any of the conveniences, and even the necessities were often lacking. The furniture was meager. It was apt to be crudely made or cheaply ornamented. It did not always have even the primitive quality of solidity. The chairs were not made to loiter in, and the beds were not made to rest on. Some had feather beds, but many more had mattresses filled with straw. When the straw had been ground into chaff under the sleepers, there was always more straw in the stack. The cookstove furnished all the heat for the family, with an occasional fire made in a bed room. If there was a rocking chair — seldom more than one — even a tired mother might feel it an idleness akin to sin to spend much time in it. Time was wasted that was not spent in work. When there was nothing to be done, it was the task of the diligent and the conscientious to find something to do. The Devil toyed with idle hands, making mischief in the world. To do nothing was to do wrong. To work was the duty of all. Children were not taught to play, but they were set to do chores. Little girls had no dolls, except the later children of the family brood. At nine or ten boys were advanced enough to hold the plow. If God did not forgive their parents, still He blessed the children with strong and healthy bodies. These conditions are not overstated. Hamlin Garland, who was a boy in the Iowa of that time, wrote later that looking back he could do nothing but think of "our ugly little farmhouse, with its rag carpets, its battered furniture, its barren attic, and its hard rude beds." He said that everything they had "seemed very cheap and deplorably commonplace."[2] These tragic remembrances made him unhappy and bred in him a spirit of revolt.

But there was another world — the one out of doors. It was wide under blue skies, and fresh winds blew through it. Boys often ran away from tasks and attics to live in that world. The aspects and the aromas of wildness had not yet entirely vanished. Many waterfowls passed through that world in spring and again in autumn. They brought with them visions of other lands far away. To the imagination there was still another world somewhere. There were quail in the stubble fields and prairie chickens in the corn fields when the snow was on the ground. The boy followed strange tracks in the snow. He pursued all manner of wild creatures. He was a hunter and a trapper, and what victor of the great wars brought home his spoils with more rejoicings? In summer time there were still berries in the copses, wild cherries and plums and grapes, and all manner of nuts in the timber. A gun in his hands, and a dog by his side, summer or winter, spring or autumn, what mattered it? The joyous freedom was the same under blue skies or gray ones, in fields of green or brown or white. What boyhood days, after all, can be compared with those in Iowa when the wildwood was still in bloom?

There was so much work to do, and so much to worry over in those days that art and literature and the amenities of life were little cultivated or observed. We are speaking of the mass. There were exceptions of course. In the average home

[2] Hamlin Garland's *A Son of the Middle Border*, p. 215.

there was little that ministered to the artistic instincts of children. There were few pictures on the walls, and they were atrocious daubs out of which a Doré might have constructed his conceptions of the Inferno, or Dante have composed his poem. Wax flowers in glass cases were esteemed adornments. There were few picture books for the children, but a few Bible pictures might be found in old volumes, and the subjects antedated the flood, when Adam was forlorn or Cain in distress. Even music was in a state of neglect, although gospel hymns and a few maudlin, sentimental ballads were in vogue. There was an occasional violin to be found, some instrument left over from other times and other states or lands, but those who fiddled in a busy world were not always considered well-witted. On Sunday afternoons one might have heard an accordion, or even a little broken organ. The pianos still belonged to the cities, and there were not many of them in the towns. The local newspapers were filled with neighborhood gossip and virulent political articles. There were a few newspapers of general circulation, like the New York *Tribune* and the Toledo *Blade*, one taken in memory of Horace Greeley, and the other for the traditional witticisms of Petroleum V. Nasby. The New York *Weekly* was a somewhat lurid story paper, and the *Hearth and Home* printed articles on artificial flowers and how to make them, and on crocheting.

In the larger towns there were lecture courses, and in what were called the cities, they were beginning to build opera houses, without operas. Many of the lecturers were men of national fame. Men like Horace Greeley, Henry Ward Beecher, Ralph Waldo Emerson, and T. Dewitt Talmage had not yet become high priced. Electricity, the magic and mysterious power of the future, was still explained and exploited on the lecture platform. A current generated by a revolving glass disc was strong enough to impart a shock to a whole audience standing with clasped hands. Little did they dream that the same currents would light the world and turn the wheels of transportation and industry. The motion picture was almost foreshadowed in what were called "peep-shows," where thousands found amusement and even instruction staring into stereopticons. That was marvelous then. In winter time every town had a season of roller skating for the sinners and a revival for the saints. The curious went to the revival meetings to see who would be the next one "converted." It was the sole "excitement" in many lives. At all such meetings timid boys, and even young men, under the first impulses of love, which made them sheepish, waited at the doors to ask to walk home with equally timid girls — even courtships partook of the primitive. A few of the older women still smoked pipes, a habit that had been somewhat general in pioneer times. Women wore long dresses, many of which were buttoned to their chins. Their street shoes had low heels and overshoes were worn in winter. When a house had a bay window with flowers in it, the family was rated as either rich or aristocratic, or both. The wife of a merchant who accompanied her husband as far as Chicago was envied and those who went as far away from home as New York excited even wonder. A divorce suit shocked communities almost more than a murder trial in later times.

The almanacs issued by the houses that made patented medicines, with which thousands cured their ailments, imaginary and real, were found in every home and they were regarded as the true family compendiums. They were consulted not only when they felt aches or pains, but for the weather on the morrow, and for the time of the rising and the setting of the sun, which was standard time in those days. The almanacs furnished not only pre-dated weather, but also ante-dated jokes. But boys with vigorous minds and some with sickly minds, wanted something more, and when they were not directed into proper channels, what were known as dime novels came into their hands by various forms of stealth. There were also Beadle's novels. Many of them had yellow covers. Boys read them in haymows, where they also learned to play cards in a dire time when many persons regarded cards as the devices by which the Devil obtained recruits for his dominion in the mysterious and dreaded world after death. Hair-breadth and hair-raising adventures filled these yellow-backed books, and the social exploits in them were true to a very untrue conception of life. But other publishers alleviated the mental and moral distress of literature by issuing cheap reprints of classics from the pens of Jules Verne and the classic English novelists under the titles of *Seaside* and *Lakeside* libraries, which also sold for a dime. Those publishers were missionaries, even if it was for profit. Their reprints were formative influences in the lives of many young men and women.

Games and amusements were not in much vogue. Men and older boys sometimes pitched horse shoes, and women and younger boys sometimes played croquet. Tennis had not been heard of. There is the tale of some boys who played croquet with the round tops of discarded bed posts for balls — or were the balls secretly sawed from a proud mother's most valued piece of furniture? Boys dug themselves into caves, or built houses in the tree tops in Iowa long before Mr. Barrie made such exploits into literature. On the farms the older folks seemed to have forgotten all about games and mere amusements. In those days men and women were apt to be older than their years. The light and the joy of youth are in the mind, and they were minded to be old. Eyes looked for chinch bugs in the fields of wheat more than for the fairies in the beds of flowers.

On stated days farm families went visiting, or received visitors. Those were days that were like ordeals. The visiting aunts brought keen eyes with them and wagging tongues. They were so many Mrs. Poysers. Those who received them were like Martha, troubled about many things. And what room was there in so practical and so critical a world for the Marys? They also gathered often in vast "picnics." These were neighborhood or Sunday school affairs. There hundreds came together and all imagined they were happy. There were swings for the children and baseball games for the boys. The men might be found in groups chewing tobacco and talking about steers. There were also county and district fairs, where thousands spent a happy day, although there were no exhibits more important than big pumpkins or samples of needle work, and nothing more exciting than a merry-go-round to travel in.

But the event of all events in those days was the coming of

the circus, the American institution called vernacularly a show. Going to the show was akin to going to heaven for the boys. In those days most of them still traveled along the wagon roads, although Barnum was putting his mammoth exhibition on railroad cars. The main circus of that period was probably not bigger than a modern side show — but how big it seemed to the youth of that era. From the time when the *avant couriers* scattered the first flaming handbills along the country roads to the morning when the boys walked out to meet the aggregation on the road, there was suspense and excitement. And when the band began to play and bespangled men and animals came forth — how could eyes see it all? Blessings on them still, on the clowns — there were clowns in those days — on the bareback riders and the tumblers, on all the acrobats and those who hung in the dizzy trapezes! What desolation fell on the youth when the show moved on! But for weeks after that all the acts were reënacted in sheds and barns, and even astonished country dogs were taught to do tricks that had never puzzled their brains before. But the circus was the circus, and every boy in Iowa had heard of Yankee Robinson and knew about P. T. Barnum, even if only a few had heard of William B. Allison — and what was the Bland-Allison act compared with a double somersault?

Of course, rural education was at a low ebb, and education in the towns was at least tedious. The average schoolhouse in the country was an unattractive place both inside and out. It was often no better than a large pine box set on the open prairies, exposed to the suns in summer and to the blizzards in winter. No one took thought to plant a few trees in the school yards. They planted wind-breaks for their cattle, but not for their children. One was "like thousands of other similar buildings in the west," and the one in the description "had not a leaf to shade it in summer nor a branch to break the winds of savage winter."[3] Going to school was one of the tasks imposed on children, when there were no tasks to do at home. The very little folks went to school in the spring and autumn months, and the older boys and girls in the winter

[3] Hamlin Garland's *A Son of the Middle Border*, p. 95.

months. Most of the school furniture was left over from pioneer days, rude benches "so greasy and hacked that original intentions were obscured." Curtains on the windows were not thought of, and what paint was left, if any, was "a desolate drab." Beginners were taught to recite the alphabet, and the older ones to do sums in arithmetic and to "spell down." Spelling contests were the supreme social features of the period. Playgrounds were not supervised severely. The little ones played "drop-the-handkerchief," and the older ones played "blackman." Fistic combats were not infrequent among the boys and every school still had its bullies. The spirit of prairie democracy had not yet been tamed, and chivalry had not yet been bred back into the new race.

All the amenities of life were at a low ebb. All life was practical, materialistic and often tinged with coarseness. There was a social democracy that was tantamount to social indifference. Men did not always stop to help women in and out of the wagons, which were still much used as family carriages. Most families had only one spring seat for their wagons, but if they had two it amounted to some social prestige. A spring wagon was a luxury that few enjoyed, and buggies were used only by the very rich or by the very old or sick.

Fathers and mothers loved their children, but they were not habitually demonstrative in their affections. Feelings were repressed and sentiments were not uttered. Men especially were reserved and reticent and often even austere. It was not a cultivated habit, or an assumed one; it was an inherited one, inherited from crude surroundings as well as from Spartan ancestors. They prided themselves in strength, not in sentiment. Hamlin Garland recalls that he did not dare to utter what he thought of a beautiful moonlight — and he had a singing mother! He says it was enough to say, "It is a fine day," or "the night is as clear as a bell." Among them love was a forbidden word. One might say, "I love pie," but not, "I love Bettie." That would have been mawkish, silly, and sentimental, and even improper.[4] He says that terms of endearment were not habitual between even parents and chil-

[4] Hamlin Garland's *A Son of the Middle Border*, p. 123.

dren, and of those who used such forms of speech it was said that "they fight like cats and dogs when no one is around." Foreigners who used such speech, as many of them did, were looked upon with suspicion.

They did not spend a great deal of money on clothes, the women no more than the men, except in the towns where "fussy" styles then began to prevail. Many of the clothes were still made at home, and the advent of the sewing machine gave an impetus to this practice. Pattern charts were not always consulted. Men and boys still wore boots, and except on special occasions, like going to church, the legs of their trousers were tucked into the tops of their boots — it took a boy a long time to overcome his prejudice against having the legs of trousers outside. Overshoes were not worn by men; to make leather water proof it was smeared with tallow. Shoes began to come in, and in the later seventies they were worn generally, although many still persisted in wearing boots. Had they not been brought up in them, almost born in them? Fashionable shoes were called gaiters and had elastic sides. When collars were worn, they were made of paper with linen sizing. They could not be washed, but they cost only fifteen cents a box. Celluloid collars were considered an improvement on the paper ones. "Store clothes" for men were made to cover the body, not always to fit it, and when ready-to-wear garments for women began to arrive the styles became more flippant.

Life in the seventies was simple in all its ways. Some writers have described it as narrow, sordid, and mean. But it was not wholly devoid of beauty or of nobility. Men were as strong and women as tender then as now, although they were more reticent and reserved. Neither their clothes nor their words expressed what was best in them. They worked hard, but the fruits of their labors were to be garnered by those who came after them.

# PART VIII

## Social and Economic Reforms

(1884-1896)

# CHAPTER LXXI

## A New Preface for a New Era

From 1884 to 1896 are twelve years of political turmoil in Iowa. Politics seemed the principal business of the people. It was a period of violent unsettlements and readjustments. Prohibition was a continuing issue that affected not only political conclusions, but even the business of the state. The railroad rate issue for a short time was even more virulent in its outbreak. The question of a sound currency remained unsettled and culminated in the national campaign of 1896. Associated with it was the tariff issue, which was precipitated by the Republican revision of the schedules in 1889, followed by a Democratic revision in 1893, both producing violent industrial disturbances which helped to bring on the panic of that year. The period is so largely political that other matters appear of little importance or interest. In Iowa men of vital influence appeared on the scenes of combat.

The author of this history is no longer dependent upon the memories or the writings of others. He was an on-looker, and often a participant in these events, and all the time a chronicler and commentator. He came upon the scene as a young man taking notes for what was then the most influential newspaper of the state, the *Iowa State Register* of Des Moines. He found himself somewhat precipitately thrown into the vortex and maelstrom of state politics, with the odor of the new mown hay of an Iowa farm still in his nostrils, and with the smell of a musty college library still upon his garments. He had served as editor of a college paper[1] with enough of youthful zeal and enthusiasm to attract the attention of James S. Clarkson, and at his suggestion he abandoned the study of

[1] The *Central Ray*, published by the students of Central University, now Central College, Pella.

law, in 1887, to become a reporter. The first thing he learned was that college journalism was one thing, and every day newspaper work another. His first assignment was to the state house. That is, he made daily rounds of the state offices to pick up items of news for the paper. In the performance of those duties he soon learned some of the secrets of the politicians. He was not an inapt pupil, for as a college student and even as a high school boy the bent of his mind had been somewhat political. For a newspaper beginner the assignment was a most fortunate one, for it brought him in touch with matters of pith and moment in the state, instead of with the mere routine of police and justice courts and the trifling things of the streets.

The first man the new reporter interviewed professionally was William Larrabee, who was then governor of Iowa. He remembers the whole incident, but most of all the timidity and the ignorance of the tyro reporter. He had thought of governors as something different — they had seemed so big when read about on the Marion County farm, hardly fifty miles removed from the golden dome of the state house — but Governor Larrabee was not different at all. He was kind, sympathetic, and helpful. He was simplicity itself, so wholly unpretentious and so modest, and in certain ways almost shy. He was a man who thought more of duty than of the limelight of high office. He wanted what he did put into the headlines, and not himself. And so the almost daily visits to the governor's office — the doors of which always stood open in those days — became pleasures anticipated, and the influences of them were lasting ones. The governor knew more about books than the college man turned into a reporter, and he knew a great deal more about many other things. And yet he always presented himself in the rôle of a man who was eager to learn. "I want to know," was a Yankee phrase that was often on his lips — and he really wanted to learn. He asked more questions than he made statements. The paper for which the author wrote was very hostile to the policies of the governor on the railroad question, but that fact never marred the relations between the governor and the reporter.

The friendship between the two men lasted as long as the life of the governor, and among the most cherished recollections of the author are the mornings and afternoons and evenings they spent together under the trees of Montauk, the home of Governor and Mrs. Larrabee, overlooking the valley of the Turkey River. That they were seldom of the same mind made arguments possible, and arguments sharpen the wits of men.

There were giants in those days — at least certain men then on the public stage seemed so to the young reporter. And some of them seem so still to him. They are men who stand out big in the history of Iowa, and some of them big in the history of the nation. Most of them are dead and gone, but the memories of them pass through the mind of the author now as vividly as when they passed before his eyes in the flesh. The old *Register* office, with its clockless tower, was the meeting place of many of these men. There many of the most important conferences in Iowa politics were held. Orators met there to rehearse their speeches, platform writers to submit drafts, and editors of lesser note to receive their blessings, or absolutions. They were the days of the "Register Regency," as it was called. Mr. Clarkson was the regent imperial, and he was the kindliest and kingliest of all the great men of Iowa in that day. If he ruled for a time in the politics of the state, he did it by the only divine right known among right thinking men, that of brains and heart. "Ret," as he was familiarly called both by those who knew him intimately and by those who did not know him at all, thought more and thought more quickly than other men. When he wrote out his thoughts and they appeared in printed columns, with leads between the lines, on the editorial page of the *Register*, there was a finality and authoritativeness about them that his admirers praised and that his opponents almost despaired to answer. Even the type setters coveted his "takes" of copy, and they prided themselves on the fact that they could read off hand the hieroglyphics in which they were written. No one could be long in the same place with Mr. Clarkson without being touched with his genius and inspired with his powerful purposes — and even to think of or praise a good and great man is to partake something of the qualities that made him good and great, and potential and powerful.

Senator William B. Allison came often to the *Register* office. He never came to Des Moines without making a call on Mr. Clarkson — if that were not the purpose of his coming. Benign and serene, wise and few of words, a listener and not a talker, he was a man fit to be looked up to and worthy of admiration. At his approach all doors stood open, and all hearts met him on the stairway. He had in those days, as he always had, a wonderful personality, and his presence was like a benediction. He had the head of a thinker and the eyes of a poet. It was the author's good fortune — due to his newspaper position, no doubt — to come within the intimate reach of his friendship, and he recalls many week-end visits with him in his home at Dubuque, and an occasional visit with him in Washington. They remain most cherished memories of a man who was truly great. If it may seem vain to speak of such associations, what better form can vanity, which is part of every human being, take?

There were others, many others, who flitted across the scenes under the Des Moines clock tower of journalism and politics. There was the volatile and bubbling "Dave" Henderson, whose more stately name was Colonel David B. Henderson, then a congressman from the Third district and afterwards speaker of the house of representatives in Washington. He oozed with humor as he walked — the Civil War had left him with one cork leg. He was full of droll sayings, badinage, and gentle raillery. He often had the manners and speech of a swash-buckler, but he had the vitality of a genuine man and conquered all by his good will and tender heart. No one was ever so familiar with another colonel, William P. Hepburn, who was the exponent of an intellectual cynicism, but who was in many ways one of the stronger men of that period. He lacked the good fellowship of Colonel Henderson, and so he did not go as far on talents that were greater.

It was the period of the railroad contests, and so railroad attorneys often strayed into the *Register* office, for they also wanted to have a hand in shaping public policies. Judge

Nathaniel M. Hubbard, of the Chicago and Northwestern, was one of the most notable of these men. He was then one of the keenest minded men in Iowa, and he had a tongue like a rapier. He was analytical and relentless in his logic. He was the supreme strategist among the politicians and he had the audacity of a pirate. By his side could often be seen a somewhat portly young man with a big head covered with reddish hair. He was Joseph W. Blythe, who represented the C. B. & Q. He was then known as the son-in-law of former Governor Gear, but later, Mr. Gear, even when he was a United States senator, was known as the father-in-law of J. W. Blythe. He was a man of superb mental equipment, a man who could see at least two sides of a question and who never betrayed a friend or a principle. He loved books and read Thomas à Kempis, and esteemed Erasmus as the intellectual prodigy of all times. The evenings spent with such a man were like old Greek afternoons in the groves of Athens. If he had been free to serve a whole state as he served his corporation, he might have been a governor and a United States senator, and the presidency itself would have been within his scope. There were many other corporation men on the scene, among whom "Tom Potter of the Q" was regarded as a wizard, and W. P. Brady as a diplomat of that period, and John S. Runnells, who became the general counsel of the Pullman Company, who had the grace of a courtier, and the speech of one who fed on Attic honey.

Among the editors, of both parties, who dropped into the *Register* office, was Sam M. Clark, of the Keokuk *Gate City*, a man with a brain as brilliant as a diamond, and whose scintillations were the envy of even Mr. Clarkson. In other settings Mr. Clark might have been a Keats or a Shelley. George D. Perkins was still struggling to make the Sioux City *Journal* the great newspaper that it became later. He was a quiet man, a philosopher in whom cynicism was sweetened with a smile that was ever lurking in his face. He was not one of Mr. Clarkson's satellites, but a man who aspired to create a sun of his own. "Lafe" Young was still lingering in the suburbs of fame in Atlantic, and Harvey Ingham was striving to harmonize outwardly a Republican paper at Algona with inward free trade premonitions. He was still in the boyhood of his journalism. Al W. Swalm of the Oskaloosa *Herald*, Bernard Murphy of the Vinton *Eagle* and Ernest Hofer of the McGregor *News* came often, but always to burn incense, and D. N. Richardson, the scholarly man of the Davenport *Democrat*, who had written a scholarly book of travels that the critics praised, and M. M. Ham of the Dubuque *Herald*, were Democrats who were among those who also called, and that often.

Among the younger men in statesmanship, but still beginners, the most conspicuous by talent were Jonathan P. Dolliver and Robert G. Cousins. When Dolliver "dropped in," all reserve was thrown off. Like the elder Hamlet, he was the observed of all observers. He did the talking. Wit and humor, stories and incidents, snatches of poetry and excerpts from his own speeches, delivered or still undelivered, fell from his lips in torrents. He was a master of conversation. He was in those days more emotional than intellectual in his utterances; the depths of him yet had to be stirred. He was still a bubbling boy, and it was a sense of boyhood that never became wholly extinct in him. Mr. Cousins was different. He was reserved and often reticent. Fine as his oratory had already become, he always seemed to be thinking more than he could express. Dolliver's thoughts came in words, but Cousins's words came in thoughts. Cousins's face in those days wore the expression of the young man who carried the poet's strange device with the word "Excelsior" inscribed on it — he saw the heights which he yearned to ascend — only to find them impossible.

Albert B. Cummins was not in the inner circles of those times. He came on the scene a little later. He was out of harmony with his party and he was not ready to affiliate with the other. He entered the general assembly by the back door, defeating the regular nominee of his party. He stalked outside the regular camps, nurturing an ambition that was to outlast all others of that period. But if Mr. Cummins was *persona non grata*, Frederick W. Lehmann, another Des

Moines man of public mind, and the undisputed leader among Democrats, was not so. His intellectual equipment was such that all doors stood open for him. He seemed to know all history, all philosophy, all poetry, and all law, Greek and barbarian. He was a collector of books, and he stored his books away in his mind as well as on the shelves of his library. He was encyclopedic in knowledge and brilliant in conversation, while as an orator he was as powerful as either Dolliver or Cousins, though he had neither the classic grace of the one nor the fervid eloquence of the other. Mr. Lehmann was a master, and all the intellectually ambitious young men of the professions in the Des Moines of that time were his eager disciples.

The author's participation in political affairs was multiplied by promotions which came to him in his profession. Within two years he became city editor of the *Register* and within three years of his advent as a reporter, associate editor of the paper and editorial writer, under Richard P. Clarkson, who succeeded his brother, James S. Clarkson, as editor of the paper of which he had been business manager. In that capacity the author of this history was made the receiver of all the political confidences in the Republican party, and he succeeded in prying into a few that belonged to the Democratic party, with many of whose leaders he was on intimate social, if not political, terms.

The author might fill a volume with the stories of the machinations and manipulations of politics, how men were nominated and elected or defeated, and how measures were advanced or retarded, but to do so would be to depart from the scope and the purpose of this history. It would be placing the emphasis on methods, and not on results. The machinery of the politicians is of no more permanent value than the scaffoldings which the workmen use to erect the house, or than the false work in which the forms of steel and concrete are moulded. He will avoid also the influence of the obsessions that afflict men who have taken a part, though it be a minor one, in certain events. Men are prone to exaggerate events in which they were actors or on-lookers. But as time and men move on to other things, what were volcanic eruptions at one time appear only as bubbles on the surface of the waters. Each generation has its own problems. The problems of its predecessors interest it only to the extent of the irreducible minimum of wisdom evolved from them.

The student of history is constantly confronted with the ephemeral nature of human contests and achievements. Even results are so unlasting. What concerns men today, tomorrow is of little or no importance or even interest. The worth of recording them is constantly challenged. Who cares today about the vendor of liquors whose arrest in 1887 threw the state into an uproar? And who cares now that then men were tarred and feathered and even shot down on the streets for attempting to enforce laws that others did not like? And as for the results of big economic battles, have not the railroad rates and regulations that were then achieved all been obliterated by world events that no one then dreamed of in Iowa, and certainly did not think of participating in? But then they were of so much importance that men were defeated for governor and even president over them.

In "this batter'd Caravanserai" of politics, as in the poet's world, Sultan after Sultan with his pomp abides his destined hour, and then passes on, and the hopes that men set their hearts upon turn to ashes, or prosper for a while, and then "like snow upon the desert's dusty face," are gone. And yet the strife in human affairs is as necessary as is motion in the waters to keep them pure and wholesome. Error comes and flourishes as naturally as weeds in gardens, forever threatening the fruition of the right. As the labors of the husbandman must be unending, so must be the labors of public men who serve the common-weal to create the common-wealth. The politician and the statesman are both necessary in human affairs — and, perhaps, one may speak of politics as the scaffolding, and of statesmanship as the structure that is reared and that remains. The issues of those days are continuing ones — prohibition even, transportation, the currency, and the tariff. In fact history, after the manner of human life, is only repetition — it varies only as men and nations have sought to solve the same eternal problems in different ways.

# CHAPTER LXXII

## IN THE YEAR 1884

The year 1884 is a marked one in the history of Iowa. To begin with, the new state house was opened on the seventeenth of January when the Twentieth General Assembly in solemn procession marched from the old brick capitol to the new one to participate in the second inauguration of Buren R. Sherman as governor. As the law-makers of the state filed out of the old building, which had served the state for twenty-six years, or since 1858, a fitting record of the event was made in the journal of the house. On these rough old walls "scarred and nicked," so ran that entry, "seamed and worn by the work of weary years . . . silence fell like leaves from memory's journal upon the beach of years, whispering a regret, yet sighed relief that time had worked such change." The figures are a little mixed but the pathos is unalloyed!

The change was typical of the state that had grown up around her capital city. The old building belonged to the primeval period. It was never anything more than a homely pile of brick with bare and ugly walls. The new building was classic in architecture, three hundred and sixty-three feet in length, two hundred and forty-seven feet in width, and two hundred and seventy-five feet in height; finished in granite and marble and surmounted with a golden dome. It was erected at a cost of $2,871,682.95, with the "constant boast" that there was not "a dishonest dollar from base course to the crown of the dome" in it.[1] The credit for this was given to the three commissioners in charge of the work, John G. Foote, Peter A. Dey, and Robert S. Finkbine, but it belonged to the inherent integrity of the people of Iowa whose spirit the com-

[1] Kasson's address printed in *The Proceedings of the Iowa Pioneer Lawmakers' Association*, 1896.

missioners represented in their work. The dedicatory address was delivered by John A. Kasson, whose influence in the legislature had been the decisive force in securing the early appropriations for the building. Mr. Kasson's address was scholarly and classical. It was delivered in the presence of what had been part of his own life work.

In the new state house, on the twenty-third of January, William B. Allison was for the third time elected to the United States senate. By length of service and solid abilities, the Iowa senator had already come into national recognition as a great law maker. The same general assembly bestowed on labor a first substantial recognition by creating the bureau of labor statistics, to serve as a basis for future legislation. The industrial laborers of the state were still few in numbers, and up to that time almost wholly unorganized. But the women who had been clamoring for recognition in law did not fare so well. An amendment extending suffrage to them which had been passed by the previous general assembly was rejected.

The suffrage movement in Iowa began in 1854 and 1855, when Frances Dana Gage of Ohio and Amelia Bloomer of Council Bluffs delivered a series of lectures on the subject.[2] It was this Mrs. Bloomer whose name remains attached to a form of dress which to her represented a part of the emancipation of her sex. In 1869 the first suffrage association in the state was founded at Dubuque, and in 1870 the Iowa Woman Suffrage Society was organized in a state convention held in Mt. Pleasant. In the same year John P. Irish, a member from Johnson County, introduced a joint resolution for an amendment to the constitution striking out the word "male," which was passed by both houses, but only to be defeated in the next assembly. Year after year the politicians toyed with this issue in the same way. The status of women in official or even clerical positions was not well defined until 1876 when the Sixteenth General Assembly passed a law enabling women to sit as school directors and to serve as county superintendents of schools. In 1872 Governor Carpenter made

[2] Gue's *History of Iowa*, Vol. III, p. 252.

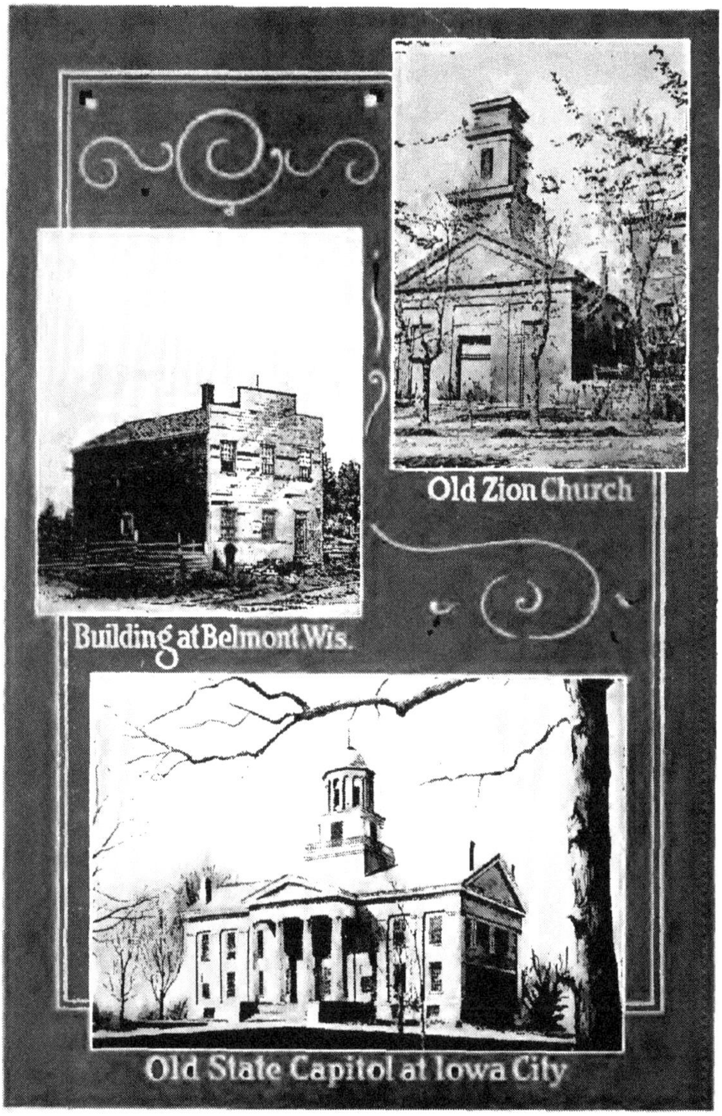


The Early Capitols

Ada E. North state librarian, probably the first woman in America to hold such a state office.[3] The organization of clubs for various purposes among women did not begin until late in the seventies. The rejection of suffrage by the general assembly in 1884, however, did not retard, but rather accelerated women's activities, and a meeting in 1885 of the Association for the Advancement of Women was notable.

But the reënactment of prohibition is the most important legislative act of 1884. The Republican party, willing or unwilling, had been compelled to accept in the election of 1883 that horn of the dilemma following the decision of the supreme court on the unconstitutionality of the amendment. Governor Sherman and the general assembly accepted the verdict of the people at the polls and two liquor laws were enacted. The first law repealed the wine and beer clause of 1857-1858, which had been grafted on the prohibitory law of 1855, and the second law modified and strengthened the provisions of the law of 1855 itself. The penalties added were of the most drastic nature and were extended to those who owned the premises upon which liquors were sold. It was also provided that one-half of the fines should go to those who acted as informers in a desire to make law enforcement a matter of profit instead of merely principle. The new laws went into effect on the fourth of July, but in many cities and in some whole counties their provisions were ignored from the start. In some instances those who sought to enforce the law were tarred and feathered for their reward.[4] The state was soon in a greatly perturbed condition over this issue.

On the sixth of June the Republicans in their national convention, held at Chicago, named James G. Blaine as their candidate for president and John A. Logan for vice-president and on the tenth of July the Democrats named Grover Cleveland and Thomas A. Hendricks for the same offices. The Greenbackers, who still survived, and the Prohibitionists, also, named candidates for president, the former, General Benjamin F. Butler, and the latter, John P. St. John. In Iowa the

[3] Gue's *History of Iowa*, Vol. III, p. 255.

[4] *Iowa City Republican*, July 21, 1884.

Democrats and the Greenbackers effected a fusion on both presidential electors and on state offices, on the basis of Cleveland for president and Butler for vice-president. The nomination of Blaine was popular in Iowa. The Maine statesman had been the idol of the politicians who were under the influence of the *State Register*, the editor of which, James S. Clarkson, had been extreme in his admiration of Blaine. In 1876, and again in 1880, the Iowa delegations to the national conventions had supported the Maine man. But in the east the nomination was not so well received. To vast numbers of influential men Mr. Blaine was unacceptable. They objected to his political morals. They soon formed themselves into a distinct movement. They were in vain styled prudes and purists and eventually "Mugwumps," for their numbers went on growing and so did their influence.

In Iowa, beset as the Republicans were with the evidences of a national revolt against Blaine and a state revolt against the enforcement of the new prohibitory law, they were fortunate to disclose a new man who with his matchless eloquence was able to relight the old fires of party enthusiasm. This man was Jonathan P. Dolliver, who made himself famous in a day. Two years before he had attracted momentary attention in the state convention by a speech placing Gilbert B. Pray in nomination for the office of clerk of the supreme court. But in 1884 he was to electrify the whole state and to make himself heard in the nation. The opportunity and the man had met.

The convention was held at Des Moines on the twentieth of August, for the purpose of nominating candidates for the state offices to be filled by election that year. It was a typical Iowa convention, composed of the representative and influential men of the party in the ninety-nine counties of the state. State conventions of the two great parties in those days were more than business meetings, more than places of political intrigue, although business was transacted and intrigue was not wanting. They were great representative gatherings, and they constituted popular forums and educational institutions. Those who sought nominations from the parties had to appear in person before the delegates and to bear their scrutiny. From these personal contacts, delegates were enabled to vote intelligently. When the conventions were called to order stress was naturally laid on oratory. The coveted position was that of temporary chairman, a position of vantage in which the holder delivered what constituted the keynote address not only for the gathering but for the campaign to follow. The man who could succeed in such a position scattered his name and his influence over the entire state.

Mr. Dolliver was still a new man in Iowa. He was also a young man. He was born on the sixth of February, 1858, in West Virginia, the son of a minister of the Methodist church. His father was a rugged man, rugged in mountain eloquence. The son received the ordinary education of his day and in due time was graduated from the university of his native state. He taught school and read law, and thus equipped he started for the west in search of fame and fortune, but with more longings for fame than for fortune. He reached Fort Dodge, his future home, in 1878 with just about enough means to hire an office and to "hang out a shingle," or a lawyer's sign. In partnership with a brother, he waited in vain for clients who did not come. The law business in Iowa cities was not highly prosperous in those distressful days, when the grasshoppers had hardly ceased to be a burden in northwestern Iowa, and Mr. Dolliver was not a diligent lawyer. He had a mind more bent on public business than intent upon his own. He was always thinking of audiences to sway mightier than juries in petty cases. But while he dreamed he also struggled with actual poverty. The brothers made their own beds and they often cooked their own meals. When they did not have money with which to pay, they worked out their own poll taxes on the public highways. A sublime optimism and a serene sense of humor must have sustained him in those days. He found the greenback craze at its highest and he prepared himself to combat its fallacies. This brought him local speaking engagements. In that way he attracted attention, among others from former Governor Carpenter. The governor interested Mr. Clarkson in the young orator and it was through this influence that he reached the dizzy pinnacle of the temporary chairmanship of the convention of August twentieth, 1884.

Mr. Dolliver faced his great audience with a speech which had been carefully prepared, almost committed to memory. But the delivery of his finished periods was so rapt and tense that they glowed like the spontaneous combustions of gray matter in his brain. The young orator — he was in his twenty-seventh year — stood before his audience strikingly handsome, tall and agile, black-haired and rosy-cheeked, in the very vigor of health and in the bloom of young manhood. And the audience matched the orator. It was made up of men who represented the leadership of Republican politics in the state, and on the stage, as the honored guest, sat General William T. Sherman. It was the hour and the honor of which the young man had dreamed, and which most of all things he had coveted. Those who had come to wonder, and the few who had come to admire, were instantly alike thrilled. They were made to realize that never before had they heard anything like it in Iowa. The very manner of the orator pleased them and his voice thrilled them. The gestures were many, not only of the arms and hands, but of the head and the entire body, but they fitted the words. The whole man was in action. The harmony was physical, oral, and mental. The sentences were stately and the rhetoric gorgeous. There were flashes of wit and ever the genial glow of humor. There was praise and sarcasm, eulogy and opprobrium, and all so rapidly and ineffably mingled and intermingled that those who listened sat spellbound and bewildered. The auditors at times punctuated every sentence with their applause. They laughed often and some times they were almost moved to tears.

Much of what Mr. Dolliver said on that day was soon forgotten. It still bore the stamp of immaturity. It was the effervescence of youth, the youth that is not required to measure its phrases with exactness, nor to chill its warmth with logic. His words were as extravagant as those of Hamlet and as superlative as those of Romeo. Even his audience was superlative. The delegates who sat in the seats were to him "the fighting strength of the Republican party of Iowa." He complimented them on the victories which they had won and on the greater victories which would be achieved under their leadership. The party to which they belonged was the party of Lincoln, of Grant, and of Sherman — and Sherman himself was sitting on the stage. It was the party of freedom, of the Union, and of moral and political righteousness. It held in its membership the manhood of the state and the nation. Those who stood opposed to them were pictured in ridicule and almost scorn. Of Grover Cleveland, he said that "to elect him president would be like giving money to a stranger on a train," while he thanked God fervently that he belonged to "a party that saves the crown of its public honor for the brow of actual leadership." The party spirit still ran strong in Iowa and those who listened heard uttered in a rapt way what they wanted to hear and to think.

It is not extravagance to say that no speech had ever so moved an Iowa audience before, and it is still true that in effect none has since exceeded it. The fame of it and of the orator spread the next morning over all of Iowa and it soon reached the nation. An orator of the first rank had been disclosed in the Iowa cornfields. Others wanted to hear him, far and wide they called for him to speak. Before the political campaign of that year was over the young Iowan was touring the country with James G. Blaine — his dreams of fame and glory had all come true and that suddenly.

But the magnetic eloquence of James G. Blaine could not lull the consciences of those who refused to believe in him, and the fervid oratory of Jonathan P. Dolliver could not hold even Iowa from wavering in its allegiance to the party that had so long controlled the destinies of the state and nation. In Iowa, in spite of the presidential interest in the election, the majority dwindled down to a meager plurality of eighteen thousand five hundred on the state ticket and the presidential ticket fell below even that, the smallest national majority in the state since 1860. In the whole country the elections were so close that day after day the result hung in the balance.

There is pathos in defeat for those who have been nurtured

on victories. On a night in that November of 1884, two men were wending their ways homeward from the town into the country, along a dusty road. The trees were bare and the air was eager and nipping, but there still lingered in it the odor of falling apples mingled with the scent of ripening corn. The one was an old man and the other was still a college sophomore. But both were Republicans. They had waited at the railroad station for the last newspapers from Des Moines. The news had been unfavorable, and so they walked away in silence. The young man had cast his first vote for the party in whose creed he had been reared, and which he believed stood for the welfare of the nation, and the old man had cast what might be the last vote in a presidential election, for he was already tottering on his legs.

"Grover Cleveland elected," the old man almost moaned. "To me the last election is like the last battle of the war for the Union — and we have lost it!"

He did not say much more. Everything seemed lost to him — everything for which one of his sons had died in the Civil War. The young man turned in silently at the home gate and the old man tottered on for he lived farther up the road. Four jubilant horsemen, all well supplied with the liquors that had been prohibited in Iowa, rode by, enveloped in a cloud of dust, shouting to the old man as they passed him, "Hurrah for Cleveland and to h—l with Blaine." The old man did not vote again, but the young man lived long enough to become, after many years, an admirer of the sturdiness of Grover Cleveland — and here he makes a record of that admiration.

# CHAPTER LXXIII

## The State Under Governor Larrabee

In 1885 the Republican outlook was not a hopeful one. The shadow of the national defeat of 1884 hung over the party. Blaine, who had been the idol of Iowa Republicans, had carried the state by hardly half of the traditional majority.[1] The fusion of Democrats and Greenbackers had resulted in the election of four of the eleven congressmen. The prohibitory law loomed as a dark shadow and the railroad situation was one of unrest.

When the Republicans met in state convention that year, William Larrabee of Fayette County, who had been defeated for the nomination four years before, was easily nominated for the office of governor. He was one of the outstanding men in state politics; one of the most potent law-makers of many general assemblies. John A. T. Hull was named for the office of lieutenant governor. The Democrats and Greenbackers, still united politically, nominated for the same offices, Charles E. Whiting of Monona County and E. H. Gillette of Polk County, the one a Democrat and the other a Greenbacker. The Republicans won the election by a bare seven thousand votes, but even that was accounted a victory.

The new governor was not a man who believed in letting well enough alone. Many were then in favor of letting the liquor law take care of itself. They said in effect that the Republican party with losses to itself had given the people the law, and let the people do with it what they pleased, and in many communities and whole counties they were not pleased to do anything with it except to violate it. But Mr. Larrabee had a different conception of his duties as governor.

[1] Blaine's vote was 197,089; Cleveland and Butler's, fusion, 177,316; St. John's, 1,472; Blaine's plurality, 19,773.

He believed that it was the business of a governor to enforce the laws. His own views were then not so pronounced as they became later. In his first inaugural address he still believed that "there is a proper demand for alcoholic liquors which should be supplied," and he discountenanced a policy "that would drive competent and conscientious druggists out of an honorable and legitimate business."

But for a while an impeachment trial attracted more attention than law enforcement. John L. Brown, who had been state auditor, had been suspended from office by Governor Sherman for alleged failure to account for all moneys which he had received. This happened on March nineteenth, 1885. Brown had refused to vacate his office and the governor had used the military power of the state to eject him. The newly elected legislature proceeded to investigate the matter, and the house framed thirty articles of impeachment against Brown, who was tried before the senate and acquitted, whereupon he was restored to his office by Governor Larrabee, and later he was reimbursed for moneys he had spent in his own defense. The trial before the senate was made memorable by a speech delivered by a young man from Cedar County, who had been elected to his first legislative office, as a member of the house for that county. Robert G. Cousins's argument was such a fine piece of oratory that it immediately brought him into public attention. He did not have the setting of a great political convention for his efforts, but merely a trial jury composed of senators. He was hailed as another Dolliver, but he was wholly unlike Dolliver. He was more reposeful, more classical, more poetical, and more philosophic as an orator. Every word in his sentences had its niche and fitted it as exactly as the bits of color in a cameo painting.

It was near the closing of his first term that the convictions and powers of Governor Larrabee were fully aroused in office. On the night of the third of August, 1886, the Rev. George C. Haddock was shot down in Sioux City by those whom he had offended through activities in liquor law enforcement. He had not only denounced the law breakers from the pulpit of his church, the First Methodist church of Sioux

William Larrabee

William B. Allison

Horace Boies

James Wilson

City, but he had helped to bring some of them to the bar of justice. Throughout the state public mass meetings were held to denounce the crime of his death. The liquor men in getting rid of him placed a greater stumbling block in their own way, for the blood of the martyr became the seed of a new spirit of law enforcement throughout the state. But the perpretrators of the infamous crime were never punished. Governor Larrabee was most profoundly moved by the Sioux City crime. It was the challenge, written in blood, to the law and order of the state of which he was governor.

About the same time the governor had another experience in office that deepened his purposes. He was most diligent about the state's business. He went into every detail of it, as he was in the habit of going into his own private business. He made every expenditure of the state his concern. He audited accounts and figured how to reduce all possible expenditures. In the course of such self-imposed duties he came across some railroad switching charges, in connection with fuel supplies for the institution at Glenwood, that he deemed excessive. He called the railroad company's attention to them and asked that they be made more reasonable. But no heed was paid to his suggestions. He then turned the matter over to the state railroad commissioners for adjustment, but the commissioners had to tell him that under the law they were powerless, all their functions were merely advisory. That incident convinced the governor that the state needed reformed railroad legislation.

In 1887 Governor Larrabee was reëlected by a slightly increased majority. He seems to have accepted this reëlection with his mind made up for more stringent enforcement of the prohibitory law and for the re-making of the railroad laws of the state, for these were the burdens of his second inaugural address, one of the clearest and most fearless among Iowa state documents. The railroad note he struck was for their managers a shrill one. It was a challenge to combat. He accused them of having used undue influence in the shaping of laws and in the creation of public sentiment. "By granting special rates," he said in his address, "rebates, drawbacks, and other favors here and there to men of influence in the respective localities, they have secured the favor of many who, after having divided with them their spoils are ready to defend their wrongs and to advocate a policy of neutrality on the part of the state." That was a bold statement, but the governor had fortified himself with many facts before making it. He held that vested rights did not include vested wrongs. He outlined a legislative policy that included the abolition of all railroad passes, root and branch of them, maximum passenger rates of two cents a mile on the first class roads, and higher ones for roads less favorably situated, and reasonable maximum freight rates, the same to be enacted by the legislature and to be amendable, from time to time, by railroad commissioners elected and paid by the people, instead of being appointed by the governors and paid by the railroads.

In a day the state was thrown into a turmoil. The railroads protested, and so did many shippers. No one among the legislators or among the people could avoid the issues which the governor had raised. Everyone was challenged to choose his place. The newspapers of the state also had to take sides. The *Register,* which had championed the candidacy of Mr. Larrabee as governor, at first deplored and then denounced his radical policies. The paper's choice of position was not without reason. Mr. Clarkson had been a railroad promoter and builder. He believed in them as he believed in Iowa and in her commercial greatness. To him the railroads were vital for the upbuilding of the state. It was through his efforts that the Wabash had been built into Des Moines and that the Burlington and Northwestern roads had sought Des Moines connections. He knew that the Wabash had never earned a dollar on its Iowa investments. To hamper and harass the railroads while they were still developing their systems was to him a grievous wrong, and the wrong was done to the state as well as to the roads.

But Governor Larrabee had grounds as ample for his crusade. Railroad conditions as they then existed would at any other time have been not only intolerable but impossible. There was neither system nor justice in freight rates. Rate schedules were Chinese puzzles and many of them were secrets well guarded. Stockmen in the western half of the state could obtain lower rates to Chicago by first shipping to Omaha, and from there re-shipping to Chicago, instead of shipping direct without loss of time. Certain communities were favored over others, so that some flourished and others perished. Competitive points had low rates and non-competitive ones high rates. Favored shippers drew rebates that constituted a liberal profit in their business. Passes were issued to favored patrons or to men of influence in politics. Railroad men admitted these things, but they believed that they were inevitable in their business. Governor Larrabee knew that they existed — he had been both railroad owner and railroad manager, and he insisted that rates must be equalized and be for all alike, alike for communities and shippers. What railroad men then regarded as revolutionary would now be considered only common sense and common honesty. But instead of using reason, they went into a combat that distressed the whole state — and that cost Iowa the presidency in 1888.

The Larrabee reforms were soon embodied into legislative bills. The railroads brought all their resources to bear on public sentiment and on the members of the legislature. The members were flooded with letters and petitions pro and con. The upshot of it all was that the whole program outlined could not be enacted. Railroad passes were not extinguished, passenger rates were not disturbed, and the attempt to make freight rates by legislative enactment failed. But the power to make reasonable maximum freight rates was conferred upon the railroad commissioners, who proceeded forthwith to do so. The commissioners were Peter A. Dey, Spencer Smith of Council Bluffs, and L. S. Coffin, but as the term of the latter expired, Governor Larrabee displaced him with Frank T. Campbell, the author of the old Granger Law. Mr. Campbell was a radical reformer, Mr. Dey was a conservative, and Mr. Smith was at first colorless, but gradually he took on color from the agitations. The hearings before the commissioners exceeded in interest the sessions of the general assembly. Railroad presidents and managers, and shippers of all degrees appeared as witnesses. In due time the commissioners evolved schedules of rates, based largely upon charges for similar services in other states. When they were put into effect the railroads began suits in the federal courts to resist them. But the right of the state to prescribe such rates was already established in court decisions. The roads gradually accepted the situation and they had many assurances that if the rates after trial should prove unremunerative they would be modified by the commissioners.

The roads doing interstate business practiced rate retaliations that eventually greatly injured Iowa's development. Instead of the through rates that had obtained they broke all shipments at the borders of the state and added to the rates the local distance tariffs of the Iowa commissioners. Iowa was a pioneer in such legislation and it was advertised to the disadvantage of the state, so that railroad and other corporate investments were retarded. Iowa paid dearly, but it was never successfully shown that the rates in themselves were unjust. On the contrary, the roads that did business wholly within the state prospered on them as they had never prospered before.

# CHAPTER LXXIV

## Iowa in National Politics

In the midst of the railroad turmoil, in March 1888, the Republicans held in Des Moines their state convention to select delegates to the national convention. Senator Allison was a candidate for the nomination for president. He was easily of presidential stature. His place in the senate had made him one of the marked men of the nation. Two other senators were seeking the presidential nomination, Sherman of Ohio, and Harrison of Indiana, while the name of James G. Blaine could not be suppressed.

Jonathan P. Dolliver was again summoned to deliver the keynote address as temporary chairman of the convention. He had the good will of all factions in Iowa politics and the eloquence to sway the convention along the desired lines. So subtle and so prevalent was the Blaine sentiment in Iowa that the orator did not dare to mention his name, for fear that such mere mention would sweep the delegates off their feet, impairing the prestige of Senator Allison. The votes of Iowa were to be cast for Allison, but the heart of Iowa was still true to the Maine statesman, as it had been since 1876. Mr. Dolliver was equal to his own reputation, but he did not surpass his first effort.

In the afternoon session Governor Larrabee was reported for the permanent chairman of the convention, without the sanction of the men who were managing the campaign for Senator Allison. They were thrown into consternation. The governor's hands were red with the blood of the railroads and it was feared that his participation in the convention would alienate national influences. He was looked upon as the reincarnation of the old spirit of Grangerism which was unacceptable to the business world. To make the best of an awkward situation that had been created, a motion was made and carried that the temporary organization of the convention be made the permanent one, by which Mr. Dolliver was continued as presiding officer. Nor could the managers for Mr. Allison carry through their "slate" of delegates-at-large. The men picked for these positions were James S. Clarkson, David B. Henderson, John Y. Stone, then attorney general of the state, and George D. Perkins, the editor of the Sioux City *Journal*. When the balloting began the name of Dolliver was freely used. From the chair he protested that he was not a candidate for delegate-at-large and that he must not be voted for. But the more he protested, the more votes he received. The convention literally went Dolliver mad, as it might have gone Blaine mad upon the slightest provocation. Mr. Dolliver was elected and Mr. Stone was defeated for the coveted honor.

When the national convention was held, after Mr. Blaine had withdrawn his name, by cable from Scotland, where he was the guest of Andrew Carnegie, it soon became apparent that the contest would lie between Allison of Iowa and Harrison of Indiana. At noon of the decisive day of the convention an adjournment until four o'clock was taken to give the delegates time for conferences. What happened in a conference participated in by the delegates from the influential states is best told in Senator George F. Hoar's book, his *Autobiography of Seventy Years*. He records that he made "a very earnest speech in favor of Mr. Allison," presenting him as a man who would make a popular candidate and a wise president. In this conference the state of New York was represented by three of its delegates-at-large, the fourth one, Chauncey M. Depew, being absent. Mr. Depew had been a candidate for the nomination, but he had been compelled to withdraw his name on account of the opposition to him as a railroad president. "Finally," says Mr. Hoar, "all agreed that their states should vote for Mr. Allison, when the convention came in the afternoon," but the consent to that arrangement on the part of the three New York men was made contingent on Mr. Depew giving his assent to it. When this conference adjourned, Mr. Hoar says that every one was confident that

Mr. Allison would receive the nomination. The senator received congratulations on that basis and the news of the impending victory was wired to Iowa.

But they had not counted Mr. Depew. He refused to give his consent to the arrangement. Half an hour before the reassembling of the convention another conference was held "to make sure that the thing would go through all right," says Mr. Hoar. There Mr. Depew balked. He said he was opposed to it. In the words of Mr. Hoar, "Compelled . . . by the opposition of the agrarian element, which was hostile to railroads . . ." he had withdrawn his own name. "He said this opposition to him came largely from Iowa, and from the northwest, where was found the chief support of Mr. Allison; that while he had withdrawn his own name, he would not so far submit to such an unreasonable and socialistic sentiment as to give his consent that it should dictate a candidate for the Republican party." It was in vain that he was told that Mr. Allison least of all men represented such sentiments. His opposition was final and fatal. New York went with his decision and the lesser states followed New York. "If it had gone on," says Mr. Hoar, "New York, Illinois, Wisconsin, Pennsylvania, Massachusetts, Iowa, California, and perhaps Missouri, would have cast their votes unanimously for Allison, and his nomination would have been sure." "I think no other person," comments the historian, "ever came so near the presidency of the United States and missed it . . . The result was the nomination of Mr. Harrison."

Senator Allison accepted his defeat with good grace, however keenly he may have felt the disappointment of it, or whatever he may have thought of the causes that brought it about. He was too wise a man to quarrel with fate. In Iowa some bitterness was felt, and Governor Larrabee and his railroad crusade were held to blame for the defeat. They did not stop to think that Mr. Depew's opposition had been much more unreasonable than Mr. Larrabee's railroad reforms. Governor Larrabee was in many other ways made conscious of the fact that the rôle of a reformer has hardships in it. To break down his prestige and influence he was even subjected to a prosecution for libel. A young ne'er-do-well by the name of Chester Turney had been imprisoned for a series of crimes. His mother, or foster mother, sought his release. Governor Larrabee refused to listen to her importunities and the importunities of those who for one reason or another befriended her. Largely, no doubt, to annoy, the case was converted into a popular agitation and the governor was charged with meanness toward a suffering boy and mother. In self-defense he caused to be published a pamphlet setting forth the crimes of the young convict and his reasons for refusing to pardon him. The statements in this pamphlet were then seized upon to frame a libel charge for which the governor had to stand trial, though personally excused from appearing in court. Of course he was acquitted, but the trial had served its purposes without securing a conviction.

But neither such petty persecutions nor the more formidable opposition of railroads or liquor interests could swerve the governor from his course of persistent law-enforcement. He called upon sheriffs to do their duties. When the jails were filled with law-breakers the governor was always ready to pardon those who would pledge themselves to abandon their evil ways to engage in honorable work or business.

When Mr. Dolliver returned from the national convention with added prestige, he entered for the second time the race for the nomination for congress in the Tenth district, which he won on the one hundred and tenth ballot. In spite of his popularity as an orator, the politicians of the district were not ready to accept him as their leader. Two years before he had been defeated on the one hundred and eighty-eighth ballot, making two of the most memorable political contests in Iowa politics. He was elected and started on his distinguished congressional career.

Mr. Clarkson, the Iowa member of the Republican National Committee, was made vice-chairman of that organization and took an active part in the management of the campaign. Many who had been alienated in the Blaine-Cleveland campaign, refused to return to their party. They were still known as "Mugwumps." The Republicans, however, carried the election. In Iowa they elected ten of the eleven congressmen, Walter I. Hayes, a Democrat, being elected from the Second district, largely on the record he had made in the liquor case. In the state election proper, one Democrat only was elected, Peter A. Dey, Democratic candidate for railroad commissioner, who defeated John Mahin of Muscatine. Mr. Dey's election was interpreted as a recession from extreme anti-railroadism. The railroads, however, had not been so much crippled by the new rates as they had predicted, and as they retained the right to issue passes they soon recovered much of their former influence over public sentiment and also over legislation.

In recognition of his services in the campaign, and perhaps, also to compensate Iowa for the defeat of Senator Allison, President-elect Harrison tendered to Mr. Clarkson the position of postmaster general in his cabinet.[1] But Mr. Clarkson united with other members of the national committee in recommending John Wanamaker, the noted Philadelphia merchant and philanthropist, for that position. At a critical time in the campaign, when the funds were low, Mr. Wanamaker had volunteered to raise a quarter of a million dollars to carry on the work of the committee. No promises were made and no pledges were exacted, but it was understood that Mr. Wanamaker should share in the honors in event of victory. To Mr. Harrison his appointment looked like bartering, but he finally asked Mr. Wanamaker to take the office. Mr. Clarkson then accepted under him the position of first assistant, and proceeded to remove from the postoffices of the country the Democrats with whom the Cleveland administration had filled them. They were still the days of spoils in politics and as an axeman in decapitating Democratic postmasters Mr. Clarkson for a season set the country aghast, thereby giving a new impetus to civil service reform.

[1] Upon his return from the east Mr. Clarkson made a statement to the author of this history to this effect, and he asked him to make a personal record of it, saying, "Sometime you may be able to use it in a history of Iowa which I hope you will write."

## CHAPTER LXXV

### A Great Reaction

The consistent and conscientious administration of Governor Larrabee was not sufficient to overcome the prejudices that still existed against sumptuary laws, like prohibition, neither did the railroads accept without protest what had happened to them. In the closing year of his administration a violent reaction set in. But it was not wholly a state reaction; it was national also. Monetary conditions were still disturbing ones, and the attempt of the Republicans under the leadership of Wm. McKinley to revise the tariff schedules was made the occasion of a new crusade for free trade, or tariff for revenue only.

When the campaign of 1889 opened the Democrats assumed the leadership by finding a new man who fitted the complicated situation of politics. This man was Horace Boies of Waterloo. To begin with, he had been a Republican who had disagreed with his party over the tariff. When the party took up prohibition he left it entirely, because he was opposed to coercive sumptuary legislation. In point of abilities, Horace Boies was a man of the first class. By profession he was a lawyer, and a very able one, and by proxy, he was a farmer, that is, he was the owner of large tracts of land in the management of which he took a personal interest. He had been a man of an inconspicuous life. He was modest to the very verge of shyness. He hated the glare of publicity. He was not an office-seeker and he almost resented being placed in such an attitude before the people. But that exactly suited the purposes of the Democrats that year, who coveted the advantages of his clean and honorable personal and political records. They called him as the Romans called Cincinnatus, almost from the plow. They made him see the calling as a duty imposed on him, and when he had accepted that duty he showed a certain kind of fearlessness accompanied by adroitness that made him a political factor to be reckoned with. All of it was shrewd and some of it was dramatic. Human interest and public curiosity were alike aroused. The coming of no mere politician, but of a patriot, was announced. The people were looking for that kind of a man in a time of doubt and trouble. They flocked to hear him, and those who heard him liked him. To see him was enough to create a liking for the man. He was clean-looking, and he talked like a clear thinker. They soon called him "the man with the affidavit face," while one adulator spoke of him as a man who had both the Ten Commandments and the Sermon on the Mount stamped on his face.[1] His speeches were subdued and sincere, logical and rational. He did not make a great deal of noise, after the manner of many politicians; and he did not use many gestures, after the manner of many orators. It was soon made apparent that he represented a leadership that his friends admired and that his opponents feared.

Against this accomplished man and shrewd politician, as he became, the Republicans pitted in the race for governor J. G. Hutchison of Ottumwa on a platform which declared that prohibition " has become the settled policy of the state . . . upon which there should be no backward step." Politically, this was for them the correct position to take, for the party had become committed to that issue and there was no way out except to go through. There was more to be feared from prohibitionists who might be alienated than to be hoped from anti-prohibitionists who might be coaxed back into the party. Mr. Hutchison fitted the platform. He was an upright man who had distinguished himself in the state senate. He was a business man, a wholesale grocer, rather than a politician. But on the hustings he was poorly equipped to contend with a man like Mr. Boies. His face was serious, almost severe, and his speech was matter of fact, without the magic of utterance. He talked to the consciences of men, but he did not appeal, as did his opponent, to their imaginations — and in politics, as in other matters, imagination is often more than conscience.

[1] Credited to the late Colonel Chas. A. Clark.

The Democrats had the advantage not only in the personality of their candidate, but they had the advantage of a united party, while the Republicans were sorely divided. In spite of their unequivocal platform declaration, the extreme prohibitionists placed a third ticket in the field. The Democrats also had ample funds to carry on their campaign. It was said that the liquor interests of the nation spent money in Iowa to help defeat prohibition at a critical time, deeming that such a result would be of national benefit to them. The railroad interests also saw gains by the defeat of a party that had enacted such radical legislation. In short, the Democrats that year had not only the best actor, but the best stage settings for an agressive campaign. And they were successful, Horace Boies receiving 6,573 more votes than were cast for J. G. Hutchison.

For the first time since 1851, a democratic candidate for governor was successful in Iowa. However, it was a one man victory. It was Horace Boies and not the Democratic party to whom the victory was due. The Republicans were able to count in the rest of their candidates for state offices, but by slender majorities. For the general assembly, the Republicans elected fifty members in the lower house, and the Democrats fifty, while the count in the senate stood twenty-eight Republicans to twenty-two Democrats, giving the former a majority of six on joint ballots. But this slender majority was due to senators who had been elected two years before.

With the lower house evenly divided, it was not until the last days of February that an organization was perfected with John T. Hamilton of Linn County, a Democrat, as speaker, and on the twenty-seventh of that month, Horace Boies was inaugurated as governor. In retiring from office, Governor Larrabee submitted an able defense of his policies. He showed that railroad earnings under the new rates, during the first year, had not been decreased, as had been feared by the railroad managers, but had, instead, been increased by $139,689, as compared with the last year under the old rates. In favor of prohibition he exhibited the statistics of population in the state's penitentiaries, showing a decrease from 756 to 604, which he attributed to the decrease of drunkenness. Governor Boies in accepting the office announced no proposed changes in railroad legislation, and on prohibition he said it was not the purpose of his party to disturb the law where it could be enforced, but to seek relief in the form of local option for communities where the law was still contrary to public sentiment.

Having lost the governorship, the Republicans entered on a protracted effort to bring their factions into harmony enough to save the United States senatorship. Many Republicans in the legislature were dissatisfied with Senator Allison, largely because he had rendered no aid and given no comfort to those who had put through the Larrabee railroad reforms. On prohibition also, the senator's attitude had been that of mere acquiescence. Instead of returning Senator Allison for the fourth time, many were in favor of sending Governor Larrabee to Washington where, they believed, his aggressive policies would work a wholesome change. They insisted that tested by state results and aspirations, Senator Allison had forfeited his high office, and Governor Larrabee had earned it. The Democratic leaders were assiduous in encouraging such factional divisions in the Republican party. Some tendered their aid to Governor Larrabee, if he would become a candidate for the senate, but, fortunately or unfortunately, they could not have their votes counted in the Republican party caucus where the senatorship would be decided.

And so for a season, Governor Larrabee and Senator Allison were uppermost in the public mind, and they stood, in popular conception, pitted against each other in the senatorial race. They were easily the foremost men of Iowa at that time. The one was as prominent and influential in state affairs as the other was in national ones. Personally they were, as they had always been, friends, but there was a marked and even sharp conflict between them in their attitude toward public questions. They still wished each other well, but the exigencies of politics created a barrier between them. Senator Allison wanted Governor Larrabee to say that he was not and would not become a candidate for senator, but Governor Larrabee sat as speechless as the Sphinx. According to the rules of politics, he owed the senator nothing for the senator had almost wholly withdrawn himself from the bitter contest that had been waged in Iowa. And the senator may have felt that he owed to the governor his loss of the presidency in 1888.

Probably it was the high personal regard that each had for the other, and the love that both had for the Republican party, that prevented an open rupture at that time. There was much to predicate such a breach upon. It inhered in the very natures of the two men. Mr. Allison was cautious, Mr. Larrabee aggressive. Mr. Larrabee believed that right was a definite moral entity in politics as well as in other things, while Mr. Allison believed that right partook of the nature of a political equity. Mr. Larrabee was ever ready to tear out the old foundations to build anew, while Mr. Allison believed in repairing the old structures on their old foundations. In short, one man was a radical and the other a conservative, and the *quasi* contest between them was a recurrence of the old conflict between these two forces.

But while Governor Larrabee maintained a long silence, he was at no time minded to enter the race against Senator Allison. He had neither the ambition nor even the willingness to become a United States senator. He had given twenty-five of the best years of his life to his state as senator and governor. He was tired of public life, and he was anxious to devote himself to his private affairs, which he had been compelled to neglect. Nor did he look upon the senatorship as a promotion from the governorship. He esteemed the governorship the higher office. The outcome was that Senator Allison was reëlected, and entered upon his fourth term with a superb equipment for public service. He returned to Washington to become the senator oracular. There was no man in the senate to dispute thereafter his premiership. But true to his instincts, he still moved from precedent to precedent. His mental and political processes were all evolutionary; none were revolutionary. If he was always sure of his aims, he was always equally sure of his footings. If he looked at the stars, it was with his feet on the earth. His cautiousness passed into proverb. It was said of him that he could walk from

Washington to San Francisco on eggs without breaking a shell of them. His touch was gentle and his speech was soft. There was in him no violence, no vindictiveness, no vituperation. He loved men and men loved him. Nor was he always complaisant either. He had his own views and his own viewpoints. His integrity was deep and his sincerity profound. He dominated without domineering. A suggestion from his lips was as potent as a command from others. He made men believe that his ways were their ways. Even so aggressive a leader as Theodore Roosevelt leaned on the counsels of the man he called, affectionately, "Uncle Billy." Outside of the White House, he became the most influential man in Washington.

But Governor Larrabee in his retirement was no less serene and influential. Having put his own house in order, he viewed the world from his pine-clad hills overlooking the village of Clermont and the valley of the historic Turkey River. He read, studied, and reflected. He kept his finger on the public pulse, and those who made laws and those who enforced them kept in touch with his thoughts. Nearly every one who was anything in Iowa, or who aspired to anything, sooner or later made the journey to Clermont to talk things over with the sage and mentor who there kept his public vigils. His influence was broadened and deepened. No finer life was ever lived in Iowa, or anywhere, than the twenty years of the retirement of William Larrabee.

# CHAPTER LXXVI

## New Issues and New Defeats

The year that saw the return of Senator Allison to Washington and the retirement of Governor Larrabee to Clermont, was filled with Republican wreckage the nation over. The revision of the tariff under William McKinley had reacted disastrously. The business world was unsettled and the financial world was in doubt. In the congressional elections in Iowa that year the Republicans elected only five of their candidates while six Democrats were successful. Colonel David B. Henderson and Mr. Dolliver were two of the men who escaped the disaster, and J. A. T. Hull and George D. Perkins, of the Seventh and Eleventh districts were new men who were successful. Among the Democrats elected were Walter H. Butler of the Fourth district, and Fred E. White of the Sixth, two radical free silver men. But the Republicans in Iowa fared better than the Republicans of the nation. When the membership roll of the new house was made up it contained only eighty-seven Republicans, and two hundred and thirty-seven Democrats. Among those defeated was William McKinley in Ohio.

The victories of 1890 made the Democrats bold and the Republicans timid in the state election of 1891 when Horace Boies was reëlected governor by an increased majority, and this time he carried the whole Democratic state ticket with him. S. L. Bestow became the first Democratic lieutenant governor in the history of the state and L. G. Kinne, the first Democratic supreme court justice since the early fifties. In this disastrous state campaign the Republicans had laid new stress on prohibition, but the Democrats had laid most of the stress on national issues, favoring saloons only "where . . . a majority of the electors" desired them. They endorsed the Larrabee railroad legislation, and talked of "equal taxation," and a fair division of "income derived from a union of labor and capital." The Democrats had an aggressive policy, while the Republicans had a defensive one. But Horace Boies, inured to politics, was the adroit genius of the campaign. His opponent was Hiram C. Wheeler of Sac County, who had been president of the State Agricultural Society, under which the state fairs are conducted. He was heralded as the farmers' own candidate, but his farming operations were soon belittled by his opponents. It was said of him, and that truthfully, that while he owned vast tracts of land, he farmed them through tenants, or by telephone orders. But the candidate's greatest handicap was his utter inability to make a speech, while Horace Boies had become a "spell-binder."

Horace Boies became a national figure with his second election. In the east his party compatriots hailed him as the wizard of the west. He had broken down the Republican bulwarks in an agricultural state that had always been Republican. He was to them the prophet of a new dispensation in national politics. He was invited to speak in New York, at Madison Square Garden, where he made a speech in which he used Iowa statistics, compiled by the state labor commissioner, J. R. Sovereign, to prove that in Iowa, under the protective tariff, corn had been raised at a loss of sixty-seven cents an acre.[1] It was that which had impoverished the west and created the agrarian discontent that filled it. The Republican newspapers in vain combatted the influence of the governor's speech by calling it slanderous and untrue.

In their many defeats and partisan despair, the Republicans began to take new counsel. Many began to ask whether prohibition, indifferently enforced, if enforced at all, was worth the price the party had paid for it, for they blamed their defeats to prohibition rather than to the national issues which had been exploited. Why should a party continue to cling to an issue that the people had repudiated at the polls? Another presidential election was impending and the desire

[1] Mr. Sovereign's conclusions were based on many reports which he received from farmers.

arose for a reunited party. In many places the younger men became active. They asked for a new deal. They made overtures to men like Albert B. Cummins — men who had stood aloof from the party on prohibition, if they had not given actual support to Horace Boies. They were opposed to all tests of party fealty except those that were national. James E. Blythe of Mason City, who was chairman of the state committee, was in active sympathy with this movement. He believed in party reconciliations. Mr. Cummins was asked to act as temporary chairman of the state convention for the selection of delegates to the national convention of that year. This at first gave great offense to those Republicans who had remained loyal to the party. They objected to the bestowal of honors on men who had faltered in allegiance. So strong was this resentment that an effort was made to shut Mr. Cummins out of the convention over which he had been called to preside.

In 1892 the Republicans lost the presidential election to Grover Cleveland, who was for the second time elected to that office. President Harrison's administration had not met with favor from the politicians. James S. Clarkson, who had resigned his position as assistant postmaster general, led a movement to nominate James G. Blaine in his stead. It was a futile effort that helped to disrupt the party. Mr. Clarkson had sold his interest in the Des Moines newspaper, but he continued to serve as the Iowa member of the national committee. In the Democratic convention, Horace Boies was one of the candidates for the nomination for president. In Iowa, Benjamin Harrison received a plurality of about twenty-four thousand votes over Grover Cleveland, but not a majority of all the votes that were cast, General James B. Weaver receiving over twenty thousand votes in the state as the Populist candidate for president, and over six thousand being cast for a Prohibition candidate. But in the congressional elections the Republicans were successful in all the districts except the Second, in which Walter I. Hayes was reëlected. Among the Republicans elected to congress were Robert G. Cousins of the Fifth district, John H. Gear, the former governor, of the First district, and John F. Lacey of the Sixth, all men who were to attract national attention. In the Eighth district Colonel William P. Hepburn succeeded in making his return to congress.

Encouraged by these successes, the Republicans in 1893 were determined to recover the governorship of the state. In their new plans they included a modification of the prohibitory law. The enforcement of this law under Governor Boies was far from a matter of state pride. The law was flagrantly violated in all the larger cities. The governor issued many pardons in favor of men convicted of liquor law violations. Conditions were deplorable. Liquors were sold in hundreds of secret places, which were called "holes in the wall." Barns, cellars, and even outhouses were utilized for such purposes. Spies and informers infested the state. They worked for the fees involved. Justice court proceedings became farcical. Justices of the peace earned more than justices of the supreme court, and constables grew rich. Arrests and seizures were the order of the day, and fees were the only things thought of. Officials pilfered, the lawyers were busy, and even city councils trafficked in licenses.[3] Disregard, disobedience, and disrespect for the law alarmed all thoughtful men. They said it was political immorality to continue such a system.

When the Republican state convention was held that year, the veteran statesman, James Harlan, appeared as the spokesman in the rôle of temporary chairman. He made the event historic by his presence, by what he said, and by what was done. At the age of seventy-three, Harlan was still stalwart and vigorous, and he spoke with all the fervor of his past. He reminded his hearers of the fact that he had stood by the cradle of the Republican party. "If I do not know what Republicanism is, who does?" he asked. He then proceeded to tell the assembled delegates that Republicanism is national, and not local; that it is a national faith which may not and cannot be proscribed or modified by factions. He beseeched

[3] The author of this history at the time prepared a somewhat extended exposure of these practices which was printed in the *Register*.

the Republicans of Iowa to throw out all discords. Speaking specifically of prohibition, he said that whatever its merits, it could not and should not be made a test of party fealty.

Mr. Harlan's speech was the prelude to what followed, when the party declared that prohibition was not a test of party fealty. The question itself was relegated to the general assembly. "The retention, modification or repeal" of the law, it was declared, "must be determined by the general assembly, elected by and in sympathy with the people." But it was stipulated that the law should be maintained "in those portions of the state where it is now or can be made efficient, and giving to other localities such methods of controlling and regulating the liquor traffic as will best serve the cause of temperance and morality." On such a platform the party pitted Frank D. Jackson of Butler County against Horace Boies who was for the third time the nominee of his party.

Mr. Jackson was young and popular and a good speaker. He covered the state with a campaign that moved like a whirlwind. Mr. Boies was soon placed on the defensive. He had been governor for four years, and he had been able to bring about no relief from prohibition. The state was filled with law violators and public regard and respect for law had never been at so low an ebb. A Republican victory pointed both ways. It would save prohibition where the law could be enforced, and it would give relief where it could not be so enforced. Even the liquor men could see that it was to their advantage to support the Republican party's proposals. Industrial conditions also operated against Mr. Boies. The country was in the beginnings of a panic, and the Democratic administration was becoming every day more unpopular. When the votes were counted it was found that Mr. Jackson had an unexpected plurality of 32,161 over Mr. Boies. The man who had been an idol in Iowa, and a talked of man in the nation, suddenly realized how fickle is political favor.

When the general assembly met in 1894, the prohibitory law had grafted on it what became known as the mulct law. The prohibitory law was left in full effect, except in cities of over five thousand population where a majority of the voters signed a petition to the contrary, and in counties where sixty-five per cent of the voters so signed. The law was variously assailed, both by prohibitionists and anti-prohibitionists. Among other things it was said that for a price the state permitted the violation of her own laws. But it was sustained by the courts, and in practical operation it was so successful that the liquor question for a time disappeared from politics.

Under the operations of the new law, two-thirds of the counties of the state remained prohibition. The saloons were confined to the larger cities, and in these there were limitations placed on their numbers. Originally one saloon was permitted to be licensed for each five hundred inhabitants, and the ratio was gradually increased until it stood at one for each thousand inhabitants. The amount of the mulct tax which was left to the judgment of the municipalities, was also increased gradually. In many cities it was placed as high as two thousand dollars a year. Concurrently, there was an ever active propaganda for temperance and prohibition, under the influence of which there was a gradual extension of prohibition territory. The mulct law, inconsistent as it had seemed, was in effect an educational influence, and when, after twenty years, the law was repealed, the change affected but few communities.

# CHAPTER LXXVII

## Dark Days and then Daylight

The industrial and financial panic that began in 1893, grew worse in 1894. The whole country was in dire distress, and the party that happened to be in power was blamed and discredited. For Iowa there was a change made in the United States senate. In 1894 the legislature elected John H. Gear to succeed James F. Wilson, who had represented the state for two terms. Mr. Wilson's health had been failing and he was not a candidate for reëlection. In this election Albert B. Cummins made his debut as a senatorial candidate.

In the same year the Republicans elected the entire list of candidates for congress, George M. Curtis of Clinton defeating Walter I. Hayes whose vogue was ended by the modification of the prohibitory law. The Iowa delegation in the lower house as then made up was one of unusual strength. It included two orators of national repute, Dolliver and Cousins, two distinguished free-for-all debaters on the floor of congress, Henderson and Hepburn, and two distinguished publicists, George D. Perkins of the Sioux City *Journal* and Sam M. Clark of the Keokuk *Gate City*.

In the state election of that year the Republicans emphasized their return to popularity and power, but the Populists polled 34,907 votes, indicating the fact that there was a deep-seated industrial unrest. In the following year, Governor Jackson refused a renomination, desiring to return to his private and corporate business, and the nomination went to General Francis M. Drake of Appanoose County. Mr. Harlan that year sought the nomination. He had never been satisfied with his retirement from politics, in the senatorial campaign of 1872, and it was his desire to "round out his career" by at least one term in the office of governor. The party owed him a new debt, for had he not composed its differences in 1893? But General Drake's war record and his many philanthropies, including the founding of Drake University at Des Moines, proved stronger than Harlan's historic claims. He not only won the nomination, but the election, defeating W. I. Babb, the Democratic candidate, by more than sixty thousand votes.

The industrial and financial distress was then at its worst. The people suffered, and the politicians quarreled about both causes and remedies. Some blamed Grover Cleveland, the president, others blamed the Democratic revision of the tariff, which the president himself had called a piece of "party perfidy" and had refused to sign, and still others blamed the Bland-Allison free coinage act of 1878.

But whatever the cause, the evidences of the panic were widespread. Gold went out of circulation and credit declined. Factories were closed and farm products went down in price far below the cost of production. In the cities men could obtain neither work nor wages, and soup houses and bread-lines were the order of the day. The cheaper things became the harder they were to procure, for the people were without money. Many banks had to close their doors and great corporations, including railroads, went into bankruptcy.

When the distress was at its height, the unemployed in many places banded themselves together and became marching armies. By some they were called organized "tramps," but they styled themselves "Commonwealth Armies." They subsisted on the charities of the highways. At first they were not compelled to beg, for the people out of pity carried food to them. They were the creations of fate and they were impelled by a strange fanaticism. Their destination became Washington — they were going to storm the national capital for relief.

One of the largest of these armies came into being in San Francisco early in 1894 and in its eastward march reached Iowa in the summer of that year. Its leader was a man who was called "General" Kelly. Cities and communities through which it passed hastened them on, each desirous to be rid of the men, and each willing to pass the danger and burden of them to its neighbors. In some cases the railroads transported them free, and in others they seized trains and operated them for their own convenience for they had engineers as well as laborers among them. The most alarming reports preceded the march of this army. Some feared general uprisings along the way as it was about to enter the more populous parts of the country. As it drew near the borders of Iowa, Governor Jackson with legal advisers and members of his military staff proceeded to Council Bluffs. It seems to have been the governor's first intention to stop them from passing through the state, or at least to safeguard their passage through it. The national guard companies in the western part of the state were summoned to their armories. But on fuller consideration, the army was given the right-of-way.

"General" Kelly and his army finally reached Des Moines. Socialists and sympathizers made many preparations to receive them. They were kept west of the city for a few days to enable them to make a Sunday entrance, to be hailed as an army of protest against industrial conditions and as the proponents of a new dispensation. General James B. Weaver was selected to act as an escort for "General" Kelly. On a misty, drizzling Sunday afternoon, the two generals rode into the city at the head of a thousand men on foot. It is recalled that "General" Kelly sat on his horse in imitation of the pictures of the Saviour entering Jerusalem. He affected the postures of a self-imposed martyrdom. He was a wiry man with a keen eye, but an eye of uncertain gaze. There was about him the vagueness and vacuity of a fanatic. The long, ambling, and wavering procession of men was cheered by many, but by others the men were viewed in silence akin to unspoken pity. Tin cups and tin pans constituted their only paraphernalia. The homeless ones were not permitted to stop in the city; they were escorted to an improvised camp east of it, where an abandoned factory served them as a headquarters. Those who remained to visit with them found among them many men of human interest. They were not all outcasts or tramps. Among them were professional men and mechanics of high order. They were men who had left their homes because they had nothing else to do, and they were impelled by motives for which they themselves could not account. There were also fanatics of various kinds; dreamers, reformers, enthusiasts, and even lunatics, and young men, almost boys, whose interest was that of adventure.

But in Des Moines sympathetic and socialistic interest in the army soon began to wane. Being well fed and cared for, pitied and petted even, the men overstayed their welcome. At first it was suggested and then it was said that they ought to be going on. The charitable found it every day harder to provide so many hungry men with food. If they had a mission in Washington, why did they linger in Des Moines? But the railroads were obdurate. They would not provide them with free transportation. As for more marching, the men balked on that. They were foot-sore and weary, and had they not found a resting place where food was carried to them? "We are here, and what are you going to do about it?" became the attitude of the army. There was no work for them in Des Moines, even if they had been willing to work. There were idle men enough in the city. At last some one hit on a solution of the city's problem. It was to provide the men with rafts and let them float leisurely down the Des Moines to the Mississippi. To this the commanders of the army agreed. The lumber was provided and the rafts were built. And so on the morning of a hot summer's day, escorted by the sheriff, Joseph McGarraugh, they started down the river — and some of them tried to sing! The sheriff accompanied them to the border of Polk County, but even by that time many of the rafts had been stranded, for the water in the river was low, the channel tortuous and full of snags and sandbars. The farmers along the river were in some alarm and they loudly questioned the policy or even the right of Des Moines and the state to turn so many wandering men loose on the country.

The Iowa through which Kelly's "Industrial Army of the Commonwealth" passed that year was a desolate one, perhaps the most desolate in the history of the state. There was stagnation everywhere. It was the year of a great drouth. In many parts of the state it did not rain that summer for nearly two months. It was an affliction of nature added to the other afflictions of the time. In August, for three or four days the hot winds from the southwest, coming from the sandy plains five hundred or a thousand miles away, literally curled and shriveled up the blades of the corn. Even the leaves on the trees were left in a withered state. As a result there was a partial crop failure. The oats ran sparingly out of the threshing machines and the corn crop was reduced to almost half of a normal yield. Of corn only one hundred and twenty-eight millions of bushels were harvested, as compared with two hundred and eighty-five millions in the following year.[1] There was not corn enough to fatten the hogs for market and not enough forage to carry the horses and the cattle through the winter months. Cattle and hogs, as a result, were rushed to markets where there was no demand for them, and where prices were low. Hogs were sold below two dollars and a half for a hundred pounds. Good horses sold down to fifty dollars a head, and many more were sold for twenty dollars. Some of the older and more useless animals were killed to save them from starvation.

It was the year of the Gethsemane. Every one cried to Washington. But the government itself was as poor as the people. There was not enough money to pay the normal expenses of the government, and so bonds were sold to provide the necessary funds. The man who succeeded in placing the bonds, J. Pierpont Morgan — and he succeeded because he could both command and demand foreign credits — was denounced as an arch-traitor to his country. Some believed that he and his associates had brought on the panic to reap a financial harvest! The name of Grover Cleveland became anathema. It became the more so when he forced through congress the repeal of the Bland-Allison act, which financiers believed would strengthen the credit of the nation.

At that time a dreamer by the name of Harvey wrote a book which he presented and which thousands accepted as the solution of the riddle of the times. It was a sophistical book, called *Coin's Financial School.* Harvey took the whole nation to school, and the lesson he taught was, coin more silver into

[1] Gue's *History of Iowa,* Vol. III, p. 176.

money. Open the mints and flood the land with silver dollars so that any one could have them almost for the picking up — and then what? But many men did not reason to the what. They swallowed the sophistries and even reputable newspapers kept spreading them by republishing Harvey's doctrines. In due time a David appeared to combat with this free silver Goliath. He was George E. Roberts, known in Iowa as the editor of the Fort Dodge *Messenger*. He was then still a timid man, but he had a rare reasoning faculty and the power of clear and forceful expression. He called "Coin" Harvey himself on the schoolmaster's carpet, and refuted his sophistries and taught others — for "Coin" himself would not or could not learn — the honest A-B-C's of finance. He showed that what the people needed was earning and purchasing power; not more cheap silver dollars, but more earned dollars. Let labor create assets, not printing presses turn out liabilities. Mr. Roberts's book gained the author a reputation as an authoritative writer on business and finance.

And then came the year of judgment — 1896, a year that was eagerly awaited by the people as well as the politicians. It was the year of the presidential election — and every one still had faith that another American election had magic of some kind in it. But to begin with, there were divisions in both of the great parties. In the midst of industrial casualties they could not agree on the remedies. In Iowa both parties had candidates in the field for the presidential nomination — the Republicans put forward William B. Allison and the Democrats, Horace Boies. But when the Republicans held their national convention in St. Louis, they named William McKinley as their standard bearer, on a gold standard platform, but with more stress laid on the tariff. They proposed to open the mills instead of the mints. The gold standard produced a schism in the party. The western delegates, whose constituents had silver they were willing to sell, withdrew under the leadership of Senator Teller of Colorado. The withdrawal was a dramatic event — one hundred or more men rising in their seats and walking out of the convention hall in a body.

When the Democrats held their convention in Chicago,

Horace Boies was as completely forgotten as Mr. Allison had been in St. Louis, when a young man by the name of William Jennings Bryan of Nebraska swept the delegates from their feet and out of their senses by declaring that "You shall not press down on the brow of labor this crown of thorns," and "You shall not crucify mankind on a cross of gold." On that phrase Mr. Bryan was nominated for president in a delirium of enthusiasm that spread to all the surrounding country. If the election had been held the next day or the next week, he might have swept the country. But a long and arduous campaign of education followed, at the end of which William McKinley was overwhelmingly elected.

In Iowa there was at first consternation over the gold in the St. Louis platform. The state had been more or less committed to free silver, or at least to bi-metallism in some form. It was said there were only two wholly sound gold standard men in the Iowa congressional delegation, Mr. Updegraff of the Fourth district, and Mr. Cousins of the Fifth. Even Senator Allison was still tainted with the free silverism of the Bland-Allison act. The congressmen hastened to their districts to begin the new campaign of education, timidly at first, but more boldly as they began to realize that the people were not afraid of gold. The congressmen had underestimated through their own fears the courage and the intelligence of the people.

But there appeared in Iowa that year an unknown orator who won his first renown. He was Leslie M. Shaw, a lawyer of Denison. He was a banker as well as a lawyer and he had studied finance, as bankers seldom study it. He was a Vermont Yankee who had acquired a western idiom. He scattered no flowers of speech, but homely sayings — the truth expressed in words that all men could understand. He was literally the miracle man of the hustings that year. When the votes were counted, the fearful ones in the Republican party were surprised to find that in Iowa two hundred and ninety thousand votes had been cast for William McKinley and the gold platform, and only two hundred and twenty-four thousand for William J. Bryan and free silver.

# CHAPTER LXXVIII

## Education and Literary Progress

The financial and industrial conditions during the decade ending in 1897 retarded growth and progress. During many of the years the people were glad to eke out an existence. The Columbian Exposition held at Chicago in 1893, in which Iowa took a creditable part and to which people from the state flocked in thousands, gave an impetus to travel and study. The thoughts and the inventions of the whole world were unfolded before the gaze of all visitors. Many new ideas as well as new devices were carried back to the remotest corners, but with it all some moral filth also was broadcasted over the land. But, on the whole, it was a helpful and invigorating influence.

Two new devices that came into general use during these years need to be mentioned — the bicycle and the telephone. The first bicycles had one high wheel and one low one which served as a trailer, the rider sitting astride the high wheel. The equi-wheeled machine called at first the "safety" soon followed and with its introduction the use of the device became general. A simple device, a plaything and often no more than a pleasure vehicle, it still exerted a large influence in business and in industries. The telephone also was at first regarded as a mere plaything, and by many as a nuisance, but its development and adaptation to the uses of widely scattered peoples was rapid. Within a few years what were known as farmers' lines covered the state with a network of wires, and later these lines were combined into systems which made long distance talking possible. To talk with a neighbor, or to call a doctor over a wire saved many weary miles for both men and horses. Socially alone, the telephone was worth a great deal, especially to the women on the farms. To talk with a friend or neighbor about a sick baby, or even about a brood of chickens, was often a refreshing experience.

The most significant forward movement in both education and agriculture was made at Ames. For twenty years the college that had been established to promote scientific agriculture had languished. Politicians directed its affairs and conventional educators taught the lessons. In 1887 congress imparted some new influences by providing additional funds and by establishing agricultural experiment stations. But funds and laws were of little benefit without men to vitalize them. By 1890 the conditions had become so deplorable that the farmers of the state, among whom the college had become almost a by-word, through their various organizations united in a demand that the school be restored to the purposes for which it had been founded.

The outcome of this movement was the election of William M. Beardshear as president and James Wilson, known in politics as "Tama Jim," to distinguish him from another Wilson of concurrent political fame, as professor of agriculture, with two agricultural scientists, C. F. Curtiss and David Kent as his assistants. As a professor, Mr. Wilson himself was an experiment. He was not a college bred man, and his knowledge of agriculture was experimental rather than scientific. He had farmed in Tama County since he had come as a boy to Iowa. He had developed distinct theories of agriculture and being possessed of a missionary spirit he had exploited them in a newspaper at Traer. He was sent to the state legislature and then to congress where he developed a capacity for public service that made him a marked man. In his college work he supplied enthusiasm, and projects and purposes, and his young assistants furnished the theories and the science. The combination of talents produced marvelous results in a short time. President Beardshear added a superb educational administration. He was a man with the heart of a boy. He opened the doors of the college to many who had before shunned it. Under the new régime, manhood was blended with science and science with manhood. To farming they added scientific and speculative interest, and the zest of a business pursuit. The college grew in prestige and influence by leaps and bounds. There is no other single development in the state at that time that deserves more to be written into history.

In connection with the State University, Dr. Samuel Calvin was doing notable writing on scientific subjects. Long noted as an educator, he wrote a series of articles and monographs on geological subjects that attracted national attention by reason of both their literary brilliancy and scientific worth. Dr. Calvin was born in Scotland, but he was reborn in Iowa. Coming to the state, with his parents, before the war, he worked for a time at the carpenter's bench. He drifted into Hopkinton College, where he became a professor. In 1874 he was called to the State University as the head of the scientific schools, specializing in geology. In 1882, when he was at the height of his fame, he was made state geologist. In his writings he re-created the Iowa that lies buried in the rocks of the ages. It was a distinct and distinguished contribution to the literature that is accredited to Iowa. Associated with him were two men who have added to these literary contributions as well as to scientific research, Dr. Thomas H. MacBride, and Professor Bohumil Shimek. At Cedar Falls, Homer H. Seerley was placed in charge of the college for teachers, in 1886, giving it new scholastic and literary prestige.

Of literary development there is not much to record. Books were written in Iowa, but they did not belong to literature. At that time it might have been asked, Who reads an Iowa book? A state so productive and progressive in other ways could boast little or nothing in these fields of higher endeavor. Johnson Brigham, who had been editor of the Cedar Rapids *Republican,* and a man of both taste and achievement in literature, felt the lack of the literary spirit in the state and undertook to foster it by establishing the *Midland Monthly,* in Des Moines, which he fondly hoped to make for the people of Iowa a literary medium. The magazine was an ambitious effort and it was well-born, for the editor's taste was discriminating. In the course of a few years many notable articles were printed in its pages, but for want of support and interest in so worthy an effort, it soon began to languish and finally perished, Mr. Brigham transferring his services to the conduct of the State Library by appointment of Governor Shaw.

Working in connection with that library, Charles Aldrich was making extensive literary and historical collections. He revived the old *Annals of Iowa*, and in what was styled the third series thereof, he published source materials on the history of the state that have become of inestimable value. His work became the foundation of the State Historical Department for which a commemorative building was later erected. Mr. Aldrich was in many ways a successor to Mr. Parvin, who was still continuing his work in connection with the Masonic Library which he had founded in Cedar Rapids, and which remains one of the ranking institutions of its kind in the world. Mr. Aldrich was well fitted for the work he undertook to do. He was himself a pioneer editor of the state, a man of never satiated curiosity and of indefatigable industry.

A somewhat similar but more analytical work was at the same time being done at Iowa City by the State Historical Society which had been founded in 1857. In 1895, Benjamin F. Shambaugh became professor of political science in the State University and subsequently superintendent of the society and editor of *The Iowa Journal of History and Politics*, an organ of research and applied history. Dr. Shambaugh devoted himself to writing and edited much state documentary material. In recent years he has directed the work of many historical investigators and writers. The publications of the society today constitute an Iowa library in themselves. Dr. Shambaugh has added scientific research and scholarship to the industry of Mr. Parvin and Mr. Aldrich.

Of historical writings there was no dearth. In connection with the Columbian celebrations, Dr. William Salter published a volume on *Iowa, the First Free State in the Louisiana Purchase,* a series of connected papers, constituting a purposeful history of the state. His *Life of James W. Grimes*, published as early as 1876, had already become an Iowa classic. It was biography written in the form of autobiography. In 1888, upon his return from a long consular service in Europe, Major S. H. M. Byers, the author of *Sherman's March to the*

*Sea,* undertook to re-write the history of the Civil War under the title of *Iowa in War Times.* The word "re-write" is used because Iowa's part in that war had already been exhaustively treated in *Iowa in the Rebellion,* written by Lurton Dunham Ingersoll and published in 1866. Mr. Ingersoll was a distinguished war correspondent. He wrote his monumental volume from actual contact with the regiments and battles he described. He was a fluent writer and many of his descriptions are unsurpassed. Major Byers in writing his history seems to have had in mind his own sufferings in the Columbia prison where he composed his famous war ballad, and he recalled the acts of those who were disloyal at home while the men in blue uniforms were fighting to preserve the Union, and often he expressed himself in bitterness that marred the historical tone of his work. William Larrabee, after retiring from the governorship, published a volume on *The Railroad Question,* that may be ranked as both history and economics. He epitomized the history of railroading to set forth his own positive views on their management and operation as factors in the industrial life of the people. Though somewhat controversial, his viewpoint was so authoritative that his volume was extensively used as a college text book. At that time Benjamin F. Gue, who had played a conspicuous minor part in the politics of the state, was engaged in writing a history of the state which he later published in four volumes. His writing was done at separated intervals and while, partly for that reason, it often lacks continuity and literary definiteness, it is none the less a monumental work, and for the period immediately following the Civil War, and before it, it has authoritative source material, for he himself was an actor in those events. Irving B. Richman appeared with a slight volume on *John Brown Among the Quakers, and Other Sketches,* and later he published a noted analytical history of the state of Rhode Island.

A man in a class by himself during this period was Robert J. Burdette, familiarly known as "Bob" Burdette. He was in the direct line of the great humorists of the American press. He began as a local editor on the Burlington *Hawk-Eye,* a paper which he made famous. His humor was human and genial, depending on no mere tricks of spelling or phraseology. He soon severed his connection with the Iowa paper and entered the fields of lecturer and author, and while successful in both undertakings, his humor lost some of its spontaneity and effect when transplanted from the settings of daily journalism. In his later years Mr. Burdette entered the ministry and for a time filled a Baptist pulpit in Los Angeles.

A volume of poems, *Toil and Triumph*, published during this period by J. L. McCreery, is interesting, if not noteworthy, because it contained the poem, "There is no Death," beginning, "There is no death! the stars go down to rise upon some other shore," a piece with a literary history. According to the author's own account, he wrote it in 1863, while he was editor of the *Delaware County Journal*.[1] It was printed in the July number of *Arthur's Home Magazine*, where it seems to have attracted attention, for it inspired some one to write a rhapsody on "Immortality," which he closed with this poem, attaching to the whole article the name of "Eugene Bulmer," which the printers reduced to "E. Bulmer." In due time some editor with a penchant for correcting errors, printed the name as "E. Bulwer." When Harper Brothers printed their *Fifth Reader* they used this poem and credited it to Lord Lytton, meaning Sir Edward Bulwer Lytton, the English author, a mistake which they corrected after correspondence. But as late as 1889, the authorship of this poem was one of the questions in literature submitted by *Lippincott's Magazine*, which resulted in the conclusion that McCreery was entitled to the honor of its authorship.[2] The poem is one of intrinsic merit, but the controversies, no doubt, added to its prestige, as did its association with the name of the distinguished author of England.

Another poem of somewhat similar fame, and even greater age was "The Little Brown Church in the Vale," which has passed into popular hymnology and was extensively used by the glee clubs of that period. It was composed in 1857, by Dr. W. S. Pitts, a student and teacher of music. The lines

1 *Annals of Iowa*, Third Series, Vol. I, p. 196.

2 *Lippincott's Magazine*, June, 1889, p. 918.

were inspired by a little church in Bradford, Chickasaw County, where an academy was founded and flourished for a time. The school has passed away, but the poem still lives and the church itself, typical of pioneer times, has been preserved as a shrine, literary and historical.[3]

But the first great note in what may be called Iowa literature was struck by Hamlin Garland, who made his debut in letters about 1887. Born in Wisconsin, he came with his parents to Mitchell County, where he grew up on a farm and received a preliminary higher education in the academy at Osage. His father interested himself deeply in the Grange movement, and when the chinch bugs destroyed the wheat fields of Iowa, he went with the immigration of that period to South Dakota where he resumed his occupation as a wheat grower, but with disastrous results. The son shared in the agrarian discontent of those days and espoused Populism. He drifted to Boston where he was brought into fortunate literary contacts and became a follower of William Dean Howells, who was then developing his school of realism in fiction. Young Garland thought of the stage as a career and he tried lecturing for a living. Finally, while in search of an ambitious career, a friend suggested to him to try writing fiction. He was urged to undertake to do for western life what Mr. Howells was doing in New England. At first he feared that he could not "manage the dialogue" part of such writing.

But with that idea in his mind he came to re-visit Iowa after a prolonged absence. As he re-crossed the Mississippi his imagination was stirred by thoughts of "The redman's canoe, the explorer's bateau, the hunter's lodge, the emigrant's cabin," all of which he associated with the "romance of the immemorial river." He must have been almost persuaded to become a writer of historical romances. But when farther on he began to see "the lonely box-like farm houses on the ridges," and thought of the drudgeries and the meager livings of the settlers, of his father bent with labors and his mother spiritually exhausted by ceaseless household cares in crude surroundings, the romance went out of his thoughts, and the

[3] *Midland Monthly*, Vol. V, p. 310.

hard and harsh realism of life came into them. He felt embittered against man's institutions and almost against life itself. Even "the Cedar rippling over its limestone ledges" between Charles City and Osage could not bring the music of beauty or gladness back into his soul. When he shook hands with his old time friends he felt only their "hard crooked fingers" and the "heavy knuckles."[4] He contrasted them with the soft hand of Edwin Booth, which he had been privileged to touch in Boston, and with "the flower-like palm of Helena Modjeska." He was like the poor child who having supped with the fairies in her dreams could not relish her homely porridge the next morning.

It was in this state of mind, in this rebellion of spirit, that he began to write his first stories of mid-western and Iowa life, which he printed under the title of *Main Travelled Roads.* His roads were real enough. When it did not rain they were covered with "the bitter and burning dust," and when it did rain they were "the foul and trampled slush." At one end of these dreary stretches there was "a dull little town" and at the other end "a home of toil." And those who did the toiling did so "hopelessly and cheerlessly to make the wealth that enriches the alien and the idler and impoverishes the producer." We have here the creed of the Populists — Garland's writings were Populism turned into realistic literature. When his master, Mr. Howells, reviewed these writings, he said that his disciple in the west still had "to learn that though the thistle is full of unrecognized poetry, the rose has a poetry, too, that even overpraise cannot spoil." Mr. Garland had gathered the thistles to make his literary bouquets, although at that time there were still wild roses that bloomed in his land.

But morose as his thoughts were, and pessimistic his Populistic preachings, Mr. Garland wrote well. His descriptions of farm life were good. In threshing time he wrote of the "beautiful yellow straw entering the cylinders," and of "the clear yellow-brown wheat" pulsing out of the side of the machines. The "pulsing" movement can be recalled by every farm boy of those days. In one of his first stories the young

[4] Hamlin Garland's *A Son of the Middle Border*, Chapter XXVIII.

man who pitches the sheaves from the stack quarrels with the blue-eyed girl who works in the kitchen to feed the hungry men, and as a result he runs away without leaving a trace of himself. Years afterwards he returned to find her the wife of the other man in the story, a greedy, grubbing, profane man who was grinding the life out of her. The old lover persuades her to run away with him, deserting her husband and home, but taking the baby with them. That was the price of emancipation and spiritual freedom.

The women in the stories all seem "tied right down to a churn or dishpan." Every one is engaged in an almost hopeless "struggle for a place to stand on the planet." Something is "eating the heart and soul out of men and women in the city, just as in the country."[5] "Mortgages are scattered all over Cedar County." The men can not stand upright to breathe, they are so ground down, and one woman boasts that she is "jest as lame in one laig as t'other"—the dialect is necessary to the realism, although it was probably more imaginary than real. If the folks in these stories can do nothing more they at least clip their "g's" in fictional conversations. One woman is made to speak of herself as just "rackin' around somehow, just like a foundered horse." Everywhere in these tales we encounter "the ferocity of labor," although farmers used to say of their neighbors that they idled away much of their time. The slaves of the old Roman galleys are invoked to make horrible comparisons, or contrasts, for, on the whole, they were better off than those who toiled in the fields of the middle west in those days.[6] The author should have called his stories *Les Miserables,* they are so full of miserableness.

There is so much of all this, that we shall not follow it. Much of it is fiction in more senses than one. Such things were findable in the west of that period — just as they are findable in all places and in all times. But to return to Mr. Howells's admonition, there were roses as well as thistles, and to leave them out was not to write realism for that must imply

[5] *Main-Travelled Roads,* "Up the Cooly."
[6] *Ibid.,* "Under the Lion's Paw."

all the things which are real, the whole constituting the truth, and parts of it constituting distortions of it. All men were not so hopeless as the Populists were in their platforms, and all the women were not lame in both "laigs." There were men who whistled behind the plows, and women who listened to the thrushes and the larks, and who had time to look for violets and to admire the lilies of the prairies which were as fair as the lilies of the fields which Christ moralized into fame in Judea. It is to be regretted that the first interpreter of Iowa life wrote out of the heart of Populism, which was a creed of discontent that soon died in the mouths of its exponents — but in literary form it has some immortality. Those who did not know Iowa, accepted it as the whole truth and so the ban and brand of ugliness and sordidness was placed on a region of natural beauty and on men and women who abounded in generosity.

Concurrently with Mr. Garland, Miss Alice French of Davenport, under the pen name of Octave Thanet, made her debut in the literary world. She caught popular favor and received critical approval in a series of stories which included *Knitters in the Sun*, in 1887, *Expiation*, in 1890, and *Stories of a Western Town*, in 1893. A gifted and talented woman by nature, and finely educated, Miss French told her stories and portrayed her characters with a delicacy of touch and keenness of insight that continue to hold the readers of them. But, unfortunately for her state, she dealt but little with Iowa subjects, and she did nothing with her literary sanity and mental and moral wholesomeness to set right what Mr. Garland had set so awry. Eventually she became almost more southern than mid-western, but her name and fame will always be associated with Iowa in literature.

# PART IX

## "Unto This Last"

(1897-1920)

# CHAPTER LXXIX

## A New Beginning

The country accepted the election of William McKinley as a settlement of its financial and industrial issues. The single gold standard was recognized, and for the third time in a decade, the tariff was revised, the new law bearing the name of Dingley, after Nelson Dingley, a congressman from the state of Maine who was chairman of the committee that framed the bill. After years of political turmoil over these two questions, the people were glad to return to work, and soon the song of prosperity was heard all over the land. The new prosperity was psychological, and not altogether political, but the national administration received the credit for it.

President McKinley called two Iowa men to high places in his administration, James, "Tama Jim," Wilson to be secretary of agriculture, and George E. Roberts, director of the mint. Mr. Roberts owed his appointment to the book which he had written, and Mr. Wilson was selected wholly on his merits. He was the president's own choice for the office. The two men had served together in congress, and Mr. Wilson's fame as a professor of agriculture at Ames had extended far beyond his own state. When he was summoned to Canton, Ohio, to meet the president-elect, Mr. Wilson was touring and lecturing on the first dairy train operated in the state, or the country. The idea of running a train with exhibits and lecturers to arouse interest in dairy farming was evolved by E. F. Farmer, then an assistant freight agent of the Minneapolis and St. Louis Railroad.[1] Prices at that time were so low that it was profitable for neither the farmers nor the railroads to haul the crude products of the farms to market. The underlying theory was that farmers were wasting their resources selling raw products,

[1] Wallace's *Uncle Henry's Own Story*, Vol. III, p. 79.

and the railroads their car space hauling them. When Mr. Wilson opened his office in Washington he found in it a few roll-top desks and a few antiquated scientists who were doing, they hardly knew what. The practical application of the energies of the government to the promotion of agriculture was the unsolved problem that confronted the new secretary. The Iowa farmer and college professor was to do for this greatest of all industries what Alexander Hamilton had done for the national finances. He proceeded to do it.

In Iowa, Governor Drake announced that he would not be a candidate for reëlection. His short administration of two years began in a time of gloom, and it ended in a time of returned gladness. His administration had been successful in all its undertakings. An historic incident in it was the launching of the battleship Iowa, which was christened by Mary Lord Drake, the youngest daughter of the governor, at the Cramp shipyard near Philadelphia. Captain Robley D. Evans, "Fighting Bob," commanded the ship in the war which was soon to follow.

The Republican party was again in high favor, and many men sought the nomination for the office which Governor Drake had renounced. Matt Parrott of Waterloo, then lieutenant governor, was at first the preferred candidate of the politicians. He had long been prominent in state affairs, serving in the senate with distinction. A. B. Funk of Spirit Lake and J. B. Harsh of Creston, who also had made distinguished careers in the senate, announced themselves as candidates; also H. W. Byers of Harlan, who had been speaker of the house, W. E. Fuller of West Union, a former congressman, and finally Leslie M. Shaw of Denison, a new man in state politics, and one who had no other claim or credentials than the series of sound money speeches which he had made in the memorable campaign of 1896.

The state convention, which was held in Cedar Rapids, was so largely attended by delegates and visitors that to accommodate all it was held in a tent on the campus of Coe College. Among the candidates it was the "field" against Mr. Parrott. Mr. Shaw was the "dark horse" in the race. The slogan of his supporters was "Keep an eye on Shaw," borrowed from a cryptic and epigrammatic editorial which had been printed in the *State Register.* It soon endowed his candidacy with the prestige of success. It was said in vain that he was a new man and that the party owed him nothing. But nothing could stop the triumphal progress of the new man, and on the third ballot in the convention he was nominated, receiving seven hundred and ninety-three votes, which was two hundred more than two principal competitors combined received.

In the general assembly of 1898, by far the most important bill passed was the one creating the State Board of Control, into whose care and keeping all the state institutions, with the exception of the educational ones, were placed. The old system of separate boards for each had long been unsatisfactory. Appropriations were made by favor and through legislative bargaining. The communities affected and the various boards were at first opposed to the change, the credit for which belonged largely to Thomas D. Healy, a senator from Fort Dodge, a brilliant young man whose possible career in political life was cut short by an early death. Governor Shaw called to serve on this board former Governor Larrabee, as its chairman, and John Cownie and L. G. Kinne. Mr. Larrabee was reluctant to reënter public service, but he was made to see that it was his duty to do so. He accepted the office on the understanding that he should be permitted to resign as soon as the work had been well organized, which he did at the end of two years, returning to the public all moneys paid him, above his expenses, in the form of a gift to one of the institutions. Mr. Cownie was a farmer and a business man, and Mr. Kinne had been eminent as a judge on the bench of the supreme court. No board was ever better constituted for so important a work.

In the meantime there had been increasing friction between the United States and Spain over Cuba, where Spain had maintained a medieval colonial government which had long harassed the peace of the island. On the fifteenth of February, 1898, an American battleship, the Maine, lying in the harbor of the city of Havana, was blown up, killing a large number of sailors. The war ship had been anchored in a place designated by the Spanish authorities, and it was believed that it had been over a submarine mine. But others believed that the explosion was internal and accidental. The event made an American furore. Retribution and even vengeance were demanded through a large portion of the press. President McKinley remained calm and counselled caution. A naval court of inquiry soon reached the conclusion that the ship had been blown up by design, by Spaniards if not by the Spanish authorities. It had been their answer to American interference in the affairs of Cuba. There followed a popular clamor for war against Spain. "Cuba libre" became the cry of the press and of all the radicals in congress. Free the oppressed of Cuba. Rid America of a menace in her ocean dooryard. Such were the cries from one end of the country to the other. In the White House, the president hesitated. He had served in one war and he abhorred all wars. He thought a peaceful settlement was still possible. Then they cried all the more, saying that the president lacked sympathy for the distressed and courage to defend American honor.

In that tense hour an Iowa congressman, Robert G. Cousins, delivered a brief speech on the floor of the house of representatives that electrified the whole country. Already famous as an orator, he awoke the next morning to find his fame national, and even international. In length the speech was a mere trifle, hardly longer than Lincoln's Gettysburg Address. But in substance and in spirit it was tremendous. Every word of it was in its place, and every sentence had a meaning. It read like a poem, and it flashed like lightning. It touched the hearts of America because it was a tribute to Americans who had gone down to death at their posts of duty. It was the simile of the American eagle guarding his own, circling over the scene of desolation where a lifeless hull projected over the waters, marking the burial place of the dead. Mr. Cousins added even to the fame of Kipling by quoting his admonition, "Lest we forget, lest we forget." Both the occasion and the matter made it one of the great little speeches in American oratory.

But the American people did not forget. The president, still solicitous for peace, if that were possible, referred the matter to congress, and congress replied with a declaration of war, April twenty-fifth, 1898. In Iowa this act was well received. The legislature had already placed half a million dollars at the disposal of the governor for any needful purposes. The first requisition for troops from the state included three regiments of infantry and two light batteries. But Iowa clamored for more recognition. The state had four regiments in the National Guard organization and she wanted all to be called. The war department assented to this, but eliminated the batteries, and limited the regiments to eight hundred and thirty-four men each. But later this number was increased to thirteen hundred and thirty-six men each, and the two batteries also were restored to the state's quota. The four regiments were promptly renumbered the Forty-ninth, Fiftieth, Fifty-first, and Fifty-second, the numbering beginning where it had been left off in the Civil War.

The regiments were assembled at Des Moines to await the orders of the government. The pride and panoply of war filled the state capital. Governor Shaw and the adjutant general, Melvin H. Byers, served the soldiers in camp in every way possible. On the eleventh of June, the Forty-ninth regiment, Col. W. G. Dows commanding, left for Jacksonville, Florida, where it was assigned to the third brigade of the second division, seventh army corps. It was taken to Cuba, December nineteenth, after tedious waiting, but it was only to witness the evacuation of Havana by the Spaniards. The regiment remained on duty during the winter and was mustered out in April, 1899. The Fiftieth Regiment, Colonel Douglas V. Jackson commanding, left for Camp Cuba Libre, Jacksonville, Florida, on May twenty-first and was returned in September, without having seen the Cuban shores. The Fifty-first Regiment, Colonel John C. Loper commanding, left Des Moines June fifth, going to San Francisco, where it was kept at the Presidio until November third, when it was transported to the Philippine Islands, where it was landed on December seventh. First at Ilolo and then at Cavité, the regiment participated in skirmishes, but all of them minor ones. During the Filipino insurrections, the regiment was in eight distinct engagements with the enemy. On September sixth, 1899, the regiment was returned to Manila and to San Francisco, October twenty-second, and was mustered out, December second. The welcome home at Des Moines, four days later, was made a memorable event with speeches by Governor Shaw and former Governor Jackson. The Fifty-second Regiment, Colonel W. B. Humphrey commanding, left Des Moines May twenty-eighth and was taken to Camp McKinley, Chickamauga Park, where it was kept until the twenty-eighth of August when it was returned to Des Moines. The camp was poorly located and the regiment suffered severely from typhoid fever in consequence. The two batteries, the Fifth, Captain George W. Bever commanding, and the Sixth, Captain Frank S. Long commanding, were both mustered in July eighth at Des Moines and mustered out on September fifth, without further service. Captain Frank E. Lyman was in command of a signal corps which was privileged to see actual service, and Captain Amos W. Brandt was in command of a company of colored immunes, attached to the Seventh U. S. Volunteer Infantry, but without being called upon for actual war duties.

The war was a short one and its battles were fought largely by the naval forces, under Admiral Dewey in Philippine and under Admiral Sampson in Cuban waters. The losses of the Iowa regiments were about two hundred, through camp diseases. Only one man, a member of the Fifty-second, the regiment that served in the Philippine Islands, was killed in actual warfare.

# CHAPTER LXXX

## AN ERA OF GOOD WILL AND PROGRESS

A few ugly scandals, growing out of the conduct of the war, followed the declaration of peace. There were also problems to be solved in connection with the disposition and administration of the freed islands, Cuba, Porto Rico, and the Philippines. A period of good will and prosperity followed which was almost likened to the golden age of tradition. Nationally, it was not the consciousness of a victory won, but the consciousness of a duty done without material reward exacted. Even the Philippine Islands were held in trust, to be given self-government as soon as the people were fitted for such duties, and Spain was paid liberally for whatever property rights she had held in them.

The twenty years that have since elapsed are crowded with great events in history, but what happened in Iowa is much of it still happening and the actors in it are still living. A mere running account will suffice for the present — historical judgment must be pronounced later, and by others.

In those happy and abundant days there was brought to Davenport the first horseless vehicle, a plaything of that day, but something that has revolutionized the world of travel and transportation. It was called a locomobile, and its motive power was steam. It was built like a horse buggy, with the dashboard included. The device was laughed at, and its owner soon grew tired of it for he sold it for one thousand dollars to Willis G. Haskell of Cedar Rapids. Mr. Haskell was cradled in Chickasaw County, in the days of the last Indian uprisings in northern Iowa. He had in him left over from a former generation the spirit of a pioneer. He was the embodiment of the eternal boyhood which Mr. Barrie later sublimated in his Peter Pan. And so the discarded plaything of one man became the prized possession of another. He succeeded in bringing the contrivance on its own wheels to Cedar Rapids. In a spirit of adventure he started with it to the state fair in Des Moines, reaching the end of a toilsome journey on the second day.

About the same time, in 1899, another Cedar Rapids man, Colonel William G. Dows, returning from the war in Cuba, seeking the adventures which had been denied him in the war, purchased and brought to Iowa a Haynes gasoline car, probably the first operated in the state. It was in 1893 that Elwood Haynes had invented the first car propelled by gasoline, which is now one of the nation's curiosities in the Smithsonian Institution in Washington. His car was not perfect; on the contrary, it was full of troubles. It was ridiculed and denounced. Even if it could be perfected so it would run, it would still amount to nothing, so the wise men said. For one thing, its use on the roads would be forever forbidden, because it would be a menace to horses, and were not the roads made for horses? It was not dreamed that horse sense would ever be developed enough to withstand the shock of horseless vehicles on the roads. But such have been the arguments against new devices and the impediments on the road to human progress! So little and so slowly had this idea of unlimited possibilities progressed, that in 1899 Colonel Dows was able to buy number sixteen in the output of the Haynes factory. When the car was taken into the country, its advent was like the coming of a circus in the olden days. Hundreds came to see it and the rural schools along the roads traversed were dismissed. Men had to be sent ahead to help farmers restrain their horses from running away on the approach of the monster. Even with such precautions there were runaways. Many cursed it and vowed they would see to it that laws were made in Des Moines to keep such contrivances off the roads. The little district fair held at Fairfax in Linn County in 1899 is historic because it was there that steam and gasoline competed for supremacy in the horseless world.

Little did the spectators at that fair dream then that within two decades every tenth person in the state of Iowa would be operating such cars. If any one had at that time predicted the half of what has been developed out of those primitive horseless devices, he would have been deemed fit for an insane asylum. But so is the future ever hidden from the present, and industrial revolutions also come unawares.

It was only a few years later, in 1904, that a first impetus was imparted to the making of better roads, an idea that has grown with the development of the automobile and the motor truck. In that year a man from Missouri, D. Ward King, who had invented a road drag, was brought to Iowa under the auspices of R. H. Aishton, of the Chicago and Northwestern Railroad Company. A special train was made up to carry the drags and the lecturers, including Mr. King. The first of a series of meetings was held at Onawa and the last at DeWitt. The coming of the train was widely advertised and thousands gathered to see the new device and its application to road making. It was simple enough, too, a split-log dragged at such an angle that it elevated the loose dirt toward the center of the road, filling at the same time the crevices and smoothing the entire surface. But simple as it was, it has never been improved upon, though in many ways modified, for the upkeep of dirt roads. It was the harbinger of the improved roads which were destined to become the furore of the horseless era. It was then still too early for any one to think, much less to speak, of paved country roads. In a world which is to be filled again with the strife of politics we must not lose sight of the humble beginnings that are of much more meaning in the affairs of men.

# CHAPTER LXXXI

## Slates Smashed and Scores Settled

Governor Shaw was reëlected in 1899, on the theory that one good term in office should be followed by another. But Senator Gear's first term in the senate was about to expire. He was an old man and his health had become enfeebled. The politicians were well aware of this. He had been a diligent and an efficient senator, ever mindful of the least of the wishes of his constituents. But he was not accounted a great senator. He was a practical politician and a utilitarian legislator. Mr. Cummins, who had opposed him in his first election, early announced himself as a candidate for his seat. In 1896, Mr. Cummins had succeeded James S. Clarkson, who had removed his home to New York, as Iowa member of the Republican National Committee. The position was one of influence and through it he had made himself the leader of a numerous personal following, made up largely of younger men who had aspirations in public life, and of older men who had been disappointed in their ambitions. Senator Gear's own political friends, or many of them, wished that he would step aside and permit them to win the battle with a man who would outlast his own victory. They were politically wise enough to realize that with overwhelming party majorities and conflicting ambitions there would be two factions in the Republican party of the state, and Senator Gear was too old to serve as a leader of one. The contest over the senatorship was fought out in the legislative districts in 1899, and in the general assembly which met in 1900. The preliminary victory was won by the Gear men in the election of Dr. D. H. Bowen of Allamakee County over Willard L. Eaton of Mitchell, as speaker of the house. The reëlection of Gear followed, but on a close vote.

In 1900 the Republicans of Iowa entered the presidential

campaign by presenting Mr. Dolliver as a candidate for vice president. It was known that President McKinley looked with favor on this movement. The Iowa outlook wore the aspect of victory until the name of Colonel Theodore Roosevelt was suggested for the same nomination. He had come home from the Spanish War the most visible hero among the land fighters. He had been triumphantly elected governor of New York, and he was already regarded as of presidential proportions. The colonel himself at first looked with disfavor on the second place on the ticket. He spoke of it as a place of political burial. But the politicians of New York, whose plans had been disturbed by the aggressive and militant governor, were in favor of that sort of an interment for him. They clamored for his nomination, and when he still refused, they made more clamor. The result was that Colonel Roosevelt was forced to yield, nor was the yielding entirely unwilling, for the glamor of even the second place was alluring to him. The Dolliver candidacy, which at one time had so much hope in it, was thus automatically cancelled, and Lafayette Young who was to have presented him to the convention, re-wrote his speech and made it serve instead the candidacy of Colonel Roosevelt, who was elected vice president and within a year, through the assassination of Mr. McKinley, became president. Mr. Dolliver might have been that president.

But if Mr. Dolliver lost both the vice presidency and the presidency, by the death of Senator Gear in 1901 he found himself lifted into the United States senate through appointment by Governor Shaw. For the governor, the death of Senator Gear was most inopportune. He had his own eyes fixed on a seat in the senate. But it became his official duty to appoint another man to the seat he coveted. Factional lines in Iowa had not yet been wholly hardened, or even defined, and an alternative proposition was presented and that was to appoint Mr. Cummins, in return for which Mr. Cummins and his friends would later help the governor to achieve Senator Allison's seat. But that course involved some risks. It was akin to exchanging a bird in the hand for one in the bush.

And it would leave out of the accounting the immense popularity of Mr. Dolliver. By this appointment, Governor Shaw closed the doors of the senate to himself, for the two men belonged to the same congressional district. Senator Dolliver could boast that his high office cost him only two cents, the price of a postage stamp on a letter thanking the governor for the honor conferred on him.

But in the making of that appointment the factional die was cast in Iowa Republican politics. If Governor Shaw felt that he had closed the senatorial door on himself, Mr. Cummins felt that it had been slammed shut in his face. He felt that he had nothing to hope for at the hands of the men who seemed to control the destinies of Iowa politics, or who at least seemed to control the distribution of the offices. But if no doors would open for him, perhaps he could force them open. If the magic circle of power would not admit him, perhaps he could break the circle itself and reshape the fragments of it into a halo for his own head. He did not wait long to perfect his plans. He announced himself as a candidate for the nomination for governor to succeed Mr. Shaw. To his friends he admitted that he did not care for the governorship itself, but that he would use it as a stepping-stone to the senate, on which his heart had been set since 1893. His announcement was sensational, and his coming out was more sensational. A monster meeting was staged for him in Des Moines in which he formally defied the men who, so he charged, had conspired to keep him out of office. He said that instead of asking permission of Messrs. Blythe and Hubbard, who were the most visible representatives of what was still called the railroad power in Iowa politics, he would appeal to the people direct.

Mr. Cummins's dramatic announcement covered his opponents with so much confusion that they could not concentrate on one candidate to oppose him. The alternative course was to place several candidates in the field, each one selected for his strength in a particular part of the state and then to concentrate the delegates to the convention so elected on one man. It was a hazardous policy, and it proved a disastrous one. The two strongest candidates in the opposition to Mr. Cummins were James H. Trewin of Allamakee County, later of Linn, and W. F. Harriman of Hampton. Both were men of distinction in Iowa politics. Mr. Trewin had been chief maker of the Code of 1897, a creditable piece of work, and with Thomas D. Healy had shared in the leadership of the senate. Edwin H. Conger was at that time on his way home from China where he had served as United States minister during the Boxer Rebellion, winning an international fame by his fine conduct of American affairs. The politicians saw in him possibilities for the campaign. Major Conger's candidacy was therefore launched in heroic ways, but the effort to capitalize his foreign fame did not meet with much response, if it met entirely with his own approval, which was doubtful. Only forty-two votes were secured in his name, while Mr. Trewin received three hundred and sixty-nine and Mr. Harriman three hundred and fifty-nine, but the three combined had not enough to offset Mr. Cummins's eight hundred and sixty votes. Mr. Cummins's first victory was so overwhelming that it left the opposition to him in a disorganized condition.

In re-writing the Republican platform that year the victors laid stress on reciprocity, then a current but still somewhat academic idea, and they stipulated that tariff schedules should not be so high as to afford shelter for monopolies. This was branded as "the Iowa idea," but they disavowed any differentiation of party doctrine.[1] The Democrats that year nominated as their candidate for governor T. J. Phillips of Ottumwa, a man who amounted to nothing politically and whose only fame was notoriety. Mr. Cummins in the election had eighty thousand votes to spare, although the prohibitionists that year polled over sixteen thousand votes.

As the incoming governor was elated, so the outgoing governor was depressed, for in some ways the sudden and overwhelming vogue of Mr. Cummins was interpreted by many as a condemnation of his rejection for the senate. But unexpectedly, President Roosevelt called Governor Shaw to the

[1] At the McKinley birthday banquet, Omaha, 1903, Governor Cummins said: "There is no 'Iowa idea,' if that phrase is meant to convey that the Republicans of my state hold any idea that distinguishes them from the Republicans of other states." He styled it a mere epigram.

exalted office of secretary of the treasury, to succeed Lyman J. Gage, who had resigned. In an instant the halo was transferred to the other head. The man who had been a country banker five years before was exalted to the seat of Alexander Hamilton. It was the ever recurring miracle of American politics. The politicians in Iowa did not comprehend it. Only President Roosevelt knew. He had heard Leslie M. Shaw expound finances — it was in South Dakota — and that one hearing fixed him in his mind as a man fit for the office to which he called him. The tender to Mr. Shaw came through Senator Allison and it was with the assurance that his entrance into the cabinet would in nowise affect Mr. Wilson's seat as secretary of agriculture — Iowa was to have two places in the cabinet instead of one.

But while Albert B. Cummins was more than ever thinking of the senatorship, and while the presidency itself was not beyond the dreams of Leslie M. Shaw, another Iowa man in an exalted place, Colonel David B. Henderson, surprised the state and the nation in 1902 with the announcement that he would not be a candidate for reëlection to congress. He had represented the Third district for twenty years and he was then serving his second term as speaker of the house, the highest office within the reach of a man of foreign birth. It was a bare announcement and the politicians were left free to speculate on the reasons for such an act. It was said an old army wound was distressing him.[2] Others said he wanted to mend his private fortunes by the practice of law in New York. But a cryptic sentence, "Let the new lights shine," was interpreted to mean that he was in a state of protest and even disgust over some of the new ideas which were being written into party platforms to serve factional ends. Colonel Henderson served out his term as speaker, at the end of which he was given a farewell in Washington such as few men had ever received.

In the office of governor, Mr. Cummins was a commanding figure. He was a governor in fact, and he spoke and acted like one. If his eyes were constantly fixed on Washington, he did

[2] This explanation of Henderson's resignation was given by Judge Oliver P. Shiras of Dubuque.

not neglect the state's business. But while he served the state he also served his own ambitions. He soon reclothed himself in the railroad issue which Governor Larrabee had created. In his second inaugural he made an appeal for national recognition by an extreme advocacy of reciprocity, which was some indefinite system of fair and equal international trade, something more than free trade and less than protection. He also espoused the primary system of making nominations and he used that as a tribute he paid to the people.

By a change from annual to biennial elections, Governor Cummins's second term was lengthened to three years, but when the five years were up, the senatorship was still in the offing and the prospect of an interment as ex-governor was before him. George D. Perkins, the editor of the Sioux City *Journal*, with a good career in congress behind him, looked with favor on the governorship and he was persuaded to announce himself as a candidate, if not on the solicitation at least with the approval of many of Mr. Cummins's political supporters. He was a more or less neutral minded man between the two factions, although his affiliations had been mostly with those who were then called the "standpatters," a phrase that had its origin in opposition to premature tariff revision. He was the logical man for the place, both geographically and politically, and also by party deserts and personal ability.

But with Perkins's candidacy under way, Mr. Cummins announced himself as a candidate for a third term. Senator Allison was old. They said he was in failing health. Should he die, whom would Mr. Perkins as governor appoint as his successor? Mr. Perkins was too high-minded a man to make a pledge, or to have one exacted from him. The presumption was that he would appoint Mr. Cummins, but would he do so? Could the senatorship be risked in his hands? In what was then known as the Cummins faction there was no one big enough to cope with Mr. Perkins except Mr. Cummins himself. Issues to meet their needs were not wanting. They said he alone could complete the program of reforms.

Governor Cummins's friends and followers rallied to the bold plan. Even those who had committed themselves to Mr.

Perkins withdrew their commitments. Mr. Perkins was stunned. He hated a factional fight and he had been placed where he had to make one. He had been urged as a peace maker, and he was forced into a war. Those of Mr. Cummins's friends who had urged him to enter the race had told him that he "might serve to check the rancor of factional strife."[3] But they passed him by when their own chief called them to rally once more around his standard. Mr. Perkins felt like one who had been "left well nigh alone to bear the cross."

The fight was waged in every county and precinct in the state. Senator Allison's friends eventually felt that his reëlection to the senate was involved, for they thought they saw a senatorial project in Governor Cummins's third term. To these suspicions Governor Cummins replied with assurances made verbally to Senator Dolliver and others, and in writing to Mr. Torbert of Dubuque, that his candidacy involved no opposition to Senator Allison's reëlection. When the convention met the contest was still undecided. One candidate seemed to have as many delegates to his credit as the other. The outcome finally hinged on the seating of two delegates from an obscure precinct in Jasper County, where no one could tell who had been honestly elected, if any one had been so elected. The Cummins men won control of the committee on credentials which meant the seating of their delegates.

With the Republicans divided into two embittered factions, the Democrats nominated Claude R. Porter of Appanoose County as their candidate for governor. For a time his election seemed certain. A preliminary poll of the state returned such a verdict. In the face of those returns a peace was patched up and the party was brought together. The result was that Mr. Cummins was elected for the third time as governor. But the Republican party had fought itself so groggy that instead of eighty thousand votes to spare, it took days to count Governor Cummins in by a small majority.

[3] Quoted from an autobiographical statement left by Mr. Perkins.

## CHAPTER LXXXII

### The Shifting Scenes

In Washington the prestige of Iowa had never been so high as it was at that time. Two of the state's ablest men were in the cabinet, Leslie M. Shaw, secretary of the treasury, and James Wilson, secretary of agriculture. In the senate were William B. Allison, loved and trusted by all and foremost among the statesmen of the period, and Jonathan P. Dolliver, an orator with whom there was none to dispute supremacy in the senate or out of it. George E. Roberts was director of the mint and a recognized authority in finance. In the lower house of congress the speaker was an Iowa man, Colonel David B. Henderson. Robert G. Cousins was at the height of his fame as an orator and he stood high in the committee on foreign relations. Other Iowa men held many chairmanships. It became a by-word that the way to influence in Washington was through the Iowa delegation.

But the dean of Iowa in Washington, Senator Allison, was growing old. His leadership had been wise, just, and effective. His sixth term would expire in 1909 and by a change in the election laws, his candidacy would have to be decided in a primary election, to be held in June of 1908. It was his ambition, as it was the desire of his friends, that he should be given one more term, making seven in all, breaking all records of senatorial service. Even if his last years should be enfeebled, it would still be worth while for the state so to honor him and so to honor herself.

But in January, 1908, an unexpected thing happened. Governor Cummins announced that he would contest the right of Senator Allison to a seventh term. The announcement caused a furore. Mr. Cummins was at once accused of bad faith. The Torbert letter was recalled. Senator Dolliver reiterated the verbal promises made to him. The governor made no explanations,[1] but persisted in his candidacy, but many of his friends felt too strongly bound to Mr. Allison to follow him in this new aspiration.

Senator Allison was too old and too feeble to make his own campaign against an active and resourceful campaigner like the governor. It was not necessary for him to do so. His colleague, Senator Dolliver, volunteered his services in his stead. "The fight I am inviting," said Senator Dolliver, in effect, "may later cost me my own seat in the senate, but I would rather lose that than have Senator Allison lose his in such a way." The senator left Washington in the midst of his duties there and made a speaking tour of the principal cities of the state. There were no halls large enough to hold all who wanted to hear him. He had spoken well on many subjects and on many occasions, but the speeches that he made for Senator Allison's retention in the senate were, probably, the most superb efforts of his life. Into no other subject did he ever put so much of his heart, so much of himself. He drew upon the whole range of literature, from the wisdom of Solomon and the raptures of David; from the philosophies of Cicero and the wit of Franklin. Shakespeare himself had described Senator Allison for him as a man who was "every inch a king." But if Senator Dolliver poured praise and eulogy on Senator Allison, on his adversary he heaped sarcasm and invective. There had never been such a theme in Iowa oratory, and there had never been such an orator as Mr. Dolliver was in that brief campaign. But oratory alone did not account for the victory. An association of politically disinterested business and professional men appeared as intervenors, with John T. Adams of Dubuque as the organizing genius. They appealed to state pride. Mr. Adams attained such success in his first venture into political management that later he was

[1] Mr. Cummins's friends understood at the time that he had been assured that Senator Allison would not be a candidate again, and Mr. Dolliver had so informed the governor, after a somewhat serious break in the old senator's health. That he had received such information through Mr. Dolliver was confirmed by Mr. Cummins in a letter to the author of this history, under date of November 22, 1920.

made Iowa member of the Republican National Committee, succeeding Mr. Cummins. Senator Allison without making a speech in his own behalf, won the victory in the June primaries, a victory which he prized above all others for it came from the people direct.

But the suspense and the stress and the strain of that primary election had drawn too heavily on the aged senator's strength, impaired as it had been. He died in August, within two months of his great victory. He was buried on the eighth, in the presence of Vice President Fairbanks and many senators and representatives of the nation. Messages and tributes were poured into Dubuque. Willam Howard Taft, who was then a candidate for president, wired: "I loved him as everyone did who came within the influence of his sweet nature and strong character . . . I have consulted him as a father." That was the attitude of the great men of the nation. He had served in congress forty-three years, thirty-five of them in the senate. "During all that time," wrote Senator Hoar of Massachusetts, "he has done what no other man in the country . . . could have done so well . . . He has controlled, more than any other one man, indeed more than any other ten men, the vast and constantly increasing public expenditures . . . It has been economic, honest, and wise expenditure . . . He has by wise and moderate counsel drawn the fire from many a wild and dangerous scheme which menaced the public peace and safety . . . He is like a naval engineer, regulating the head of steam but seldom showing himself on deck. I think he has had a good deal of influence in some perilous times in deciding whether the ship should keep safely on, or should run upon a rock and go to the bottom."[2] Nothing needs to be added to the tribute of one who served so long with him in the senate of the United States.

To fill the vacancy caused by the death of Senator Allison, Governor Cummins soon convened the general assembly in an extraordinary session. He resigned his office, turning it over to the lieutenant governor, Warren Garst, and became a candidate for the senate. But when the legislature met, forty-

[2] See Hoar's *Autobiography of Seventy Years.*

three members stood together in opposing a settlement of the matter, except according to the new law, that is in a primary election. Accordingly a special primary election was called, in connection with the regular November elections, when John F. Lacey contested with Mr. Cummins for the vacant seat. Contrary to expectations, the interest in this election was small, and Mr. Cummins won it by receiving 135,579 votes against 95,871 cast for Mr. Lacey, and thereby he became a senator of the United States sixteen years after announcing his first candidacy for the office.

That the new senator was fitted for the office which he had so long and so strenuously sought, none of his opponents could deny. If it could be said of him that he had made issues to suit his own ambitions, it could also be said that he had made them to serve the people. His administration as governor is a distinct period of state progress, and if in that office he served himself and his aspirations supremely, it must also be said that he served the people extremely well. It did not take him long to find his place in the United States senate. He had long been a man of national views. He had no apprenticeship to serve. He went into the senate at an important time, when the Payne-Aldrich tariff was pending. The Dingley tariff had filled the country with so much prosperity that a revision had been demanded. The people had "waxed fat and kicked." An industrial equalization was the demand of the times. President Roosevelt had avoided the tariff, in the midst of his many other vigorous policies. He looked upon it as a trouble maker.[3] And so the task of revising devolved on the Taft administration. President Taft, together with other troubles then pending, picked up the reciprocity issue out of the national platform and out of many state platforms, including that of Iowa. But many who had talked about the benefits of reciprocal trade, balked when it was concretely presented to them. Congress enacted it, but Canada rejected it.

The Payne-Aldrich revision of the tariff was looked upon as the "standpat" expression of the big business interests of

[3] Senator Allison quoted President Roosevelt to that effect in a statement to the author of this history.

the country.[*] Senator Cummins soon aligned himself with those who were opposed to it. A railroad bill, amendatory of the interstate commerce act, said to have been prepared by the attorney general of the United States, and approved by the president, met with no more favor at the hands of the Republican insurgents, as they began to be called. They said they did not want tariff bills made in the mills of Rhode Island, nor railroad bills prepared in the executive offices of the government. The turmoil became supreme — and the Republican party was going on the rocks, with former President Roosevelt in the offing.

Senator Dolliver returned to Washington deeply perplexed. His friend, his political father and mentor, Senator Allison, was gone. In his place sat a man whom he had bitterly denounced on the stump. His friends wondered what he would do — and so did Senator Cummins. Would he remain "regular," or turn "insurgent?" He had already come under the influence of the times. He had been touched by the discontent. He was a sincere lover of the people. If Allison had been alive he would have counseled cautiousness, for he was by nature suspicious of new issues. But Allison was dead.

While Senator Dolliver stood hesitating between the old and the new, he was profoundly aroused by what he considered a slight and an insult. Senator Allison had been chairman of the finance committee, and Senator Dolliver aspired to a place on that powerful committee. It was due him and he felt it was due the memory of Senator Allison. It was within the gift of Senator Aldrich, and Aldrich gave it to Senator Smoot of Utah. It was to Senator Dolliver a breach of faith and a lack of trust. He resented it. It separated him from the men who had been the co-workers of Senator Allison. He at once made his peace with Senator Cummins. He aligned himself with the insurgents. He went over not as a follower, but as a leader. What impelled him most to take this step does not matter, but having taken it and having placed his hand to the plow, he did not turn back. He spent weeks and months in preparing himself to attack two of the schedules in the new tariff bill, those on cotton and wool, which were alleged to be the hobbies of Senator Aldrich. He employed experts to instruct him in the intricacies of such manufactures. He made himself master of his subjects. He realized it was a momentous step for him to take. He had stood by the side of McKinley the protectionist, and his speech in defense of the Dingley Bill had become a classic in the defensive structure of the tariff. But new times make new issues. His speeches in opposition to the Payne-Aldrich bill were long sustained efforts and brilliant ones. The nation almost sat up to read them. Wit and ridicule, philosophy and aphorism fell from his lips in almost unwonted multitudes, for he had the zeal of a convert to a new faith and he was called upon to defend himself as well as the issue he had espoused. He spoke of President Taft as a man who was surrounded in the White House by men who knew what they wanted. He made the whole nation laugh, and those who could not laugh could grieve. By many these speeches are regarded as the apex of his oratorical efforts, the expression of his best convictions. But he himself may have had misgivings and regrets. He may have felt like a man adrift. "You voted for the tariff bill," he said to a friend in the lower house afterwards, "and that was all right for you to do, but I had committed myself too far to the other course."

But the labors and the strains were telling on him. He had a weak heart. He literally thought and talked himself into his grave. He lived in stormy days when he needed reposeful ones. He was welcomed back home from his new triumphs as he never before had been welcomed. But they were new friends; the old ones stood aloof. When the next state convention, that of 1910, was held in the Coliseum at Des Moines, Senator Cummins presided over it in the morning and Senator Dolliver in the afternoon. Each defended his course. One-half of the audience listened to Senator Dolliver in silence — and at one time some one hissed. He spoke in defiance, but there was a pathos in his words that showed the yearning for his old friends. At the conclusion of his speech he talked about assembling all his old friends and all his new friends around him in his home in Fort Dodge. He wanted to bring about a great reconciliation, and to live the rest of his days in the love of all whom he loved.[4]

But it was not to be. He did not live long enough. Mr. Dolliver was born politically in the great Republican convention of 1884, and he died almost literally in the convention of 1910. They were the beginning and the ending of his career in public life. And between those two dates were twenty-six years of superb service, years filled with momentous achievements. After his speech in the convention, he made a few more oratorical efforts, but he died suddenly on the tenth of October, 1910. There was no death in the ordinary sense; he merely ceased to live. The heart which he had so long overtaxed simply refused to work longer. It could no longer supply the energy for his great body and his great brain. His death was a political tragedy. It left a great void in Iowa, and also in the nation.

"Great men are plentiful in this country," said Senator Tillman of South Carolina, "but not as great as Dolliver." It was the tribute of a political opponent. "Beyond any possibility of doubt," said another senator, Mr. Beveridge of Indiana, Dolliver was "the greatest orator of the contemporaneous English-speaking world."

4 Mr. Dolliver proposed such a meeting in his last conversation with the author of this history, in the Chamberlain hotel, Des Moines, after the convention.

# CHAPTER LXXXIII

## The Whirligig of Politics

With the death of the men who had created it, the older order was passing away. But what were called new ideas were merely the old ones with a new shading in color. There are said to be only thirteen basic stories in the world, and that all the tales that have been told and re-told are only variations of these primary ones. There are probably fewer ideas of government and of possible social and industrial compacts. Every possible form of government has been tried at least once, or many times. Even the recall of judges and of judicial opinions which startled some Americans at that time, it was found had been tried long before. It has been said that all the moral government possible may be read out of the Ten Commandments of Moses, and all the social ameliorations possible out of the Sermon on the Mount preached by Jesus Christ. But as the twenty-odd letters of the alphabet may be arranged to form the literature of a world, so concepts and compacts and ideas may be arranged and re-arranged without end to form new laws and new governments. The study of history ought to be the most profitable occupation of mankind, but those who make the laws and who project them are not always students of history. In their equations human desires count for more than human experiences. The impossible is always appearing as the possible. But it may be that out of the attempt to reconcile them, human progress comes.

In Iowa the older order was passing away. Colonel David B. Henderson, a valiant fighter but not a far-seeing man, gave up in despair, and Robert G. Cousins, one of the sanest thinkers among the great orators of the state and nation, went into retirement. Leslie M. Shaw, who had been governor and secretary of the treasury, found no more work to do except to

Jonathan P. Dolliver

Albert B. Cummins

Leslie M. Shaw

Robert G. Cousins

moralize on *Vanishing Landmarks*. In 1912 William Larrabee died, regal-minded to the last in his retirement watching the parorama of politics. Colonel Henderson also soon joined the great majority. With the election of Woodrow Wilson as president, "Tama Jim" Wilson, already enfeebled with age, returned to his rural scenes in Iowa, his great work done.[1] No men as big as those who were passing away seemed to be in sight to take their places. But somehow the world provides for its own continuation. Men come and go, but the world of men goes on forever.

Warren Garst, who inherited Governor Cummins's unexpired term, was not able to succeed himself in the governorship. An indifference which was tantamount to a reaction had followed the violence of the senatorial contest. B. F. Carroll, who had been an editor in Van Buren County, and who had served in the legislature of the state and as auditor of state, was elected governor. By political affiliations he belonged to the older order. The politicians could not account for his election, but the people in the new primary elections decreed it. It devolved upon him to fill by appointment the vacancy caused by the death of Senator Dolliver. He selected Lafayette Young, the editor of the Des Moines *Capital*, a man with a political ancestry long enough to date back to the era of the Grange Law. The new senator was a foremost publicist, and an orator of renown enough to attract attention in the United States senate. But factionalism was not yet dead in the state, and so when the senator asked for an election to the office to which he had been appointed, an interminable deadlock resulted in the general assembly. The solution of the Republican *impasse* was the election of William S. Kenyon of Fort Dodge. The new senator was a lawyer by profession, long connected with the legal department of the Illinois Central Railroad. Politically, he was largely an unknown man, a conservative with progressive proclivities. In a primary election that followed, he and Mr. Young were pitted against each other in what was another major contest in Iowa politics. He won the victory, and Mr. Young wrote in his paper the obituary of the

[1] James Wilson died at his home in Traer, August, 1920.

vanquished, but what was deemed the corpse of the old order refused to accept the burial tendered it. Their exponents die, but ideas do not. The old order also was founded in an idea, the idea which is expressed in conservatism as contrasted with radicalism in political government. Both are eternal ideas and forces in human affairs, and neither one will ever die. Each has its ups and its downs and the best that is attainable in government is probably the result of the two forces in conflict.

In national politics the great eruption between the ideas of the conservatives and the radicals came in 1912, when the Republican party was split in two parts, with William Howard Taft and Theodore Roosevelt as the candidates. Through the chasm between them, Woodrow Wilson drove his scholastic political chariot from Princeton College to the White House, via the governorship of New Jersey. In Iowa the line of cleavage was more or less indistinct, insofar as it affected the governorship. George W. Clarke of Dallas County was the duly nominated candidate in the party primaries, but Judge John L. Stevens of Boone County entered the race as a Republican radical, in the stated interest of the presidential candidacy of Colonel Roosevelt. Mr. Clarke, a man of indistinct affiliations so far as the factionalism of that period was concerned, was elected. He proved a man of a great deal of common sense and of reconstructive abilities, and he was reëlected in 1914.

While Governor Clarke was pleading on the stump for his own reëlection, the German army marched through Belgium, laying waste the country, and General Joffre's French soldiers were forced back on the Marne, where with their backs to Paris, the immortal city of western civilization, they fought and routed the German army which then intrenched itself in the chalk banks of the Meuse. The president of the United States issued a proclamation of neutrality, and the American people went about their business. In 1916, while the French were closing their heroic defense of Verdun, Iowa staged the political contest between William L. Harding and Edward T. Meredith, the candidates of the Republican and Democratic parties for the office of governor. The legislature had repealed the mulct law, and Iowa was under the prohibitory law of 1855, as modified in 1884. Mr. Harding was accused of being so reactionary that his election would mean the restoration of the saloons under the mulct law, while Mr. Meredith as the candidate of the party which had been opposed to prohibition since 1854, espoused in the name of his party, the most ultra doctrines of prohibition. The Republican press itself was divided, one-half of its daily papers opposing the candidacy of Mr. Harding, who was nevertheless elected and that by a majority then the largest in the history of the governorship.

In progressive state legislation the administrations of Clarke and Harding were important. The State Board of Education was created and organized in 1909, with James H. Trewin, later succeeded by D. D. Murphy of Clayton County, as chairman, and William R. Boyd of Linn County as chairman of the finance committee. The advent of this board meant a new era in the development of the state's educational institutions. The board was the corollary of the State Board of Control for the penal and reformatory institutions. It brought the State University, the State College at Ames, and the Teachers College at Cedar Falls, as well as the minor educational institutions under one uniform and coördinated direction. With useless rivalries abolished and public confidence established, all the institutions made more rapid progress than ever before. In the development of the professional school of medicine at Iowa City, the first public hospital for crippled children was established under what is known as the Perkins law.[2] It was provided that all children congenitally or otherwise deformed should receive surgical and medical care at public cost in all cases where parents and guardians were not able to provide such treatment. Under this system thousands of children who might otherwise have been compelled to go through life handicapped, have been restored to almost normal

[2] It should have been called the Boyd law instead. The idea was evolved by William R. Boyd, the chairman of the finance committee of the board. But it was the good fortune of Mr. Perkins of Delaware County to be asked to sponsor the bill.

conditions. Of all the state's charities this is in many ways the sweetest and the noblest. The law has since been extended to adults under similar conditions.

Another significant law provided for the creation of a system of state parks, for the purpose of preserving and maintaining for the people all the places of great historical associations and of admitted scenic natural beauty. The first of the parks established under this wise law is known as the Devil's Backbone in Delaware County, a projecting and high ledge of rock almost encircled by the Maquoketa River. Other parks have since been established, and eventually the state will have a completed system of reserved lands for the pleasure and the recreation of the people.

In the industrial sciences, including applications of science to agriculture especially, Iowa has made great progress. But in art and literature the progress has hardly been commensurate with her wealth and material prestige.

In poetry, two men have attained national fame, George Meason Whicher of Muscatine and Arthur Davison Ficke of Davenport, and the latter is rated among the coterie of foremost writers of verse in the nation. In fiction, Rupert Hughes, a member of the Keokuk family of that name, is often counted among the "best sellers." His novels are cosmopolitan, and very modern. He is a master writer of whom much is yet to be expected. Emerson Hough of Newton has produced a long list of novels of rank, many of them dealing with historical subjects. Edwin L. Sabin, who many years ago collaborated with his distinguished father, Henry L. Sabin, in the writing of *The Making of Iowa*, has specialized in juvenile fiction with western historical settings. In the allied field of fiction, with humor as its basis, Ellis Parker Butler of Muscatine has made himself one of the successors of the great American humorists. He won his first fame with *Pigs is Pigs* in 1906, which literally made a nation laugh. He has fully sustained himself since.

Among the writers of fiction accredited to Iowa two women are conspicuous, Susan Glaspell of Davenport, now Mrs. George Cram Cooke, and Mrs. Eleanor Hoyt Brainerd of New York. The former has followed the serious in fiction, with later emphasis on playwriting, while the latter has accepted the lighter forms of fiction. Mrs. Brainerd may be described as social and Miss Glaspell as socialistic. Both still hold out the promise of highly sustained achievements.

Major S. H. M. Byers, of a former generation, has been writing poetry in southern California, and Mr. Garland, still in vigor, has produced *A Son of the Middle Border*, which has been ranked among the dozen or so best American autobiographies. It is a book that has much to do with Iowa. In theological literature Newell Dwight Hillis, born in Magnolia, and successor of Henry Ward Beecher and Lyman Abbott in Plymouth church, has written a long list of books and Dr. Edward Thomas Devine, of Hardin County birth, has achieved fame as a social welfare writer. Herbert C. Hoover, of Cedar County birth, has reduced a few of his many works to writing, and Dr. Joseph Fort Newton, at least re-born in Iowa, has attained international fame not only as a pulpit orator, but as an author. In dramatic literature the state has to her credit Willard Mack, one of the most successful producers of the times. He was born in Cedar Rapids as Charles Willard McLaughlin.[3]

In the domain of practical legislation a series of road laws occupy easily the first place during this period. The construction and maintenance of adequate roads is a problem that dates back to territorial days. For three-quarters of a century practically no progress had been made. Under various systems, good, bad, and indifferent ones, dirt roads have been maintained. Rain and frost and travel have undone what was done each year. The development and increased use of automobiles and motor vehicles of all kinds at last gave the needed impetus toward a more permanent construction of highways. By successive enactments the work of draining, grading, and crowning the roads has been accomplished, and in 1919 the decisive step was taken of listing the roads as primary and secondary state highways and county and town-

3 No attempt is made to list all the more or less successful writers claimed by, or credited to the state — many of whom, as a matter of fact, are not of Iowa birth.

ship roads. It was provided that the primary roads, connecting the county seats and the principal cities, should be hard surfaced by the use of either stone, concrete, or brick, or other compositions of like durability. The funds for this purpose are to be derived from three sources, federal aid, taxes levied on automobiles and motor vehicles, and taxes levied on property directly or indirectly benefited. The work thus legally outlined is in progress, but many years will be required for its completion.

In the regular session of the legislature, in 1919, Iowa ratified the eighteenth amendment to the constitution of the United States, making prohibition national. The state had been under complete prohibition of the liquor traffic for four years and so the change was not important here. In an extraordinary session, called by Governor Harding, the legislature also ratified the nineteenth amendment, extending suffrage to women on the same terms as to men. The leader in this important national campaign was an Iowa woman, Mrs. Carrie Chapman Catt, who appeared on the scene in Iowa in 1889, when she was chosen state lecturer, in recognition of her abilities as a speaker and organizer. In 1890 she left Iowa and soon became identified with the national suffrage movement.

In national affairs Iowa's influence became less marked. Few of the outstanding men in national politics were left and the newer ones did not have the opportunities for development, being members of the minority party. In the lower house of congress, James W. Good of the Fifth district in 1919, with the return of a Republican congress, became chairman of the committee on appropriations, giving him a power for the exercise of which he was well fitted by reason of long study he had given while in congress to national finances and expenditures. Mr. Good has made the creation of a national budget system the end and aim of his congressional career and when that is accomplished, as it will be, it will stand out as one of the most notable pieces of legislation in a decade.

In the Senate Mr. Cummins was at the same time favored by being advanced to the position of chairman of the committee on interstate commerce. In that office it devolved on him to take the leadership in framing a bill under which the railroads, after being operated under the government for twenty-six months, as a war measure, were returned to their owners. There was opposition to such return, and also differences as to the conditions under which they should be returned. For a while this was the storm center of politics, resulting in a somewhat formidable movement for his defeat through various labor organizations. But in spite of these, Senator Cummins was renominated and reëlected, defeating Claude R. Porter.

For the nomination for governor in 1920, Lieutenant Governor Ernest R. Moore of Linn County and former Congressman Nate E. Kendall of Monroe County were the principal contestants in the June primaries, with J. F. Deems of Des Moines County and Attorney General H. M. Havner of Iowa County, in third and fourth places. Mr. Moore's candidacy was largely based on his record as lieutenant governor and his record as a business man, and Mr. Kendall's vogue was much enhanced by his acknowledged abilities as an orator. Mr. Moore led in the primary, but having failed to receive the necessary thirty-five per cent of all the votes cast, the decision was left to the state convention where Mr. Kendall won the victory. His election followed in November, defeating Clyde L. Herring of Des Moines. In national affairs, President Wilson summoned E. T. Meredith of Des Moines to take the office of secretary of agriculture, to fill a vacancy in 1920.

For president in 1920, Iowa's delegation was instructed for Frank O. Lowden, governor of Illinois, a recognition not only of his abilities as an executive, but of the fact that he had a personal Iowa connection, having been reared in Hardin County and been graduated from the State University. In the final balloting in the Chicago convention the vote of the state was cast for Warren G. Harding of Ohio, and for vice president for Calvin Coolidge of Massachusetts, who carried Iowa in the November election by majorities of over four hundred thousand, the highest of record in the history of the state.

# CHAPTER LXXXIV

## Part of the World War

We must return to France to write the last chapter of this book. We went there to find a beginning for the history of Iowa. But we return in the twentieth century not as they came in the seventeenth. Joliet and Marquette came unheralded. We return in the company of more than a hundred thousand men in the panoply of war, their marching lines stretching from the Des Moines to the Marne and the Meuse, their vanguards before Sedan and Metz, and their rear guard still in Camp Dodge. Their explorers came in two birch bark canoes; our liberators went in transports convoyed by battle cruisers, torpedo boats and seaplanes.

How strange and how wonderful are the mutations of time! How could Father Marquette have dreamed on the twenty-fifth of June in 1673, when he first set foot on Iowa soil, that two hundred and forty-four years later a hundred thousand armed men should spring up from that soil in readiness to go to defend the country from which he came! In France in 1917 they may have repeated the salutation which the Indian chief gave to Father Marquette in 1673 — how beautiful is the sun . . . when thou comest to visit us!

It is not our purpose, nor does it come within the scope of this work to review the World War, or even to write the record of Iowa's share in that great adventure in arms. It is enough here and now to pay a tribute to those who went to the front, and to those who remained at home to do their work in like spirit with them, if not in like suffering and sacrifice. All history belongs to the future — Iowa's part in the World War must be written by those who follow the men who enacted it.

It was on the twenty-eighth of June, 1914, that three fatal shots were fired in the streets of Serajevo, in Bosnia. The dead were Archduke Francis Ferdinand, heir to the throne of Austria-Hungary, and his wife. That was not the cause of the war; it was the pretext. On the twenty-third of July, Austria's ultimatum to Serbia was sent, making demands that included the abrogation of her sovereignty. It was worded to be rejected. Vienna was jubilant over a prospective war, and there were joyful echoes in Berlin. On the twenty-eighth day of the same month, Austria declared war on Serbia. Russia moved to stand by Serbia. Germany in an ultimatum demanded that Russia desist, demanding for Austria the right to fight out her differences with Serbia, and Germany also demanded neutrality of France, whose adherence to Russia was historic. Russia and France refused to bow, and so Germany declared war on Russia on August first and on France on August third. Peace overtures had been made, under the leadership of Great Britain. The Hague Tribunal was invoked and a conference of all the powers was suggested. France and Italy gave their assent, and Russia also, but the German condition was that Austria and Serbia should have their battle out. So nothing came of the efforts to restore peace, and on the fourth of August, Great Britain declared war on Germany on behalf of violated and invaded Belgium. Great Britain pleaded the observance of treaty stipulations, but she was not unmindful of the menace of having the Germans at Antwerp. Soon Turkey and Bulgaria were drawn into the war and on the side of Germany and Austria, and Italy and Roumania, and subsequently other nations, on the side of the Allied Powers. All Europe was at war and civilization was hanging in the balance. By day and by night the soldiers of Germany marched in the perfect panoply of scientific war across prostrated Belgium, and on the twenty-first of August they met the French and British armies in France, routing the one and driving the other back on the Marne, within twenty miles of Paris. The French government in flight went to Bordeaux. On the sixth of September, General Joffre faced about, calling upon his men to die rather than surrender. Many of them died, but none surrendered, and the final victory drove the Germans back forty or more miles to the Meuse where they intrenched themselves in the chalk cliffs. There was a race for the channel ports, in which the remnant of the Belgians and the British held a tiny bit of unfortunate Belgium, all the rest falling under German sway. In the meantime, a grand duke of Russia led his army across Poland and invaded East Prussia, where on the twenty-sixth of August, and on the days following, the battle of Tannenberg shattered the Russian armies and made the fame of von Hindenburg. The Russians turned and invaded Austrian Galicia with astounding success. And then month after month and year after year the battle lines surged back and forth, the German dreams of supping in Paris, and the Franco-Russian dreams of meeting at Berlin alike thwarted.

That was the World War in its terrible beginnings, while in America the president issued a proclamation of neutrality, which was then in consonance with the majority thought of the people. But all Americans did not think alike. Many were in mental protest and some in even moral revulsion. To many the success of Germany, which they held to be the aggressor, would mean the reincarnation of autocracy over the ruins of western civilization. Thousands of young men rushed across the Canadian line to enlist.

But it was Germany herself out of the exigencies of her relentless war which made American neutrality impossible. On the seventh of May, 1915, with submarines she sank the Lusitania, off the coast of Ireland. When the great British liner went down, twelve hundred men, women, and children perished, including one hundred and fourteen Americans. To sink passenger ships was contrary to the rules of war, but Germany's defense was that the Lusitania was armed and carried war materials. An exchange of notes between Washington and Berlin resulted in the verbal stipulation that thereafter international law would be observed with respect to passenger ships. But on the twenty-fourth of March, 1916, the Germans sank the Sussex, plying between England and France, and two Americans were among the injured. Another series of notes resulted in the written pledge signed by Germany that thereafter merchant ships "shall not be sunk without warning and without saving human lives, unless these ships attempt to escape or offer resistance," when overtaken.

Once more America gloried in her neutrality, and a grateful people reëlected the president who had kept the nation out of war. But the intervening time of peace was utilized by Germany to prepare what her own minister of foreign affairs, Dr. Zimmermann, in a note to the German minister in Mexico called ruthless submarine warfare. On the thirty-first of January, 1917, Germany through her ambassador in Washington, Count von Bernstorff, informed Washington that on the following day she would enter on unrestricted submarine warfare in all the waters surrounding Great Britain and France, thus shutting American ships from the high seas, except that it was stipulated that one American ship a week might proceed to Falmouth harbor under certain conditions, which included distinctive markings that German submarine masters could recognize.

America, which had gloried in her neutrality, then found herself confronted with the fact that the high seas were not open for neutrals. More notes were exchanged and on the grounds of violated pledges, given verbally in the case of the Lusitania and in writing in the case of the Sussex, Count von Bernstorff was handed his passports and the American ambassador at Berlin, Mr. Gerard, was recalled. This was on the third of February, three days after the notification by Germany. Diplomatic relations were thus broken off, an act apt to be preliminary to a declaration of war. Then followed the publication of the Zimmermann note to Mexico, including an effort to array Mexico against the United States, with Japan as a possible ally to Mexico and Germany. It was even proposed that Mexico should seize Texas, New Mexico, and Arizona, while Japan might have as her possible spoil of war, California and the whole Pacific coast of the United States, for aught Germany cared. Revelations of plottings for American disturbance, with the knowledge, if not at the instigation of Ambassador von Bernstorff, followed and all these combined to leave America in a warlike mood. The fall of the Russian autocracy, and the establishment of a feeble republic under Alexander Kerensky, aided the growth of the war sentiment in America, for with Russian czardom gone the World War became one of democracy against autocracy.

And so on the second of April, 1917, congress met in special session, and President Wilson read before the assembled houses his war message, a message thoughtfully phrased and nobly shaped to a great national crisis, and four days later congress passed a formal declaration of war against Germany. In many ways it was the most momentous declaration made on American soil since the Fourth of July, 1776.

The whole heart of America responded at once. All party and nearly all racial differences were forgotten in the national duty. There were outbursts of patriotism from the Atlantic to the Pacific and from the Great Lakes to the Gulf. Volunteers enlisted and money could be had for the asking for all war purposes. Those who lived then have lived in one of the holiest hours of American history.

But none were unmindful of the fact that it was a great adventure upon which the nation had embarked. It was a nation almost wholly unprepared for war. During the nearly three years of neutrality hardly a preparation for war had been made. The navy alone seemed to be in order. It was an armless nation that had sprung to arms. But American optimism prevailed. America had unbounded resources and what she did not have she could make. American money and American energy, we told the world, can conquer all things, including the armies of Germany. The draft was invoked, not to supply the necessary men, but to distribute the burdens of the war that were to follow. Liberty bonds were oversubscribed almost over night. General John J. Pershing was selected to lead what became the American Expeditionary Forces. With his staff he journeyed to France to lay a tribute at the foot of the statue of Lafayette, who had come to America to fight for her freedom. He was probably not the first to say, "Lafayette, we are here," but the whole nation said it with him. To help France became the sentiment of the war, but the fact of the war in which America had entered was to protect her own rights on the seas, and to safeguard her own frontiers against a Europe dominated by a German autocracy. The logic of the situation was that it was easier to help the Allied nations fight that autocracy than later to encounter it unaided. While America went to aid the Allied nations, America also invoked the aid of those nations to fight the battles that seemed inevitable.

In Iowa, for that is the theme of this history, the response to the call of war was instantaneous and it was overwhelming. Her volunteers were so many that in many cities and in whole counties the first draft was avoided. The three regiments of the National Guard of the state were immediately summoned to duty. The place of rendezvous was Des Moines, where Camp Dodge was named after General Grenville M. Dodge of Civil War fame. Out of them a war strength regiment of three thousand six hundred men was created, composed of almost equal parts of the three regiments. This became the 168th regiment of the United States army, which was assigned to the Forty-second or famous Rainbow Division. The Iowa regiment constituted one-fourth of the infantry strength of the division. Colonel Ernest R. Bennett of the old Third regiment was succeeded by Colonel Matthew A. Tinley, who led it at the front. It was the one large distinct unit of the state in the great war, the other Iowa troops being scattered through many organizations.

But with all her resources it was not until the spring and summer of 1918 that the American forces began to count on the frontiers of the war. The miracle of transporting two million men through seas imperiled by submarines and mines was accomplished, which was the greatest miracle of the war and one of the greatest in the history of the world. When the first American troops were rushed to the front, France stood with her back to Paris, while the Germans were again driving their wedges across the Marne, and the British stood with their backs to the Channel.

The Americans entered the war at the point nearest Paris. They were not many but they were determined. They faced the trained shock troops of the Germans. Some Frenchmen called to them, "Don't go in this direction. There are machine guns there." "That's where we want to go," the Americans answered. "That's where we have come three thousand miles to go." And they went into Belleau Woods.[1] That was the frenzy of courage on ground that American blood has made sacred for all time to come.

We pay our tributes — others must write the history. But in Iowa the people were thrilled, as well as saddened, when the news came that of the first three Americans to die in the World War, one was Private Merle Hay of Glidden. It was a mother's loss, but it was Iowa's gain — if men must die to keep open the portals of human liberty. It was over his remains, and over the remains of his two associates, that France pronounced the gratitude of a nation. And over their combined graves may fittingly be inscribed the heroic legend of the Greeks, "Go tell them who live in Lacedaemon, that we lie here in obedience to her laws." For Lacedaemon write America. Write also, Iowa!

Iowa's men were in the fighting lines, on the Marne and on the Meuse, in the St. Mihiel Salient, in the Argonne Forest, before Sedan, and before Metz. As we cannot name all, so we will name none — but all collectively in this brief mention of what stands as one of the most glorious episodes in Iowa history, as well as in American and world history.

Nor must we withhold a tribute from those who did their work in like spirit at home. Iowa failed in nothing in those glorious days. She did not forget even the destitute in Belgium nor the orphaned in France. A sacrificial altar was erected in every home. Those who lived and labored as well as those who marched and fought in those days will cherish the spirit in which all things were done as long as they remain on this earth and, dying, they will carry some of the glory of it with them to heaven, and the glory of it will not be dimmed even there.

[1] Otto H. Kahn, in *When the Tide Turned,* address upon his return from France, November 12, 1918, before the Boston Athletic Association.

# CHAPTER LXXXV

## A Postcript Personal

I have gathered the materials for this history from many sources; from newspapers yellow with age; from musty pamphlets; from books in decayed bindings, and from lips that quivered when they spoke of the things of long ago. But most of all, I must acknowledge the indebtedness to my own mother. She told me so much about early Iowa that even as a school boy I thought of writing a history of the state — her story of Iowa.

She came to Iowa in 1847, before the state was a year old, and while she herself was still a girl. Sitting by the side of her father on the front seat of a mover's wagon, she first saw the wonderland of the prairies in the waning summertime of that year. To her eyes it was like the unfolding of a dream in some fairy land. Blashfield's picture in the state house at Des Moines, with the winged spirits hovering over the pioneer's wagon, might have been painted from her visionings. Her father, Mathias de Booy, grandson of Cyrenus de Booy, of ancient name, was a man already burdened with years, but he was permitted to live in the land of his adoption until he had increased the psalmist's limit by more than a score. I can just remember him — a man who had participated in the wars of Napoleon in Europe, and who might have witnessed the inauguration of Washington, had he been an American citizen. It takes only three generations to encompass all of the marvelous history of America.

They journeyed from Keokuk up the valley of the Des Moines River, following, perhaps, in part the route of the Dragoons in 1835. There were scattered settlements, but the country generally was still an open prairie. It must have been a hard journey, but my mother always spoke of it as a beautiful one. In her old age she seemed to think of it as something she had dreamed when she was a girl. She was young and she was impressionable, and all the things of earth and sky were lovely in her sight. The skies were so vast and so blue, and the flowers were so many and so fair. Doubtless she added to them something of her own loveliness, and sweetened them in her remembrance. But I have tried to write of the prairies as she saw them then, and as she remembered them afterwards. Nor have I found her personal impressions of them at variance with the testimonies of any of the earlier writers, whether French or American. George Catlin, the artist, said over and over that he could find no words to describe the beauties of the prairies, and so did Albert Lea, the soldier and engineer.

I have written not only of the prairies, but I have written of savages who paddled canoes on unmapped rivers; of explorers and adventurers and missionaries; of men who felled the forests and subdued the land; of those who toiled and fought and died; of the sturdy and the strong; of the determined and the valiant who helped to make this state; of the wise and the unwise who made and unmade her laws — but with all my writings I have felt that there was something omitted, something left out of the story. And that something is the part that women played in the making of Iowa.

History is largely made up of the visible deeds of men. It omits the invisible deeds of women. What wives and mothers suffered and endured and achieved in the seclusion of their homes did not always find its way into the narratives. The pioneer women did as much as the pioneer men. They ventured as far and often they hazarded more. By so much as their bodies were weaker and their souls more sensitive, by that much they suffered more. If the labors of men and of women differed in kind, yet were they equal. Men's labors were sometimes done, but those of women were unceasing. Mothers were busied with their household cares while the men dozed before fires, or slept in their beds. And what the women contributed to the future was as much, or more. They were the conservators of the traditions of the human race, and the perpetuators of the things that are in all times holiest. If the men made the farms and built the cities, the women made the homes and re-created the race. And so I have thought, and I am still thinking, that anything that I may write about my own mother may stand as a tribute to all the pioneer women of Iowa.

In many books that have been written about pioneer life in the middle west, it has been pictured as petty and monotonous, and as steeped in the melancholies of isolation and despair, but while it often partook of such qualities, there was much more in it. Pioneer life had a sweetness and a nobility of its own. It was vast in visions for those who learned to love it, and who by that love were reconciled to its hard labors. But it was worse than misery for those who despised their surroundings and who quarreled with their fate. Its hardships were indeed many, and its discouragements were multitudinous. There were dismal days in summer and stormy ones in winter. Drizzling rains and driven snows found every leak in the roofs and every crevice in the walls of the cabins. In a few cramped rooms the women had to carry on the interminable work of living. Cooking and washing and sewing and sleeping all had to be done in a few rooms, and often in only one. Broods of children had to be cared for, and there must always be a welcome for even the stranger. But for the best of them and for the noblest, labor was love, and love was labor. In such surroundings and so hampered, even the golden threads of romance were woven into the textures of life, although the romances might be of their own thoughts and of the future. At least I like to think this was true of the mother of whom I am writing. Over her memories of the past in Iowa there always seemed to linger the scent of roses, of faded petals in a beautiful jar.

The mother of whom I am writing was not born, nor was she reared, in the west. The blood of the movers did not course in her veins. To her a home was not something on four wheels; it was a fixed place where year after year the same flowers bloomed like familiar faces returned, and where year after year the same birds came to nest and to sing. She belonged to one of the oldest and proudest civilizations of Europe. She came out of surroundings that were ages old, to live in those that were ages young. If the new things thrilled her, the memories of the old must sometimes have depressed her. She was often bewildered. She spoke of wandering out into the prairies like a child lost in a strange land. They seemed so wide and the sky stood so high over them. At night their stillness broken by the howlings of the wolves made her think of death. And when the winds moaned through the grasses by day their billows reminded her of the seas which she had crossed.

I never fully understood what she told me about such feelings and impressions until many years afterwards when for the first time I heard Dvorak's *New World Symphony* — as I listened to that beautiful music I recalled what she had told me, and the meaning of it was made plain to me. She had been homesick amid her new surroundings; she had longed for the old scenes. The composer of that music had lived on the same prairies and he had mingled their moanings with the same memories and longings of an alien soul.[1] As she might have painted Blashfield's picture, so she might have composed Dvorak's music, if the gift and the genius of the painter and the musician had been hers.

But when she had children of her own, the past must have vanished from her mind, for children belong to the future. She was soon dreaming and planning for them in her new and multitudinous land. She hoped for them better things than had befallen her — for that is the ever recurring hope of all mothers. When they began to build a college in the town near which she lived — a university they called it in those days — she dreamed and hoped all the more.[2] The projectors of that college thought of it as a voice crying in the wilderness, but she thought of it as a doorway and a gate for her children, for the born and the unborn. In that doorway

[1] Dvorak lived for a time in Winneshiek County and is said to have composed portions of this symphony while under the spell of the Iowa prairies. His Iowa home was in the village of Spillville, near Decorah.

[2] Central University, at Pella, which was founded by the Baptists of Iowa.

they would stand on the threshold of other worlds, and by that gate they would enter the future which she craved for them. Glimpses of other worlds had come to her, and dreams of places whose walls were wider and whose roofs were higher than cabins on the prairies. She told me that as she watched the builders of that college she thought that every brick they laid in mortar was like a kind and comforting word spoken to her. And perhaps her happiest and proudest days were those when her children went to school in that college.

And they were beautiful days — they are still beautiful to me in memory. Bright mornings, noondays steeped in sunshine, and lingering twilights. Balsams and four-o'clocks blossomed in the gardens, verbenas and portulacas crawled out of their beds to burst into bloom, mignonette sweetened the air, and holly-hocks and sunflowers and trailing morning-glories vied with each other. Creaking wagons passed slowly by and disappeared on dusty roads. No one was in a hurry, and, perhaps, no one was worried over many things.

How times and manners and customs have changed! How simple were human wants in those days, and how complex they are today! What was then a luxury is now hardly a subsistence. What was then a day's journey is now the flight of a moment. In those days they still scanned the almanacs, and every year they read the Bible through to their children from dewy morning in the Garden of Eden to the effulgent splendors of the New Jerusalem of which the seer dreamed in the sunset of his life on Patmos Island. Now in every home in Iowa they read what happened in the world yesterday. The rising sun brings the messages from the four corners of the world, and from the seven seas thereof. What was done in Africa or Asia last night is talked over at the dinner tables of the four corners of the state. Marvelous and miraculous! But if we think of things they dreamed not of, have we not forgotten others which they knew? Even in her day, George Eliot sighed because leisure was gone—"gone where the spinning wheels are gone, and the pack horses, and the slow wagons, and the peddlers who brought bargains to the door on sunny afternoons." [3] Men, and women also, live

[3] The quotation is from *The Mill on the Floss.*

faster now. They think they live. And yet do they take time to live?

But those days are gone. They will not return. Three hundred thousand automobiles have displaced the creaking wagons. Humanity is now on wheels. It is going up into the air. We call it progress and we boast of it and rejoice in it. But if we must think of those other days as slow and prosaic and uninteresting, still let us not forget that we are the beneficiaries of those who lived so leisurely then, and who planned so much for the future. We are their debtors — let us pay our debts to them at least in the tokens of remembrance. And let us not despise their ways, lest those who come after us despise our ways. May not the historian of 2020 moralize over the old fashioned things of 1920, even as we now moralize over the past! All wisdom has not yet been garnered, neither has all progress been achieved. And in the meantime, folly, as Satan among the sons of God and men, is also present.

Ah, yes, they were old fashioned days and old fashioned ways! But there were in them many beautiful relations between parents and children. If much was then exacted of children, much was also bestowed on them. Mothers would have lived on crusts rather than deprive their children of schools. They measured their passing years not by the riches which they had accumulated in twelve months, but by the growth and progress of their children. Stocks and bonds were less, but flesh and blood were more. The mother of whom I have been writing, and of whom I am still thinking — and there were many such in Iowa then — was happiest when her children were gathered around the evening lamp — and one lamp served all — each one with a book or slate. All idleness was waste, and all waste was sin.

And books! What a supreme veneration that mother had for books! What was the secret message she discerned as her children pored over printed pages? Was there some magic power in them which she coveted for them; some key to the riddles of the future — the key which she did not find herself? She often told me that her brother who had died in his youth had written things which might have been printed in books had he lived to perfect them — and I thought she wanted me, who had been named after him, to finish his work. And years later, when I placed in her hands my own first little book — a mere pamphlet which I had bound in covers to please her — what a delight she took in it! Of such trifling things was happiness made in those old leisurely days that are gone. And yet is there anything that has come into the world that is better or more divine than the love between mothers and their children?

But books around evening lamps were not all of life. The out of doors in the sunlight and the twilight were also much, or even more, to that mother. She taught me to love the fields and all that in them is. She was mindful of the flowers and the trees, of the growing corn and the lowing cattle; of the larks in the meadows and the eagles soaring in the skies. She watched for the coming and the going of the water-fowls when the sun changed in his course. And all these things are forever associated with my memories of her. I never see a prairie lily in bloom, and I never hear a whip-poor-will calling, that I do not think of her in the beautiful days of old. My delight in them comes from the delight she had in them. And could any of us "have loved the earth so well if we had had no childhood in it?"

When I went away to do the things which she would have had me do, if she had not planned them for me before I was born, as often as I returned to the old home we walked through the fields, by the hedges and the rail fences, and under the trees which she never ceased to love. And always, back of the orchard, she would point out to me where the sweep of the prairies had been, when she was young and when Iowa was young. And always she tried to tell me how beautiful they had been to her — and if any things had been ugly or bitter, she seemed to have forgotten about them. She remembered still the nesting places of the birds, and the nooks in which the fairest flowers bloomed. She talked about the robins in the apple trees and the thrushes in the hedges; of the violets in the hollows and the roses on the ridges. She knew where the wild lilies still bloomed in patches of sod which the plows of men had never upturned, and where grew the clusters of pale gold which the Indians called puccoon, but which she called fillette, out of another language. And when darkness fell, until late into the night she talked about the past, her own more than fifty years in Iowa, of Indians and settlers, of wolves and storms. Some of these things I have tried to write into this book — but not all of them, for there are things that a mother can tell her son that he can not tell to others.

But she never finished telling her story of Iowa, for one afternoon in the spring of the year, the threads of her remembrance and of her life were broken. She passed away while waiting for a cup of tea, the social afternoon cup which she herself had poured for so many others, for four o'clock had always been tea time in her home. It was the best way for her to leave the earth which she had loved so much through nearly four-score years.

She was only one of many pioneer mothers in Iowa. She did not live in the sight of the world. She died unknown to fame. But after having written so much about so many others, I could not do less than write something also about her — and how poor is the little I can do for her, compared with the much more which she did for me!

# INDEX

www.ingramcontent.com/pod-product-compliance
Lightning Source LLC
LaVergne TN
LVHW012208040326
832903LV00003B/195